Life On Earth

(Past, Present & Future!)

(From a Revolutionary-Humanist & Gaia-centric Perspective.)

Roy Ratcliffe

Copyright © 2025 Roy Ratcliffe

ISBN: 978-1-918264-66-1

All rights reserved, including the right to reproduce this book, or portions thereof in any form. No part of this text may be reproduced, transmitted, downloaded, decompiled, reverse engineered, or stored, in any form or introduced into any information storage and retrieval system, in any form or by any means, whether electronic or mechanical without the express written permission of the author.

Hitherto, 'life on earth' in general has always been studied from the particular perspective of humanity.

The study of humanity from the general perspective of life on earth, has hardly begun.

All knowledge of reality starts and ends with the observational experience of reality.

All subsequent understandings of reality start from; a critical and self-critical contemplation of that experienced-based knowledge; as confirmed or modified by comparison with observed reality.

CONTENTS.
Acknowledgements.
Foreword.
Preface.
Introduction.

Chapter 1. The inorganic elements of life on earth.
Chapter 2. Cells. Bio-chemical (organic) beginnings.
Chapter 3. The inorganic/organic composition of Soil.
Chapter 4. Plant and photosynthetic organisms.
Chapter 5. Insect Organisms.
Chapter 6. Animal Organisms.
Chapter 7. The social evolution of Hominid life.
Chapter 8. The social evolution of Homo Sapiens.
Chapter 9. Hierarchical Mass Societies.
Chapter 10. Hierarchical mass society reflected in ideology.
CONCLUSION.

Acknowledgements

I would like to acknowledge the following individuals who despite their busy lives have given me invaluable support by reading all the draft chapters I produced during the writing of this book. My heartfelt thanks are therefore extended to Pat Clarke, Graham Dunn, Richard Machin and Sian Fletcher. Their many helpful comments and suggestions throughout this process have assisted me greatly in completing its final production. They are all individuals who I came across at various times because of our common love of making music and songs in local music groups. They have since become a valued group of supportive friends. My daughter Jan Boden deserves a special mention for without any prompting by me and despite her own extensive family and work commitments, she has taken it upon herself to read and comment upon everything I have written in this book and also on my blog (www.critical-mass.net) over recent decades. Furthermore she has also undertaken the task of preserving the electronic versions of my writing as well as transferring many of them onto the more tangible medium of paper.

Of course, all the conclusions, lines of research, suggestions and any limitations resulting from this process are entirely of my own making and they are bound to be many. In addition any form of serious critical appraisal concerning the evolution of anthropocentric exceptionalism within the history of humanity is likely to stir up considerable defensive feelings among many readers. Furthermore, defensive feelings invariably take the form of either total silence or concerted attack upon those criticising mainstream sensibilities. That is to be expected. The full reality of what is taking place on the evolutionary basis of all species of 'life on earth' is as yet being largely ignored. It will take the courageous and concerted efforts of many more future Greta Thunberg's to raise awareness to the detailed levels necessary to form a critical mass capable of preventing further environmental catastrophes and of reversing the current and future losses of essential species. Nevertheless, alongside such activists, the reality of such losses and their knock on effects, will sooner or later force a reappraisal of humanity's future role upon more than the relatively few who have so far become its Gaia-centric advocates.

Roy Ratcliffe (October 2025)

FOREWORD

As far as we humans can ascertain, life as it appears on our planet, is an occurrence which is an *exception* within the entire universe. This is both with regard to the huge expanse of our solar system which lies within the even larger expanse of the Milky Way Galaxy of which the huge solar system is merely a small part. Moreover, the Galaxy in which our solar system resides appears to be just one of many millions if not billions of other Galaxies within the vast expanse of inter-stellar space. Clearly, there is as yet, no tangible evidence that life in any form, let alone the forms which exist on our planet, exists beyond the outer gaseous boundaries of the planet we call earth. Yet life, as it exists in its many various forms and myriad of shapes on earth, is actually not exceptional. Life is everywhere. Life is under our nails, on our skin, in our mouths, within our stomachs, up our noses and even living in our butts. In the form of microscopic cells, organic life forms make up our skin, and are inside and outside of our bones, our body organs and tissues, blood, urine and faeces. Furthermore, life in the form of plants assisted by pollinating, wind, insects and animals, captures the sun's energy and transforms this and other inorganic gasses and minerals into the air we breathe and the food we eat. We humans could quite literally not exist without the ceaseless activity of millions of life forms both symbiotic and non-symbiotic within us, upon us and all those billions of forms existing outside us.

Life in some form or other also exists in the coldest, the hottest, the driest, the wettest, the most acidic, the most alkaline, the highest and deepest parts of the planet, whether on land or in the sea. Indeed, it is estimated that life on earth has existed in single celled bacterial forms for billions of years, and in multicellular forms for multiple millions of years. On planet earth, life is literally almost everywhere. Consequently, in contrast to what we know of the universe beyond the planet earth, 'life on earth' cannot be regarded as exceptional at all. Indeed 'life on earth' is normal, quite routine and ubiquitous. Yet despite this fact and in spite of the fact that humanity is totally dependent upon the whole interdependent chain of life forms on earth, from the smallest cells and microorganisms, to the largest plants, insects and animals, a problematic trend was set in motion during the previous five or six thousand years of human existence. Sections of the human species during a particular historic part of its evolution came to see themselves as so exceptional that they needed only their own skills and intelligence to survive and prosper. This trend was a form of anthropocentric exceptional arrogance and conceit which was (and still is) totally at odds with the actual existential dependency of humanity upon every other aspect of organic and inorganic life on earth.

So human life on earth is in a very real sense, the opposite of the anthropocentric ideologies humanity has created concerning its own exclusive and 'privileged' place on earth. Although the rest of life on earth is not at all dependent upon humanity to survive, humanity is certainly totally dependent upon the rest of the interconnected and inter-dependent organic/inorganic support functions of life on earth as a whole. Despite the concept of Gaia, (life as a whole planetary system) being suggested in ancient Greece and re-stated in the 20th century, we humans are only just beginning to understand that we absolutely need the complex inter-connected web of life to exist. Minute life forms harness energy from chemicals or the sun and convert this energy into forms suitable for human and animal life to process internally in order to continue to exist and to reproduce. Therefore, although humanity, as a life-form species, is far from exceptional in this bio-chemical dependency regard, this realisation has yet to thoroughly sink in and be sensibly acted upon. Moreover, the exceptional and narcissistic, short-sighted self-regard and ecological disregard of some human beings reached a tipping point in the 20th and 21st centuries. It was then that some people were encouraged to not only damage and destroy each other by the millions, in two world wars and do the same to most other forms of life on earth, but to do so in pursuit of personal or collective acquisition and satisfaction. This damage and destruction was done at the most extreme levels to plant species (by forest and prairie clearances), to insect and animal species (by chemical dumping and spraying) and to the human species at the levels now known as crimes against humanity and genocide. In the course of examining the information and evidence presented in the following chapters of this study, the biological origins and organisational impetus for this myopic process of human, self-conceit, self-destruction and ecological devastation will also be explored.

PREFACE

From the earliest historical times, the study of life on earth has been motivated by many considerations; economic, religious, military, industrial, commercial and scientific, but whoever produced these studies and whenever they produced them they have always been filtered through and adjusted to the anthropocentric perspective of hierarchical mass society class of educated elites. Only individuals from the elites were provided with the time, resources and skills necessary to both study and record their findings and of course they did so from their class perspective. Therefore, the study of life on earth (nature) from the perspective of life on earth – as a whole - has been consistently neglected and is well overdue. Furthermore, I suggest that what is also long overdue is the reverse of this human-centred process – a critical study of humanity from the broader perspective of 'life on earth' or nature. Moreover, in the 21st century I would go further and suggest, a study of mass society humanity from the perspective of life on earth – as a whole - has become not only a possibility, but a pressing necessity!

The natural sciences have revealed sufficient evidence to confirm that nature in general is not a separate realm from humanity, but humanity (as a late development of multicellular life forms), is only a part of a networked continuum of life linking all organic and inorganic materials into an interconnected, inter-dependent global system. The planet earth is therefore more than just a bio-sphere, clinging onto a sphere of inorganic rock, liquids and gasses. This is because the organic, bio-chemical elements of earth, life itself, depend upon the inorganic contributions of energy and materials, provided by the earth's rotation around its own axis (creating weather patterns) and around the sun (creating consistent, but alternating levels of solar energy transmission) enabling biological life to renew itself. This book is therefore, the author's contribution to challenging the dominant anthropocentric human obsession with its own species and with its view of the rest of nature as an interesting and useful backdrop, plus convenient food bank supply, but otherwise as an infinitely exploitable source of raw materials.

At the same time I hope the book will contribute to a process of revolutionising and integrating the study of all species of life on earth, by encouraging new generations to look critically at the role of the human species in its treatment of its own species members and all the other species of life on earth. Therefore it seeks to replace the current egotistical motivation for the study of life on earth, along with its many glaring contradictions. In its place, I hope to encourage a revolutionary-humanist, post-industrialised, post-capitalist and Gaia-centric motivation to the current and future understanding of life on earth. Furthermore, I hope that such motivations will ultimately lead to a large-scale active desire to protect and nurture this amazing and possibly unique planetary system.

Since the twentieth century, with its accumulated wars, pollution, ecological destruction and climate changes there has been a developing awareness of the need for a new perspective on the role of the human species within the totality of life on earth. The embryonic biological awareness of species inter-dependence and the growing problem of a consistent human alteration of ecologically determined evolutionary balances, was initiated and sustained by explorers such as Humboldt, Bonpland, Marsh, Muir and others in the 19th century. However, I suggest that this formative perspective now needs a different form of social motivation and needs to be combined with a radical readjustment to humanities eco-destroying production practices. A century or more of government reforms by limited acts of 'Conservation' and 'National Park' exclusion zones, have failed to halt the insatiable appetite of entrepreneurial exploiters for ever new natural resources to extract and productively consume. Preserving limited areas of undisturbed 'natural beauty' or 'pristine wilderness' to protect 'endangered species', as occurred during the 19th and 20th centuries, is no longer good enough to ensure the long term viability of life on earth.

It has become glaringly obvious, to those who are not blinded by excessive self-interest or ideological dogmatism, that we humans, sooner or later, (preferably sooner) need to embrace a more appropriate level of intellectual humility and a more sustainable level of practical interaction with the amazing galactic occurrence of the animated material we call 'life' or 'food on this planet. Given current levels of individual self-interest, whether such a radical re-adjustment of general thinking and acting will come before or after a huge natural or human assisted cataclysmic climate or extinction event is impossible to say. However, it is possible to say that the accumulated material evidence now available means a serious readjustment in thinking can at least be started by those with sufficient motivation. As long as large-scale human communities continue to exist, an alternative perspective on life on earth to the current hierarchical, exploitative one, may well be a valuable resource to be aware of and to have on hand.

In Spring 2022, as I commenced researching and writing for this study of *life on earth, from a revolutionary-humanist and Gaia-centric perspective,* sixty years had elapsed since the publication of a remarkable piece of writing entitled the 'Silent Spring' by Rachel Carson. It was a book addressed in 1962 mainly to the intellectual middle classes of the advanced industrial countries. Its purpose was to warn them to act to prevent a problem she identified as the *"alteration of nature"*. This alteration, she argued, was being affected by the production and distribution of dangerous and lethal materials within the natural environment. These toxic materials were being increasingly deposited onto the land and dispersed into the air and seas. The implications of the detailed information provided by Ms Carson, competing as it did with post-war middle-class concerns for salaries, investments, holidays, professional careers and offspring futures, was effectively ignored.

Immediate human self-interest satisfied by the then existing Marshal and post-war reconstruction plans, assisted in continually expanding the economic systems ability to produce. That economic expansion and self-interest was, as so often in the past, the main concern of the ruling and emerging middle classes. The heads of capitalist industries producing and distributing such life destroying materials were similarly indifferent to their effect upon the condition of the planet. They were more concerned with exploiting their chosen commercial or financial niche to make profits for themselves and their shareholders. For most if not all of these 'captains' of industry, making the environment safe for 'life on earth', was the last thing on their minds. Earlier still in 1941, Ms Carson had already written *'Under the Sea Wind'*, a book warning the literate classes of the misuse of pesticides in agriculture. That message also largely fell on deaf ears and was effectively side-lined by agribusiness, government, academics and politicians.

Previous to the publication of 'Silent Spring', in 1939-45, a world war had raged in which the elite sections of humanity ordered, invented and had working people produce extremely dangerous materials to be designed, manufactured and delivered at breakneck speed. For those five or six years of total war these dangerous materials were dropped, almost daily, as explosives or released as chemicals around the globe on military and civilian targets alike. When the German-led capitalist Axis elites were finally defeated in 1945 very little changed in this respect. For practically the whole of my teenage and adult life, without any serious mainstream questioning, dangerous and lethal materials have been produced in huge quantities for use in military wars and in ever expanding industrial, agricultural and commercial activities.

Those materials have caused unintended as well as intended damage to the global environment. This continuous, almost frenetic, productive activity and waste product dumping in rivers, seas and on land, has occurred at the same time as information regarding the serious consequences that such activity does to the planet and its life-forms was also circulating within the public domain. Those among the middle and upper classes in government, politics, academia, science, economics, and education, with the time, education and resources to read such books and begin to act in order to prevent the dangers described and outlined in their contents, actually continued to do little or nothing. Going by the lack of action, they obviously preferred instead to focus on themselves and ignore the wider implications. By the time a collapse in the UK engineering industry in the nineteen seventies shook me out of the job of producing and inspecting post-war civil aircraft parts, very little had been done to prevent further damage to the climate, to pollution or the ecology of the planet.

The many protests in various forms, during the 1960's, 70's, 80's and 90's, that I attended were not lacking in seriousness but despite the many 'ban the bomb', 'stop the war' demonstrations, numerous 'acid rain' and environmental protests and in spite of the occasional political rhetoric, no serious heed was taken by heads of government and their 'establishment' support staff. Those who were educated and amply rewarded to advise and govern modern mass societies, still preferred to employ their brains anywhere but to consider the future animal, insect and human welfare of 'life on earth' in general. Sadly, despite the exponential growth in scientifically sound information that publicised the growing problem, this indifference is often still the case. Using their combined power and influence, the particular personal or family interests of the elite were enthusiastically pursued and invariably outweighed the general interest of the mass of their citizens and the welfare of the many key species contributing to production of essential gases and food chains. Throughout my 70 plus years of experience in school, industry, politics and higher education, I have learned not to expect any form of serious elite concern for the welfare of the bulk of their citizens or any serious degree of self-criticism of their own active role in the eco-destructive 'progress' of the hierarchical mass society system based upon the capitalist mode of production. In the main, the ranks of the ruling elites and their middle class supporters have remained focussed almost exclusively upon themselves and their own immediate families.

Over multiple generations, the governing classes have through their ideas and actions supported the accelerating deterioration of environments, working and living conditions of ordinary people - across the world – and did so caring only that their own lifestyles were enhanced by the process. It is an undeniable fact that the entire global population now lives in an interconnected world in which there is a relatively small elite group at the top of the various socio-economic pyramids of national aggregations. It is these elites who exercise considerable power both to cause things they support to happen and the power to prevent things they object to, from occurring. In this process of governing and ruling, the elites at the very top are aided and abetted by those chosen from the educated middle classes in the ranks of civil services, military establishments, legal practices, governmental departments, educational institutions and law enforcement agencies. I will maintain in later chapters that it is the domination of these two classes who have individually and collectively guided the world to its current situation despite mounting evidence of existential future disasters. Even in 2024 a majority of this class are still more concerned with themselves than by initiating an eco-stabilising change in the mode of living and producing that we humans are currently entangled within.

It was in 1973 at a Lancashire (Chorley) Teacher Training College for mature students that I first became aware of the 'Silent Spring' and where my previous on-the-job engineering 'training' ceased and my new teacher 'training' began. Fortunately, some of the tutors and students at my college were not only exponents of 'educational' subjects, but they mixed this with a desire to encourage critical and self-critical thinking, rather than rote learning and its reliance on 'borrowed' thinking. Training their students to regurgitate education establishment platitudes and sophistry was something a number of these tutors consistently resisted. This critical thinking element complimented my earlier *'crap-detecting'* experience in industry as a worker and trade union shop steward who needed to regularly deconstruct management double speak and duplicity. At my college in Chorley, student's critical thinking was rounded out and honed by exposure to alternative opinions and a few subversive writings. Interestingly, only a few of which were mildly critical of the capitalist mode of production, whilst some were severely critical of the system of education. So even at my 'radical' college, very few individuals were exceptionally concerned about the continuing degradation of the planet, the ongoing oppression and exploitation of native and indigenous working people and animals around the globe or the pollution and ecological damage done to near and distant land, air and sea. Yet regular strolls and cycle rides across the many Lancashire or Yorkshire, roads, fells and fields around my home in the UK revealed that pollution and ecological damage was clearly proceeding at an ever increasing tempo.

At a national level during that period, medicines declared unsafe in the UK were being cynically repackaged and exported to countries with less discerning medical officials. Their eager, subservient bureaucracies were just content to trust first world assurances of safety and to make a little bit more than an average living. As the decades rolled on, local landfill refuse sites were bursting at the seams and local re-cycling solutions were introduced, which were almost as quickly outsourced to foreign lands. The problem of 'waste' was literally 'dumped' into someone else's foreign land-fill destinations. Toxic chemicals and plastics were daily settling in the deep ocean sediments, in sea life stomachs and on sea shores on which ever increasing mass society untreated excrement was dumped after it had polluted rivers and streams along the way to the coasts. The blue planet was rapidly turning orange and brown and its rivers and lakes heading toward a messy blue/green end, whilst media outlets broadcast positive spin polemics based upon the notion that 'science' would sort these problems out'. Throughout that whole period it was a notable fact that banal excuses for not preventing ozone damage or chemical run-off in rivers and seas were routinely made by politicians and industry leaders and their salaried in-house scientific and medical advisor's. Given that in the 21st century, knowledge about climate change, pollution, and ecological destruction is now more widespread and undeniable than in the past, but still continues, it is worth considering the following, neglected, or studiously ignored, extract written by Rachel Carson back in 1962.

"To a large extent, the physical form and the habits of the earth's vegetation and its animal life have been moulded by the environment. Considering the whole span of earthly time, the opposite effect, in which life actually modifies its surroundings, has been relatively slight. Only within the moment of time represented by the present century has one species – man – acquired significant power to alter the nature of his world.....The most alarming of all man's assaults upon the environment is the contamination of air, earth, rivers, and sea with dangerous and even lethal materials. This pollution is for the most part irrecoverable; the chain of evil it initiates not only in the world that must support life but in living tissues is for the most part irreversible. In this now universal contamination of the environment, chemicals are the sinister and little-recognized

partners of radiation in changing the very nature of the world – the very nature of its life." (Rachel Carson 'Silent Spring'. Chapter 2. Penguin. 1962)

It could not have been put more concisely or succinctly than that. During that period or even now, it does not need years of painstaking documentary research or hours of ploughing through reams of statistical reports to understand the seriousness of the problem. Rachel Carson had done the heavy research lifting for the reader. The two or three minutes needed to read the above is all it took for the essence of the problem to be firmly contained in a proverbial nut shell. But that was clearly not enough then, nor is it yet. Business as usual, was the open or hidden mantra for practically everyone among the elites during the last 80 years and business as usual is still the default position for those in positions of power and influence today. The only thing missing from the above précis by Rachel Carson is a deeper and more inter-connected and detailed understanding of the inter-dependent essence of life on earth, and the reasons why her warning was either, totally ignored, rigorously denied or strenuously subverted. This 100 plus years of industrial level of bio-chemical interference with nature and the social reasons for ignoring it will be considered in the following chapters. As I write, I suggest that it is no longer an actual absence of knowledge which is a problem, but the fact that there are too many vested interests in conserving the profit-based system, plus a woeful lack of a deeper understanding of the entire cycle of life on earth. It is those characteristics, along with insufficient motivation, which prevents serious solutions from emerging. I hope this study will help to overcome both.

It seems obvious that the first premise in considering the history of 'life on earth' is the existence of living organisms or even more accurately communities of living organisms. However, there are some crucial prerequisites without which 'life on earth' - as we know it - could not exist. The concept of 'Life on Earth' is so wide ranging and overwhelmingly fundamental that these prerequisites are often taken for granted and are therefore frequently overlooked. The phenomenon of life on earth has puzzled successive generations of humanity and has produced a wide spectrum of ideas and causes ranging from the supernatural to the natural. Until the 18th, 19th and 20th centuries, historical evidence suggests that the supernatural and magical 'explanations' (sic) for life on earth have overwhelmingly dominated anthropocentric focussed thinking. In contrast, this present contribution to understanding the processes of life on earth is firmly based upon as much understanding of the 'material' fabric of the natural planet and universe, as current discoveries and the hypotheses based upon them, have established. I therefore start from the proposition that life on earth, despite its complexity, individual variation and species diversity, comprises an animated mixture of common elements and energy sources that existed prior to the origin of life on earth. These inorganic elements (gases, minerals and metals) and energy sources (radiation, electricity and gravity) existed when the planets and the solar system were formed from whatever, solid or gaseous material pre-existed before its eventual amalgamation into the solid bodies orbiting around the star we call the sun.

Consequently, from this perspective, life on earth consists of those materials which have actively combined due to the chemical, gravitational or friction based electrical properties of those materials. Thus, although it is as yet unknown how 'life on earth' got started, we can confidently say that 'life on earth' at its most basic is an animated mixture of gases, liquids and mineral particles that associate with each other bio-chemically in manifold forms and replicate, or reproduce, their own material existence. These initial bio-chemical forms eventually evolved to become self-replicating multi-cellular species of many, many kinds. Of these various inorganic gases and minerals, two gases in particular stand out as the foundations upon which most life on earth has been supported if not initiated - Oxygen and Hydrogen. These two gases also combine (as H2O) to form water which is also indispensable to all forms of life on earth. Oxygen at a 21% mixture with other gases makes up a crucial component of the air which the bulk of non-aquatic life-forms need to breathe. This constant intake of energy rich material in solid, liquid or gaseous form assists the essential interactions within and between cells and organisms. This intake of non-organic material and energy and waste exclusion in order to create tissue and other membrane and bio-chemical substances (by metabolic processes) is essential for survival and species replication.

The exception to these aerobic (air breathing) forms of 'life on earth' are the many anaerobic forms which continue to exist in places which lack oxygen and yet even these are still essential to life on earth, particularly those in the digestive systems of many life forms on the planet - including our own. For this reason, after the general introduction, the first chapters of this book will deal with the inorganic 'elements'; in particular the water that exists within us, the air we breathe, the minerals, proteins and carbohydrates we absorb as nutrition (N) and which our cells metabolise (M). Consequently, I conclude that the subsequent facts and processes to be established as a basis for the study of life on earth from a revolutionary-humanist and Gaia-centric perspective are threefold. A) the biological organisation of individual organisms; B) the social organisation of the various species; and C) the relationship of each species to the rest of the natural world.

The introduction which follows is somewhat longer than I originally anticipated but I decided that since the perspective I have chosen is radically different than the usual anthropocentric bourgeois influenced one, some preliminary remarks might be useful to the reader. They consist of some references to issues and opinions which I and other people have found lead to confusion in the understanding of many things of importance and relevance to ourselves and the rest of life on earth. Of particular difficulty was how to promote a broad understanding of life on earth conceptually - but in an abbreviated form. My solution to this difficulty was to reduce it to a simple formula which is included in the following extract from the general introduction. So with the exception of the following extract from the introduction, the reader should feel free to skip the rest of the introduction and proceed immediately to chapter 1 on the inorganic material upon which everything living rests and is ultimately derived from. The crucial extract is as follows.

"The first point to address is the introduction of the condensed characteristics I have chosen to distinguish the life cycle of each organism and species, and to also indicate the common bio-chemical characteristics and sequences which

*make all life on earth part of the same fundamental interconnected evolutionary phenomenon. As a conceptual tool to use for that purpose I have chosen six biologically based and linked phases of living which I consider apply to all organisms, from the smallest single celled life form such as bacteria and some viruses, to the largest multi-cellular forms such as the elephants and whales. The essential phases of life on earth which I have chosen to condense or abbreviate are the following; Nourishment designated as **(N)**, **M**etabolism as **(M)**, **G**rowth as **(G)**, **R**eproduction as **(R)**, **A**geing as **(A)** and **D**eath as **(D)**. I have further abbreviated these as the sequence; **(N-M-G-R + A-D) = life**. My reasoning is as follows: All living organisms need Nourishment; all nourishment sources must be internally Metabolised; all metabolism enables Growth, whether as basic bio-chemical tissue and molecular renewal or as an incremental increase in organism size or complexity. Furthermore, all species of organisms must Reproduce (R) and all Age (A) and Die (D), albeit in the patterns and sequences appropriate to their species evolution." (Extract from the general Introduction)*

It is commonly understood that the nutritional (N) source for all life-forms (from the smallest to the largest) is a mixture of inorganic substances (water, gasses and minerals) and organic substances (plants, insects, animals or fish). However, what I consider is often overlooked or taken for granted are two crucially important facts. The first crucial fact is that the organic material used for nutrition (N) is itself a bio-chemical organism that is going through (or has already gone through) the (N-M-G-R + A-D) process of living. The second crucial fact is that the nutritional intake for most life forms is more frequently required than the rate of reproduction (R) of their particular sources of nutrition (N). Put crudely, if the nutritional need (N) for organisms is for a daily intake and the organic form of nutrition they generally or absolutely depend upon, reproduces on a much longer time scale say over months or over a climatic season, then this represents a massive contradiction. Put even more crudely, if as a vegetarian I needed a carrot a day to survive and carrots take months to grow, I would have a huge problem unless there were proportionally far more of them available to consume until new ones grew.

This contradiction between the need for most life-forms to consume organic food sources far more frequently than they grow or can reproduce themselves has only been overcome by two additional biological and planetary factors. The available sources of (N) in terms of each species are part of a much larger species pool comprising of millions of plant, insect and animal species and the additional fact that some species, (such as microscopic plants and insects) reproduce themselves in such prolific numbers that they form a mass foundation of (N) for the basis of many food chains. The contradiction between the rate of (N) intake and the rate of reproduction (R) therefore only seriously manifests itself when a species arises whose numbers consume the available (N) sources in larger amounts than these can be naturally (or artificially) reproduced. Life on earth has encountered such problems before and such species have either adapted to different sources of nutrition or migrated to other locations of preferred or alternative nutrition, before nutritional supplies ran out and existential problems arose. However, once the limits of even a flexible ecologically based (N-M-G-R + A-D) biological system have been reached or exceeded, the historical record demonstrates that the rare contradiction between the relative rate of consumption of (N) and the relative rate of reproduction of (N) by (R) is resolved by partial or total species extinction. Humanity is, of course, the only species capable of understanding this fundamental contradiction and of potentially acting in such a way as to prevent species extinctions or where they occur to offset them. Whether humanity has enough accumulated and combined wisdom and motivation to do so in future is a different matter.

INTRODUCTION

Some General Points.
Most studies of life on earth seem to start from an assumption that the current hierarchical mass society system is the best that humanity can not only conceive, but also practice. The few mainstream criticisms concerning the deteriorating state of the natural world are invariably directed at one or more symptoms, but never against the system of production – as a whole. Therefore, most authors, writing on the various species in danger, tend to consider that any problems experienced by plants, insects, animals and humans must be inevitably solved by political and social reforms or additions to the existing hierarchical regulatory systems. For this reason, whatever their personal politics, from a revolutionary-humanist and Gaia-centric perspective, most authors are, therefore socially, essentially 'conservative'. This is because once the economic system is critically studied it becomes obvious that it is the existing hierarchical mode of production that is the cause of the existential problems that all forms of life on earth now face.

Conserving any system which is perpetuating systemic problems is not a way of solving them. The elites, through their wealth, power and connections determine the 'what', 'when' and 'how', most things are produced, consumed and in what manner the continuous manufacturing 'spoils' and refuse is disposed of. In other words, most authors writing about the dire conditions of animals and nature do not fundamentally question the socio-economic system as a whole. In most cases they actually occupy a social position of institutionalised relative superiority within it. In a very real sense they therefore personify the contradiction at the heart of all hierarchical modes of production. They are part of the problem even when some of them are advocating marginal solutions. The contradiction that even those jetting around the world, with multiple camera crews, making documentary series concerning the ecological destruction humanity is creating, seem not to recognise the contradictions they are simultaneously perpetuating. They are adding to the overall pollution and resource destruction themselves whilst visiting as many far off places as possible to point out the destruction 'humanity' is causing.

The practical ecological 'footprint' for this study, however, is quantitatively different. Its practical production involves no private or public transport travel and has used existing literature, a second hand laptop and a single fan heater. Its philosophical stance starts from recognising that the existing socio-economic system is the main problem for life on earth and that continuing it cannot produce any kind of authentic solution. The hierarchical mass society system of producing what are the bio-chemical essentials for human and animal life Nutrition (N) is largely determined by the personal needs and desires of the hierarchical elite, whose control is focussed upon wealth and privilege accumulation, not on the general needs of life on earth. These hierarchical systems, as will be considered in Chapter 9 and 10, have long undermined the previously existing ancient inorganic and organic foundations of life on earth. The pollution of air, land, sea and fresh water together with resource depletion and the destruction of key organic species such as forests, soil microorganisms, insects and animals, has always resulted from hierarchical mass society systems, it has merely been enhanced by modern industrial methods of production, consumption and waste disposal. These key species, as will be demonstrated in the following chapters, are the essential base line producers and circulators of the inorganic and organic prerequisites for all life on earth. The distortion, depletion and destruction of such fundamental species are now the combined results of the continuous profit-producing over-production, over-distribution and over-consumption of goods and services orchestrated by the elites of the so-called advanced countries of the world.

Yet even within the advanced countries the production, distribution and consumption of goods and services is also disproportionally creating a relatively small number of extremely wealthy citizens who have far more than they need, alongside a great mass of extremely poor and discontented citizens who have far less than they need to even keep healthy and survive comfortably. This poverty of available resources applies to more than just the human species. Fertile land, wild grassland, forests and jungle habitats have been fenced in, cut down, stripped bare or made uninhabitable for wild life by bulldozer, digger, chain saw, insecticides or monoculture production. The consequent lack of adequate diverse nutrition and shelter also inhibits and kills plants, insects, animals as well as humans. Disproportional distribution of land, goods and services is replicated in every hierarchical mass society community and within every country in the world.

In response, the solutions to such eco-destruction and disproportional wealth distribution suggested by the system's elite supporters are currently two fold. Either to essentially continue with things as they are (conserve), but increase employment by lowering salaries and wages, or to 'level up' income (reform), so that the poor can buy more goods and services. These types of anthropocentric focussed suggestions do nothing positive for the plants and algae, which produce the air we breathe; the insects which do most of the pollination for the plant food life eats; they do nothing for positive the birds and animals which keep pests down and the microorganisms which break down all the larger detritus of dead and decaying matter. Just advocating more of the same type of anthropocentric responses and the future outlook for life on earth in general, and for humanity in particular, is as stark as it possibly could be.

Solutions based upon continuing the present hierarchical mass society mode of production, will only perpetuate into the future what has happened over many decades in the past and is still happening, while the fires and floods are still burning and drowning habitats and species. Tinkering at the margins type solutions such as flood barriers, fire breaks, water dowsing by aircraft, will not dampen down or correct the adverse weather patterns causing rising temperatures, either. However, such suggestions, if implemented, would allow the rich to continue for a further period, to invest in production, transport and retail and get even richer and enjoy their conspicuous consumption. Those types of suggestions also ignore the fact that since existing production, distribution and consumption levels are already exhausting the atmospheric, water and mineral resources and depleting the ecological balance of life on earth, then continuing as usual and/or increasing production and employment offers no short or long term solution. Worse still further economic expansion will not solve existing problems but exacerbate them. Also it is obvious that 'levelling up' incomes would only lead to increased production, distribution and consumption and therefore also accelerate the accretion of inorganic pollution and the simultaneous extinction of life on earth. There is already overproduction, over consumption and disproportional class-based distribution, to sensibly suggest more. Consequently, to avoid catastrophic levels of extinctions for our future plant, insect, animal and human communities (and families) a different and revolutionary solution such as a 'levelling down' of the rich and to decrease non-essential production and consumption will be required. Without such an intentional radical de-construction of hierarchical mass society systems, logic and emerging authoritarian tendencies suggest there will be a subsequent unintentional or intentional de-construction of them by ecological collapse, climate catastrophe or further wars and civil wars.

However, before considering solutions it is essential that the integrated and inter-dependent 'nature' of life on earth is properly understood. In following discussions and debates over the last decade on pollution, climate change, species loss and sustainability, it has become clear that among the general public and even among the political class, there is very little understanding of life on earth as an integrated, interdependent whole. Solutions based on half understood systems invariably produce ineffective or unintended consequences that can be as bad, or even worse than the problems they are intended to solve. There is a huge mass of information in the public domain on individual species and nature which goes into intricate detail in many cases, but most of it fails to see life on earth as an integrated, interdependent system. The usual approach to life on earth, in popular or academic life sciences studies, is to focus on one species or on one category of life and consider it in as much minute detail as is possible given available resources, time and final document size. An alternative approach, as in encyclopaedia's, is to briefly describe as many species as possible with very little analysis of the integrated and inter-dependent 'nature' of life on earth as a whole.

The approach presented here is different to both those regards. Using the limited time and resources available to me, I will therefore provide a provisional analysis of the integrated and inter-dependent system of life on earth and then the effects upon it by the actions of hierarchical mass society communities of human beings. Of necessity this approach will mean many details and nuances of species and organisms will be ignored or insufficiently covered. Nevertheless, if the overall connections and inter-dependencies are sufficiently covered and the links adequately demonstrated, then further details can be added and integrated to the readers own understanding of life on earth at another time. However, in taking this approach there are a number of introductory points I feel it necessary to make to help prepare the reader for the radically different approach I have taken. For understanding the complexity, the unity and the increasingly precarious condition of 21st century life on earth will be essential for any sustainable future for life on earth.

The first point to address is the introduction of the condensed characteristics I have chosen to distinguish the life cycle of each organism and species, and to also indicate the common bio-chemical characteristics and sequences which make all life part of the same evolutionary phenomenon. As a conceptual tool to use for that purpose I have chosen six biologically based interconnected phases of living which I consider apply to all organisms, from the smallest single celled life form such as bacteria and viruses, to the largest multi-cellular forms such as the elephants and whales. The essential phases of life on earth which I have chosen to condense or abbreviate are the following; Nourishment (N), Metabolism (M), Growth (G), Reproduction (R), Ageing (A) and Death (D). My reasoning is as follows: All living organisms need Nourishment; all nourishment sources must be internally Metabolised; all metabolism enables Growth, whether as basic bio-chemical renewal or as an incremental increase in size or complexity. Furthermore, all organisms must Reproduce (R) and all Age (A) and Die (D), albeit in the patterns and sequences appropriate to their species evolution.

What distinguishes each life-form from each other are the types of nourishment, their body morphology, their form of growth, their methods of reproduction, their rate of ageing and the final sequential stages of death. The evolutionary form of these distinguishing characteristics, have produced the bewildering multitude of small and large differences between the billions of species of life on earth. Yet despite that spectacular variation of organisms and species, it is the above noted N to D phases of living (the common bio-chemical sequences) which identify them as part of the living material of planet earth. Since, for each species, these phases of life are connected in a common type of sequence I have therefore linked them in the abstract sequential and abbreviated form of **(N-M-G-R + A-D).**

This abbreviation will appear in each chapter throughout the book and serve as a reminder of both the importance of each of the inter-connected sequences and phases which are necessary for all species of life on earth to live, but also a reminder of their essential inter-connectedness. So based upon the available evidence it is impossible not to conclude that every living organism, of every species, needs inorganic nourishment consisting of minerals, liquids, gases and direct or indirect energised particles from solar rays, to supply materials and energy to renew its structure. This fact together with the evidence that every living organism must include some organic material in its nourishment intake in order to live, also establishes a crucial fact. The bio-chemical material produced during every organism's life cycle of (N-M-G-R + A-D) also is, or at some point becomes, the (N) part of another organism's life cycle of (N-M-G-R + A-D). Every form of Nourishment (N) for every living thing is either part of, or the whole of, another living or once living organism. Life on earth is therefore not just externally connected to the inorganic and organic material available on the planet, but each species body material is also internally connected to both.

The commonly used phrase *'we are what we eat'*, turns out to be more than a simple 20th century cultural metaphor. It embraces, perhaps unintentionally, part of a literal truth, for we are not just what we eat but also what we breath and drink.. For these reasons, the common term 'nature' used to describe all life on earth, is far too abstract to reveal the inter-dependent bio-chemical reality of life on earth. Consequently, I shall repeatedly emphasise this alphabetically abbreviated sequence (N-M-G-R +

A-D) and use it throughout each chapter. Organic nature in all its manifold and varied aspects, involves the process of (N-M-G-R + A-D) so as already noted, this abbreviation will be used continually in order to underline and stress the essential biochemical sequences necessary for all life on earth to fulfil, as well as the commonality and inter-dependence of all the species of life on earth. The usual dualistic division between those aspects of life which are biologically determined and those which are socially determined will also be avoided at this stage. It is clear to this author that among all social forms of life on earth, there are varying degrees of biologically and socially determined aspects of living, which are best dealt with in subsequent chapters.

Two specific Points.
The following two specific points are somewhat detailed and whilst I have included them because I think they are useful introductions to some of the points made during the subsequent chapters, they are not essential. They can be bypassed without detrimentally interfering with the information contained in the main chapters.

1. **Assigning purpose to biological functions.**

A further point which I wish to alert the reader to is the fact that the approach I have adopted will probably make those who have uncritically accepted the Darwinian and neo-Darwinian ideas about the evolution of life on earth, uncomfortable. This is not because I am an advocate of religious ideas of 'creation' of life on earth or a supporter of their semi-agnostic fellow travellers who suppose some other form of 'intelligent design' to explain the complexity of body organs. Not at all! I am a firm advocate of the evolution of life on earth concept and feel comfortable with my questioning and evolving understanding of its functioning. Not having an answer for everything is fine by me as is resisting the temptation to fill in knowledge gaps with guesses or imaginary made up explanations. Until sufficient substantiated evidence proves convincing enough to assume a factual probability rather than simply an imaginary possibility I prefer to remain agnostic, so to speak. Equally, I prefer to follow the sound advice of Bertrand Russell in this study - and in life in general. *'Whenever you are sure of something; maintain it with doubt'.*

So I hope absolutist believers in Darwin's explanations will at least give my sceptical rejection of his anthropocentric and proto-racist theory subtitled the 'Preservation of Favoured Races' a serious consideration. I do think on serious reflection, and I hope other readers will agree that Darwin and his evolutionary theory - at its outset - rested far too firmly and comfortably upon the racist and class-based assumptions of Malthus and other Victorian eugenic influenced thinkers, not to be seriously challenged. However, this tainted connection of Darwinism with the eugenics trend of 'pure stock humanity' and racial 'true breeding' phenomenon and a number of other unwarranted Victorian assumptions, does not involve throwing the evolutionary baby away with the undoubtedly polluted bath water. The fact that evolutionary theory was and often still is, immersed in the most distorted ideologies of prejudice and discrimination, does not mean abandoning it entirely. To continue the neonate parenting metaphor, the fact that a quantity of poop has been bobbing around the evolutionary intellectual bath water since 'Natural Selection's birth in the 19th century does not involve rejecting the potential of direct observations of life forms to increase the understanding of the bio-chemical structure and subsequent incremental evolutionary trajectories of 'life on earth'.

However, since the discovery of the function of Gene's and DNA in the reproduction of life on earth, there has emerged an almost universal tendency among those who comment upon it, to understand its bio-chemical functions from within the Darwinian anthropocentric paradigm of Natural Selection. This particular paradigm of evolutionary thinking contains an assumption that changes in the form and function of life on earth are fulfilling a supposedly evolutionary purpose of self-improvement. This tendency of assuming purpose to natural bio-chemical changes has also meant its inappropriate application to the content of microscopic cells. The dualist framed 'survival of the fittest' and 'death of the weakest' assumptions by Malthus, Darwin, Galton, Haeckel, Ploetz, Gunther and others, (including the Nazis) is deeply flawed. Looking beyond selected phenomena it is not true that life on earth in general mimics hierarchical mass society competition and warfare. (This issue will be taken up in greater detail elsewhere for those interested in pursuing a critical appraisal of this trend of thinking about evolution.) Meanwhile, during this study, with the exception of predatory species) I have found no reliable evidence establishing the fact of a universal general struggle of organisms against nature in general (i.e. other life forms) and against certain other organisms in particular nor for establishing that 'purposeful' changes occur within species, rather than 'functional adaptations'.

I suggest the distinction between 'purpose' and 'function' is important to consider as something can have a functional relationship to something else without that being a deliberate or intentionally purposeful relationship. I reason that dictionaries have so many thousands of word definitions is a seriously purposeful and useful one. Distinctions between words and meanings can have serious implications in many areas of human life. Since 'purpose' is generally defined as a 'conscious', 'deliberate intention', or a 'pre-planned and thought out action'; a cognitive pre-processing ability is a necessary faculty to act purposefully. Purposeful behaviour is undertaken to 'realise an intended result'; it is an intended condition or situation toward which human beings strive', in order to 'implement some intended result'. If these definitions are sufficiently accurate, then to assert purposeful behaviour is a process which must be provable by verifiable evidence. I wish to stress this point because in everyday usage the difference between the two terms can be frequently blurred. For this reason I consider the burden of evidence required to substantiate purpose in non-human life forms, is much greater than the evidence required to indicate a functional relationship.

The reader can self-check their own use of this word as well as mine to see what evidence or lack of it they normally attached to its' use. Since the use of the term purpose, therefore, presupposes a conscious intention for a result, then in serious studies, it is self-evident that convincing evidence must be able to be provided for any such assertion. To provide a non-organic example of this difference between function and purpose, from a scientific and physics perspective, I suggest that it is valid to say that; 'a function of the moons mass orbiting around the earth is the attraction of large planetary bodies of (mainly) water resulting in the tides. Tides are a functional result of the gravitational attraction of the two masses. However, the moon lacking consciousness does not intend to do this. The moon has no purpose and the tides are just the result of the proximity of earth and moon and the other gravitational forces acting between them. Therefore it would obviously be wrong to assert that the moon's 'purpose' in orbiting the earth is to cause the tides. I remember my very knowledgeable father explaining to a young me that the 'purpose' of the cams in my motorcycle was to lift the valves so petrol could go into the cylinder and exhaust gas come out. However, in retrospect it became clear that cams do not themselves have a 'purpose' in that particular sense; they have functions. They are purposefully designed and made by engineers to accomplish an intended human purpose. The cams just rotate according to the position of the timing gears. The point I am making is the obvious one that language can get harmlessly misused (a great deal of humour depends upon it) but in serious matters such as the study of life on earth from a biological perspective, accuracy is required. Therefore, assumptions based upon human imaginings and experiences of 'purpose' cannot simply be attributed to non-human organisms or to inanimate bodies in 'nature' and still be classed as scientific.

At times in this study it may seem overly pedantic to take to task the popularisers of 'nature' programmes and documentaries for applying anthropomorphic terms such as 'purpose' and other such terms, to life on earth. However, the reason I do so is a serious one. I do so because the use of purpose, rather than function, perpetuates the general anthropocentric attitude which in the main dominates hierarchical societies and is frequently applied to nature in general. Anthropocentric thinking assigns purpose to nature (species life on earth) and considers it has discovered and established a purpose that already existed in nature. But nature (evolution at the bio-chemical levels) has no purpose, only functions. These functions contribute either to the organisms' survival and are replicated during reproduction; or are modified by bio-chemical alterations, without detriment to it; or they function to the detriment of the organism and lead to a difficulty or its demise. In contrast, however, the common anthropocentric attitude also often assumes that much of nature is purposefully detrimental to humanity. By this assumption many insects, plants, birds and animals are negatively designated as 'pests' and 'weeds' which purposefully obstruct agricultural production and profits. Or like bees or wasps attracted by our sugary diets, seeming to purposefully spoil our summer picnics. Rats attracted by our over abundant organic waste resources in cities are imagined as purposefully destroying property.

Thus the existence of many life forms are seen not as species which are essential to life on earth in general and in particular, but as something to eliminate by chemical or mechanical destruction. Virus life forms, for example, are becoming the 21st century equivalent of the campaign to get rid of any tiny organisms designated as 'germs' in the 20th century period of so-called heightened hygiene consciousness. This was before the idea of beneficial bacteria became more commonly understood and before a recognition that the life cycles of many tiny internal and external organisms were also absolutely essential to a healthy life. Insects and animals are of course purposefully seeking nutrition, it is functionally necessary for them to live, but they are not consciously trying to help or hinder any other form of life on earth. If life on earth was consistently treated as 'functional' and organisms 'essential' to life on earth in general by those who should know better, then their protection would be more likely to feature in human decision-making concerning their actual existence and role in nature.

That is why I consider the internal bio-chemical functions of microscopic cellular life that are frequently incorrectly attributed to purposeful activities in the maintenance of life, and need to be challenged and corrected. I consider the only justification for attributing purpose to life on earth is in an organism's pursuit of Nourishment (N) and in some cases Reproductive activity (R) in the ongoing overall processes of (N-M-G-R + A-D). But even then such a human designated 'purpose' is merely a human assumption. I consider that for the rest of life on earth the natural phases (M) through to (D) are best described as functional and sequential, rather than purposeful activities in general or that the results of certain activities are purposeful, rather than functional.

I reason that just because these bio-chemical 'phases' are clearly functional and sequential, does not provide any or sufficient evidence to conclude that they were either intelligently created or at any point are intentionally or consciously purposeful. The function of seeking nutrition (N), by all forms of life on earth, is to satisfy bio-chemical system imbalance, not in the exclusive to humans knowledge that they must purposefully do so in order to grow (G) and reproduce (R), even though these other phases when functioning correctly, do result from the energy obtained from adequate nutrition.

The one exception to this general observation is in the reproduction (R) phase of some human beings who do not always copulate for pleasure but purposefully when intending to produce offspring. However, I contend that this exception is socially determined and not bio-chemically determined. For the rest of life on earth (including many if not most human beings) the function of sexual activity is to experience comfort, intimate proximity and intense pleasure with another organism, not to ensure reproduction. This is so even though sexual satisfaction by copulation can of course result in reproduction. The available evidence suggests that apart from the (N) phase of living, the processes of life on earth, (with the exceptions noted above) are functional phases which have evolved from the origin of single celled organisms which without intending to do so, reproduced by cell division or budding. It is therefore the case that these basic bio-chemical functions, although modified, have been retained within all multi-cellular organisms and species of life on earth. I have found no actual evidence whatsoever of any intent or purpose informing the bio-chemical actions and interactions, within cells, between cells and between organisms.

I also conclude that the Metabolic processing (M) of absorbed nourishment (N) by the organelles within cells were not 'designed' to fulfil that function and did not purposefully evolve in order to provide energy for growth (G) and that growth hormones were not 'designed' to enable the reproductive (R) phase to be reached. In the absence of evidence otherwise, I suggest it is best to consider these sequential occurrences as 'functions' or 'sequences' and are simply how the phases have incrementally evolved, through successful combinations, recombinations and symbiotic inclusions. To imply or assert that the sequence (N-M-G-R + A-D) phases of life were purposefully linked to ensure Reproduction (R) or Ageing or Death (D) of organisms or species, as some people do, is to do so without any convincing evidence. It is to commit the long running human mistake of assuming and insisting that an invisible guiding power is operating throughout the galaxy or in secular terms that a clear correlation of certain events equates to a clear causation of these events.

I consider it is by means of such mistaken assumptions, that the basic bio-chemical functions of existence have been incorrectly given not only the attribute of purpose but a 'knowing' consciousness of this purpose. Thus, some modern biological science professionals incredibly assert that life forms engaging in reproduction activities are doing so for the purpose of "passing on their genes", which is sheer anthropocentric nonsense. They are indeed passing on genes but knowingly is an anthropocentric imposition on a biological function. It is an obvious fact that life on earth was reproducing for billions of years, before the concept of 'genes' were suggested in the late 19th and 20th centuries and not all humans know of their existence or understand their function even in the 21st. Passing genes on is a function of life but there is no evidence of any prior intention of doing so. Species of life on earth from cells to multi-cellular species have been functionally reproducing for millions if not billions of years, with limited or no obvious form of conscious understanding, so it is sheer nonsense to apply such anthropocentrically derived conscious reasoning to animals then or now. But such nonsense repeated in studies of life on earth doesn't come out of thin air. It stems from the logic of Anthropocentric Darwinian orthodoxy that assumes an evolutionary struggle of organism against organism for so-called limited resources, (an purely imaginary form of competition) which minutely but continually modifies them and 'rewards' (sic) the so-called 'fittest' by guaranteed breeding.

Such ideas about evolution have still not been freed from contamination by earlier teleological assumptions and constantly appear among some 'celebrity' and highly regarded 'popular' nature watchers and commentators on nature. Such 'borrowed thinking' should be returned to the original owners literature long before it becomes indistinguishable from a wilful act of deliberately misleading the modern public. Deliberately harbouring borrowed thinking until it resembles a cache of stolen artefacts from the past is an unnecessary and counterproductive form of intellectual hoarding. For example, some modern enthusiasts of Natural Selection imagine that as a consequence of this anthropomorphic assumption, sexually reproducing species are purposefully selecting partners with the 'most' advantageous genetic structures' to copulate with. A few of these 'naturalists' seem to imagine that many of these female insects, fish and animals are choosing (i.e. consciously weighing up the so-called fittest mates based upon the size or shape of their appendages) or to mate with - based on their, energy, colour, plumage etc.

Insects, fish, birds and animals are presumed by such observers to have the same aesthetically admiring tastes regarding plumage as their human observers. By the same assumption they imagine that male organisms have been somehow persuaded (by nature) to grow colourful or unusual attributes simply to be able to signal to potential female sexual partners their so-called biological advantage by these visual attributes. Or worse still some think that 'nature' (the term is actually a linguistic abstraction with no actual or potential agency) is rewarding the appearance of such outstanding morphological characteristics with increased sexual activity, by these characteristics 'turning on' the female sexual receptivity. The presumed corollary is that those with diminutive size or unspectacular visual attributes may therefore lose out in these imaginary competitive reproduction stakes and fail to attract a mate thus causing a dull variety of the species to die off.

The fact that after millions (or billions) of years of evolution the spectacular specimens of species are still in a small minority and the ordinary 'plain' specimens such as birds, ants or flies, still exist in greater numbers and still take essentially the same unspectacular form appears not raise a quizzical eyebrow by many naturalists in the direction of the survival of the fittest concept. Despite billions of years of so-called struggle to exist, the continued existence of the varied range of organisms of each species does not cause a 'convinced' Darwinian to completely dismiss the teleological assumptions upon which Darwin's natural selection theory is based. In this way borrowed confirmation biased ideology can select and manipulate what is observed and what is understood. It is in this way that the imagined purpose of life on earth, previously assigned to an imaginary god, has been intellectually transferred to an equally imaginary abstract 'selection' process in nature which supposedly affects the genetic aspects of the bio-chemical evolution of life on earth. Not surprisingly imagination can be too easily used to fill any gaps in scientific knowledge as well as to fill in any otherwise boring interlude between observations. Too often the bio-chemical processes of Reproduction (R) in the overall (N-M-G-R + A-D) processes of life on earth have been assigned a conscious or semi-conscious purpose when outside of imagination and speculation, there is actually no evidence to base this on only borrowed outdated opinion.

This simplistic human based assignment of evolutionary purpose to bio-chemical functions has been naively done, I suggest, because the heightened levels of human consciousness and study assigns purpose to almost all human actions and then these anthropocentric assumptions are applied to all forms of life on earth. This assignment of assumed human purpose to reproductive activity is also the shared basis of what I consider the flawed assembly of factual evidence contained within the Darwinian hypothesis of a competitive evolutionary struggle of life on earth. It seems that religiously influenced naturalists, such as Malthus and Darwin, clearly needed a mechanism to replace the earlier idea of a god who had 'created' everything in perfect forms. The fact that sequences of ancient fossils sufficiently proved species were obviously not perfect from the start, but changing or gradually evolving. To reconcile God's imagined creation and the reality of obvious examples of anthropocentrically observed development and thus 'imperfection', some other unseen agency of change was required. The idea appears to have intellectually evolved into the idea of a god who had deliberately intended gradual improvements but had delegated the process of such improvement 'selection' toward perfection to the agency of the terminological abstraction 'nature'. Of course, the term nature does not designate anything in particular so has no agency to act or 'select' anything. However, by this virtual reality invention, organisms and species could be imagined to evolve by means of an intervention by a linguistic abstraction 'nature' (or by an individual insect, bird or animal) 'selecting' certain preferred characteristics. Imagination is amazingly flexible and creative in that it can imaginatively produce one non-existent human abstraction with agency, (a male god), and then think that that non-existent abstraction can create another abstraction with agency – (nature} - all without requiring a shred of practical material or evidence to substantiate any of it.

It is perhaps relevant at this point to make clear the problem of understanding the real world – as it really is - from within the framework of human thinking – as it is invariably conceptualised. The human intellect using the evolved bodily senses observes and considers real material things, then collectively assigns words (graphic signs) to them. However, these words are also just symbolic abstractions and do not exist outside of the brains of human beings or exist beyond these representative symbols on paper or other material. This process has given rise to a common mistake of taking the word socially attached to the thing as being an actual part of the real thing. A simple demonstration of this potential confusion on a day to day basis was provided by the philosopher Fredric Hegel. He pointed out the obvious fact that living organisms can eat cherries and plums and can smell, feel and taste them; however, no organism can eat, taste or smell 'fruit'- or 'vegetables' for that matter.

The word fruit (along with the plural vegetables) are just linguistic abstractions humans make so as to collectively include all types of such organic life forms in everyday conversations. So while people can frequently say they eat lots of fruit and vegetables and be understood, such a statement could not possibly be literally true. To be accurate they would have to say they eat lots of 'carrots' and 'apples' or whatever. For a further example, an animal can 'select' a ripe fruit and a convenient mate, but 'nature' can do neither. Of course abstractions will usefully suffice in general conversations as well as specific ones, but may not always have a place in serious matters particularly in the areas designated as science. It is when abstractions are confused with real things in more serious matters that problems start to emerge. For example, in this study the terms 'time', 'space' 'universe' and 'species' will be used as abstractions but not in the sense of identifying them as entities that can be physically seen, touched, smelled, weighed, measured or directly studied.

Yet some commentators and writers talk as if these abstractions actually exist. Thus astrophysical comments by scientists such as 'since the beginning of time', or the 'creation of the universe' are obviously virtual abstractions which do not actually exist, yet are frequently referenced as if they did. Time, for example, is simply the human measurement of movement of earthly and solar system bodies; first by observing and calibrating shadows, (tree shadows, sundial's) and later measured by mechanical and electrical means (clocks). Of course, planetary movement existed before humans, but time did not exist until humans invented it by calibrating planetary and orbital movement in various physical ways. Similarly, an act of creation is the known and evidenced production of something from something else by human or animal activity. It is totally inappropriate, within the scientific paradigm, to apply the term 'creation' to explain the existence of the solar system, galaxy or universe based upon an imaginary entity. The use of creation presupposes a known and tangible 'creator'. Of course, abstractions, like 'nature', 'struggle', 'species', 'cells' will be frequently encountered in this study also, but the reader should not consider these as anything other than collective nouns and should expect that nothing really specific in a material sense can be said about them precisely because abstract words relate to nothing specific.

These (and many other such abstractions) are the equivalent of 'fruits' in the earlier example suggested by Hegel and refer to nothing specifically concrete or real in the world or the universe. The real important observations in any study of 'life on earth' (another useful three word abstraction) will need to relate to a specific organism or group of organisms to be of any real value. Which 'part' of nature, what 'specific' organism or species, what 'type' of cell, what 'evidence' is there for 'struggle' are questions which need to be seriously considered and pursued before accepting any assertion as valid simply because it has been uttered by some celebrated intellectual. Of course, humanity could not converse effectively without the use of abstractions, but as the world of politics demonstrates, abstractions can also be deliberately or unthinkingly used to confuse an unwary audience into assuming an issue has been or will be addressed. Every failure due to negligence or wilful neglect is followed by 'we will learn the lessons'.

Therefore, in terms of humanities understanding of nature it should be absolutely clear that apart from some humans, no other species of life on earth understands life on earth as a whole or even their own (N-M-G-R + A-D) phases of living or their interconnected sequences. Their awareness of life on earth no matter how acute their sense organs have developed does not extend to a conscious understanding and a collective symbolic reconstruction of its integrated functions. Humans know that animals need to breathe oxygenated air, but birds and other animals don't. Outside of the human species, animals are not aware that what they consume as Nutrition (N) consists of inorganic and organic material which will be metabolised by their internal cellular organelles (M) and that the resulting energy and mineral peptide forms will be shared around their cells and passed to other cells – even though that is what biological science has determined is occurring. Life forms are not aware that their successful reproductive activity (R) will reproduce a close copy of themselves – even though it does. They do not know that they will age and die. They simply eat (N) because their body cells signal various forms of discomfort or disequilibrium until nourishment creates a sensation of satisfaction. The rest of their (M-G-R + A-D) phases follow as a result of past multi-cellular evolution, not as a pre-determined result by an imaginary heavenly research and design bureau, or by the action of abstractions such as 'nature'. Even humans, the most conscious and most purposeful forms of life on earth, generally do not always copulate to reproduce a next generation. They do so because copulation satisfies a physical, social and sensual need or desire.

Apart from humans, mature life forms do not nurture and protect their new offspring so as to ensure that the next generation of their species survives. They would need to have a grasp of evolutionary theory to protect them for that reason. Instead, they probably do so because of physical and emotional attachment to this entity which at birth has emerged from them and smells and looks like smaller versions of themselves. Likewise life does not Age and Die in order to make way for future generations. It is perhaps convenient that death of organisms provides nourishment for others and also makes way for new life, but when most life forms struggle against dying they are not doing so to prevent others from taking their place. These long- term phases of life on earth and their sequences happen the way they do because this is how life on earth has evolved. Purpose and design are entirely human concepts developed late in the post-hominid and post-hunter-gatherer sequences of *Homo sapiens* social evolution. They are characteristics which should not be anthropomorphically forced into areas of nature (life on earth in general) in which they do not belong. Suggesting that any of the bio-chemical sequences of life on earth, are purposefully created rather than functional modifications or evolutionary adaptations of previous life forms, is to reintroduce mystical religious considerations (or God) into the arena of secular science by the back door having previously ushered them (and God) politely out via the front door.

2. Speculation to fill in knowledge gaps.

The third characteristic I shall draw attention to in this introduction and throughout the book is the filling of gaps in knowledge and understandings with imaginative possibilities whilst implying or insinuating these 'imaginings' are actually real. It is obvious that the majority of events in history and prehistory are not fully known and never can be fully known. No living person has had direct experience of what happened before their own existence, and even those who have experienced certain events in their own lifetime can easily miss, forget or unintentionally alter the detail. Even contemporary records of events are only abbreviated interpretations by the recorder of what has taken place. It is often the case that even two people experiencing and viewing the same event - at the same time - can have differing understandings and accounts of what took place.

So accuracy can never be fully realised even when observational evidence is examined with forensic levels of due diligence.

If this is true of contemporary events concerning life on earth, then how much more so must it be true of events hundreds, thousands or millions of years ago? The best we can realistically ascertain from critically studying the available evidence concerning the past in general and the ancient past in particular, is a general outline of possibilities or sometimes probabilities. Yet imaginative gap-filling tendencies are so frequently resorted to in the fields of archaeology, pre-history and history that it is almost ubiquitous and allowed in books which are passed by editors and reviewers without censure or comment. Whilst it is a frequently heard and read expression that we can 'learn from history', it is less frequently heard and read, that we can also miss-learn or be 'misled', either intentionally or unintentionally, by historically inaccurate narrative assumptions. As in other areas of modern life and the internet in particular, it really is a case of 'buyer (or reader) beware'.

Consequently, historical narratives (fictional and non-fictional) are full of imaginative inserts to fill the vast numbers of gaps that are inevitable. In some more obvious cases these imaginative possibilities are preceded by the words 'clearly' or 'must'. A typical example might be paraphrased as the following;

'In one pre-historic grave we found a very decorative object so the occupant was clearly a king or chief'.

'In another grave we uncovered several gold vessels so it must have been the high priest of this tribe.'

By providing these two above paraphrased examples, I have simply reduced the many hundreds of such similar statements I encountered in the research for a later chapter in this study. Of course, there could be many other explanations for why a decorative object is included in an unmarked grave. The person could have been a beloved parent, grandparent or popular community helper. Or it could have been a fortunate individual buried with some of his accumulated treasures, gifts or thefts. Alternatively, the goods could have been hidden in some persons grave until needed later or until the coast was clear and forgotten. The reader can no doubt add their own list of speculative possibilities, but in serious studies such possibilities should not be presented as facts or probabilities without conclusive and independently verified evidence to support such assertions.

As noted, the problem with encountering such conclusions is that it is almost always the case that the evidence and conclusions are being 'used' to 'fill in a gap' of knowledge or in such a way as to favour an author's pre-conceived idea or pre-determined narrative. For example, if some official tomb diggers/robbers (as modern archaeologists in fact are) think ancient societies always had kings and queens, then decorative grave goods are often presented as evidence of ancient kings and queens and no other possibilities are considered. But the desire to fill gaps with plausible assertions, is also motivated by professional competition and pride. A well salaried professional in any subject has an inbuilt reluctance to admitting a lack of knowledge, so conjecture, imagination, assertion and occasionally a string of long Latin-based words can be used to fill any blank knowledge gaps or save any possibly "I don't know" embarrassing moments.

Being 'blinded by science' occurs in far more areas of life than science; and prejudiced opinion smuggled in by being 'obscured by imaginary and well rehearsed detail' is apparent in far more areas of life than just politics. I write this on the basis of long experience. I have worked among such representatives in engineering, academia, education and politics, many of whom uncritically borrow opinion from any superficially acquired or 'plausible' source and uncritically pass it on as valid and as their own. Incidentally, pressure to prematurely fill knowledge gaps comes from the fact that being the first to declare a plausible (but insufficiently examined) link in a chain of evidence has promotional and/or tenure extending possibilities. This, of course, happens to be a really perverse incentive to appear doubly certain of an untested hypothesis or conclusion.

Finally, the guidelines I adopted for this study were threefold. First: To consider and understand the chemical and biological organisation of the individual organisms. Second: To consider and understand the social form of organisation within the various species. Third: To consider and understand the bio-chemical basis of the relationships between the various species. I hope the reader will find these three guidelines and the above noted points helpful and the rest of the chapters interesting and challenging.

They are certainly intended to be both - and radically so, rather than being entertaining and popular. I also hope the reader will creatively and critically use the conceptual tool of (N-M-G-R + A-D) and the points made in this introduction to; a) check any unwarranted assumptions or assignment of purpose, or speculations that I may have inadvertently included in this book; and b) to use them to explore their own particular focus on the part of life on earth they are most concerned to understand.

Although this introduction has been intentionally rather long, I hope dear reader that it has by this means sufficiently equipped each of you to make sense of the variety, complexity of the material presented and at the same time prepared you for the reasoning process contained in the following chapters. As a social species I suggest we should be collaborating in order to understand and change the world for the better, not competing to get ahead within the existing eco-destroying system. And as an intelligent species, we should all be on a journey of evaluating what we once thought was valid against new evidence and of actively assisting each other to overturn the many prejudices we have undoubtedly inherited from previous generations.

CHAPTER 1

THE INORGANIC ELEMENTS OF LIFE ON EARTH.
At first glance it may seem to some readers that the non-living subjects of this first chapter - the gases, liquids, minerals and rocks - have little or nothing to do with the important world of active living things. As far as we generally understand them, like the stars and planets these inorganic elements are seemingly relatively inert materials that just move according to mechanical, chemical, electrical or gravitational forces. Life on the other hand, with its self-replication and self-animated activity can seem to be something completely different. The two domains are phenomena, which seem simply to be physically and therefore intellectually considered poles apart. Whilst for some purposes, there is good reason for continuing to make this distinction, for the purposes of understanding life on earth in general, at this particular stage of understanding the evolution of life on earth, I think there is not.

In fact there is a very good, long overdue reason in the study of life on earth, to seriously consider the intimate interface and interconnection between inorganic and organic material. All organic life contains vital quantities and qualities of inorganic material and could not function without them. The now familiar 'vitamins' are indeed the vital minerals that all life on earth requires for their cells to function normally. Indeed, life on earth is a self-organising composition of organic and inorganic material, and as will be covered in the subsequent chapters, it is in many ways of a qualitatively different order to non-organic material. However, the important interconnection of the organic with the inorganic should not be ignored or taken for granted as is often the case. For a very long time the separation of *'animal, vegetable and mineral'* categories of the earth's contents has described not only the name of a once popular parlour game, but has satisfied a common sense way of looking at the world. I suggest this too is no longer a sufficiently rigid demarcation even from a common sense perspective.

The fact is that all 'life on earth' has key elements of inorganic material as functioning parts of its inner and external structure. For this study to focus on the amazing phenomenon of 'life on earth' we need to be aware at least of some of this interconnected complexity. As animals we humans obviously need to breathe the combination of inorganic gases we call air and we need to drink the mixture of inorganic gases we call water. Both are absolutely vital. Without air we humans, (as with practically all life forms), die quickly; without water we die slowly; without nutritional material we also die slowly. The importance of relatively unpolluted air and water has long been known, but that these substances are 'mixtures' of other molecule groups is a fairly recent level of human understanding. Previous common sense understandings might have concluded that combining two gases would simply result in a mixture of gasses and in many cases it would. The combinations resulting in what is known as laughing gas and butane gas for example. However, despite the fact that for thousands of years' people using their 'common sense' thought water was a single liquid element, it turned out that water is also a mixture of gases - Hydrogen and Oxygen. But not mixed in just in any proportions but specifically in the ratio of two to one, (i.e. H2O). It is now the case that practically everybody knows the H2O symbol. So even before we get to the even greater complexities of real life, it turns out that not everything humanity has thought in the relatively recent past is either true or what it seems to be. As we consider 'life on earth' throughout this book, this conclusion will become something of a recurring theme.

We do now reliably know that 'life on earth' in all its forms, consists of various mixes of organic and inorganic materials and that these inorganic materials are not only all around life on earth, but in different states and proportions are also within us humans and within all organic forms of life. In fact the term inorganic should not now be understood as meaning inert. Most, if not all, inorganic materials contain forces of energy which can be released in one way or another. Most common everyday inorganic fuels are sources of easily released energy. Each species of life on earth needs to constantly absorb and metabolise these gases, minerals and electro-magnetic sources of energy (sunlight) in order to remain active, to grow and to reproduce.

There is a reasonably sound deduction that these inorganic materials condensed out of the original interstellar gases and material which went through a process of concentration and condensation which resulted in the formation of the gaseous and then solid surfaced objects we generally call stars and planets and in particular, the planet we call earth. Using the same reasonable presumption, these materials coalesced into the roughly spherical shapes not only of our own planet, but all the other solid orbiting bodies within our solar system. In other words, those inorganic gases and assorted solid materials existed before the start of 'life on earth', and are clearly its indispensable chemical basis. Those inorganic materials known to be essential to life on earth include Hydrogen, Oxygen, Nitrogen, Helium and Carbon.

These particular gases, in different nuanced forms, are essential to life on earth, again not just in any amounts, but only in particular proportions or ratios. For example the atmospheric gases that air breathing life forms have evolved within, comprises Nitrogen (78%), Oxygen (21%) and Argon (0.9%). However, Oxygen is a potentially dangerous gas even at such low percentages, easily causing fires and explosions. Therefore, some things so essential to us to survive can, in different proportions, be also detrimental. We tend to take for granted the composition of air and frequently forget which other life forms are ensuring the production of it. Too much or too little oxygen can also be detrimental to plants and animals. For life on earth to continue, the inorganic environments, temperatures, atmospheric ratios and electromagnetic radiations, need to be within the general oscillating parameters which have existed during the evolution of life on earth. Yet it is the evolved biosphere made up of a complex of plants, insects and animals that has up to modern times helped maintain these proportions, within a manageable dynamic balance. For example, one group of organisms (animals, bacteria and fungi) absorb oxygen and expel carbon dioxide and another group (plants) absorb carbon dioxide and expel oxygen. This balance between animals and plants is not the only balance crucial to life on earth, but it is crucial to the composition of the air most terrestrial life needs to maintain itself. Nitrogen, the main component of air, is not a biological product and undoubtedly came from volcanic sources. Therefore it is suggested that;

"The original source of oxygen in the atmosphere was not biological photosynthesis, however, but a chemical equivalent ... .Solar energy, especially the ultraviolet rays, can split water to form hydrogen and oxygen without the aid of a biological catalyst. Hydrogen gas is light enough to escape the Earth's gravity. Oxygen, a much heavier gas, is retained in the atmosphere by gravity. On the early Earth, most of the Oxygen formed in this way reacted with iron in the rocks and oceans, locking it permanently into the crust." (Oxygen: 'The Molecule that made the World'. Nick Lane. Oxford. Chapter 2)

Nevertheless, biological photosynthesis by plant based communities now keeps it refreshed. It is the so-called human produced greenhouse gases which have caught most attention over the last few decades because of their effect on the climate and on life on earth in general. For millions of years these natural gases recycled from within the network of life on earth have maintained a life supporting balance by being absorbed by the planet's natural materials at roughly the same rate as they have been produced by their natural sources. These gaseous products are; Water Vapour, Carbon Dioxide, Methane, Nitrous Oxide, Ozone and several types of fluorocarbons. The effect they have in the atmosphere is to prevent the normal cooling of the earth's temperature by natural means. The consistent release of these gaseous products causes the average air, sea and land temperatures to increase and ice to melt in glaciers, causing rivers to flood. Ice loss at the earth's poles, also causes a loss of reflected solar heat and raises sea levels. The higher atmospheric temperature, beyond a certain point, causes plants, animals and humans to lose the ability to cope and the chain of food and habitat resources they rely upon to survive and can also shrivel and deteriorate.

Although these gases are products of natural materials, the activities of humans since the start of the industrial period of production in Europe some 250 or so years ago, have produced them at a rate far higher and faster than the planetary life-forms and biosphere could absorb them and thus maintain its previous balance. Indeed, the problem has further accelerated since sometime after the First and Second World Wars, (1914-18 and 1939-45) when new war-time inventions and productivity increased due to automation, mass production techniques and the many petro-chemical driven inventions. These industrial 'tools' and 'techniques' were combined to pave the way for humans to rapidly cause forest clearances, increase fossil fuel production and consumption along with the global production, distribution and consumption of commodities on a massive scale. Mass travel in automobiles, ships and aircraft let loose a never ending torrent of pollution and greenhouse gas emissions. In the life-time of practically one generation (or perhaps two) a reasonably healthy planet and its natural resources has been reduced to the equivalent of an individual human being with a degree of asthma (air pollution), blood cancer (fresh and sea water pollution), diabetes (soil contamination), vital organ damage (ecological species destruction) and multiple other planetary co-morbidities.

It should not be forgotten that the materials listed in the above extract are all those inorganic parts of organic life on earth which are not optional to life on earth, but essential. In addition, the one already mentioned vitally important inorganic compound formed from a combination of two of them - water - is absolutely essential. Water, mixed with other organic and inorganic substances is in every cell, of every living life form on earth. Much of life on earth, including humans at a molecular level are made up of Hydrogen, Nitrogen, Carbon, Oxygen and Water in appropriate proportions and which have been energised by the inorganic rays of sunlight also in appropriate amounts. Some minute cells and anaerobic bacteria can live without oxygen as a gas and without sunlight as an energy source, but as far as I am aware, none can live without atoms of oxygen and hydrogen mixed in the molecular form of water. Even deep below the earth, bacteria in rocks can survive without oxygen, sunlight or plant material for nourishment, by drawing energy from chemical reactions, but apparently they cannot survive without contact with some molecules of an aqueous based mixture of gases which have seeped into the rocks.

Moreover, most of the earth's surface is covered with water which is currently estimated to amount to around 70%. Half of many animal bodies, including human bodies, contain water in some form. Water is also of crucial importance in being almost a unique universal solvent with direct enabling consequences for the cellular structure of all forms of life on earth. The hydrogen bond with oxygen not only gives water its amazing characteristics but in the replication of cells, it is now known that waters' complex molecular arrangement assists in the necessary connection and disconnection of links in the strands of DNA in living organisms, when they replicate to form copies of their bio-chemical structures. Until the late 18th century, it was thought by every intelligent enquirer into the materials crucial to life on earth, that water was a single element. It was only, in the late 18th century, that it was established by Lavoisier that water is itself a compound of at least the two key gases, Oxygen and Hydrogen, mentioned earlier. The understanding of Chemistry at that stage was much disputed, particularly between the French and English based scientists over whether theories should be the simplest possible explanations or the most complete. Discoveries and historical debates such as these, serve to remind us that knowledge is never absolute, fixed and final, it is always provisional and it is always relative. The assertion of the existence of absolute truths is a mistaken or short-sighted promotion of anthropocentric opinions or figures of speech - not a representation of actual realities.

The further amazing thing about water is that within the temperature range on planet earth, it can exist in more than one form. It can exist in the form of a liquid (fresh and sea) which can absorb many things, a solid (in the various forms of ice) a semi-solid (in the forms of sleet and snow) and a gas (in the forms of steam or vapour). All these forms (or states) of water play a crucial role in supporting life on earth, or rather life on earth has evolved in relationship to these different forms of H2O established by the planet's inner heat and its position relative to the sun. Incidentally, it has been claimed that Oxygen is not unique to planet earth but is the third most abundant element in the universe. Although this claim, as with many astronomic assertions, can of course only be an estimate based upon visual evidence gathered by light sensitive instruments and estimated using complex calculations. There is no practical way to verify either the actual evidence or the accuracy of such calculations. However, on earth;

"Water plays a unique role in chemistry. The special properties of the different forms of water — from ice and snow to liquid water — are due to hydrogen bonding between the H2O molecules,...The hydrogen bond is of fundamental importance in biological systems since all living matter has evolved from and exists in an aqueous environment. Hydrogen bonds are involved in most biological processes as little energy is needed in forming as well as breaking of these bonds. Without hydrogen bonds, no water can be transported from the roots to the leaves in the trees!" ('The Wonder of Water'. Preface. I. Olovsson.)

Life has utilised water so consistently and effectively that chemists specialising in understanding the complexity of water, consider that it should be considered as more than just a semi-inert inert liquid compound but as a sympathetic biomolecule which is essential to all forms of life on earth. Given its apparent role in binding and releasing water molecules in the functioning of haemoglobin and entropy in protein folding within cells, it perhaps should be judged as more than just an extremely useful solvent, but of course, sympathy is a human concept, not a characteristic of water. I only mention such detail to indicate the extensive and all-embracing importance of water, not just for everyday human washing, cooking and drinking but for the crucial role it plays within the bio-chemical cellular process of all life on earth. Once its importance is understood, the realisation should dawn on more of us that water is just too important to life on earth to be treated as a commodity to be bought and sold for profit or to be polluted by agricultural, industrial and domestic run-off and negligence. Many plants, insects and animals live in it, all animals and plants need it and it is within the cells and bodies of all species of life on earth. And;

"....no other fluid possesses all the properties that make water so biologically versatile. Not only does it provide a broad and flexible canvas for life to paint its full multifaceted tableaux, it is itself part of the palette." ('Water and Life' Edited by RL Lyndon-Bell and others. CRC Press.)

In this context, it should be mentioned in passing that for millions of years, access to water for all life forms was natural and for at least three hundred thousand years (300,000) the relationship of humans to water was entirely natural. Perhaps this is where I should point out that all the numbers relating to years mentioned in relation to past events before recorded history are also extremely approximate and frequently disputed. The sources used to estimate the dates of pre-historical events such as the age of the earth or the appearances of certain species, even when utilising radio-chemical dating are not all completely accurate or reliable. Therefore, the assumptions often made when considering or calculating them are best understood as useful approximations and are therefore not always valid in terms of accuracy. Consequently, the accuracy of any assertions made which are mostly dependent upon dates or periods of time to support them should be viewed with some degree of scepticism. However, we can safely say that all species of life on earth, not already resident in water, no matter when they existed or for how long they existed still had to locate themselves within easy reach of water. With the expansion of settled agriculture between ten thousand and five thousand years ago water was understood to be so vital to human agricultural production that it was socially engineered to be relocated near human settlements. River diversions, canals, dams, reservoirs, irrigation ditches began one of the many re-orderings of the natural environment by human intervention or interference, which for good and bad will be considered in later chapters, but it is undoubtedly a change of crucial importance.

Minerals and Sediments.

It is worth ending this section with a short description of the nature of the inorganic material which make-up the surface of the land and the ocean beds of the sea, both of which are necessary to the life forms that live within the biosphere of earth. Without venturing deeply into the realms of geological science there are two basic forms of material classed as rocks. These two basic forms are 'igneous' rocks and 'sedimentary' rocks. The Igneous rocks have been formed from molten material (as exists in the earth's core and the sun) and were cooled down and solidified by contact with air or water. This solidification was an analogous process to the ones that occur in volcanic eruptions or underwater tectonic plate cracks, where liquid lava is forced out by plate or magma pressure in one form or another and becomes cooled to a solid condition. The Igneous rocks are mostly in the form of Granites, which contain various mixes such as quartz, mica and feldspar. They are present in haphazard formations in various parts of the world and are mostly of extremely ancient formation. Some of the Igneous rocks have been around for so long that a combination of heat and pressure has changed them into what are known as Metamorphic rocks, the most familiar one being the various seams of Marble, from which columns, temples, monuments and even modern counter tops have been fashioned.

The sedimentary rocks are made of material such as dust, sand, grit held in suspension in air or water before settling down and being compressed by successive layers of solid material or water. The commonly used sedimentary ones are slates, limestone, sandstone, millstone grit, clays, shales and carboniferous limestone. The latter in large quantities, was held in suspension in the seas and it is from this that the many sea creatures obtained the material to form their protective shells. Not surprisingly, life was absorbing and using the inorganic material of the planet from its earliest beginnings. So prolific were these ancient forms of life on earth that their shells accumulated on the bottom of sea beds and under great pressure for millions of years were eventually transformed into limestone. Due to gravity, sediments were initially laid down in horizontal strips and many previous life forms were preserved in the sediments and are now found as fossils in various places. Not knowing in detail the weather patterns and volcanic activity we cannot assume that these sedimentary deposits were laid down in a regular incremental pattern, so dating fossils by layers, may not always be accurate. However, because of tectonic plate shifts many of these layers were also tilted at all kinds of angles and elevated to places of considerable height. The fact that fossils of sea creatures were being found on ancient mountain tops provided evidence, not only that life on earth was indeed very ancient, but that the solid surface of the planet had changed radically over the eons of time.

Nevertheless, fossil dating aside, scientific studies have also established that living things contain many essential inorganic elements within them that, as already noted, 'life on earth' depends upon. Indeed, the rocks ground down by the action of winds, rains and tides are the basis of the vitamins, minerals and metal oxides that the organs and cells of all living things need, when they have passed through the metabolism of other life forms and been re-absorbed. Thus the vitamins, A, C, D, E and the B's, are chemical compounds of bonded atoms obtained from these planetary materials. The minerals from Calcium through Magnesium, Phosphorus, to Sodium, along with trace elements such as Zinc, Copper iron and Selenium that our organs and internal and external cell structures need to keep us and other plants and animals alive and healthy are all derived in one way or another from the inorganic materials located on planet earth. Ground down by wind, water and gravity erosion, these particles are carried by wind, rain, rivers and deposited in and on the top soil around the planets' surface. As one popularising educational organisation puts it;

"Minerals, also called mineral elements, are those elements other than carbon, hydrogen, oxygen and nitrogen that are found in the body. These minerals are derived from the breakdown of the rocks of the earth's crust which are then dissolved in water." ('Nutrition: vitamins and minerals'. Open University Learning Publication. Section 2.1)

During its pre-organic stage of existence, planet earth was already evolving, both physically and chemically. The earth was moving and changing itself by mechanical, chemical and electrical forces implicit in all matter. Some parts were cooling down, some parts were heating up, some parts were breaking down, whilst other parts were coalescing and combining. Gases were becoming liquids and liquids were becoming gases, solids were dissolving in liquids and particles were settling out of liquids. Even before organic life forms appeared the inorganic planet itself had evolved from a gaseous swirl to a hot liquid magma and onto a mix of solid surface crust and water over which formed a mixed gaseous atmosphere. At a certain stage, somewhere, (possibly near deep, ocean vents) a process of inorganic chemical reactions and combinations morphed into a combination with bio-chemical properties. A further process of discrete organelle integration took place and self-regulating chemically active cell-like structures emerged. The discipline of biological science has classed these early life forms as archaea and proto-bacteria. It is conjectured that some inorganic but reactive and energy containing material on the planet had been transformed into the earliest known form of organic material. In other words, the inorganic planet had been slowly, very slowly, changing itself not only by means of alterations to its chemical and physical structure, but now by alterations and transformations to a new form of bio-physical structures.

Inorganic material becomes organic.

Nevertheless, reasonably plausible scientific speculation suggests that some billion plus years ago, the inorganic materials on our planet mixed and combined in such a way that the bio-chemical foundations of life on earth, particularly protein molecules, became actively self-reproductive. How and when these gases and substances bio-chemically combined and recombined to form living organisms, is the subject of considerable speculation and much controversy, particularly between religious and secular thinkers. The idea that some invisible male superman set the whole 'life on earth' thing off, still has an extensive, but evidence-absent grip on the thinking of millions of human beings. In secular terms, it is conjectured that since many inorganic compounds once mixed together can release energy stored in their atomic structures either slowly or rapidly without any biological agency involved then this natural energy release was probably involved during the first stage of producing inorganic chemicals capable of further stages of synthetic refinement. In chemistry it is known that some metal Sulphides can actually catalyse organic molecules from inorganic ingredients and studies of single cell life forms have produced evidence that some bacteria still only use inorganic material for nutrient and metabolic energy purposes.

Therefore it is reasoned that in some water-based, geo-chemical and mineralogical reactions, organic compounds were by some bio-chemical means anciently formed. However, there is no tangible evidence that these associations between atoms and molecules were anything other than just potential random events. In addition there are as yet no plausible suggestions that such associations were or are purposeful. Suggestions by evolutionary sceptics that the occurrence of self-replicating bio-chemical organisms could not have happened by random associations, once considered in detail, are unconvincing ones. The crass analogy provided by a well-known radio astronomer that a random occurrence of life on earth is as unlikely as a hurricane blowing through a scrap yard could assemble a car or an aeroplane is entirely spurious. This is because, if for no other reason, the random assembly of inert manufactured substances by humans is a completely different proposition than the random mixing of natural liquids, gases, chemicals and bio-chemicals.

There is no parallel between the areas of self-replicating bio-chemical life and the millions of meticulous physical stages of research, prototype testing and evaluation required for any complex form of mechanical or civil engineering. Such illogically constructed broadsides against evolutionary explanations ultimately stem from a stubborn defence of creationist type ideologies. In actual fact, many aspects of inorganic nature demonstrate that under specific circumstances, different qualitative transitions do emerge from the random association of various different material quantities. For example, two commonly available inert powders or liquids when mixed deliberately or accidentally can cause an explosion; two different materials or metals when heated by magma can produce an alloy or even gemstones. Even before life on earth began, the random association of (or natural mixing of) two or more chemical substances, under certain volcanic (heat or pressure) circumstances, did for example produce the Granite, Diamonds, Gold and Silver etc., that we are thoroughly familiar with.

Under the appropriate circumstances, quantitative additions of substances can produce different qualities. The fact that other inorganic substances will not mix, conjoin or react with each other is immaterial. Just because many substances coming together do not result in a new quality, does not mean that others do not actually do so. Chemistry and much of industry is based entirely on the search for and discovery of new materials by combining, splitting and mixing quantities of various existing substances. When this combining occurs this confirms that they are physically able to do so, not on the basis of alchemy or magic, but based on the propensities of their natural atomic structures. Therefore, the question arises; why should affinities and potentials, under the right circumstances, not merge naturally among bio-chemical substances as they do in chemical and metallic affinities?

Furthermore another important characteristic of the natural world (both inorganic and organic) should be noted at this point; the production of organic as well as inorganic substances, (new and repeat) always requires the consumption of other material and energy substances. To produce inorganic metals other inorganic substances must be consumed; to produce inorganic granite, other inorganic minerals which they contain must be incorporated. To produce new (or repeated occurrences of) organic life, other organic material must also be incorporated. In this sense production is not separate from consumption it is often simultaneously consumption; and consumption is often simultaneously production. Intellectually, the two moments can be separated, but in the real-world of practice they cannot. As will be covered in later chapters the consumption of nourishment (N) by cells produces energy and proteins and the consumption of energy and proteins produces cellular growth and its bio-chemical renewal. In addition, as will be demonstrated in the following chapters, the characteristic of symbiosis and endo-symbiosis among life on earth organisms provides evidence that bio-chemical affinities and synthesis do occur naturally and indeed do (and logically did) merge to create new forms of living multicellular entities.

From an evolutionary perspective, it is suggested that the origin of 'life on earth' was an accumulation of these chemical associations which eventually transformed themselves into bio-chemical organic compounds and then by a further process became a bio-synthetic composition of cells, capable of self-replication. Then by using energy from various available sources, these bio-chemical processes continued to combine, evolve and merge. The term now used for the way life forms gain energy in the sunless depths of the deep ocean is termed 'Chemosynthesis'. That process is the deep sea alternative to the Photosynthesis method used by plants within range of the energy transmitted by sunlight. Although this is one of many logical deductions starting from known and tested chemical experiments, in actual fact no one really knows how life on earth began. So exactly how inorganic material was synthesised into continually self-regulating and continually self-replicating organic material has still to be uncovered, nevertheless the reproduction (R) stage of life on earth is remarkable for its often high rate, particularly within cells. Nevertheless, such 'origin' speculations, interesting as they might be, need not entertain, confuse or otherwise delay us from focusing on what we can and do know about life on earth. Unlike previous generations we now know, with a high degree of certainty, that life on earth is made up of interconnected cellular associations (organisms) based upon cell type structures and their numerous organelles. We now also know that;

"Cells are made up of carbon, oxygen, hydrogen, nitrogen, phosphorus, and sulphur as the major ingredients, with a whole suite of trace metals and other elements as well. All of these compounds are critical in the construction of basic cellular components like the cell membrane, genetic material (DNA and RNA), and all of the proteins and other molecules used in running the cell's machinery." ('Oxygen' 'A Four Billion Year History' D. E. Canfield.)

Life on earth at the cellular level will be considered further in a later chapter, it is introduced in this first chapter merely to emphasise the foundational and continuous ongoing interconnected link between the inorganic aspects of the planet and the organic. For many generations, knowledge has been separated into different disciplines which has allowed exceptional detail to be pursued, but often at the cost of understanding the vitally important connections. Too often the two domains of materials science and the life sciences, in particular, have been viewed as disconnected areas of study. Even each particular discipline has been subdivided into smaller and smaller fields of study until the holistic world itself is viewed through the often restricted prisms of a particular narrow subject based paradigms. This micro-division of knowledge has continued across the generations, until a large detailed amount is understood about a little portion of existence and little is understood about a large portion of existence. In this way each specialist area tends to continually focus down onto its own detailed research areas and problems.

Yet, from the stage of the beginning of life on earth, there were two inter-connected forms of change taking place on the planet; inorganic changes and organic changes; and both were continually affecting each other. A change in one could cause a change in the other. An inorganic atmospheric change beyond a certain point would engender a change in the organic life form dependent upon it. A change in temperature or soil acidity would favour or not favour an adaptation or mutation within life forms living in or on it. From this observation we can safely conclude that change, either very slow or reasonably fast, is therefore the only real constant on the planet and that this is likely the case for the entire universe. However, the importance of this observation for the purpose of this particular study is to register the fact that both these forms of change took place naturally, often slowly and without any form of conscious intervention or inbuilt purpose. The natural changes to inorganic material which occur in the form of combinations or disintegrations are due to natural causes of physical phenomena such as pressure, heat, cold, erosion or electrical or chemical reactions or attractions.

In response to these inorganic changes, the changes to organic forms were therefore either compatible with the inorganic surroundings, (including any changes) or else organisms would have failed to survive and thus ceased to exist. We can conclude from the proliferation of fossilised life forms in sedimentary layers and the vast numbers of life forms known to modern research that many such changes were successful and that many were not. The number of failures cannot be known for obvious lack of evidence, but those that survived are evidence of successful changes by adaptations of one kind or another. Throughout those billions of years the two categories of material substance (organic and inorganic) were constantly interacting, whilst, as we shall see in the next chapter on cells, the organic material was absolutely dependent upon the inorganic.

The only conclusion possible from the above descriptive scenario, if it is at all accurate, is that it is only those inorganic changes, that are compatible with the existing inorganic and organic conditions of the earth, that will allow life, as we now know it, to survive and evolve. Too much air or water pollution, too much nuclear fall-out, too much heat, too little photo-synthetic vegetation and, one by one, life forms dependent upon them adapt by mutation or will die out. Therefore, if changes in the inorganic conditions of the planet are made to occur, which are not compatible with the entire spectrum of organic material of the planet then it will be the organic material which will become extinct, not the inorganic. A dead orbiting planet Earth, (such as Mars), will still be a planet, but not one that earth adapted life could survive on - nor how an intelligent species would want it to be. The fact that for billions and millions of years, the above process of change and adaptation was an unconscious unfolding of bio-chemical processes by the numerous organic species of life on earth is not altered by the later arrival of humanity. The fact that a species has evolved whose consciousness has developed to such a degree that a few of its members have begun to understand the delicate balance achieved by the organic material within the parameters of the inorganic material, does not alter the absolute necessity for such balance to continue. The inorganics; the composition of the atmosphere, the levels of solar radiation, the temperature ranges, the water quality and distribution, the wind cycles and the soil composition, all need to be compatible with or tolerable to, the whole network of integrated and inter-dependent organic life forms.

When it is fully understood that 'life on earth' (including human life) is essentially a variety of inter-connected inorganic materials energised and animated into self-activated motion and replication, then the false dichotomy of life versus non-life; or of important forms of life versus unimportant life or inert 'stuff' we can afford to pollute and destroy, then humanity can begin to move on beyond its current Holocene and Anthropocene self-obsession. Until this understanding becomes more widespread, we will continue to find that most studies of life on earth start from an ancient historical assumption that human life is something distinctive and can be considered and treated as something separate from other forms of life. The focus of many short-sighted studies is on what differentiates human life from other forms of life, whether this is in the form of language, tools, culture, art, music or whatever. Although I accept that these are radical differences between humans and non-human organisms and inorganic materials I do not accept that they negate the essential continuity, similarity and physical interdependence between all forms of organic life on earth and the planet. My decision to utilise the abbreviated formula (N-M-G-R + A-D) as a conceptual tool to assist in considering the phases that life on earth goes through, will hopefully bring to attention the main stages of all life on earth and will encourage further consideration of the essential interplay between the inorganic and organic at each stage of life and evolution. As already noted I hope this abbreviation also helps to keep in mind these fundamental species similarities and inter-dependencies whilst considering the multitude of less fundamental differences, as will be discussed in each subsequent chapter.

I consider the bio-chemical sequences of life on earth so important to keep in mind throughout this study that I shall include frequent repetitions and reminders of it. Here I will note some questions which I found useful to consider at each stage of the (N-M-G-R + A-D) processes of life on earth. Nourishment (N); the intake of the inorganic and organic material needed for metabolism by the organism. *(Where does it come from? How is it recycled?)* Metabolism (M); a stage of relative external stasis while internally the organelles actively break down and assimilate what is needed from the ingested nourishing material. *(How does this occur? What can impede it?)* Growth (G); the replacement, extension or expansion of the organism utilising the metabolised materials ingested. *(What regulates this? What distorts it?)* Reproduction (R); the process of internal sequencing required for cellular replication and species continuity. *(What triggers it? What interrupts it?)* Ageing (A); the gradual deterioration of the organism's various cellular and multicellular organ functions. *(What accelerates it? What delays it?)* Death (D); the end of the organism's 'active processes' leading to the immediate or eventual recycling of its materials. *(Should we accelerate it? How should we celebrate it?)* Each phase or stage has its own evolutionary developed parameters for each particular species, but these can all be usefully condensed or codified into the abbreviated form of (N-M-G-R + A-D). All life on earth must constantly interact with these organic and inorganic materials throughout the first phases of (N-D-G-R) of the process of living which retains a dialectical balance within a limited range of chemical and thermal limits.

In insect, plant and animal species this internal balance varies and in humans and other organisms it is known as homeostasis. Within these varying limits 'life on earth' can function well. However, beyond them 'normal' life is detrimentally affected and that with excesses to these limits, all but the most adaptable or robust of life forms will eventually cease. For example, a few of the bacterial cell forms of life on earth can exist in extremes which would extinguish most other forms of life hence they are commonly called 'extremophiles'. However, extremophiles are the exception and not the rule on planet earth. Therefore, in this study we will focus upon those interactions which fall into the normal range of (N-M-G-R+A-D) for each of the species covered. It needs to be stressed that the pre-industrial organic and non-organic weather influenced material (gases, liquids and solids i.e. non-organic nature) had evolved naturally over billions of years.

During this period they settled into a dynamically balanced system of winds, tides, rivers, lakes, seas, aquifers, flood plains and swamps, with their patterns of gas and water absorption, evaporation, condensation (storms, rains etc.). With the rare exception of large external cosmic induced extinction events, around and upon these dynamically balanced inorganic planetary systems, organic life had also evolved alongside them. Again it is important to understand that this evolution took place over extremely long periods of slow geological changes and during long periods of relative stasis. This evolution occurred within sea based plants and animals and within land based plants, insects, animals and on to four limbed mammals and semi-bipedal animals, including humans. So, with the rare exception of major extinction processes, organic evolution reacted to and adjusted to earth's periods of extremely slow patterns of inorganic change and environmental stasis. After the following couple of paragraphs of summary, a broad range of different realms of life on earth will be considered in the following sequence of chapters.

Summary of Chapter 1.

This first chapter has briefly described the inorganic materials, from which planet earth was originally formed, such as gasses, liquids, igneous and some sedimentary rocks. At the same time, the point was made that the term 'inorganic' does not mean completely 'inert'. The different often 'active' states of water, gases and minerals, was noted along with the propensity - under certain conditions, - to mix and be altered by natural forces such as heat, gravity, chemical erosion or explosion. It was proposed in this chapter, that at a certain unknown point in the the multi-billion orbital circulation of the earth around the sun, inorganic materials (active or otherwise) became combined in such a way that the structural mix of inorganic and organic material became self-reproducing molecules, organelles and archaic cells, eventually taking the form of the bio-chemical structures we know as 'life'. It was noted that the self-replicating, bio-chemical structure of life needed to be consistently supplied with additional sources of inorganic material by absorbing energy, gases, liquids and minerals along with additional organic material. This replenishment is achieved through a process of each cell absorbing Nutrients, (N), Metabolising them (M), Growing (G), Reproducing (R), before Ageing (A) and Dying. (D). For convenience, this bio-chemical life-cycle process was condensed into the abbreviated formula of (N-M-G-R + A-D) = Life on Earth.

CHAPTER 2

Cells - bio-chemical beginnings and essential components of all 'life on earth'.

In the previous chapter the sequence (N-M-G-R + A-D) as life cycle phases common to all forms of life on earth, was presented as a condensed or codified form of recognising their fundamental similarities. It seemed to me that these phases and sequences were obviously true from the knowledge gained from within the life cycles of animals, plants and insects. At that point in time, however, I had not come across a reference which would confirm that a six phase life cycle as a provisional working hypothesis also existed in the case of minute cells. However, late in the research for this chapter I came across the following two extracts;

"...cells share many characteristics with all kinds of animals, plants and fungi. They grow, they reproduce, they maintain themselves.." ('What is life?'. P. Nurse. Chapter 1)

And;

"A living cell is a dynamic chemical system, operating far from chemical equilibrium. For a cell to grow or make a new cell in its own image, it must take in free energy from the environment, as well as raw materials, to drive the necessary synthetic reactions. This consumption of free energy is fundamental to life. When it stops, a cell decays toward chemical equilibrium and soon dies." ('The Molecular Biology of the Cell' . B. Alberts; A. Johnson; J. Lewis. Sixth Edition. Chapter 1)

I had previously come across evidence that cells took in material from outside their surrounding membrane and excluded unwanted material from within. The above quotations from authors specialising in cellular biology, therefore, confirmed my logical premise that a form of the sequence (N-M-G-R + A-D) also existed for the life-cycle of cells. If we consider that *maintaining themselves,* includes (N), (the intake of needed material) and (M), (breaking down and processing that material in forms to be used inside the cell), then the first two are confirmed. It is obvious that cells grow (or renew their parts and functions) and it is common knowledge that they reproduce as will be described below. However, within the books I consulted during this research on cells I also came across considerable anthropomorphic language applied to cells along with a modern trend of inapplicable teleological assumptions also being applied to cells. Thus cells, for example, were described as 'factories' having 'command centres' and 'miniature power plants' in one book and 'Teleonomic' (teleological: a compound derivative of the Greek 'telos' meaning 'end' and 'logia', meaning logical) in another. The latter Latin derived term assuming a 'logical end' to the process was asserted as an 'irrefutable biological phenomenon'. However, logic itself is purely a human construct and even human life does not always follow a set pattern such as what human logic would anticipate, let alone any pattern that life in general may appear to follow. Such assertions are invariably based upon anthropocentric assumptions that everything in existence has a humanly imagined (and class-based) purpose and is designed to fulfil that humanly imagined purpose.

That anthropocentric way of viewing the world ultimately stems from the fact that humans and many animals frequently do exhibit purposeful behaviour (i.e. have an anticipated outcome to their actions in their consciously directed activities) and this phenomenon is applied unscientifically to everything that exists. This view is transmitted and imposed universally and consistently within the religious ideologies of many peoples, where gods or spirits are imagined to have 'motivated' 'designed' and 'created' everything living (and not living) for some human imagined purpose. Revealingly, it is always a purpose which requires a simple or complex human imagination to conceive it. I have dealt with this phenomenon more fully in the introduction, but perhaps a cautionary reminder here will be useful. I urge caution so as not to make the common mistake of assuming that all human and non-human active 'functions' of material 'things' inorganic or organic, imply the existence of a prior active 'purpose'. Certainly, the pursuit of the nutrition phase (N) of life is purposeful in most species but I repeat from the evidence of the additional (M-G-R + A-D) sequential phases the latter are not purposeful in the sense of functioning with regard to some intended outcome.

In any study of life on earth, other than the study of human history, I suggest, therefore, that the two concepts, 'functional' and 'purposeful', should not be confused or used interchangeably, particularly in serious attempts to understand life on earth. For example, there is no evidence that a cell's complex metabolising internal organelles in the metabolic (M) chemical processing phases have been 'designed' to purposefully metabolise the nutrient material (N) in order that the cell or organism can meaningfully fulfil the growing (G) phase. Also cellular and multi-cellular growth has not been 'designed' in order to purposefully enable the reproduction (R) phase to be reached and accomplished. Nor are cells and organisms designed in such a way as to purposefully age (A) in order that they can then die (D). There is absolutely no material evidence anywhere to suggest that Life in general has been designed, and much to suggest life and its functional complexity has just 'evolved' within natural biological success or failure parameters and constraints. Similarly, the process of dying is a functional result of the energy sapping, material exhausting process of living - not the unfolding of an external or internal intended purpose.

From an evolutionary paradigm of understanding, the previously noted phases of a cell's (N-M-G-R + A-D) life cycle are the interconnected and accreted functions of cellular life's entire evolutionary development. It needs to be remembered that the properties of many material things have just occurred, either by random (chance) interactive events or by pre-existing chemical (or other attractive) affinities, and any active functions associated with them have just functionally evolved from such events or affinities. In the case of life on earth (or organic nature) if we are to resist the urge to imagine an invisible higher intelligent power (male or spirit) to explain what is not yet understood, then caution against anthropomorphic and teleological assumptions are necessary. A form of sensuous awareness of surroundings is clearly exhibited by most cell organisms enabling those with the physical means to move toward or away from familiar or unfamiliar material, but we should not assume at this level of microscopic cellular life that this anything within it other than chemical, lipid or ionic attraction or repulsion. There is absolutely no grounds in biological or chemical evidence to assume the cell organelles or some molecular association within it 'knows' what it is doing, simply because it is doing something functional and sequential. When a child asks how a compass needle 'knows' how to point north, if we are sensible we explain it does not 'know' it merely generally moves to that position as a result of magnetic attractions operating upon its molecular structure, not as a result of ferrous metals 'knowing' where north is. I only labour this point because during my working and non-working life I have witnessed the confusion between function and purpose across all professional and non-professional levels of society, particularly with regard to understanding (and misunderstanding) the existence of 'life on earth'.

Returning to practicality of the abbreviation of (N-M-G-R + A-D) as evidentially valid material phases of life on earth, the phases of Aging (deterioration) and Death (cessation of living) of cell's, is also corroborated by those who study them in detail. Thus I suggest, as noted earlier, that despite its abstract presentation, the sequential abbreviation is universally relevant for all living organisms. Consequently, questioning the usual idea of death being the end of *life on earth* in general does not require the consolation of a mystical invention such as an imaginary everlasting soul and an imaginary 'god governed' heaven to be resurrected into. That the individual organism, cell or multi-cellular organism when ceasing to be self-determining and self-renewing the bio-chemical material frequently becomes recycled as a metabolised, potential organic nutrient addition within some other organism that is already living, is undeniable. This assumption can also be reasonably asserted from the evidence accumulating from a materialist investigation. Once understood, it emerges as an obvious fact that the deliberate predatory or accidental death of living organisms, (cells, plants, insects and animals) is a crucial part of the nutritional intake of most if not all other species of life on earth, whilst what remains becomes inorganic.

Therefore, it is perfectly valid to consider that the death of an individual multi-cellular organism is not an end point in the organic cycle of life on earth, but the continuation of material within the larger metabolic cycles of life on earth in general.

Indeed, animal and vegetable organic food intake, living or dead, is an absolutely essential element for much of life's existence. The literary research I have undertaken on cells suggests that there are three basic means that cell evolution has adapted to obtain its energy and nutritional needs. There are Litho-trophic variant cells that obtain their energy needs from inorganic nutrients; Organo-trophic variant cells that obtain those needs from most types of organic molecular substances; and Photo-trophic variant cells which obtain these necessities from transforming energy from light sources. Some extremophile Prokaryotic bacteria exist purely by metabolising available inorganic energy-containing material such as Gases, Liquids, Sediments and Minerals within various Rocks.

So in the case of the smallest and earliest forms of 'life on earth' and on to the most complex, there is an essential requirement to obtain external material and energy sources to enable the elemental phases of a continuous process of organic survival and biological replication to take place. Since I consider these phases as the important, but frequently neglected phases of life on earth, I will continue to repeat them frequently, throughout this book. Repetition being a well authenticated aid to memory absorption. The elemental phases are: 1, obtaining sources of nourishment 'N' (in the form of liquids, inorganic minerals, gases and organic material) suitable for the organism: 2, a suitable period for metabolism, rest, digestion and security 'M' (within a membrane, nest, cave, den or home): 3, a period of uninterrupted developmental growth to maturity 'G'; 4, a reliable method of reproduction 'R' (in the form of sexual or asexual replication). It is during these first four continuous cell processing phases of living (N-M-G-R) in single-celled organisms and multi-cellular organisms that differentially, but progressively, reduces the ability of the organism to continue to cycle through the process without a pivotal degradation and/or sequence failure.

Some species have short cycles (the May fly) and live only for a day, others (Tortoises, Whales and Trees) have relatively long ones and can live for hundreds of years. Life on earth in its various species forms keeps on going, but **all** particular multicellular organisms have evolved with general 'average' limits as to how long they can exist, before the stage 5, of serious detrimental ageing '(A) begins (in the form of an individual or sequential degeneration; of cell structure in part or whole): 6, Death 'D' (in the form of the cessation of organic self-activity.). It is clear that the latter two phases (A-D) can often be extended or shortened by certain circumstances but never avoided. These six essential and interconnected phases of existence (N-M-G-R + A-D) are necessary for all organic entities, from the smallest to the largest. They must be fulfilled, and need to occur in patterns and on a sequential scale appropriate to the evolved life-cycle of the particular organism and species to which it applies. I consider the idea that the human species should now do all it can to try to indefinitely prevent ageing and death, is a form of anthropocentric arrogant exceptionalism.

So again from a scientific and secular perspective this sequence of phases taking place within all species should not be presumed to be purposeful. Organisms are not absorbing nourishment (N) for the purpose of metabolising (M) these substances in order to grow (G). Nor are they reproducing (R) for the purpose of continuing the species. Neither are the phases of ageing (A) and dying (D) purposeful acts in order to provide nourishment or make space available for other life forms. This denial of purpose may seem glaringly obvious in the case of microscopic cells, but so prevalent is the human assumption of 'purpose' in our own anthropocentrically focussed practical and intellectual lives, that, as we shall see, it is constantly applied to the world of nature in general. Plants, for example, do not re-cycle nitrogen etc., in order to produce oxygen in order that other life forms can breathe. The production of oxygen as a bi-product of plant photosynthesis provides the gaseous products which other organisms and species have emerged within and are developed or adapted to breathe (absorb the oxygen, etc.) but this evolved function was a result, not a prior intentional or purposeful bio-chemical process.

I again stress that seeking and inferring intentional 'purpose' and meaning within life in general is purely a direct or indirect aspect of the religiously inspired anthropocentric consciousness or a borrowed habit of earlier thinking obtained from some previous members of the human species. Therefore, just because there is more often than not a purpose attributed to most human actions, it should not be assumed that any effect which has an identified cause and an identified result must be caused by an 'intended' effect. However, knowledge and understanding of life on earth, once seriously considered and confirmed, reveals a substantial material continuum to reality rather than an amalgamation of understood reality and imagined unreality. We do know, of course, that the tides on the earth are a result of the moons gravitational attraction (high tides by the addition of the suns gravitation) but at the same time we no longer assume that this is the purpose of the moon's (or suns) existence or the purpose of the invisible (and as yet unknown) phenomenon known as gravity.

Only the ancient belief in an invisible, mystical creator God or some imaginary conscious force might construe that everything that exists has been created with an intended purpose to fulfil. A general secular viewpoint is content to consider that things may have a functional effect (positive or negative) without considering it to be intentional. Nevertheless, rejecting the miss-use of the concept of purpose does not mean that connections and inter-connections do not exercise a vital or essential 'functional' relationship to life on earth. Therefore, the (N-M-G-R +A-D) functional sequence of such fundamental bio-chemical facts (or phases) of existence, noted above - with all their individual and collective significance and implications - need to be given their full importance. I keep stressing this point early in this book, because these biological phases (and not social developments) are the underlying material (earthly) basis of all species as well as human history and of course also the pre-history of all 'life on earth'.

If the integrated phases of (N-M-during the G-R + A-D) are given their full importance then research on one phase should not be considered in isolation from the other phases. For example in this chapter on cells, it is clear that life on earth (in the form of single cells) without means of motility will, with other things being equal, have less need for Nutrition, will need relatively less internal bio-chemical processing for Metabolism, with consequent repercussions on the cells rate of Growth, Reproduction, Ageing and Dying, than cells with motility-enabling flagella and/or cilia. Of course, again assuming all other factors remain the same. All these phases of the cycle in single cells take place continuously within the cells, often multiple outer membrane layers. Also serious consideration of all the phases indicates the following crucial observation. Any lasting changes in the form, content and function of the cell and its organelles (caused by external circumstances) may have repercussions in the more complex and nutrition-dependent Metabolic, Growth and Reproductive phases, or as a result of deficiencies in nutritional content. Since material and energy produced during Metabolism will be degraded or dissipated by movement and change due to Growth and Reproduction, the requirements for intermittent but appropriate levels of Nourishment will vary. So too will be the number of cycles of (N-M-G-R) possible before essential parts of the cell will also Age, (degrade and be dissipated) before finally ceasing with – (D) Death. Since energy and material are required for all forms of life on earth, this same essential bio-chemical pattern of effects will obviously apply to multi-cellular organisms, which are in fact - associated cellular collectives - of varying complexity and size.

Moreover it is how these phases are secured, which to greater or lesser extent determine the level of awareness or increased consciousness exhibited by the life forms considered. In general there is a molecular and organ level of interactive sensitivity to, or cellular awareness of, surroundings by all forms of life on earth, including (as we shall read) in the cellular category of life considered in this particular chapter. However, given the domination of the anthropocentric ideology of 'individualism' in hierarchical mass society thinking of humans it is worth pointing out at this early stage the fact that the ideological paradigm of 'individuality', consistently ignores the reality of 'life on earth' on so many levels and to a considerable degrees. Although individual organisms can be distinguished and studied, separately from their species and environments, they are interactive multi-cellular forms of life. Even the most basic prokaryotic cells demonstrate by their internal structures and in their external energy and material requirements, that there are no examples of a truly individual self-dependent organism in organic life. In the case of a virus even this minute form of bio-chemical organism needs another life form cell in order to complete its reproductive phase. As will be demonstrated, throughout this chapter, the basic biological fact of cellular reproduction also demonstrates that each organism emerges from another organism by budding or mitosis (with or without the addition of mixed genetic material). Current evidence suggests that this basic inter-connected asexual or sexual reproductive fact of division at the cellular and organelle levels is now an undeniable and universal factor in the phases of all life on earth.

The modern, unrelenting human focus on individuality within life, I suggest, is the result of a neglectful or insufficient understanding of the complexity of the essential interdependent network of connections within all so-called individual and collective life forms and between them. This misperception was understandable at some early stages of human knowledge, but its continuation now appears to be a form of a lazy anthropocentric habit or an ideological act of wilful ignorance. The ancient social introduction of this misperception, embodied in monotheistic religions - as the mythical first individual human, Adam - was later promoted by the ancient and medieval church authorities. It was then adopted by the bourgeoisie along with their preferred mode of production. It was, of course, mystical nonsense. In any group of organisms its so-called individual forms are slightly or fully social individual forms and thus dependent upon each other for their initial reproductive existence and for their continuing life-cycles.

The inter-dependent social nature of most species and their absolute nutritional dependence upon some, or all, other life forms, once studied further consolidates this observation. What was formerly classed as an individual cell, whether prokaryotic or eukaryotic, once examined in detail by powerful electron scanning microscopes reveals itself to be an internal symbiotic ensemble of many active sub-units (organelles, tubules, membranes, etc.) which interact, coordinate and process their functions in order to exist and replicate their existence as a minute membrane enclosed bio-chemical units. However, elements of that membrane bounded social unit which is kept 'alive' by its own circuit of (N-M-G-R + A-D) will at some stage become part of the (N) or potential (N) for another organism either before or after it ages (A) and dies (D). Consequently, the recycling of organic and inorganic material is fundamental to the origin and continuation of species life on earth in general and to the evolution of individual organic life forms in particular.

In the animal species this intake is motivated by the individual bodily sensations of discomfort, known amongst humans as hunger and thirst. We cannot know whether the metabolic need for biological and mineral nourishment for internal, collective metabolic processes such as rest, growth and reproduction are also triggered by sensations of physically communicated instability or disequilibrium in cells. However, we do know that the internal bio-chemical units (organelles, mitochondria or chloroplasts, etc.) that associate together within cells collectively function around an homeostatic equilibrium, in which energy and material is constantly used up and constantly needs replacing. It may be that when a bio-chemical imbalance is detected, the cells internal membrane and sub-units allow material from outside the lipid barriers to enter and the organelles and internal connections process (metabolise) this material into usable forms. From within the material I have been able to access for this study, four phases of the cells internal processes have been so far described: 1. a phase in which chromosome and DNA replication occurs; 2. A phase of Mitosis, a bi-polar sub-assembly process; 3. One of Cytokinesis; organelle distribution; and 4. Meiosis; Chromosome segregation. Therefore, at the present level of understanding;

"A living cell is a dynamic chemical system, operating far from chemical equilibrium. For a cell to grow or to make a new cell in its own image, it must take in free energy from the environment as well as raw material to drive the necessary synthetic reactions. This consumption of free energy is fundamental to life. When it stops, a cell decays toward chemical equilibrium and soon dies." (Molecular Biology of the Cell. .B. Alberts; A Johnson; J. Lewis. Sixth Edition. Chapter 1.)

So even at this microscopic level of life on earth, physical activity requires an energy source and its metabolised consumption, which in turn initiates the function of metabolic chemical energy transformation and appropriate molecular production, and this process of energy transformation enables cellular activity and energy consumption to continue. In regard to the transformation of external energy sources into biochemical useful forms for organic life in general, the role of the cells with photo-synthetic capabilities is remarkable. These cell organelles absorb the radiated energy of sunlight, gasses and minerals and metabolise them into forms suitable for maintaining the functions and survival of all cellular and multi-cellular life forms. What is also remarkable is the astonishing rate and form of reproduction (R) for many species of life including the cells within multi-cellular organisms. The reproduction phase (R) of species is a vital part of the process of life on earth and will be considered in further chapters.

Meanwhile, between bacterial cells and algae in the marine environment, there are some critically functional and revealing inter-connections and interactions. Some bacteria attach themselves to algae which exude material which the bacteria can utilise as nutrients for energy supply. At the same time the bacteria exude a growth inducing hormone which the algae ingest to supplement or replace its metabolic processing and grow. At a certain stage or point in the process, the Algae dies and the bacteria detach, descend and move on. It is easy to understand how such behaviour could be viewed as purposeful until it is realised that what is exuded by the algae was not intended to be nutritious; it was just waste material retaining some active nutrition and the hormone exuded by the bacteria was just surplus to its requirements. The fact that these wastes became beneficial to some other organism was not intended. Neither organism was purposefully producing targeted material to attract the other. Such exchanges are probably best understood as accidental encounters which evolved sensory awareness functions to allow that particular interaction to continue among many other actual or potential sources.

This example illustrates the fact that life on earth at its most microscopic level has a degree of sensory awareness and organelles and materials within them functionally interact to keep the organism alive, but this does not in any scientific or evidential way suggest any form of teleological purposeful activity. The consumption of inorganic and organic material and the production of organic material is a necessary functional result of life on earth in general as well as for individual organisms, but it is certainly not a prior premise for its existence. This circular process, 'consumption-production-excretion, consumption-production-excretion' (C-P-E -C-P-E), is maintained by one continuous cycle of momentarily discrete, but intimately linked and continuously inter-connected (N-M-G-R + A-D) phases of life on earth. One phase must always, sooner or later, follow the other for the cycle to continue. In this regard, we should note that the common modern dietary expression 'we are what we eat', also applies in essence to cells. Cells, by a similar bio-chemical process of absorbing, metabolising, growing, and reproducing, are literally made up of what the material they commenced with at reproduction and have absorbed and metabolised since they formed. If they absorb viruses or unsuitable material that cannot be processed they can also cease to function as before (i.e. malfunction) or even cease to exist in their original form. When cells link together to form multi-cellular organisms, these processes are also linked together and the total homeostasis of the organism (via pili and molecular connections) becomes a collective internal response to internal and external environmental activity. We should perhaps further note at this point also that not one element of this process dominates the entire integrated system. Life on earth at this microscopic level functions as a non-hierarchical inter-connected collective of bio-chemical activity. Assigning levels of importance to elements of a system which absolutely requires every part to function is merely transferring human hierarchical social concepts and prejudices to the realm of cells.

"If a cell is to grow and reproduce, it must be able to import raw materials and export waste across its plasma membrane. All cells therefore have specialised proteins embedded in their membrane that transport specific molecules from one side to the other. Some of these 'membrane transport proteins', like some of the proteins that catalyse the fundamental small-molecule reactions inside the cell, have been so well preserved over the course of evolution that we can recognise the family resemblances between them in comparisons with even the most distantly related groups of living organisms. (ibid; 'The Molecular Biology of the Cell' .B. Alberts; A Johnson; J. Lewis. Sixth Edition. Chapter 1)

Since these needs are common to all multi-cellular individual organisms of a social species then in such cases, these needs are generally sought and obtained collectively. Such individual processes will be described in general here and how this process is collectively manifested within all the categories of life on earth will be considered in the appropriate chapters. Although being flexible and adjustable to a certain extent, all six phases of living (N-M-G-R + A-D) are interconnected and interdependent. For example, abundant, inadequate or insufficient Nourishment (sources of material and energy) may affect the later phases of Growth and Reproduction. Similarly with Digestion, (internal absorption and protection) may positively or negatively affect later phases. Even deterioration (aging) and death can be extended or accelerated by excesses or deficiencies in any or all of these four earlier phases.

The structure of Cells in a little more detail.

So the basic units of all forms of life on earth are the tiny organelle, containing bio-chemical active cells which are invisible to the naked eye but whose ability to associate and integrate together is overwhelmingly evident in all living organisms. At least those we can see with or without optical or electron magnification. As noted, some biological cells can exist independently from other cells or can link themselves together in complex structures and in this way, form and make up the bodies and organs of all living things, ranging from internal and external organelles and on to micro-organisms in plants and animals. As noted, under a powerful microscope, the simplest ones, the Prokaryotic cells are made up of discrete active internal elements contained in a cytoplasmic material, surrounded by a plasma membrane and sometimes reinforced with a tough protective outer layer. Imagine a tiny soap bubble filled with an aqueous liquid, with even smaller active organelle assemblies inside. That outer layer and membrane acts as a permeable barrier protecting the internal structure and multiple contents of the cell and functions to keep out material detrimental to the cell. However, this membrane is not just a passive impervious form of material but is itself an active bio-chemical part of the cell.

The active membrane therefore allows useful material into the cell and enables the jettisoning of unneeded material out of it - as waste - or as unprocessed material surplus to requirements. More often than not the cell has hair-like cilia and tubular type filaments that are embedded in the inner or outer membranes which assist in the sensing of its surroundings, can connect with material external to its membrane and is capable of moving microscopic amounts of material through its internal environment. An interesting example of the bio-chemical ability of a minute single cell is provided by the existence of a single coral cell. This cell also has cilia protruding from its membrane which oscillate in such a way as to mimic an erratic form of swimming. However, the cell is also obviously capable of sensing vibrations passing through the sea water for when certain fish transmit sound vibrations in that immediate area the single coral cells cease swimming randomly, head for the bottom and settle to adhere there and grow. The observational interpretation of such behaviour is that the form of awareness of surroundings contained in or on the coral cell has triggered a functional response to that location as one in which the (N-M-G-R + A-D) process becomes possible - for that is exactly what then transpires; the coral cell then takes in material from that fish-deposited waste environment, metabolises it, grows and reproduces, until it ages and dies.

The cell thus obtains sources of nourishment for energy and growth by engulfing or allowing in waste or other material through its membrane that is encountered within its immediate surroundings. Indeed, as noted above, it must absorb such sources of replenishment or Nourishment (N) and further Metabolise (M) them in order to survive, to grow and to reproduce. Therefore, at the cellular level of life on earth, there appears to be a built in, fundamental active pattern of 'sensing' and 'engulfing' (internalising) material, utilising it internally, 'excluding' excess material and then the triggering of a process which involves reproducing (R) itself. So again in the hope that repetition will help the reader to remember this crucially important process, in its shortened form, I shall repeat the basic phases of microscopic cellular life. They are Nourishment, Metabolism, Growth, and Reproduction, then Ageing and Dying;

or as noted throughout (N.M-G.R. + A.D.) for short. However, the complexity of life on earth does not end there for the interconnectedness of cells with each other and with the rest of 'life on earth', needs to be carefully considered in order to be fully appreciated. Therefore, it is now suggested that;

"At some point before 2 billion years ago, small colonies of bacteria began to adopt the habit of living inside a common membrane. It began when a small bacterial cell, called an archaeon, found itself dependent on some of the cells around it for vital nutrients. This tiny cell extended tendrils toward its neighbours so they could swap genes and materials more easily. The participants in what had been a freewheeling commune of cells became more and more interdependent....Cyanobacteria specialised in harvesting sunlight, and became chloroplasts – the bright green specks now found in plant cells. Other kinds of bacteria devoted themselves to releasing energy from food and became the tiny pink power-packs called mitochondria which are found in almost all cells that have nuclei, whether plant or animal." ('A very short history of life on earth'. H Gee. Chapter 1)

The phenomenon of tiny micro-organisms (or organelles) existing and beneficially functioning inside of another cell or multi-cellular animal is called endo-symbiosis and perhaps points to one of the earliest stages of pre- or post-viral bio-chemical forms of life on earth. As already noted, some of these, semi-independent life forms, such as viruses, are not capable of reproduction (R) on their own and need to interact with a cell capable of its own reproduction, this lack of internal self-sufficiency can have either positive or negative effects upon other multi-cellular life forms. These semi-independent viral life forms are generally classed as Viruses if they harm the multi-cellular structures they enter, and are classed as Phages if they are neutral or if they are functionally beneficial in some way. Again these minute, semi-independent bio-chemical life forms are not intentionally harmful or intentionally beneficial they are just repeating the evolved (N-M-G-R + A-D) processes (minus self-replicating R) they have previously bio-chemically inherited. Despite, the usual amount of unnecessary anthropomorphic language being used in the above extract (*habit, adopt, neighbours, swap, freewheeling commune, harvesting, devoting*) I decided to use that quote because it does sum up the most recent understandings I could find of the symbiotic nature and complexity of life at its most minute and earliest forms even though it drags along with it inappropriate anthropocentric terms that only apply to human activities.

The extract could have been written with a language more suited to the real interactions within cells, but as indicated, it is almost impossible to find popular accounts of science which do not resort to misleading, anthropomorphic stereotypical language. Economists also do it when they write and talk about *'growing the economy'* or countries *'balancing the books'* as if countries were gardens or abstract accounting books. Professors of astronomy declare that *'stars are born'* and *'die'*, that telescopes *'probe into the beginning of time'*, that the universe was *'turned on'* by a *'big bang'*. Contemplating, the immense universe is addressed by some in language more appropriate to a high income family home where humans are born, lights are switched on, fireworks explode, children probe in cupboards for lost toys and a family pet eventually dies. Presumably such language is used in a patronising assumption that the average reader would not understand what was being described without such homely, familiar - but of course completely misleading terms.

When cells do not succeed in passing through the first four elements (N-M-G-R) of the above noted cycle, and remain undigested by other organisms then they could - in some cases - become dormant or as in the case of some multicellular animals, exist in a state of torpor, in which cells re-balance their internal rhythms for a period of stasis or an organelle form of hibernation. Of course in extreme cases within deficient environments cells and multi-cellular organs and organisms could ultimately die. But in that latter case, as already noted, they would still become potential or actual recyclable organic and inorganic material available to other life forms. Although the precise nature of this internal and structural coordinated triggering needed to progress through these stages is as yet unknown, its effects are sufficiently strong enough to cause its operation in all viable cells whether they exist as single membrane bounded units or as multicellular connected collectives. And this process occurs whether they are associated together in minute multicellular microorganisms, or within larger organisms such as insects, plants and animals.

So to once again I repeat, the available evidence suggests that a pattern of Nourishment, Metabolism, Growth, Reproduction and then Ageing and Death, in whatever particular form these take, is fundamental to the life cycle of all cells (and all life) whether they are considered separately or, as will be indicated in later chapters, when combined together in the multi-cellular bodies of plants, insects and animals. Many cells are so adapted to be interactive with the environment they exist within, that as noted above, they have Pili (strands that can connect with other cells) and cilia or flagella which are little tail-like strands which wiggle or turn (as on the male sperm cell) and help propel the cell through any not too dense material it is situated within. I suggest that the importance of understanding cells and their role is not yet generally promoted in popular education and culture and is consequently overlooked, at least among the general population. Yet in really understanding life on earth, as a whole, it is becoming clear that;

"Only by understanding microorganisms and microbiology can we predict and minimise the effects of human activity on the biosphere that sustains us. Though diverse habitats are influenced strongly by microorganisms, their contributions are often overlooked because of their small sizes. Within the human body, for example, there are between one and ten microbial cells (mainly of bacteria) for every human cell and more than 200 microbial genes for every human gene. These microbes provide nutritional and other benefits that are essential to human health." ('Brock; Biology of Microorganisms' Fifteenth Edition. Page 42)

It is in an understanding of life on earth, at this microscopic network, level that the anthropocentric focus of humanity is exposed as primitive and arrogant. All the so-called 'higher' organisms are supported by, resting upon and dependent upon, the continuous reproduction of life forms invisible to the naked human eye. The colloquial saying, 'out of sight; out of mind' has enormous scientific and social implications in the study of life on earth. Of course, as already noted, there is no absolutely reliable evidence on how life on earth in the form of archaic organic cells began and there are only approximations of when and where such 'life on earth' became active. But, although puzzling, I repeat that it is not important in understanding the present and future situation with regard to life on earth. The current assumption is that two of the three most basic cellular life forms, Bacteria and Eukarya branched out from a logically supposed, 'Last Universal Common Ancestor' (LUCA) of cellular life and the third Archaea, branched away from the Eukarya to form what is currently classified as having its own domain. Although all three cellular forms share similar characteristics as described above, they are considered sufficiently different enough to be placed in these separate categories. Of course the categories could all change yet again - as they already have during the life-time of this author. Similarly, there are only estimates regarding how many species of life now exist on planet earth. Most of them are actually invisible to the naked eye, but being out of sight and thus out of mind, can lead to most human beings missing the fact that they may be absolutely essential to the existence of all life on earth - including the existence of the human eye which cannot perceive them, without powerful instruments of magnification.

Estimates of species on earth vary wildly from more than 10 million to possibly up to 100 million. However, the lack of detailed evidence and numerical accuracy in these three regards does not mean there is a lack of sufficient reliable evidence to understand what inorganic and organic material life on earth is made of and from. Indeed, biological studies since the invention of microscopes of ever increasing magnifications have revealed the content and structure of the most elemental components of all living things – the Prokaryotic and Eukaryotic cells, mentioned above! Therefore, from comparative DNA evidence, it is now suggested that three general cellular forms (or branches) of microscopic life exist; Eubacteria, Archea-bacteria, (both of these comprising of Prokaryotic type cells) and finally Eukaryotes - cells with membrane enclosed Nuclei and other organelles, such as mitochondria, which have their own DNA. It is important to remember that all these minute cells - both complex and less complex ones - contain within them a variety of even smaller organic bio-chemical components (organelles) and interactive bio-chemical amalgamations.

The Eukaryotic cells are generally larger and more complex and also have plasma membranes around the internal nucleus etc., which contain its own internal DNA strand together with other organic supportive material. In a sense it is a kind of cell within a cell! The fact that one cell has DNA material from a different cell within it suggests that the ability which all cells have to engulf external material for nutritional and other associated purposes occurred billions of years in the past. However, it is conjectured that in certain cases, some of this material was not fully absorbed and then broken down by the host cell Metabolism (M) but remained more or less intact and continued to function within it. In this way, some of the bio-chemical material engulfed by the initial cell form may have stayed more or less intact and became a supplementary, symbiotic, cooperating but protected part of the host cell. Thus the term endo - symbiosis is often used to describe such beneficial associations taking place when a tiny viable complex life form unit lives inside and functions within another tiny complex life-form.

The fact that the DNA within these Eukaryotic cells has retained a membrane around it over millions of years suggests that the other cell organelles are so efficient at breaking non-resident material down that, unlike in the Prokaryotic cell, the DNA strands and molecules cannot be retained within an unprotected general membrane. In this regard, there is an amazing symbiotic characteristic with regard to the male sperm cells in some animals such as some bats where the male sperm cells are kept viable within the female body until the female reproductive process utilises them for her reproductive process. If this hypothesis is correct, it further suggests that different bio-chemical life forms tolerating or beneficially living together whether inside each other, or in close supportive proximity, are perhaps fundamental to all forms of life on earth. At the cellular level the hypothesis is that these different internal forms integrated or adapted their bio-chemical activities and thus collectively became part of the Eukaryotic cells' self-renewing, self-directing, self-sustaining and self-reproducing, biological life form.

These cell materials, once internally amalgamated, then continually produce, sustain and reproduce the cells in this altered functional form. Once having done so in the far distant past, these cells now sustain and reproduce many of the combined multicellular forms of life on earth. It may be difficult to imagine but the material of which these cells comprise are all active components contained both within and even on most life-forms, from the tiniest single cell to larger multicellular forms. The most gigantic current species of life such as whales and elephants and those which are reduced in size such as microorganisms are no different in this active bio-chemical regard. Everything that lives, grows, reproduces and dies does so due to the actions and activities of one or more of these millions of minute generalist and in many cases interacting and interdependent 'specialist' adapted cells. For example, (and to anticipate the later section on humans) complex forms of life such as human bodies, are made up of millions of cells (estimated as 10 to the 13 power) but the actual potential for reproducing a new version of a complex organisms such as a human being etc., always initially resides within those bio-chemical elements condensed and concentrated in a single cell. In humans, that single cell is carried in the female of the species and is known as the ovum. Thus in the case of;

"...cells that form a human body, the whole organism has been generated by cell divisions from a single cell. The single cell, therefore, is the vehicle for all the hereditary information that defines each species." (Molecular Biology of THE CELL. Sixth edition. Alberts; Johnson; Lewis; Morgan; Raff; Roberts; Walter. Pub. Garland Science. Chapter 1.)

In the exceptionally comprehensive book quoted above, the detailed insight provided by the author into the structure and importance of the tiny cell in reproducing and maintaining life on earth is largely the product of visual evidence obtained by modern mechanical and electro-chemical technology, via ever more powerful microscopes. Another fascinating insight into the complexity and nuanced function connected with the symbiosis of cells within multi-cellular organisms is provided by the immune systems of many animals. If a healthy functional internal cell within an animal becomes infected by a cell such as virus, or bacteria the cell continues to function for a time before it succumbs to the internalised virus, but the waste material the invaded cell subsequently discharges during this infection period is altered by the material of the bacterial or viral agent . This 'abnormal' peptide molecule discharge from the infected cell can be detected by the body's T cells so the cell and its invading content can be identified and neutralised by toxins in a process known as phagocytosis. I suggest this and many other such nuanced functional synthesis at the cellular level by life on earth, should be a reason why humanity needs to be in considerable awe and develop a protective mind-set over everything contributing to this naturally evolved interconnected reality of life on earth. Simply being in awe of the destructive capability of its own non-natural technological achievements such as atom bombs, is an example of humanity functioning in a way counter to the process of evolution of life on earth. In this regard, how far the intellectual understanding of humanity has come since the period of ancient Greece and Rome can be measured by the following observation by the Roman philosopher, Lucretius, with regard to inorganic matter.

"Bodies, again, Are partly primal germs of things, and partly Unions deriving from primal germs. And those which are primal germs of things No power can quench; for in the end they conquer By their own solidness; though hard it be To think that aught in things has solid frame;" (Lucretius Book 1 Character of the Atoms.)

Yet how little humanity has understood about the results of its practical activities, since such embryonic insights were articulated. As hard as it was in those early mass societies to think scientifically, beyond the immediately obvious, this insight by Lucretius represents an early intellectual inkling of the more modern understanding of the atomic structure of all the inorganic and organic material on the planet. Nevertheless, the development of high-powered microscopy it can now be also extended to the organic material of the planet. However, the importance I attach to this quotation and the reason for including it, is that it demonstrates the willingness of some people - even many generations ago - to seriously question the commonly held assumptions of their particular period and to pursue the idea that there remain many things yet to be discovered beyond the surface phenomenon and assumptions accepted by the current social world. The early assumption that rocks were solid when in fact they are composed of millions of tiny atoms and sub particles, which were also once in gaseous forms, liquids and sediments and are decaying extremely slowly, has now been superseded - at least by rational evidence-based science.

An almost parallel assumption that plant, insect, and animal bodies were solid flesh or fibre was undoubtedly obscuring the fact that they too are made up of millions of tiny cells constantly living, contributing, reproducing and dying. A further more modern assumption which I suggest needs to be seriously challenged with regard to 'life on earth' is the Victorian ideology of the whole of nature being at war with itself. That, in essence, is what the theory of the Preservation of Favoured Species by Natural Selection is based upon. But at its most fundamental level of the cell, life is an association of many cooperating organelles, functioning to maintain, preserve and reproduce the whole or the multi-cellular whole of which it is an evolved part. (For an extended critique of 'Natural Selection' as a deeply flawed and unconfirmed by evidence, hypothesis, I have produced further articles. See www.critical-mass.net).

Rigorous criticism of dominant assumptions was vital in the past and is still vital now. Challenging popular assumptions and so-called received wisdom, produced by individuals and groups remains important in practical terms as well as in intellectual matters. Seriously questioning many of the assumptions made by our leaders, academics, parents and grandparents is essential because ignorance, prejudice and carefully preserved confirmation bias has been - and still is - endemic among all social classes and within all subject disciplines. I hope this study of *life on earth* from a revolutionary-humanist perspective will set an example of the opposite and encourage young people on our planet to critically question the handed down ideas and concepts of past generations before simply uncritically accepting them on trust. If past ideas turn out to be reliable guides - fine! However, if they do not then they should be rejected no matter who promotes them - the present author included. Serious criticism of *everything* will be essential in order to correct the historic distortions and devastations of life on earth by previous ill-informed or prejudiced generations in general and the advocates of the current mode of production in particular.

The complexity and variety of life emanating from single and multi-clustered minute cells is a vitally important point to grasp for it establishes how life on earth - in its most fundamental units - manages to exist and that these forms continue to be the means of replicating themselves and ourselves to this day. So to recap; the basic cell comprises an outer lipid plasma membrane layer, rather like a microscopic version of a soap bubble which forms around an internal space. The membranes of cells, however, are not based upon soap and form around a regular or irregular three dimensional space of cytoplasmic material. The shape depends upon the type of cell in question, some are long, some are roundish others are dish shaped. Plant cells also have an additional strong outer membrane of cellulose. Nevertheless, contained within those three dimensional layers and spaces are certain microscopic objects called organelles, nuclei (enveloped or not), Centrioles, Mitochondria, Microtubules etc., and in the case of plant based species Chloroplasts.

However, in functional terms rather than specific organelle identification terms, the cell contains collections of bio-chemical elements some of which act as; a) catalysts; b) areas of bio-chemical synthesis; c) energy producing elements; d) endoplasmic support material and; e) replicating bio-chemical DNA strands. The cell is protected by the above noted active plasma layer and membrane and the membrane also contains chemical/biological substances which adjust to allow certain materials to pass into the cell and waste material to pass out. The membrane under the necessary stimuli is also able to expand and contract to allow for growth and any complex process of cell budding or cell division (mitosis). So, as noted, in order for the cell to survive, the cell membrane allows useful organic and inorganic material to enter through them as a means of obtaining nutritional mineral and energy nourishment. In general the membrane does not allow harmful material to enter into the cell - although some viruses and bacteria manage to enter cells when they are not recognised by the cell membrane as detrimental intrusions. It is then in multi-cellular organisms, that specialist cells, known as immune system cells 'detect' the bio-chemical difference and are able to neutralise or disable the material not useful or harmful to the system.

Other forms of cell reproduction (R) have arisen in which crucial cell components protrude from the cell and the membrane forms around them as a 'bud' but which the outgrowth is still connected to the cell. Eventually the bud breaks off and then within the external environment it now exists independently. The new cell proceeds to grow (G) to essentially the same configuration as the original cell. In other cases, some internal components reform within the cell and then form their own membrane around these before exiting from the main cell as a complete unit. The cell development then continues outside of the originating cell. The reproduction functions of life on earth, like other aspects of life have taken many relatively complex and sophisticated forms. As well as long tail like flagella, which undulate or rotate to move the cell, some minute cell forms have multiple hair-like cilia on their outsides which often move like a synchronised row of oars and allow the cell to be propelled through the environment it is in. In single cell organisms the pace of reproduction (R) appears to be related to the availability of the necessary material and energy required to function in this (R) phase and in the other essential (N-M-G-R + A-D) phases of a cells life cycle. Hence, during periods of abundance of either suitable material or environmental conditions (or both), the appearance of billions of organisms in the form of 'blooms', 'swarms' or other such high-density organic life formations occur within certain environments. The timing and pace of reproduction in other cellular life forms appears to be stimulated by such abundances of material, energy or environmental factors.

However, in multicellular life forms in which cell types have become specialised within the overall bodily structure, the reproduction (R) of cells suggests that there must be a biological feedback system which regulates and limits cell reproduction within certain organs and associated systems. Otherwise more skin (or bone, heart muscle, blood) cells would be reproduced than were needed to replace the rate of dying cells and result in abnormal (cancerous type) growths. Furthermore, logic suggests that this bio-chemical feed-back function must be a universal phenomenon because the problem and solution occurs within all or most multi-cellular life forms. The rate of reproduction for cells within multi-cellular life forms, clearly need to be regulated around an average required to ensure that the continued morphological appearance and functions of each multi-cellular organism, is maintained. Since all life forms are bio-chemical systems, the mediating agency of such cell reproduction and limitation must also be a biological, cellular level relationship. What this bio-chemical limiting function of reproduction comprises and where it is located within or between cells I have not as yet been able to locate within the literature I have so far studied. However, it does appear that it is a disruption of this normal limiting functioning of cell reproduction in multi-cellular organisms which leads to the appearance of many cancerous growths both internally and externally upon and within certain individual animals and humans. Considered individually, cells continually reproduce themselves whether accurately, or not, are just fulfilling their evolutionary pattern and function, but in multi-cellular organisms, this appears to be regulated in some way. Otherwise, an unlimited or unneeded reproduction of normal healthy cells within a multi-cellular organism could (and sometimes does) create abnormal problems within multi-cellular life forms.

A further interesting phenomenon concerning the reproduction of life on earth at the cellular level is that the process of triggering biological gender in some species can also be influenced by other external changes such as temperature. One example occurs in the case of crocodile eggs, in which the temperature around the eggs can trigger the formation of either male or female offspring. Some bio-chemical function within the egg organelles must respond to temperature by switching developmental pathways between the two gender types. This clearly suggests that in general, the species as a whole and not the gender is the fundamental determining element in the evolution of life on earth. Reproduction in terms of joint gender contributions in sexually reproducing species is perhaps a much later adaptation. Despite the important distinctions between male and female in most species (reproductive roles and body size differences, the overwhelming morphological similarity between the genders also suggests this is actually the case. Despite different relative body sizes and certain nuanced specialised organs and cells, both male and female overwhelmingly share the external body characteristics and internal organs and functions of the species as a whole. A further example of the common source, or dynamic of reproduction, is provided in the case of the eggs of bees in which unfertilised eggs become different morphological forms of the species than those from fertilised eggs. This latter example suggests that at the cellular level, both types of reproduction (asexual and sexual) can take place within the evolutionary development of one or more species.

We have now briefly considered the fundamental cellular components of life on earth along with their basic functions of replication, nutrition (organic and inorganic) waste removal, growth, and further replication, both simple and enhanced. Although the detail currently known for each of these discrete functions is enormous in its extent, sufficient evidence has been considered here to establish that cells are systems of life that utilising natural materials are self-regulating and self-perpetuating organisms of both simple and at the same time complex structures. Thus understood, it is time to turn to the inorganic and organic material that these multicellular life forms absorb from the habitat and growth medium we classify as the soil which lies upon the dry surface layers of the planet. It is here in the soil that this microscopic world of life interacts with and supports the plant life upon which the rest of life on earth depends. For in the soil are;

"..plant growth-promoting rhizobacteria, (PGPR) or biological control agents (BCA). As their names suggest, the direct effect of PGPR is the promotion of plant growth, while the direct effect of BCA is to control soil-borne pathogens, which in turn improves plant productivity." ('Bacteria in Agrobiology': Plant Probiotics' Dinesh K. Maheshwari Ed.)

So to sum up so far: Each cell in one sense, is a tiny (microscopic) social organism, surrounded by one or more permeable but protective lipid membranes containing a variety of internally active symbiotic bio-chemical organelles working together to maintain its functions and homeostasis within the environment external to it. Each surviving cell has its metabolic requirements which are satisfied during its life cycle of Nourishment, Rest, Growth, Reproduction, Ageing and Death (N-M-G-R + A-D). Reproduction (R) at this microscopic level requires no cooperation from an independent organism and as far as we know is internally regulated, by the nutritional and other levels obtained. However, when such cells combine with other cells as multi-cellular organisms, they also interact and (functionally cooperate) together and combine their efforts to maintain the functions and homeostasis of the larger multi-cellular whole. The multi-cellular organism also goes through its own particular process of N-M-G-R + A-D, but of course on a larger and more complex scale.

Despite the understandable emotional aversion to loss by death, experienced by humans and other sentient animal species, the death of an organism by natural causes or otherwise is not the end of each organism's role in the evolutionary process of life on earth. An individual death is not really the loss of life on earth in general; it is just the recycling of one particular organic phase of it. This is because the bio-chemical necessary material death of all organisms, also become the recycled essential inorganic and organic nutritional materials needed by many other forms of 'life on earth'. The common sense phrase that 'we are what we eat', conveniently misses out the organic and inorganic source, if not the substance of most of what we are eating. The fact is that we are all consuming and metabolising other once living organisms along with inorganic liquids, gasses and minerals. If we temporarily suspend the anthropomorphic, egocentric obsession with ourselves and consider the function of death from the wider point of view of life on earth as a whole, the human emotionally perceived negative can be viewed as a rationally perceived positive. Without death occurring, many other forms of life would lack necessary organic nourishment (N). Without organic nourishment, life could not fulfil the necessary phases of existence. The much repeated formula I have selected for this book (N-M-G-R + A-D) will hopefully be used by readers and serve to replace the dualistic 'life and death', 'human and non-human', or 'absolutely negative anthropocentric assumptions concerning the cycle of life on earth.

Finally, although sufficiently robust to withstand the rigours of a planet in various stages of change, living cells are not invulnerable to novel chemical combinations, particularly those created and forced onto nature by human ingenuity, rather than those emerging from more naturally evolved forces. The latter survive or fail on how well they integrate within the overall web of life on earth. In contrast, the chemicals designed by human agents to interfere with the evolved N-M-G-R process of cell life do so by being taken into the cells inner cytoplasm and once there cannot always be synthesised as normal nutrition and/or cannot always be advantageously metabolised. Thus these substances can affect the 'normal' growth (G) and/or reproduction phases (R) of the cells life cycle and either kill the cell or distort its previously evolved functioning. So important is the (N) phase of (N-M-G-R + A- D) that most life-forms are absorbing sources of nourishment for much of their non-sleeping time.

In modern profit based forms of production for human consumption, the additive materials used to 'process' foods at all stages of production are utilised to maximise profits and to slow down the natural ageing and decay of organic material. This modern chemical adulteration of soil, crops and livestock by the often undeclared additives to nutrition destined for the daily intake of human beings is not only killing the so-called 'pests' and moulds, that degrade crops etc., but are being absorbed by the cells of all human beings who eat them. Reassurances, by manufacturers and their paid 'scientists', that these additives are safe does not alter the fact that they are unnatural and their use is unnatural. The same goes for much of modern tools and utensils in food production. Micro-plastics and molecules of rare materials are shed by tools and containers during their use and end up in the environment to be inhaled or absorbed in any number of ways. Of course, the chain of life on earth when so 'disturbed' in one place does not necessarily end or stay there, for affected or infected cells may well be absorbed by other cells or multi-cellular organs and cause disturbance or deformities there. Unintended consequences nearly always attach themselves to interventions which are insufficiently grounded in a full understanding of the complexity of life on earth. In societies where control is vested in those eager to 'improve' upon nature whilst improving their own profits and standing within society, those interventions frequently have unintended negative consequences, as are recorded within the annals of modern history. Thus, lifting the lid of one profit-based innovation ever so slightly, we read;

"On a cellular level pesticides can inhibit cell division, photosynthesis, and growth; (they) can alter membrane permeability; change metabolic pathways; and inhibit the action of enzymes, including those functional in metabolising steroid hormones (i.e., oestrogen and testosterone), and the enzyme which is functional in the deposition of calcium carbonate in eggshells. (E.P.A. Report by Charles Reese. 1972.)

End note: Without human interference, the nourishment (N) sources for all cells are the naturally constituted inorganic and organic material, in the form of liquids, minerals and gases and other life forms. The metabolic processes (M) in cells take place within cell membranes, by mitochondria or photosynthetic cells and waste is ejected. The growth (G) of cells takes place in organelles, plasma content and membranes. Reproduction process (R) of cells is in the form of internal mitosis, meiosis or budding. Ageing (A) is a result of depletion or wearing out of key parts of the cell. Finally the death (D) of the cell is the result of the cessation of one or more organelle or a lipid membrane invasion by a virus or engulfment and metabolic conversion by another cell or organism.

Chapter 2 Summary.

In this chapter the form and function of individual and multi-cellular forms of life on earth have been described in sufficient detail to recognise a commonality between all the forms of life on earth. From the smallest to the largest life forms, all are made up and dependent upon external and internal cellular processes and functional relationships. These structures and relationships are the amazing bio-chemical characteristics of the microscopic cell in either its Prokaryotic or Eukaryotic forms. The internal 'organelles' within even the smallest cells are made up of smaller associating elements that have specific and/or general functions.

It is these evolved sub-units that in their combinations contribute to the cells ability to exist semi-independently and/or to exist in conjunction with other functioning cells. Life at the cellular or multi-cellular level share not only the (N-M-G-R + A-D) processes of all forms of life but all have evolved within the relatively stable conditions of the planet as a whole. Life, wherever it is situated, has adapted to survive in the varying Gravity, Atmospheric Pressures, Temperatures, Moisture conditions and Oxygen levels, distributed around the planet during the relatively slow changes within each geographical region and the environment surrounding its habitat.

CHAPTER 3

The composition of Soil.
It was pointed out in chapter 1 that the inorganic material of the planet itself was and is, essential material for the composition of all life on earth. However, for land based species, this essential material had to be first rendered into a form which cellular life can absorb and metabolise. The planet itself due to its movement, weathering, gravity and decay provides some initial breakdown of the minerals, gases and liquids but not always sufficiently suitable for plant or cellular intake. A crucial element in the further breaking down of this material has been by the activity of life itself, in the form of micro and macro organisms. Once these are provided with an appropriate and reliable form of energy, which of course comes mainly from the sun or the deep sea radiant equivalent via molten sources of 'earth core' material emissions. Much of this bio-chemical transformation of inorganic and organic material into usable forms is accomplished by the unique life forms known as microorganisms and plants. These photo-synthetic active organisms and their unique functions will be considered in the following chapter. However, since land-based plants depend upon sun, air, water and soil to provide the essential organic and inorganic nutritional material for the rest of life on earth, I have decided to consider the role of terrestrial soil and its micro organic contents before moving on to plants.

Prior to the existence of organic life on earth, the non - organic material which accumulated upon the planet's surface would, at the very least, be composed of various kinds of dust, molten lava, heavy gases, liquids and some similar, but earlier deposited interplanetary material. We can presume, this original inorganic surface material was similar if not identical to that found soon after volcanic eruptions expel lava and pyroclastic flows of dust and particles in modern times. To such ash and debris we can add the probability that there may well have been further inorganic material deposited from any non-planetary bodies which long ago collided with our planet, landing as solid or fragmented atomised dust material, depending upon any variable atmospheric resistance at the time. This accumulated inorganic material from various sources thus became the substrate material which, if not sub-ducted by the many plate tectonic shifts, is now found below the later mixed fossil bearing organic sediment deposits on the land and sediment at the bottom of the seas and lakes.

Much of this mixed surface lying material has become what we now classify as 'soil' on land and 'sediment' underwater. But this process of circulation and depositing of inorganic material still continues, because water, wind and ice constantly grind and erode minerals from rocks. Moreover, winds still blow the finest dust particles along with any other small and light enough particles high into the upper atmosphere and across continents depositing tons of nutrient rich minerals and organic material onto distant lands and seas. Rivers do a similar process of conveying organic and inorganic materials from high elevations to low elevations. In this way the natural forces of the planets dynamic climate cycles deposit new nutrients on the surface as potential soil or mineral rich sediment. Furthermore, the planets movement through the solar system and also by being carried along through far reaches of space by the Galaxy's movement ensure that any material in space (such as meteor showers, etc.) in the planet's path may be also swept onto the earth's atmosphere and eventually onto its surface. In these ways much of the inorganic material that has been utilised and transformed into, and by, the many organic life forms is continually replenished.

So considering the composition of soil and its replenishment is not such a strange place to start an analysis of the individual and social forms of *life on earth* in general and humanity in particular. For the mixture of organic and inorganic materials, we class as soil and sediment began as (and remains) the basic foundation of the expansion of land based planetary life and the many various plant forms that have been transformed during different periods of evolution. Soil is particularly important because from millions of years ago, land based life in general and humanity over many thousands years, has depended upon the quality and quantity of the vegetation growing and dying on the surface layer of soil exposed to the open air upon the earth's crust. Whole periods of evolutionary time continued with plant vegetation, growing where possible, which not only provided the base line nutrition (N) for the many land based insects and animals including the Dinosaur's but it also did far more, The decay and compression of former plant life laid down the vast seams of compressed carbon in the form of coal and oil which, until eventually extracted as a source of mass production energy by combustion, lay deep underground. Under industrial forms of human mass society extraction, this long dead and compressed organic material has become over the last two centuries, a form of inorganic pollutant which is detrimental to living vegetation and life in general.

During the long periods of slow evolution, where the soil mixture became progressively more fertile, grasses, trees, fruits and vegetation began to reproduce in great abundance and this land-based growth of vegetable matter is the form of nutrition that most land animals have for many millions of years, ingested to survive. Even those top-of-the-food-chain animals which have become carnivores can only become meat eaters on the basis of the existence of species which are not carnivores, but grazers of vegetation. Animals alone could not and cannot process the inorganic radiant energy, gasses and minerals into nutritional nourishment, so could not have survived life without the nutritional foundation of grasses, trees, nuts and fruits growing in soil which land animals, birds and insects consume. Only land plants and aquatic plants can do this amazing bio-chemical/mineral transformation of inorganic material into edible organic material, via photosynthesis. Fertile soil, air, water and sun are the minimum requirements for vegetation to grow and the quality of the vegetation - as a vital source of base line nutrition - depends in part upon the composition of these inorganic sources and in particular, the activities taking place within the soil. For, fertile soil is not inert dirt, but alive with various multicellular forms of life on earth.

"A multitude of insects such as cockchafers, bees and some flies, which spend at least part of their life in the ground, make the soil more mobile by constantly carrying innumerable particles." ('Invisible army of the ground'. Microorganisms. C. Moscow.)

A soil we humans consider 'healthy' or 'fertile' also contains moisture and many forms of organic and inorganic material. As already noted, the inorganic materials in soil comprise of minerals from ground up rocks, sands, muds, metals, oxides, and various natural chemical compositions. The organic materials consist of; bacteria, archaea, virus, fungi, algae, lichen, slime moulds, protozoa, nematodes, arthropods, worms, insects and small animals, both the living ones and the dead and decomposing ones. All these soil based microscopic life forms, like us humans, are DNA based multicellular organisms and as well as drawing nutrition from the environment, many of the insects and microorganisms have, and some actually require, interactions with other microorganisms. Micro-organisms all require their own forms of Nourishment, Metabolism, Growth and Reproduction (N-M-G-R.), before succumbing to (A-D) so some will consume other microorganisms and in turn are consumed by other microorganisms. Life on earth lives off life on earth and much of its processes take place unseen within soils. Natural soils are packed with millions of tiny life-forms which help transfer a range of organic material and inorganic minerals into useful nutrient materials, available to be absorbed into the plant species and their cells that grow in it. Consequently these nutrients are then passed on into the digestive tracts of those organisms which eat the plants that grow in and on it.

So a healthy soil contains a wide variety of organic and inorganic material delivered by organism waste, actual organism deaths, rains, rivers, floods and volcanic eruptions. All of these organic and inorganic materials exist in healthy soils, albeit in differing quantities and qualities. The multifarious plants extract from the soil, air and sun those things they need as they grow and those substances extracted from the soil are replaced by plants and other organisms when they die in or on the soil. Consequently, despite frequent opinions based upon mass agricultural production, soil in its 'natural' state does not need artificial fertilisers. For millions of years prior to mass society agricultural production, soil became naturally fertile (and could stay so) by the things living, defecating and dying on it and within it and from supplementary deliveries of materials contained in rain water, river flood dispersal, air and sunshine.

"Forests and wild natural landscapes not used by man don't need any 'fertiliser' to have abundant plant growth. This has to do with the fact that nature is taking care of recycling the necessary nutrients in eternal cycles. Dead leaves, twigs and other organic 'waste', such as animal excrement or even dead bodies, are pre-digested by the natural soil flora and prepared as plant-accessible nutrients." ('Fertile soil is not just Dirt'. Dr Oliver Platt.)

Therefore, the natural, metabolic relationship between all forms of life and the soil relies upon that complex organic vitality of the soil not being squandered or destroyed. Artificial, chemical based fertilisers have only become needed where natural fertility has been depleted by repeated over use or by contamination. This natural cycle of life and death has over millions of years been the evolutionary basis for all sustainable social and metabolic interchanges between land based life in general and the soil; and thus also between humanity and nature. To ensure the long term sustainability of land based *life on earth*, any mode of production devised or imagined by humanity, must ensure that the natural quality and vitality of the soil, air and water is sustained naturally and not squandered or destroyed by chemical polluting additives. It is a fact that chemical based soil additives used for growth by large-scale farming for profit either kill, damage or bypass the soil microorganisms and go straight to the roots of the plants fertilised in that way. Experimental evidence indicates that after many applications of chemical fertilisers and insecticides, the fields farmed in that way cannot be easily returned to organic forms of farming. This is because the soil microbiology – as a whole - has been systematically destroyed, deformed or has atrophied away. In such places, any transition to organic farming will first have to ensure that the soil is revived with carbon and other mineral nutrients and that the microorganisms that convert the dead organic matter into forms the plants can utilise are sufficiently replenished and restored.

Over the duration of millions of years the living organisms existing on the soil, managed perfectly well without such chemical fertilisers and other additives. These are simply the products of relatively recent industrialised methods of production and consumption, in which the primary motive has been the commodification of nature's organic products primarily as vehicles for the profit of the owners of capital based industry and agriculture. We can reasonably state, with a high degree of certainty, that for millions, if not billions of years, no species of organic life either squandered or destroyed the vitality of soil, air, water or permanently blocked out the sun's rays to its leaves and fruits. In terms of considering humanity from the perspective of 'life on earth' as affected by humanity, we need in later chapters to understand the previous prehistoric and historical modes of human productive activity. This is a vitally important understanding relevant to the need for humanity to conserve nature not to over consume it. In this regard, other modern economic or cultural criteria or self- interested prejudice should not be allowed to obscure this fundamental soil-based foundation of all life on earth.

The key soil characteristics that affect yield are nutrient content, water holding capacity, organic matter content, soil reaction (acidity), topsoil depth, salinity, and soil biomass. Change over time in these characteristics constitutes "degradation" or "improvement." Degradation processes include erosion, compaction and hard setting, acidification, declining soil organic matter, soil fertility depletion, biological degradation, and soil pollution. ('Soil Degradation; A Threat to Developing-Country Food Security by 2020?' Sara J. Scherr.)

It is not difficult to understand that the quality of food grown in soil is dependent upon the quality of the inorganic and organic ingredients in the soil and environment producing this growth. Other things being equal the poorer the soil the less the quantity or quality (or both) of the nutritional value of organic material grown in it. The poorest possible land for growing things is a desert or granite mountain side in which very little grows and upon which very few species can live. Furthermore, the more intensively the soil on land is used to repeatedly grow things upon it, the more is taken out of the top-soil layer than can be replaced naturally. This is why in the last two centuries artificial chemicals have been incrementally added to the land on most modern farms to compensate for essential mineral and microorganism loss due to agricultural overproduction. However, as already noted, minerals are not the only losses to soil by methods of intensive farming. The pesticides used to keep yields high, not only kill insects designated as crop pests but also kill beneficial insects, bacteria and microorganisms, which are essential for a healthy soil ecology, as well as other useful animals, vitally important pollinating insects and larger animals which circulate minerals, droppings and introduce air into the soil.

After several generations of modern intensive farming methods, soils have become less fertile and many over-used fields in some places have become virtually sterile. In the past century, the example of the over use of soil in some parts of America resulted in parts of the land becoming known as the Dust Bowl during the 1920''s and this result has been well publicised. But also large herds of non-migratory domesticated flocks or herds of grazing animals can strip grazing land to a state of permanent or semi-permanent barrenness. So humanity globally now faces two developing problems with regard to soil. First, considering that a lot of the food we eat originates on modern farms, it can hardly be surprising if it is now less nutritious than it could be and perhaps naturally should be for human and animal populations. But, second, the situation is much worse than the problem of local and regional nutritional degradation, because general soil degradation and top-soil nutrient loss is becoming a global problem.

"There is historical evidence of large-scale soil degradation in many parts of the world in the past 5,000 years (Hillel 1991; Hyams 1952). UNEP (1986) calculated that 2 billion hectares of land that was once biologically productive has been irreversibly degraded in the past 1,000 years. Rozanov, Tar- gulian, and Orlov's (1990) analysis of global changes in the humus-sphere found that there has been a loss of humus at a rate of 25.3 million tons per year on average ever since agriculture began 10,000 years ago. This loss accelerated to 300 million tons per year in the past 300 years and 760 million tons per year in the past 50 years. Nearly 16 percent of the original stock of organic soil carbon may have been lost." (Soil Degradation A Threat to Developing-Country Food Security by 2020? Sara J. Scherr.)

Of course, in this context, we need to avoid typological thinking when we examine human individuals and communities because in fact no two individuals or groups are identical even when they are doing essentially the same thing. It is the economic system which is causing the exhaustion of the soil, not the particular individuals farming crops or herding livestock. For, in real world past history, many herding communities were aware of the dangers of overgrazing and over planting and where possible reduced this by regularly moving herds to other areas or leaving fields wild (fallow) and thus allowing grazing and crop growing land to recover. However, modern profit based agriculture and animal herding tends to be practiced in fixed locations and the farm and plantation managers solve these excessive use problems by industrial chemical additives. This practice indicates that 20th and 21st century soil exhaustion and contamination is not natural or inevitable. It is a deliberate result of modern farming systems and methods. Yet throughout history and pre-history, life on earth in all its natural evolutionary forms has been a contributing part of the natural processes of soil formation and its fertility along with the attendant plant, insect and animal evolution. Only during the later periods of human evolution has humanity excessively interfered with and altered that natural process. Hence;

"Any interference by humans with the natural processes of soil formation, evolution and erosion has an effect upon these processes, often unforeseen." (Land degradation and Society. P Blake & H Brookfield.)

And;

"But while there is a recognition of land as the product of natural forces, land – and other natural resources – were considered 'free' inputs into production and did not produce value since it was only labour that was considered to perform this function." (Land degradation and Society. P Blake & H Brookfield.)

In many cases, the labour theory of value fails to recognise the role that natural species reproductive (R) processes play in the production of organic nutrition and other useful materials. To sum up: Without human interference, the nourishment (N) sources for all micro-organisms within soil are inorganic and organic material, liquids, minerals and gases. The metabolic processes (M) in micro-organisms take place within their cell membranes, by mitochondria or photosynthetic cells and waste material is ejected. The growth (G) of micro-organisms takes place in their organs, plasma content and membranes. Reproduction process (R) of micro-organisms is in the form of voluntary sexual inter-action, meiosis or asexual means. Ageing (A) is a result of depletion or wearing out of key parts of the cell. Finally the death (D) of micro-organisms is the result of the cessation of one or more organs, invasion by a virus or engulfment and metabolic conversion by another organism.

Chapter 3 Summary.

The soil which is the surface layer lying on top of the subsoils and granites making up the earth's solid planetary surface, comprises much more than the broken down inorganic materials, created by wind, storms, erosion and tectonic or volcanic activity. After billions of years of the life and death cycles of millions of species of life on earth, it also comprises the non-recycled residue of previous living organisms. Everything that dies and is not absorbed by other living organisms as forms of nutrition, becomes mixed in with the inorganic material on the land or at the bottom of lakes and seas. Even then this accumulated material serves the function being the habitat for many millions of micro-organisms, including the many varieties of fungi on land and the algae within sea beds. Those minute, invisible to the naked eye, out of sight, life forms of bacteria and fungi are the means by which multifarious life in its most fundamental, yet still sophisticated structures, contribute to the basis of the air we breathe, and the food chain links and habitats for all other species.

CHAPTER 4

Plants and other Photosynthetic organisms.
In the realms of biological science, it is currently considered that, as with all forms of life on earth, the multicellular organisms ancestral to land based plants, actually originated in the sea. Thus;

"To colonise land, plants had to find a way of acquiring mineral nutrients, in particular scarce minerals like phosphate - an essential nutrient readily available in water but occurring in extremely low concentrations in soil. On its own, a plant's ability to extend its roots to explore for nutrients is limited. Partnerships with mycorrhizae expand that capability exponentially. 90-95 percent of terrestrial plants in all ecosystems on every continent have mycorrhizal relationships." ('Wilding: The Return of Nature to a British Farm'. Isabella Tree. Picador. Chapter 1)

This quotation identifies the importance of fungi (mycorrhizae) to plant life, but its use of language once again illustrates that the modern understanding of plant symbiosis is still being linked to earlier anthropomorphic assumptions and terminology. Plant cells spreading onto unmodified land billions of years ago is described in the above quote as *'colonising'*; cellular root growth to absorb nutrients within soil is conceptualised as *'exploring'*; and beneficial associations of microscopic cells are defined as *'partnerships'*. This use of such ancient and 19th century socio-economic, business-orientated terminology is not just inaccurate, it is grossly misleading. This may seem a small point in this particular case, but it indicates and illustrates a continuing unwillingness by otherwise knowledgeable authors to dispense with outdated ideas and terminology within modern scientific understanding and discourse, particularly, but not exclusively within the biological area of study. The rationalisation that this is used because it appeals to an ordinary reader or viewer on TV is patronising and assumes that ordinary readers and viewers are not capable of understanding complexity when described by using more specific, accurate and 'relevant' words.

The reader should be aware that such uncritical clinging on to inappropriate words and concepts also frequently becomes attached to more serious matters than understanding fungi. It can then serve to distort or even obscure an accurate understanding of life on earth in general, with serious and tragic consequences. A classic example of the latter is the earlier noted use of the invented category of 'race' which was introduced centuries ago into biology as a means of distinguishing between different plant and animal species, and was then further mis-applied to different sections of the human species. In fact there are no such biologically discrete types of organisms, which correspond to a category of difference which the term *race* exists to perpetuate. Not within the plant forms of life nor any other species of life on earth, yet it is the case now that many people - in all walks of life - think and act as if the word 'race' represents a really distinguishing feature of themselves or any other living 'thing' rather than an invented, unfounded anthropocentric discriminating form of belief. They therefore continue to use this imaginary concept and categorise themselves and others in terms of something which does not actually bio-chemically or structurally exist. This abstract concept of 'race' applied to humanity was a product of politically motivated, colonial era propaganda and then foisted onto the study of the human species, where it was uncritically accepted, even by those who suffered most from being labelled as belonging to a different (supposedly higher or lower) category of humanity. This general acceptance still enables other people to use the concept as a way of discriminating against other human beings. If the social function of science is to use our five biologically evolved senses and our neo-cortical processing abilities to extract accurate understanding after studying actual reality, then fabricating and then imposing pejorative political prejudices back onto reality, is not science, but anthropocentric ideology.

Whilst on the subject of scientific failures, here is another. Ever since the scientific method of research in Europe replaced the biblical narrative of an imaginary, invisible, all powerful male who created everything, the origin of plants, as with the origin of life, has been the subject of considerable research and discussion. I do not wish to go into too much detail of 'origins' in this section on plants, or any other species section for that matter, as that level of detail would become overwhelming. However, I suggest a little biological detail will be necessary in this and other sections, to help to make clear the composition and functions of the many, invisible to the naked eye, connections between all life forms and between these and the inorganic material of the planet. So, for example, on the origin of plants we can read that;

"..at some time between 2,100 and 1,200 million years ago, the first photosynthetic eukaryotic organisms emerged. These were the first plants, and every subsequent organism on this branch of the tree of life is a plant." (Plants. 'A short introduction'. T. Walker. Oxford)

Note that even the best evidence based science in most fields of study are also not that exact, particularly with regard to astronomical based dating of pre-historic events on planet earth. In the particular case quoted above, between 2,100 and 1,200 million years, there is an enormous 900 million year gap of uncertainty about the origins of our modern plants. However, the reliability or otherwise of this or that type of estimated guess is not crucial to this particular discussion of life on earth, other than it emphasises a point made previously. The point being that even in science, there is frequently a very tentative nature to many scientific understandings and assumptions even when they are frequently asserted as reasonably or absolutely accurate findings. The advice given by the Philosopher Bertrand Russell and mentioned in the introduction is useful in this regard - and many others: *'Whenever you are certain of something; maintain it with doubt'.* The reason for this advice is simple; newly discovered evidence or newly discovered connections, may require an adjustment to the certainty of any particular previous level of understanding. Failure in this regard results in uncorrected, inaccurate knowledge becoming useless dogma with adherents of it passing it on through subsequent generations. The essential point of relevance of times scaled to this study of plants, is the fact that plants and their many interconnections have been around a long time: a very, very long time.

During those immense durations of time (or the immense number of earth orbits around the sun) the plant species of life on earth in its process of (N-M-G-R) had as its (N) source its own synthesised products of sugars, starches and minerals by means of its photosynthesising cells, a process known as Photosynthesis. This makes the phases of large and small plant life different from the rest of organic life on earth, in one vitally important regard. With one or two notable exceptions, vital plant nutritional sources (N) do not predominantly come from directly or indirectly absorbing other life forms. They come primarily from the bio-chemically processing of inorganic materials derived from the atmospheric gasses and liquids as metabolised utilising the energy radiated by the sun. This makes them not only qualitatively different from all other forms of life on earth, but it means that their growth and life-cycles are now essential to all forms of land based life on earth. For the rest of a plant's M-G-R phases, plants are essentially the same in form as the rest of organic life. They Metabolise absorbed material, they Grow, they Reproduce, they Age and they Die. In their reproductive phase most plants have also been adapted to rely on other external elements or organisms to fulfil the pollination and seed dispersal functions.

Plants are also differentiated into numerous morphological sections and these multi-cellular clusters result from a multitude of modified specialist cells. The embryonic bio-chemical information in the seed of a plant is itself a composite assembly of semi-dormant and active cells and organelles which as noted in the chapter on cells, produce the material and the eventual sequential DNA triggering for differentiated cells to combine and to eventually form and grow (G) into (in this case) the mature plant. A further important consideration with regard to plant life on earth is the incredibly prolific results of their reproductive (R) processes resulting in seed embryos which are often produced in masses by the mature organisms of all plant species. They exceed by a considerable magnitude the number of viable genetic units needed to maintain each plant species. This prolific rate of reproductive potential, considered on a superficial, single species level, might appear an unnecessary case of overproduction and thus an unnecessary waste of energy production and consumption. However, once we consider the inter-connected and inter-dependent relationships of species life on earth - as a whole – this reproductive activity and the apparent superfluity of potential new organisms has evolved in such a way as to actually supply a crucial nutritional (N) requirement for the (N-M-G-R + A-D) cycles of much of the rest of life on earth.

This fact again indicates that all life forms on earth are not completely independent entities, but, as noted elsewhere, they are to a greater or lesser extent dependent upon and inter-dependent with all other life forms and inorganic liquids, gases and minerals. Moreover each apparent individual life form as already noted, is itself made up of multiple organic cells and inorganic material. Life forms are not actually composed of only their own home grown and evolved parts, as was often assumed during pre-scientific periods. We now know that all life forms consist of multiple cooperating self-replicating cells and organelles. Many cells and the two forms of DNA contained within the Eukaryotic form are not strictly 'owned' or 'created' by the individual life form itself, they are contained within material received from the donor or donors during the reproduction (R) phase. Similarly, some are actually re-purposed in the form of re-cycled elements of organic material and inorganic material already pre-existing on earth. Due to the finite nature of individual life form existence, some of these organic and inorganic elements are simply passed on sooner or later to other forms of life. Understood in this sense, 'life on earth' is a constantly recycled part of nature and 'nature' (as the abstract collective word which includes all species) is constantly being recycled as parts of 'life on earth'. Moreover, it is a recycling process in which, as noted, results in a consistently high reproduction (R) level and this high level has played an essential nutritional (N) part in the process of evolutionary development.

It is important to stress and include within this broad planetary plant category, the flora and fauna floating or anchored in or on the sediments and rocks at the bottom of the earth's seas, rivers and lakes. Most land based creatures such as ourselves may only visit the sea or a lake occasionally for recreational purposes, but the products of creatures of the sea, rivers and lakes visit us each and every day and not just as food. The flora and fauna of the sea in the form of plankton, algae, dinoflagellates, copepods, quorum sensing bacteria and the other microorganisms, and lipid releasing organisms, which utilise these materials for various stages of their life cycles, supply the organic basis for all the seafood we eat and also contribute to the air we breathe. For example the phytoplankton drifting in the seas as huge blooms are tiny microscopic plants, which grow in the presence of sunlight, nitrogen and phosphorus. Although floating in the sea, they produce oxygen and are nutritionally the equivalent of grasses on the prairie and thus are the basic metabolic cellular building material for all ocean life. Thus;

"Plankton not only provides the food for higher trophic levels, such as fish, seabirds, penguins, seals and sharks, but produce oxygen, cycle nutrients, process many of the pollutants that humans dispose of through our waterways, and help to remove carbon dioxide from our atmosphere." (Plankton. 'A guide to their ecology'. I. M. Suthers; D. Rissik and A. J. Richardson. CRC press. Chapter 1)

This quote illustrates both the scientific advances made in recent years but, as noted elsewhere, also demonstrates the baggage of outmoded categories often dragged into text books along with the new conclusions. Relatively new is the recognition, that life on our planet rests upon the efforts of (the invisible to the naked eye) bacteria, algae, archaea, protozoa, phytoplankton and zooplankton, but the weight of human-centred tradition in the sciences has the forms of 'life' ranked into *higher* and *lower* trophic levels and categories with predators and humans at the top. This anthropocentric human-centred taxonomic labelling results in the most important and founding category for all life on the planet (oxygen producing, nutrient cycling, pollutant processing, plankton and their soil living equivalents) are ranked as the lowest forms. This contrasts to the anthropocentric assumed fact that the supposedly most 'intelligent' species is actually over-foresting, over- fishing and over polluting the rivers and seas (i.e. industrialised humanity). Yet this species ranks itself as the highest. This has resulted in an anthropocentric practice and ideology among human beings which assumes that every other form of life is less important than the supposedly superior humans and all other forms of life are therefore considered as either simply extraneous and/or available as materials to serve whatever half-baked purpose, privileged humans decide they should serve.

Nevertheless, the number of earth orbits around the sun calculated as 2,100, 000, 000 years or 1,200, 000, 000 years noted earlier, even if they are not exceptionally accurate, are nevertheless staggering lengths of estimated time for many organisms to have existed. Moreover, during such long periods of evolutionary activity, plants became ever more complex, interconnected units of active living and relocating organisms, until they have become the shape and form that we see in modern times. Moreover, plants only seem to be environmentally static but in fact they are living organisms which move their leaves, flowers and roots in order to gather sunlight, gases from the air, minerals and chemicals from the soil and which their internal cells then actively convert into fibres, sugars and proteins, which are the material (N) resources for other forms of life on earth. Hence the observation that plant nutritional sources therefore contain both inorganic and organic materials. Plant cells use these materials internally via capillary movements to produce their cell structures and seeds for future reproduction.

Most plants therefore are rooted *gatherers* of nutrition and storers of energy and use these to grow themselves, but access to this essential energy and mineral source (N) is also the attraction for insects and animals to graze on them and which at the same has also evolved to enable pollination. Here we should again note that the life-cycle of plants also adheres to the universal requirement for Nourishment - Metabolism - Growth - Reproduction, Ageing and Death; (N.M.G.R + A-D). Although they are not like some animals, *hunters* of nutrition, what some plants produce as sugary sap does attract insects, birds and some animals which unintentionally through contact assist the dispersal of pollen in the plant reproductive cycle. In some plants the sweet liquids have served to attract, then dissolve insects which enables such plants to obtain some organic substances they might otherwise not obtain, from their roots. So in a nutritional sense, the latter plants (such as the Venus Fly 'Trap' plant) are a plant version of the animal ambush predators. However, in lacking a consciousness they are not purposefully 'trapping' flies etc., that term is just another application of lazy anthropomorphism. Nevertheless, plants, taken as a whole are examples of living organisms that;

".. not only repairs its own waste and produces new material of like character to it, but it also produces new masses of living matter, which when detached from the parent mass, eventually begins a separate existence and growth. Furthermore, the plant organism has acquired, by the process of evolution, the ability not only to produce an embryo for a successive generation but also to store up, in the tissues adjacent to it, reserve food material for the use of the young seedling until it shall have developed the ability to absorb and make use of its own external sources of food material." ('The Chemistry of Plant Life'. Introduction. R. W. Thatcher)

The new masses of potentially future life forms which plants abundantly produce and detach are of course - seeds! Seeds are individual packages of 'dormant' or semi-dormant cells and nutrients, many of which in nature cannot be reliably spread very far without a whole ecosystem of animals and wind to distribute them. Therefore, plants have evolved alongside animals and insects, and animals and insects have evolved alongside plants. This form of association has proved so beneficial that in many cases it has evolved to become a symbiotic interdependence. In woodland, forest and plain the ecosystems in and around plant life has become an integrated organic mutual support network, which not only supports their immediate insect and animal neighbours but, through the absorption, transformation and expulsion of gases benefit life on earth in general. So it is worth repeating again, that plants therefore, do many of the things other life forms do, such as produce new cell material to replace worn out or damaged material, (i.e. Grow) create embryos (i.e. Reproduce) and ensure nutrition in its seeds until the seedling plant can exist independently. But crucially, they also do more. They directly absorb gases and mineral compounds as their sources for cell metabolism (M) and their cells make these into proteins, fats and carbohydrates. The Nutritional or Nourishment and Growth element of the (N.M.G.R.) plant life cycles, (more to follow) therefore is the foundation of all other (N-M-G-R) land based species life cycles.

Whilst researching material for this chapter, I came across the following interesting statement of the Metabolising period that plants undergo in a 19th century treatise on plant life, which encapsulates much of the then known detail;

"When the sun is set, the leaves of plants no longer decompose the carbonic acid of the air, but a pause takes place in the activity of their functions and they sink into a passive condition. The gaseous bodies brought from the ground by the action of the spongioles percolate through the delicate tissues of the leaf and escape away into the atmosphere. At night, also, in many flowers, the petals fold themselves together, and for a time all active processes cease. It is, therefore, through an instinctive impulse, that comes over them during this period, that all animals, except such as take their prey by night, seek places of rest." ('A treatise on the forces which produce the organisation of Plants. J.W. Draper. Chapter 1.)

So clearly, the Nourishment, Metabolism, Growth and Reproduction phases (N.R.G.R.), that were encountered in Cells, Microorganisms and which we will encounter later in the chapter on Insects, although accessed and realised differently, also occurs in plants. However, unlike the insect and animal forms of life, it is important to constantly remember that plants are unique in the fact that they use the carbon dioxide from the air along with other inorganic material for solar ray photosynthesis and then extrude oxygen. What plants produce in living out their life cycles are gasses and materials that most other life forms now need to directly breath, eat and absorb in order to sustain their lives and reproduce their species. In this integrated cycle of '*life on earth*' we animals then process this plant produced material by inhalation and digestion (M) and exhale and excrete the very gases (carbon dioxide) and mineral compounds the plants need to continue their cycles of life on earth. Furthermore;

"There are many components that affect the overall fitness of plants. The interactions and reactions that occur with and within the shoots of plants depend upon abiotic factors such as sunlight, water, temperature, atmospheric gases and wind, and biotic factors such as pollination, herbivore, and pathogen attack." ('Bacteria in Agrobiology: Plant Probiotics'. D.K. Maheshwari ed. Springer.)

And as noted in the previous chapter, below the soil surface the root parts of plants also directly depend upon soil chemistry, water, minerals and nutrients in addition to the huge number of microorganisms and fungi that exist there and play a positive role in the plants normal development. Above ground plants directly interact not only with the atmosphere but also with the crawling and winged life forms which pollinate, spread seeds and consume its fibres, fats, proteins and sugars. On both levels of sensory interaction, atmospheric and subterranean, the health and quality of the plants entire organic structure depends upon the presence and quality of the organisms taking part in the many absorbing and exuding interactions which take place in soil and environment. Too much or too little of what the plant directly needs in any of these organic and inorganic interactions of gases and minerals, can negatively affect its quality, its survival quantity and consequently also the quality of those of the many other organisms which interact with it.

Thus maintaining the ecologically dynamic *'balance'* of everything the plant has evolved with is not just a good idea or an outstanding moral sentiment, it is absolutely essential for a healthy biosphere and therefore of paramount importance to all life on earth. For example, the plants that have been more accessible to certain insects, such as flowering and fruiting plants, have survived in greater numbers precisely because the insects with the most suitable means of successfully collecting and depositing pollen or other material from them have also survived in sufficient numbers. Their different requirements for their respective metabolic purposes have been served by both the profusion and varied nature of organic and inorganic material. In this interconnected way and over many generations of organisms, a two way (or multiple adjusted) modification of plant and insect/animal parts, has often taken place. In many cases, two species have developed to become exceptionally dependent upon each other. Consequently, too few pollinators or too many caterpillars or locusts above ground can lead to decline of the affected plant: too few microorganisms, fungi or inappropriate chemicals in the soil can do the same. Furthermore, for plants the uptake of minerals and metallic elements, such as the secretion of iron by molecules such as *siderophores*, are provided by microorganisms. .

"Nutrients are extremely important and directly influence growth, yield and quality of crops. Soil microorganisms can provide nutrients to plants through the fixation of atmospheric N2 and or by enhancing nutrient mobilisation/uptake through their biological activities such as mineralisation, and through the production of siderophores, organic acids, and phosphates." (Bacteria in Agrobiology: Plant Probiotics. 2.4.1.)

The earlier example, of the gradual mutual evolutionary adjustment of the pollinating insect, bird or animal and the pollinated plant is just one of many gradual morphological (body shape) adjustments made to many other insects or plant associations which makes them become mutually dependent. In such cases, if one of the 'contributors' to this reproductive exchange is destroyed in one way or another, so too by default, is the likelihood of the other. The factual basis of the above sentences is not a recent discovery. However, in view of the 20th and 21st century reluctance by many people to recognise the threat to life on earth by the actions of the current mode of production, it is worth reminding the reader of the insights provided by a few of the more perceptive scientists of the 19th century. Here is one from 1840.

"Plants not only afford the means of nutrition for the growth and continuance of the animal organisation, but they likewise furnish that which is essential for the support of the important vital process of respiration; for beside separating all noxious matters from the atmosphere, they are an inexhaustible source of pure oxygen, which supplies the loss which the air is constantly sustaining. Animals on the other hand expire carbon, which plants inspire; and thus the composition of the medium in which both exist, namely, the atmosphere, is maintained constantly unchanged. (Justus Liebig. 'Organic Chemistry etc.)

If we accept the general accuracy of the above quotation and its many modern equivalents, then it has long been known that what happens to the plant life on earth is of vital importance to the rest of life on this planet. So in the almost two centuries between 1840 and 2020 we need to consider what overriding motive has constantly and virulently been in the way of applying the logic arising from this scientific understanding. We need to ask why agricultural practices were never altered sufficiently to address the problems the 19th century industrial methods of production, transportation and consumption were already creating. Indeed, that question will be the topic for a much later chapter on modes of production devised by human communities. Meanwhile, since the quality of plant life depends directly and indirectly upon the quality of the soil microbiome in which it grows, this is the medium for growth that we should consider as we continue this inquiry.

So although practically every human being knows that plants generally grow in soil, what is less known, at least in detail, is how they grow, the full implications of their life cycles and how plants interact with other plants and animals. Practically all organic *life on earth* exists in what are known as aerobic conditions and consequently require an intake of oxygen in some form or another. Most living things need sunlight, oxygen, and other gases to help them metabolise the intake of minerals, proteins, fibre and chemicals for energy, survival and reproduction. Plants and other photosynthetic organisms are only slightly different in this regard, because, as has been noted, plants rooted in soil and located in the sea, produce oxygen. If life began in the seas, which seems probable given the available evidence, then plant life on earth is one of the earliest multicellular forms to establish a permanent hold on the land beyond the seas. This is confirmed by the fact that the probable photosynthetic ancestors of modern plant life have been discovered as fossils in rocks dated between one and two thousand, million years ago. If that calculation turns out to be reasonably accurate, then *life on earth* in some basic unicellular and multicellular forms is indeed incredibly ancient and crucially important. Does it seem sensible therefore that whole forest plant systems are being felled globally to make way for large mono crop plantations, animal grazing ranches or logging in order to make luxury furniture items?

There are a number of pre-aerobic (anaerobic) forms of life such as some bacteria that can survive in deep muds and other places devoid of oxygen and sunlight, (such as animal stomachs) but for the vast majority of living organisms, such conditions are uninhabitable. The question of how during the earth's evolution, the planet became enveloped in oxygen is interesting and has been tentatively answered with regard to chemical transformations along with the chemical capabilities of early plant and algae metabolism. But of far greater importance, is the ability of land based plants such as trees to absorb some chemicals from the atmosphere and discharge others such as oxygen for this is at least one of the sources of the quantity and quality of the air we breathe. How this initially occurred is thought to be by an ancient form of anaerobic life known as cyanobacteria in assemblies or colonies called stromatolites. It is currently suggested that the metabolic processes of these early life forms managed to separate the oxygen out of the water (H_2O) as a gas and this accumulated in an atmosphere of mainly carbon dioxide until oxygen became a significant part of the earth's atmosphere. However, understanding the probable atmospheric origins are less important than understanding the importance of maintaining them now for ecological balance of those essential species which recycle and produce the atmosphere of planet earth and as previously noted, are the foundations of all food chains.

The other source of oxygen production on the planet is via the single or multicellular aquatic plants known as algae based in the seas. They are part of the large and varied spread of aquatic organisms which also produce seaweeds and kelp. Algae vary in size from the microscopic pico-plankton to giant kelp with fronds over 100 feet in length. Although algae have some similarities to plants they have many differences. For example, algae do not have roots, stems, leaves or vascular tissues. Some algae exist in many types of loosely or highly organised aggregate association where each basic cell can exist independently of the others and reproduce itself by cell division. Most of them obtain their metabolic needs for gases and minerals by utilising energy derived from sunlight and their carbon needs obtained from CO_2. They also form beneficial associations with other life forms such as lichens and corals. In such cases they supply their associating life form with oxygen in exchange for nutrients and an element of protection. This ability to produce oxygen has served a double functional benefit to all life on earth. First, algae in the form of phytoplankton in the seas, forms the basis of the marine food chain as they are eaten by the tiny krill upon which other ocean species feed. Second, the oxygen the phytoplankton produce supplies approximately half the oxygen all life land based forms need to survive. Among the plant-like symbiotic species are the many forms of lichens which are a beneficial association of fungus and algae. In this case the algae can exist independently but the type of fungi which associate with them are dependent upon the algae.

At this point we should further mention and lay stress on the importance of this other multi-adaptable life form, fungi. This too is not strictly a plant, lacking leaves, stems etc., but it is an (N-M-G-R +A-D) processing organism which actively collects material and makes functional connections with plants as well as algae via its hyphae and mycelium. In this way it provides and obtains nutrients in interactive processes which benefits both plants and fungi. Fungi in the form of yeasts, of course also have multiple uses to humans in fermentation processes. Of the ubiquitous nature of fungi in general, biologist Merlin Sheldrake writes;

"Today over 90 per cent of plants depend upon mycorrhizal fungi...No plant grown under natural conditions has been found without these fungi; they are as much a part of plant-hood as leaves or roots." (Merlin Sheldrake. 'Entangled Life'. Vintage. Introduction)

It is estimated that there are between two and three million species of fungi on the planet and their function is to integrate into the process of chemical transformation needed by living things which we call metabolism. Plants depend upon fungi to extract nutrients such as phosphorus and nitrogen from the soil and deliver it through their thread like tubular mycelium which connect to plant roots via their hyphae. The fungus draws from the plant roots, sugars and lipids which are produced by the plants by photosynthesis of sunlight and air. What this sparsely detailed study of life has revealed so far is the complexity, the interconnectedness and the inter-dependence of life forms, large and small on each other and on the mineral and gaseous compounds of the planet. This abbreviated account is presented as part of the process of hopefully convincing the reader that living things - as a whole - are not simply disconnected entities sharing a separate or collective space in something called the natural world, but are interconnected, interdependent elements and parts of the entire system of life on earth. We humans are not a separate part of nature and nature is not a separate entity from us. Nature is part of us and we are part of nature. We are nature and nature is us, but we are often taught to act and think as if we are completely separate from the world of plants and other life forms.

Yet everything we eat and every breath we take depends upon plants. And it is not just human life which is dependent upon plants. With the notable exception of the deep ocean vents, all insect and animal life on earth is intimately linked and dependent upon the contribution which plants provide to the environment and the ecology of the entire planet. In the deep ocean trenches algae and bacteria also provide the bridge between organic and non-organic material that land based plants provide elsewhere. The dead and decomposing elements of the prolific numbers of sea and bird life forms that existing in the sunlit regions of the ocean also sink in large quantities down to the so-called twilight and midnight zones and on to the ocean bottom, providing organic nutrition on the way down to those life forms which are adapted to scavenging which then in turn become the sources of nutrition for the predatory fish and mammals which thrive - even in the darkest depths miles away from the direct energy of the sun.

Practically everything else that is alive, eats, breathes the gases and utilises the materials produced by plants. We need to include in this broad category, the flora and fauna anchored on or within the bottom sediments and rocks of the earth's shallow seas and lakes. They, and the micro-organisms utilising these plants for various stages of their life cycles, supply the organic basis for all the food the land based insects, birds and other animals eat and all the mixture of gases everything inhales when breathing. Consequently, plants are the primary and constantly active prolific link between the inorganic material of the planet and the organic species which require both forms of material for their survival, growth and metabolic reproduction. If we accept the general accuracy of the earlier quotation, then what happens to the plant life on earth is of vital importance to the rest of life on this planet - including humanity!. However, before going further with the other categories of life on earth, it is possible on the basis of what has been described above, to preface the coming descriptions with the following observation.

In all species there are functions, intrinsic to each individual organism, which consciously understood or not, require them to absorb a range of materials supplied by organic or inorganic nature. These individual requirements are met by; 1, actively obtaining the necessary liquids, solids and gases to enable their processes of metabolic reproduction; 2, actively obtaining protection for their survival. In modern economic terms obtaining these necessary materials (1) involves some form of production and consumption as a naturally evolved basis for its species. Plants produce seeds, which sprout and consume material stored within them until the air and soil become the source from which it eventually grows and consumes gases and material in order to produce roots, cells, fibrous tissue, foliage, flowers and further seeds. As we shall see in the following sections, all animals from insects to humans produce and consume naturally produced material, in a continuously cycling snd recycling process. For all organic species, production is dependent upon consumption and consumption is dependent upon production and also upon reproduction, and this continual process occurs either quickly or slowly, depending upon the species considered. Although language and imagination can conceptualise this process as having two distinct stages, in real life, production and consumption are not separate activities, but two connected phases of one dynamically integrated process.

Incidentally, as already noted, this ability to imagine things differently than they actually are and the limitations of linguistic terms causes a common problem, particularly in bourgeois forms of dualistic idealised thinking. Language and imagination have frequently been used to separate integrated material processes and then when attempts are made to impose these imagined separations back onto a reality which is not static, problems logically occur. The temptation to do this is greatest for those intellectuals who live by the production and consumption of ideas, mainly for monetary based transactions and rewards. It is a temptation, which if it is not resisted, can lead the intellectual into a virtual world of ideas of their own and others making which does not exist in reality, or fails to accurately represent reality. Intellectual specialists, themselves, are the distinct, unique and direct product of mass societies, who have learned to obtain what they need by creating ideas and opinions, and so exist within two realms. The first is a real material realm determined by the (N-M-G-R + A-D) material processes of life and the second a virtual socially constructed one, entirely dependent upon (N-M-G-R + A-D), but indirectly determined by human culture and educational training. Professional thinkers tend to spend almost as much time in a virtual world of ideas as in the real one and therefore for them, the virtual world of their ideas frequently dominates their view of the real world.

In the most extreme cases, such as those involved in religion, astrophysics, politics and philosophy, their culturally determined intellectual world of ideas, although ultimately dependent on the real world, often becomes more real to them than the real world. They spend large amounts of time processing ideas that are not directly connected to the actual biological world, but to a virtual and social world. This is a huge socially created problem and contradiction. If intellectuals and politicians frequently seem to be 'out of touch', that intellectual bifurcation between virtual realities and real realities is most likely the reason. Devising modern schemes to visit other planets, for example, whilst their employment and leisure activities are messing up this one on earth, has become a typical example of an oscillating separation between living in a reality whilst at home and operating in a virtual reality whilst at work. Making moderate or vast amounts of money out of writing and producing fantasy novels and films, or sociological/philosophical treatise, (i.e. mentally constructing and producing virtual realities) whilst large numbers of their fellow citizens starve and shiver in various states of system produced (real life) homelessness and poverty, should be an obvious general indictment of the present system, but only if this non-virtual reality constantly informs your existence, instead of the virtual realm of abstract ideas.

However, it is as yet the case that the real world reality of hierarchical mass society forms are largely ignored by the virtual reality producers of history, philosophy, fiction and fantasy. For example, the philosophers Plato and Hegel are among such well known ancient cases of educated human beings oscillating between mentally inhabiting a virtual world of ideas and then occasionally or rarely visiting and considering the real natural one. Both the above philosophers at times considered that the real biological and social world were imperfect copies of their intellectually idealised world; rather than the opposite. It was a failure to recognise that their idealised worlds had been derived from a real world with the imperfect rough edges and contradictions having been imaginatively removed from it. A suggestion to *'Let them eat cake'* made to people who lack bread; or 'if you work hard enough you will succeed'; are examples from different mouths, classes and ages, but the symptom of imagining that something is possible, irrespective of real world planetary, material, biological or social restrictions, is similar. We will come across this tendency in the later sections dealing with the human species.

Meanwhile, to recapitulate; all living species have evolved functions to produce and consume organic and inorganic material as a natural process - even though they produce differently and consume differently. In those species of life which form groups or colonies, whether these are of short or long duration in addition to their individual functions, there also arise socially driven and created functions perceived as needs. Both of these categories of need have modified anatomical characteristics and caused behavioural modifications, by adaptation or mutation. Most individual life forms reproduced within social species can only intermittently individuate themselves within their social group. Without the group the socialised individuals sooner or later, cease to 'be' both metaphorically and literally. Although in one sense the above description is both obvious and logical (outside of creationist fantasies), it is often ignored or taken so much for granted that it is effectively ignored. However, the essence of all life on earth, including human life, is the natural and direct constant interaction between the organic and inorganic material of the planet. This interaction between insects and the rest of nature will be considered in the next chapter.

An important end note reminder concerning plants: Without human interference, a crucial nourishment (N) source for all plants are inorganic materials, in the form of natural liquids, minerals, gases and energy from the sun. Without these numerous, environmentally sensitive natural ingredients, the metabolic processes (M) in plants cannot take place naturally. However, if they are environmentally available, then within plant cell membranes useful waste is ejected by leaves or roots and the growth (G) of cells takes place normally within the tissues, organelles, plasma content and membranes of plant cells. Plant food is good mineral and energy containing nutrition. Furthermore, the reproduction process (R) of plants, in the form of voluntary sexual combinations or budding can also take place. Ageing (A) will then be a result of natural depletion or wearing out of key parts of the plant. Finally the death (D) of the plant will be the result of the cessation of one or more active cellular organelles or lipid membrane, invasion by a virus or engulfment and metabolic absorption by another cell or organism, not necessarily by chemical or nucleus destruction. Finally, A healthy, natural environment as well as a healthy soil is necessary for all life on earth.

Chapter 4 Summary.

Plants are of course multi-cellular combinations of the specialised cell structures considered in chapters 2 and 3. Their root cells absorb and process nutrients (N) from the soil microbiome, whilst their leaves, or other photosynthetic containing receptors absorb the gasses in the air and the radiated energy from the sun to both produce proteins, carbohydrates and other materials primarily for their own growth and survival,. However, due to the prolific rate of body-cell metabolism (M) and seed reproduction (R) produced by many plants, their actual body form and seeds become the nutritional (N) basis for the vast number of life-forms which cannot produce these bio-chemical and solar energy transformations for themselves. Consequently, by their own (N-M-G-R + A-D) processes, plants also sustain almost all other vegetation or meat eating life forms, whether in the form of insects, birds, fish, animals or humans. However, with regard to these primary life-cycle reproductive functions, they are assisted by wind dispersal and also by insects, birds and other animals, whose own nutritional (N) needs are obtained by consuming and internally processing grains, fruits, leaves, grasses or nectar. This (N) seeking activity by other life-forms assists plant life forms in their (N-M-G-R + A–D) processes of pollination and seed dispersal. Plants aggregated as vast forest, prairie and swampland living communities have been the nutritional equivalent of accessible, 24/7 energy, gas supply and nutritional super-stores for life on earth in general for millions if not billions of years.

CHAPTER 5

INSECT ORGANISMS.
Insects belong to a category of life forms known as Arthropods, which also contain Spiders, Scorpions and Mites etc. The latter species, however, do not consume vegetable matter and seem to have evolved to obtain their nourishment (N) by ambushing, attacking predators, or scavengers upon other insects and animals or parts of them. This suggests that these particular land based Arthropod forms only developed and evolved after the herbivore insect groups had become a sufficiently prolific and reliable source of alternative nutrition (N) to (by that point) the abundant species of plant life. So as the insect species are already an overwhelmingly large enough group to consider, and as they are crucial to so many known aspects of life on earth, I have decided to focus this chapter, as its title indicates – on insects. Insects are multicellular organisms which, although in different proportions, are composed of three basic body sections: a head and a two part body joined by a waste-like tubular connection.

"By nearly any measure, members of the class of Insecta hold no rivals, especially when the standard focuses on species abundance, efficiency, or contributions to ecosystem functioning." ('Insects: Evolutionary Success etc. DB Rivers. Chapter 1)

Because animals, plants and insects are so different from mammals and humans in body shape and other characteristics, it is easy, perhaps too easy, from an anthropocentric viewpoint to assume there are few, if any, fundamental similarities between many of the species of life on earth, particularly insects. However, even despite their different body shapes (morphology), sizes and life styles, insect multi-cellular life forms have in addition to their cellular basis, they also have heads, eyes, mouths, guts, legs and an anus in common with other life forms. That, I suggest from a life on earth perspective, is quite a few fundamental bio-chemical and morphological similarities. In addition, the reliance of insects upon the biosphere for in-organic and organic materials, upon air, various microorganisms, fungi, and their life-cycle processes (N-M-G-R + A-D), establishes not only a wide range of similarities, but ones fundamental to practically all forms of life on earth. For example, many insects, (ants, flies and beetles) just like plants and animals, even have internal and external microorganisms in contact with both their external body cells and the internal body organs and cells within them. These symbiotic associations serve essentially the same or similar purposes as the symbiotic and immune cells of plants, animal and human bodies. Thus termites, for example, have evolved internal symbiotic relationships with cellulose producing microorganisms to process the plant material they use for nourishment. And yet despite these fundamental commonalities, it is still possible to read that;

"The more insects are studied, the more unique they are found to be and the less they have in common with so many other animals. They are among the most permanent and persistent kinds of animals' nature has evolved. Even in that remote period, perhaps 500 million years ago, when mighty forests flourished that are now coal we suddenly came upon 'a wild riot of teeming insect life'. ('Insect Natural History'. A..D Imms. Collins)

I draw attention immediately to the phrase '*kinds of animals nature has evolved*' to highlight the common mistake of assuming the collective abstraction 'nature', which represents no particular organism, yet nevertheless is often linguistically assumed to have the ability to cause modifications to cell structures and morphology in insect evolution. Of course, the scope and scale of insect life on earth is so vast and astronomical in numbers that even the relatively few humans who specialise in insects have rarely tried to cover them all. There is even great difficulty in covering the detail of even one species of the estimated numbers of between two million and six million species of insects. The very best that can be attempted here, therefore, is a general view of insects as a whole and as yet their known relative place in the whole spectrum of integrated and inter-dependent organic life on earth. Such a general view, plus a criticism of some obvious errors I have encountered, is the limited scope set for this study of life on earth.

For example, although I am in general agreement with the above quotation, in some respects I also draw attention to the fact that the above author has stressed the uniqueness of insects but at the same time has asserted their lack of external commonality with other animals. Yet given the list of common bio-chemical similarities between species, insects have much more in common with the rest of life on earth, than the more obvious differences. Given the subject matter and evidence provided in previous chapters of this study, this dualistic either/or, us or them, type anthropocentric assertion should not be allowed to stand unchallenged. If the common planetary conditions, common materials, common energy sources, common DNA structures, common protein synthesis and cellular makeup of all organic species, from single-cell bacteria, through multi-cellular plants and onto multicellular insects, (animals to follow), are not enough to clearly establish the fundamental interconnected commonalty of all forms of 'life on earth - including insects - then really - what would it take? Some other intellectual anthropocentric consideration or inherited habit must have been guiding (or perhaps clouding) the thinking behind the author's first sentence above.

internal Insect Microorganisms.

"In general terms, insect associations with beneficial microorganisms are not exceptional. Most animals host beneficial microorganisms, from which they derive nutrients, protection from natural enemies, or other services (McFall-Ngai et al 2013). There are, however, two ways in which microbial associations in insects are special. The first is the remarkable diversity of form and function of associations in Insects." ('Insects and their Beneficial Microbes'. Angela E Douglas. Introduction.)

Yet once again, sandwiched between the evidentially supported facts, we encounter the anthropomorphic language based upon relatively recent human hierarchical mass society experiences. This is another common misuse of language, which in biology since Malthus and Darwin has become consistently embedded in the ways of 'popularised' and even 'specialist' thinking and assertions about life on earth. Life on earth is imagined as being a war of survival in which organisms not apparently immediately beneficial and not providing direct obvious 'services' (!) to another individual organism are classed as (natural!) 'enemies'. I again suggest that this language and thinking is a product of the narrow based, anthropocentric focussed social life of human hierarchical mass societies. As we shall consider later, only hierarchical mass society elites create enemies out of other human beings and other species, and this is not a natural development, but an unnatural social development. It is only since the onset of ancient hierarchical mass societies that the concept of 'enemies' was also applied to other groups of humans, which began competing rather than cooperating over the same resources. As will be considered later, other human life forms only became considered 'enemies' when they interfered with the ambitions of aggressive and acquisitive elites who controlled hierarchical mass societies and their settled territories. As was noted in previous chapters, bio-chemical life on earth in all its various forms does not create enemies (or friends), nor do other species (including predator species) engage in war. These anthropocentric characteristics, where they exist, are all exclusive developments within certain forms of human hierarchical aggregation.

Even among humans, as we shall consider more fully in a later chapter, most people, from birth to adulthood and death, are never 'naturally' antagonistic. Indeed, they have to be made so by socially created categories, processes, pressures and conflicts, and as was noted previously, the symptoms characteristic of warfare is absent among plants and also insects. Insects, even those considered detrimental or deadly to other organisms, are not engaged in acts which can realistically be described as war. The parasitic insects as with parasitic plants are merely attempting to fulfil the N-M-G-R phases of their bio-chemical species existence and the particular sequences that have so far evolved within their particular relationships to the cycle of life on earth. For the most part, insect life on earth finds its nutrition (N) in the most functional way it can, and this is not always by the risky process of killing other life forms. It is more often from grazing on plants, scavenging or being in a symbiotic relationship with another life form.

For example, the guts in some termites contain 'protists', whilst others contain bacterial symbionts. Some of these internal micro-organisms produce 'anti-microbial peptides' which function as part of the termite immune system. This association of two or more life forms in turn functions to differentiate between potentially pathological and non-pathological encounters and any intrusions by other non-compatible or non-digestible organic sources. So the similarities and connections of insects with other species of life on earth are fundamental to life in general and from a life on earth perspective, there are many more similarities than morphological differences. Insects also experience the world as other organisms do by the equivalent of smells (pheromone detection), touch, taste, sight and sound. Their cellular structures have evolved to produce organs such as antennae and the above noted eyes, mouths and limbs, which clearly are a commonly shared characteristic of nearly all organic forms - even down to the cilia appendages used for motility in microscopic single-celled organisms, noted in a previous chapter. Albeit the latter exist in a much differently evolved form. Clearly, when looked at beyond superficial surface characteristics, life on earth in the form of insects, shares not only a common planet, a common atmosphere, a common temperature range and humidity variations, but also common strands of DNA, common cellular and multicellular structures, and of course, a common (N-M-G-R + A-D) life cycle process. Furthermore, it needs to be born in mind that humanity has not even 'discovered' all the species of insect yet, let alone classified and fully understood their ecological function within the whole spectrum of life on earth. In terms of the species of insects known and as yet to be discovered, estimates vary widely as do the proportions of insect to animal species and this varies with regard to the location in which they are found.

Insect numbers and origins.

"For example a single tree in Peru produced 26 genera and 43 species of ants; a tally that equals the total ant diversity from all habitats in Britain....Present day species diversity results from either higher rates of speciation (for which there is limited evidence) and/or lower rates of species extinction." ('Insects: An Outline of Entomology'. PJ Gullet & PS Cranston. Section 1.3.3)

This contains an interesting observation because clearly insects, like plants, have been an amazingly prolific form of life on earth for thousands of millions of years. Firstly because not only are single tropical trees occupied by multiple genera and species, but as was recorded in the chapter on soil micro-biome, tiny insects proliferate in even small volumes of most terrestrial soils, sands and even in drops of water. Secondly, the relatively low rates of insect species extinction indicate that the insect forms of organic life are amazingly adaptable. They continue to exist in extreme cold areas, extreme hot areas and extremely crowded areas. The lower rates of insect species extinction among such massive insect populations over millions of years around an often sole nutritional source – plants - suggests competition for scarce nutrition and habitat was not fuelling or stimulating, insect evolution or insect species extinctions. These above observations once placed alongside the currently understood cause of insect behavioural change casts some interesting light upon the evolution of insect life.

It is interesting because according to the experts, insects do not alter their response to external circumstances or external event stimulation by learning to adapt as many animals do with their much longer life cycles, warm blooded adaptations or mutations and some with higher levels of cognitive understanding. Instead, the alteration of responses to external circumstances by insects, are considered to be the result of random, genetic changes (known within biology as stochastic change) across reproductive generations. If this is correct then it is these accidental bio-chemical mutations over extended generations which have changed insect structure and behaviour in an adaptive way. Hence, an accumulation of these changes sometimes results in a variation within the particular insect species and then by further accumulation of such changes evolves into what may become classified as a new species. Therefore if accidental genetic mutations and not hypothetical competitively produced extinctions and survivals have facilitated insect evolution, we have in these cases a more direct causation than the popular Darwinian evolutionary oxymoronic abstraction, classified as 'natural selection'. I write 'oxymoronic' because nature and most species cannot select, because the anthropocentric term 'selection' presupposes an advanced stage of consciousness, accumulated knowledge and a careful evaluation of results. However,, as noted, not all insects have been fully described or studied.

"A little over 1.5 million species of living organisms have been scientifically described to date. The vast majority (66 %) are arthropods such as crustaceans, arachnids, myriapods and insects. Insects represent 75 % of all animals..." (Insects; Structure and Function. R.F. Chapman Chapter 1.)

For most of us who do not focus on insects, either for a living or for a hobby, this form of life on earth is often viewed with indifference or even antipathy. Insects are frequently considered creepy-crawly, stinging, dirty, disease carrying invasive vectors, which are best stamped on or sprayed with something toxic to get rid of them. Such attitudes have been perpetuated not only by those who do not study them, but also by those educated professionals, who do. The range of insecticides which have been developed by science based specialists is testament to an attitude that emphatically demonstrates the biological and inherited cultural level of general ignorance concerning this vital and irreplaceable form of life on earth. Of course, with a jar of honey in mind, it is generally admitted that a few insects, such as bees, are good but mostly the rest have been frequently viewed as pests. Yet many other insects, not just bees, pollinate plants, including humanity's current staple crops. Furthermore the life-cycle process of (N-M-G-R + A-D) within insect species also functions to re-cycle huge quantities of dung, dead animals and organic litter.

Insects such as bees also by consuming (N) live organic material control other life forms humans consider as 'pests', and of course insects, when not chemically annihilated, are themselves a large-scale staple food (N) for birds, fish, amphibians, reptiles, bats, small mammals and frogs, and have been their staple (N) diet for millions of years. A number of these insect eating life forms are in turn used as nutritional intake for other animals and humans. The vegetables, poultry or fish (and some meat) we humans enjoy as food, all gained their nutrition, weight and even their taste and texture during their (N-M-G) phases by means of the insect assisted (N-M-G-R + A-D) pollinating process of plant forms of life on earth. The temporary profit based convenience of getting rid of insects considered crop pests by some, would not just be permanently inconvenient, but, if continued, would be an unmitigated disaster for all life on earth - including humans. What Rachael Carson asserted about Anthropocene humanity in general a generation ago, is particularly applicable concerning the indifference to, and the increasing chemical warfare against, the absolutely essential insect life of our planet.

"Man is a part of nature, and his war against nature is inevitably a war against himself." (Rachael Carson)

It is estimated by some specialists that a variety of arthropods, having different body shapes, crawled out of the sea some 450 million years ago and 400 million ago became the ancestors of the many varied insects which, although now severely endangered, still exist. As noted, the bodies of these multi-cellular insect organisms have three basic structural elements to them; a head, a thorax, an abdomen and six legs. A distinctive feature of many insects is their existence in multiple connected but changing morphological forms during reproduction; from an egg, a larva (grub, caterpillar or maggot) to a pupa and the emerging adult form of the insect. This process is known as metamorphosis and involves a system of multi-cellular decomposition and re-composition, interspersed with short or long dormant stages between the above noted structural changes. The complete metamorphosis involves stages of little apparent activity, but even then cells within each new quiescent stage are processing or reprocessing the available material which will eventually become new or re-purposed organs (eyes, wings, mouth parts).

Some authors in the field of insect studies (entomology) suggest that due to the obvious interdependence of plants and insects for nutrition and pollination that they could have emerged from the sea at around the same time. However, I personally doubt that hypothesis. Based upon the evidence I have so far come across, I suggest plants would have needed to be well established on the planet's land before insect species could supply themselves with enough nutritional (N) sourced energy and material to fuel their own (N-M-G-R) needs. The evolutionary relationship between plant and insect life, although mutually beneficial, is asymmetric in certain functions. As reasoned in the previous chapter, only plants can create organic nutritional and nourishment sources from inorganic gases, liquids and minerals and radiated sunlight. Furthermore, plant reproduction does not (and did not) always need insects for pollination (then or now) because pollination can be achieved by water currents (for sea based plants) and air currents along with birds and animals by land based plants. The life cycle process of plants (N-M-G-R + A-D) could therefore have existed for long periods of time without the association of insects. Insects, however, could not have completed their N-M-G-R phases of their evolutionary development or their global dispersal without (N) from plant material being available to them. Logic suggests that insect cannibalism, which still remains a minority adaptation of some insect life cycles, would not historically have yielded sufficient (N) to enable insect species to populate the entire globe.

Insects – the first life-forms to fly.

Some insects evolved an ability to fly and were the first forms of life on earth to do so. Other insects, such as silverfish and bristletails etc., continued to crawl or walk. Incidentally, we should remind ourselves that insects are the most common species of multi-cellular life on planet earth. There are known to be at least 1,000,000 species of insects (yes species not just individual insect organisms within a species) and there are still places on earth not visited where it is highly likely that there will be many insect species yet to be discovered. Each species may have produced millions of individual insects alive at any one time, so in earlier pre-industrial modes of production, the insect density was undoubtedly fairly high. This very high density of insects which existed until recent centuries is probably the result of three crucial evolutionary developments. First, the amazing metabolic success of plant life in synthesising inorganic materials into energy and mineral rich forms to be available for the large scale of insect nutritional needs. This, and the proliferation of plant life around the planet, provided constantly available nourishment to herbivore insects and even to parasitic insects. Second, the high levels of insect reproduction (R) and adaptation to the different nutritional qualities (N) of plant life. Third, most insect species are quite resilient to extinction type events such as climate change and land mass disturbances.

It is therefore estimated that species of insects in considerable numbers have existed for hundreds of millions of years. Indeed, fossilised remains of insects have been dated to 400,000,000 years ago. In terms of the total weight of insects on the planet in the 20th century it has also been estimated that for every one pound weight of human beings there are 300 pounds weight of insects. That is a considerable mass of available nutritional (N) resources whether the insect is alive or dead. Whether such calculations are factually correct or best guess estimates is in a sense immaterial for the purposes of this study. The point being made by quoting such estimated numbers (and being stressed here) is that from the perspective of life on earth in general, insects and plants are far more significant for the continuance of 'life on earth' in general and in a number of positive ecological and evolutionary ways, than are us humans. Life on earth in general could continue without humans, but not without insects and plants.

"Nutrition concerns the chemicals required by an organism for growth, tissue maintenance, reproduction and the energy necessary to maintain these functions. Many of these chemicals are ingested with the food, but others are synthesised by the insect itself. In some insects, microorganisms contribute to the insects nutritional requirements." (Insects, Structure and Function. R.F. Chapman .Chapter 4)

I have already indicated that there is a frequent anthropomorphic perspective introduced into the studies of life on earth in general and it is not as prevalent within the study of insects, so it is encouraging to see the term 'functions' used in the above extract, instead of 'purposes'. As noted previously, concepts such 'reason' and 'purpose' are often attached to descriptions of insect behaviour, body form and bio-chemical production which, with the absence of insect reasoning and knowledgeable intentions for purposeful actions, such unscientific terms have no place in non-human studies. Insects did not purposely develop wings so that they could escape predators. Wings certainly enable that function, once they have been acquired, but it is more logical to suggest that these appendages were the result of gradual mutations, not some prescient intention. Without reasoning abilities we can only assume that each cell and multi-cellular organism is merely following an evolutionary sequence in response to internal mutations or caused by unintended external effects from other inorganic or organic substances that are within its cellular structure or are in close proximity to its limited external sensory organs.

Molecular level pheromone material from sources of nutrition (N) may be the trigger to stimulate the intake of nutrition and begin a metabolic process of synthesising the nutritional source to be suitable for insect species. Other pheromones emanating from a compatible insect may stimulate activity leading to reproduction. Internal bio-chemical activity by organelles may stimulate the function of cell division or the removal of unneeded materials, but there is no current evidence for asserting that any form of reason or purpose is or ever was behind the gradual or accelerated evolution of those functions, in cells, plants or insects. Insect functions and sequences (as with plants and fungi) are not intentional adaptations. I suggest they are best understood as just the accidental, intrinsic, successful evolutionary genetic sequences and organelle productions, which are passed on through reproduction - as modified (or not) - by further cellular mutational outgrowths and DNA/RNA replication. I again suggest that the repeated inclusion of anthropomorphic assumptions, introduces an unnecessary distortion into the understanding of non-human life on earth. Returning to the advanced progress of insect evolution and the ability to fly it is noted that;

"Insects were the first animals to fly. They had functioning wings over 100 million years before flying reptiles of birds. The wings are outgrowths on the 2nd and 3rd segments of the Thorax. Wings are formed of the same material as the rest of the exoskeleton – chitin" ('Characteristics of the Insect Orders'. Laura Smith.)

When insects began to fly no other living organism could under its own efforts take to the air, against the force we describe as gravity and under their own bodily exertion. Other organisms could either swim in water or crawl on land and so far as we know it - that was it! Thus, for an extended amount of time (or more accurately an extended period of geological and evolutionary change), it is logical that insects had no obvious predators apart from those relative few, evolving within the insect species itself. Flight enabled quicker and further movement than crawling and for millions of years, the only limit to expanding their spread to other locations was the availability of suitable forms of plant nutrition, convenient habitat and much later a few predatory plants and insects. This perhaps adds to the reasons why, until more recent times, insects populated every part of the planet in great numbers and are now the most numerous species on earth. Interestingly, from an aeronautical perspective even the slow evolution of insect flight has still resulted in highly adapted flight characteristics in so many non-aggressive forms which far exceed the aeronautical efforts of humanity. I would suggest Butterflies and Moths as being the obvious long range examples of flight achieved on the basis of ecologically balanced and minimally acquired energy sources. Perhaps the most glaring examples of amazing flight characteristics, far beyond human ingenuity to match, are the flight abilities of the Dragonflies.

"Their four wings can move independently of one another, which is unusual in the insect world. Each wing is powered by several sets of muscles which adjust frequency and direction. This enables a dragonfly to fly both backwards and upside down, and to switch from hovering motionless in the air to speeding off at a maximum speed of close to 50 kilometres an hour." ('Extraordinary Insects'. Anne Sverdrup-Thygeson. Section; 'Multifaceted life'.)

What takes even the best aero-nautical engineers with multiple resources (involving high costs) and years to achieve or improve, comes no way near what some insects routinely achieve within a few minutes of leaving the pupation period. What costs the human species astronomical amounts for each flight in financial and material resources, time and pollution clean-up, the living cells of insects can do on a sip or two of nectar or in some cases a mouthful of dung. Their built-in bodily sensory organs, the sensory 'orientational' ability which enables butterflies and moths to navigate across entire continent's, comes courtesy of the insects cells, DNA, organelles, structure and sense organs. But of course it is not just the abilities of individual insect species which is of importance to life on earth, but the contributions the insect species - as a whole - make to that continuous cycle of (N-M-G-R + A-D) in general - which all life forms are involved in and dependent upon.

Insect collectives - 1; (swarms).

"We could not live without insects pollinating crops, controlling pests, recycling decaying plants and animals back into the soil, and producing valuable products like honey, beeswax, silk, natural dyes and shellac." ('Insects Did it First'. G.S. Paulton & E.R. Eaton. Introduction.)

In the case of insects, however, we encounter a life form which from a predetermined anthropocentric point of view can be seen as destructive to the way humanity has socio-economically evolved to structure its own (N-M-G-R + A-D) processes. Mass society living, (eating, reproducing and dying) utilising mass production techniques to obtain sources of nutrition, has introduced changes to the rhythm and functions, not only of plant and human life processes, but also to those of many insects. Mass swarms are cases where due to favourable (N) circumstances, as a whole, the reproductive rate of some species has increased to such an extent that their local 'natural' nutritional source (N) is no longer sufficient. Mass swarms of insects, which prior to agriculture and mass communities, may well have been smaller and more infrequent, then multiplied. They then occurred and were located and re-located to where large anthropocentric focussed concentrations (fields, orchards and plantations) of nutrition (N) were being produced, stored, distributed and consumed. From that point on some insects (and other life forms) could therefore assemble in plague-like (unnatural?) proportions, and as such have been recorded in the oral and written historical record of hierarchical mass societies based upon agriculture and the herding of animal livestock. Therefore, I tentatively suggest that the prerequisite for plagues and infestations may not be naturally determined ones, but socially determined events triggered by the way hierarchical mass societies of humans has produced, structured and stored its own sources of preferred nutrition.

Prior to mass agricultural production, evolutionary logic would suggest that any natural nutritional abundance in any particular environment would be met by natural increases in species adapted to consuming that source of nutrition. Plagues, however, overwhelm local predator species by the sudden appearance of insects or animals in such vast quantities. Of course, oral and written records of plagues can only go back as far back as the earliest mass societies based upon settled agricultural modes of production. It is this anthropocentrically amplified phenomenon that probably accounts for the bad reputation given to many insects such as house flies, horse flies, cockroaches, locusts etc. I have not yet come across a study of plagues from the perspective of considering whether they occur with or without mass produced crops or whether the two are linked by any cause and effect chains. The question of whether swarm collectives of insects and birds are a pre-agricultural natural phenomenon or a socially created post-agricultural phenomenon linked to the social evolution of mass agricultural producing societies, I lack sufficient evidence to conclude. However, as bad as these swarm phenomena occasionally get in modern times, the scientific study of insects by entomologists of many insect species estimate that only around two percent of the total known species of insects are detrimental to the activities of humans. If this is only approximately correct, it does suggest that over 95% of insect species are either beneficial to the existence of the human species or at the least not harmful.

Insect derived Honey, Silks, Dyes and Shellac have long been used beneficially by human communities but now other chemical properties synthesised by insect metabolic processes are being found useful in human and animal focussed medicines. Indeed, as more becomes known about the importance of insects, a new category of insects described as 'keystone species' has been identified, because it is now known, with a high degree of certainty that the loss of their critically important ecological functions and body mass would lead to a collapse of a wider ecological system balance. However, since not all insects have been studied and any ecological importance these may have, is not understood, then many other insects could also be 'key species'. For example the insects such as Bees, Ants, Termites,

Beetles, that specialise for their nutrition in recycling dead, animals, dead, plants and controlling the number of insects considered as pests, are vitally important in enriching soil and creating humus for plants. These billions of often invisible or at least unseen recycling organisms would be hard to replace.

Insect collectives – 2; (insect societies).

The other rather amazing thing that insect life has evolved is a structure of non-hierarchical mass social living. The main social insects include the Wasps, the Bees, the Hornets, the Termites and the Ants. The social wasps form communities from scores of individual wasps up to thousands of individual wasps; Honey Bees form communities of between 20,000 and 60,000 individuals; Termite communities vary from a few thousand to a million; Ant colonies exist with numbers from a few thousand to a million or so. All these social species of insects have created collective socio-economic living processes in which all aspects of their (N-M-G-R+ A-D) phases of life on earth are dealt with collectively and with very little or zero internal social conflict. There is clearly a division of labour between the various categories of the various social insect species, but the anthropomorphic terms historically used to categorise them do not in fact reflect the actual tasks involved in these divisions of labour. For example, the so-called queen (or queens), in such insect communities are not hierarchical elites and do not rule or command the community. Indeed these particular female insects are often morphologically and biologically reduced to a life of just staying in an adapted (N-M-G-R) phase continually reproducing the next generation of insects, until ageing (A) and death (D). The extra nutrition they are provided with by the efforts of the so-called 'worker' insects is less of a 'royal' privilege than an absolute species-adapted necessity to keep their rate of reproduction functioning.

These individual insects are therefore not queens at all but have evolved into multi-cellular, bio-chemical specialist egg laying organisms. The insects classed as 'workers' in such communities are not really workers either. They are just the average insect organism collectively doing various tasks that individual social insects would instinctively and ordinarily do.

They individually and collectively) forage for (N) based or (N) enabling material and return it to the collective hub, where it is stored and or individually consumed. Others collectively tend the reproduced eggs and become a supportive part of the (R) phase and in some cases, tend to the plant and other organic material (pre-M) phase, used as sources of nutrition and nourishment (N). In some cases, some social insect species have evolved exceptional mouth parts, which are used as tools for nutritional production or defence. So in general, the social insect (N) phase of life is obtained collectively, and consumed individually; parts of the external (M) phase are done collectively; the (G) phase occurs individually and the (R) phase is achieved by a much restricted number of individual female gender organisms. This is an amazing adaptation of mass society structured living and yet is also one without any continual internal friction or conflict arising. The characteristics of social insects have clearly impressed many people;

"Individually, insects, though beautifully designed, are always small; There are good reasons for this. Instead they have cooperated and formed organised groups of individuals that have evolved into societies so well integrated that they are effectively new super-organisms ." ('Social Insects' MV Brian. Chapter 1.)

Of course if we accept any part of evolutionary theory, then insects have not been "beautifully designed", they have just evolved into the form and function they currently are by cellular mutation and cellular modifications. It is only the human species which in contemplating them subjectively finds this 'beautiful' or otherwise. Beauty really is in the eye of the human beholder. Within mass societies, insect ones or otherwise, the insects are not simply individuals either, hives or mounds are collectives of 'social' individuals. Termites for example build huge mounds, with even more extensive underground structures, which result in temperature and humidity regulated conditions by the activities Termites carry out within their mounds. They also do this and forage for nutritional sources, without any form of hierarchy, managers, architects, planners and elites in control. But to my mind in my research, what many insect specialists also fail to recognise or fail to adequately draw attention to is the following. In the Termite equivalent of million plus social aggregations, (miss-named as 'cities') there are no insect equivalents of palaces, mansions, no hierarchically based dining arrangements, no unemployed termites, no intentionally starved or homeless termites, no pollution and everything produced or gathered is either utilised or re-cycled.

This may be an obvious fact, but there are also no termite equivalents of police, no termite prisons, no termite detention centres and no continuous internal termite on termite community violence. A similar pattern exists within other social insect mass communities. The misnamed army ants species, for example, do not have armies. There are no ant equivalents of generals, officers and grunts. Moreover they never plan for war or deliberately target a weaker community for species annihilation. When they are on a mass foraging trip, if any other life form gets out of their way, they are left alone and not pursued, damaged or used as nutritious food. Indeed, in some cases, if another life form mimics their group pheromone type odour in some way that organism will even be accepted as part of the group - even if they are of a completely different species - or of a different morphological body form.

Therefore, Darwin's comment on Slave making Ants, in his 'Origin of Species' is a typical anthropocentric misinformed term from a superficial level of observation and subsequently results from a purely intellectualised form of thinking. Using insufficient evidence and making anthropomorphic assumptions, is still rife at all levels. Those Ants he described were not making 'slaves' of other ants. In such cases when these ants encountered some ant eggs of a different ant species while out foraging, they then took them to their own nest and fed and reared them as a fully integrated part of their own colony. These newly acquired ants from a different nest would not be eaten, starved or forced to do anything that other resident bred ants would normally avoid doing. Describing them as slave-making ants was the conscious imposition of an inappropriate anthropocentric based phenomenon applied onto the study of another species. Here again, the so-called 'worker ants' are not a separate and subordinate category of ant either. They are not 'employed' by a colony forming elite - they are the colony! They are active members who do not give or follow orders or instructions or live in inferior accommodation or survive on inferior nutrition. Yet everything neededfor the colony to survive gets done by one or more of the colony members. The same or a similar pattern exists with the other social insects, and indeed, the gender difference is such that in social insect societies the vast majority of the individuals in a community are actually bio-chemically female and are certainly not subjected to an insect form of male domination, discrimination or male insect violence.

It would seem from this description that life on earth, in the multi-cellular form of insect mass societies, with very little in the way of cognitive abilities and communication means, have avoided all, or at least most, of the depressing problems now facing mass society humanity. In insect mass societies, there are no hierarchies, no upper classes, no unemployment, no male-on-female insect violence, no homelessness or starving individuals. Of course, in this study of life on earth, there is no intention to suggest that humanity should copy what other life forms do. However, so far in this study, there are clear indications that cells, plants and insects, with their severely limited resources, with the exception of predatory species, have also kept their own species free of regular conflict and at the same time not endangered any other ecological and weather systems. That cannot be said of either the 20th or the current 21st century stages of humanity. The species categories I have considered so far are certainly not at war with each other. Our own human species once not blinded by arrogance and self-interest, as elite humanity seems to be presently, could at least reflect upon what is natural and learn from the natural systems of life on earth with their thousands of millions of years, of what retrospectively amounts to countless trial and error experiences behind it. As we shall explore in a later chapter, humanity, thousands of years ago, also secured its own (N-M-G-R + A-D) requirements from nature, for multiple thousands of years, without internal class differences or without the mass destruction of its own and other species.

Insect parasitism.

There is another section of the insect species, whose life-cycles have not helped to gain them a favourable regard by the human species. These comprise the few insect species whose (N-M-G-R) cycle is based upon the parasitic use of other living life forms - particularly for the nutrition (N) of their offspring. The results of their species reproductive activity, from a human perspective can be seen as macabre in the extreme. Some insects after copulation insert eggs and grubs into other living organisms such as plants, other insects, animals and even humans. These eggs and/or grubs then absorb as nutrition, the surrounding living material of this other living organism in two ways. The grub consumes the host's organic material from the inside of their living bodies working toward the outside, or alternatively by consuming from the outside of their living bodies into their insides. Confronted with such 'natural' facts, this is where we humans need to hold back any repulsion and abhorrence we feel whilst reading the following information on one parasitic (Pompilid) wasp species;

"They have one of the most potent insect venoms and are able to paralyse the largest tarantulas. Their speed, life-freezing venom and skittish behaviour enable them to capture spiders several times their own size. A single sting renders their prey as putty in the mother wasp's mandibles; then she will drag the spider into a pre-prepared lair and lay a single egg on it. By the time the baby wasp is munching through its personal living larder, its mother has long since moved on to hunting and provisioning more offspring." ('Endless Forms; 'The Secret World of Wasps'. Seirian Sumner. Part 1)

We should note here in passing that apart from some social species, (Bees, Ants, Termites) only Death (D) incapacitates the role of the female in seeking adequate nutrition, not her role in reproduction. This fundamental asymmetrical aspect of female/male sexual forms of reproduction will be considered again in the animal realm. However, when considering insect behaviours, such as those above, we need to simultaneously process the following fact. The insects utilising this method of preserving their offspring and ensuring it has enough Nutrition to Metabolise, Grow and eventually Reproduce (N-M-G-R) are not aware of the nature of this process nor aware of its outcome for the host species which are used this way. They also have no awareness that they are affecting and infecting the (N-M-G-R) pattern of another form of life on earth. Some insects, for example, even eat the eggs or grubs they have produced themselves. In doing these things these rare parasitic species are not negating abstract human sensibilities, they are just fulfilling in this case a non-typical (N-M-G-R + A-D) pattern of evolution that they have inherited via their multi-cellular evolution and the sequences determined by their DNA. Life on earth at this cellular and multicellular level has no understanding of 'life on earth' and no level of aesthetic consciousness which can replicate human intellectual levels of understanding or moral qualms and conscience. Prior to humanity, life on earth, via its multifarious organisms, had no moral or 'natural' barriers, (only bio-chemical ones) to ensuring its cellular and multi-cellular nutritional or reproductive welfare, regardless of its effects upon other life forms. Such infrequent examples of life feeding off another life while it still lives are not typical of the evolution of life on earth. Also, biological and sex differences and reproductive roles were an evolutionary development, not something the organisms were consciously aware of. Yet the evolutionary role of the female of the species within insect reproductive and in the initial life support process of their offspring is remarkable.

"(1) Females oviposit exactly where the larvae will begin to feed.(2) Females construct or induce habitats for progeny. (3) Females provision cells on which larvae feed. (4) Plants provide micro-habitats for? insects and others. (5) Animals provide micro-habitats for parasites. (6) Weaving insects and spiders make nests for themselves. 7) Burrowing by adults and larvae into substrates provides shelter and food/" (*'Insect Ecology, Behaviour, Populations and Communities'. Section 2.6. Price, Denno, Eubanks, Fine and Kaplan.*)

In studying life on earth, we also need to remind ourselves of the following sobering fact. Human beings, despite having a much higher level of consciousness and moral aspirations, have not rid themselves of a careless or reckless disregard for the lives of others of their own species, let alone the lives of other species. As we shall consider in a further chapter, humans have tortured innocents and killed babies (in or out of the womb) for some real or imaginary 'higher reason' and are still doing mass killings in many parts of the world, even as this sentence is being typed or later read. Deliberately starving people, young, mature and old to death, has been practiced by ancient and modern elite citizens, since the origin of hierarchical mass societies. Moreover, those among us, who do the above, do have an advanced consciousness and knowledge of moral issues. Among human communities the general rule to; *'not do to others what you would not want done to yourself or your loved ones'* is not yet a universal one, for it continues to be ignored. Altering such unnatural minority social behaviours within humanity is a level of morality yet to be universally achieved by the human species. So yes there are also some insects that hunt and kill other insects for nourishment, there are those who do damage by eating or cutting leaves and boring holes in trees and soil. But that from such insect species is not a conscious choice, but an unconscious evolutionary developed trait which takes place within an ecological balance of life as a whole and by its results has become sources of nutrition for these and other species.

However, as noted, there are even more insects which pollinate fruit and vegetable crops and of course (M) metabolise sweet liquids from their (N) nutritional intake such as honey from bees and sugary substances from aphids. Also we need to recall that at some point in their life-cycle, insect bodies become (N) nutrition for other insects, animals and fungi before decaying into humus which then becomes nutritional material for plants. Over 80% of plants need pollination by living animals and most of that is done by insects. Grasses and conifers, rice, maize, barley and wheat, (the Grains) are among the exceptions where wind assisted air born pollination can also be frequently achieved. Furthermore, insects have already made available chemical compounds which medical researchers have found useful as anticoagulants and anaesthetic substances. The understanding of the amazing bio-chemical products of cells that have developed in insects as well as plants, is still in its very early stages, and;

"We have not even got round to naming four-fifths of the perhaps five million insect species that are thought to exist, let alone studied the ecological roles they might perform." ('Silent Earth' by D. Goulson. Chapter 2)

There are just too many ways in which these millions of insect species secure their own metabolic needs from nature to go into greater detail in this short study. Nevertheless, this immense diversity rests on the fact that insects, like all other forms of life on earth, also require the same basic phases of Nourishment, Metabolism, Growth and Reproduction (N.M.G.R.), before their final phase of (A-D). Many, but by no means all, have evolved to rest at night, when solar energy radiation is absent and, like plants, many tend to be active during the day, others at night. Insects that fly expend an enormous amount of energy just to stay airborne and so sources of energy rich nourishment and periods of rest are still needed in their often relatively short lives. However, like plants, it is the role that insects play in the nutritional requirements of other forms of life on earth such as birds and animals which also should not be overlooked. It is in this aspect of life on earth that human forms of chemical predation in the sense of targeted destruction of 'life on earth', has become widespread in the 20th century. The amount of organic material these so-called 'pests' provide for the nourishment and metabolic requirements of insectivorous animals and birds is enormous, but frequently overlooked. Their grubs and bodies have also contributed considerably to the nutritional requirements of human beings in certain places and at certain times. So consistently eliminating insects directly and indirectly also consistently eliminates those animal organisms who depend upon them for their (N-M -G-R + A-D) and so on along multiple food chains.

Insect Metamorphosis.

How most insects function by their actions and bodies to deliver the metabolic needs of other life forms, is also too extensive for this relatively short study to consider. However, a few examples of the contribution insects make to the many animal species in general and to the human species in particular cannot but reveal how vitally important they are. Nevertheless, there is one development within the reproductive phase of the life-cycle of some insect species which I suggest is truly remarkable and occurs in no other species of life on earth. For this reason I consider it is now worth commenting upon further in the context of this study. That really amazing development is known as metamorphosis. Not all insects contain or retain this ability within their life cycles, (65 percent of known insects do) but those which do illustrate the extent of the complexity that life on earth is capable of achieving without any external planning, guidance or 'intelligent' manipulation. Highly skilled human technicians can build mechanisms with two or more interconnected stages with different functions, but the mechanisms produced by humans are not self-replicating and cannot reproduce any of the complex functions achieved by life on earth. In contrast, insects and plants can. These latter functions are just a few of the many facts that should temper any human tendency toward arrogantly assuming human superior complexity over nature. No matter how seemingly amazing human achievements are, they in no way match, or exceed, the complexity of the evolution of life on earth.

Just consider such clear examples by considering reproductive metamorphosis. An insect lays an egg in which its cells first multiply and expand before reassembling themselves into a grub, maggot or caterpillar. This first stage of reproduction then involves constant eating (Nourishment and Metabolism) and after a period of time, the cells inside the grub enter a stage of life in which its internal activity changes and it protects itself by secreting a cocoon. Within the cocoon the cells continue to (Metabolise) and break down its previous contents and the cells of this material stage reassemble (Grow) themselves into another form before a final stage of the original insect form emerges. Then, if the (N-M-G-R) phases of the cycle are not interrupted the whole cycle repeats itself. For example a butterfly lays an egg which transforms itself into a caterpillar and which then transforms itself into a butterfly; similarly, a maggot is transformed by its internal genetic material into a fly. The cellular and organelle components of the structural cell materials have self-assembled, disassembled and reassembled themselves into completely different body forms. This transformation undoubtedly seemed like super-natural magic before scientific investigation discovered some of the tiny details of reproduction processes achieved by its biological intra-cell components during reproduction and evolution. Nevertheless it is still a process, which far exceeds the ability of any human intellect to fully understand or to replicate.

The process of cell division and multi-cellular reproduction is complex without the extra complication of a two stage metamorphosis. This is because each time a cell divides into two, the double helix DNA strand has to be replicated so that upon cell division each daughter cell has only one copy. This is achieved by the prior assembly of multiple proteins within the cell and then this cellular process functions to apply this enzyme complex known as (the DNA helicase) onto the DNA strand. This enzyme then moves along the DNA strand in a sense unzipping the two connected strands of DNA so that the bio-chemical molecular process can begin copying each strand. Which are then repositioned into the double form and on successful cell division each daughter cell gets the exact copy. The source for this paraphrased paragraph has been taken from a Study Report by MRC Laboratory of Medical Sciences published on 22/1/25. However, so far in my research, I have failed to uncover the finer detail on this process of insect metamorphosis, but consideration of some of this detail based also upon the chapter on cells, seems to suggest that the DNA and other genetic material which is contained within the insect egg, must have had within it at least two potential sets of (homeotic?) gene development possibilities.

Perhaps a second set of alternative DNA potentials lies dormant or semi-dormant in some form of the organelle or nucleus components whilst some internal or external circumstance triggers the first set of DNA potentials to produce the cells and structure necessary to become a viable caterpillar or grub. The second phase of genetic material needed later perhaps remains within structure as the dormant source of DNA needed for phase 2 and is awaiting some external chemical or thermally induced internal activation. After a period of absorbing appropriate forms of organic matter, some other temperature, H2O or changed chemical balance 'perhaps' triggers the cells in the first multicellular body form (the grub) to cease to function and decompose. At some point the second set of DNA potentials (?) begins to reorganise the remaining cellular components and substances within the cocoon and during phase 2 produces a different body form. This third form which if it successfully survives, replicates the form and abilities of the initial insect which previously laid the original eggs. Whatever the complexity, the extended phases of (N-M-G-R) within metamorphic transitions is undoubtedly an amazing sequence that bio-chemical forms of life on earth have evolved through millions of generations of insect species. Even incompletely comprehending such biological intricacy and complexity of 'life on earth', should temper the arrogant and narcissistic self-importance, displayed by many human individuals, with regard to their anthropocentric level of understanding and their limited range of skills and achievements.

So what to earlier forms of limited human knowledge seems like a miracle of one thing turning into another is just another amazingly detailed microscopic bio-chemical cellular form of life on earth replicating previous patterns of beneficial cellular associations and sometimes achieving 'novel' bio-chemical combinations. These interactions spread over thousands of millions of years along with complex divisions (mitosis and meiosis) and recombination of cells and by absorbing (engulfing) other organic and non-organic material has obviously created more and more viable organic structures. The reality of life on earth has enough amazing complexity to ever need any imaginative human fantasies to be invented to satisfy our curiosity. Combining and re-combining cells into one form, then triggering a further transposition of cells producing a new form, seems to be a recurring pattern in metamorphosis. Random mutations obviously continued more than once in the lineage, until some existing forms were stable enough to continue the sequence indefinitely. The new mutated or symbiotic forms clearly became viable and self-replicating and thus able to achieve viable nutritional sources for sustaining their own metabolic processes (N-M-G-R) at each stage. These immediate biological and evolutionary processes (as with many others) are well documented but as yet nowhere near being fully or generally understood. There is far more to learn about life on earth than is as yet known about life on earth. For this reason it would be a monumental form of arrogance to think that we now understand everything or that our species bogged down in wars, ecological destruction and self-indulgence, can now improve on what life on earth in the form of its species has already achieved. Instead, perhaps if enough of us can become wise enough, we need to learn from life on earth whilst we celebrate its complexity and start to do our best to nurture and protect it, rather than invent and enjoy pastimes that do the exact opposite.

Insect recycling.

Insects in general, are not bound to any one particular ecological niche. They can exist on land, in water, or in soil, and move between these environments during their life cycles. They can tolerate extremes of cold and heat and wet and dry conditions. They can exist in solitary, gregarious, partly social or highly social associations and be active by night or by day. They also pollinate plants in the sea as well as on land. Isopods, brushing among some sea weeds, pick up the sticky male spermatoids and randomly deposit them on the female counterparts. The general drifting together of male and female reproductive counterparts in the sea in this case has been part of the process of evolutionary reproductive adaptation. As with their aquatic counterparts, insects on land are essential to the following activities;

"..nutrient recycling, dispersal of fungi, carrion, dung and soil; plant propagation, by pollination and seed dispersal; controlling animal community structures...by predation." ('The Insects'. Gullane and Cranston. Blackwell)

It has been noted in previous sections, that many insects spend at least some of their life within the soil where their life, death and reproductive cycles contribute to the fertility of the soil and thus to the quantity and quality of plant life. But of course insects also depend on absorbing the nutrients produced by plants and other organic life forms from bacteria, fungi and lichen etc. Insects are essential to most forms of organic life and are the essential food source for many other insects, animals and birds. Again a general conclusion arising from this study cannot be reasonably avoided; that once established, an entire species of insect life has never been ended by the actions of another species of life - even though a large percentage of those reproduced became the food source for other animal and insect species. This conclusion is evidenced by the fact that fossil remains of many insect species indicate they have remained in essentially the same bodily structure (morphology) for many millions of years. They existed then and still existed in the 19th and 20th century in configurations which were essentially the same. Although their numbers have now been much depleted by chemicals and other anthropocentric environmental destruction, their viability and necessity within the ecological landscape of the planet, is undeniable.

The insects found trapped in the solidified sap of trees known as amber provide three dimensional examples of this fact. Successful insect species were living on plants (trees) and each other and had survived in almost (if not exactly) the same bodily form and structure for hundreds of thousands if not millions of years. Moreover, most of them then and now fulfil a particular evolutionary role; one that other living organisms cannot always replicate. Furthermore, because insects have specialised to a considerable extent, they cannot always be replaced by any other organism or inorganic processes. Once we understand the importance of the huge insect biomass in Nutritionally (N) supporting all other forms of life in complex interactions on planet earth, from pollination to recycling, then we should be concerned at what has taken place over previous and current decades. Globally, it is estimated that the planet has lost at least ten percent of all insects since 1970, and this does not nearly reflect the actual loss in certain areas of the planet. In the areas with the most capitalist developed industrial/agricultural countries of Europe insect loss is undoubtedly far greater than that.

"Studies in Germany and Netherlands have found a midsummer decline of flying insect biomass of 82% over 27 years of record keeping." ('G. Burke. in 'Rebugging the Planet' by V. Hird.)

This flying insect species loss confirms my own lived experience over a lifetime of 'entitlement' travel (largely unaware and untroubled for much of it by my own and others polluting activity). In the 1950's and 1960's on trips out on my motorcycle and I would be covered from head to foot with bugs splattered on my motorbike paintwork, my leathers, helmet and visors – lips, nose, ears – everywhere! Windscreens on our family car needed constant cleaning after every 30 or 40 miles on our trips to the Lancashire seaside towns of Blackpool, Southport and Morecambe. By the time I ended the much later 20th century 300 mile trips to see family and friends (whether by motorcycle or car) not even one tiny midge spoiled my view, dimmed my headlight or smeared my visor. When we understand that with so many insects now missing, and with the above-noted knowledge that they are essential to 'life on earth', (and have been so for millions of years), is it not now time for more of us to begin to do more than just catalogue what else is now missing and stop what we are doing to cause their loss and to the rest of nature's essential species?

The growing evidence is pointing to the fact that there is now an increasing crisis in the depleted insect population within the world's vital ecosystems. Furthermore, humanity cannot escape the accusation because they are not killing themselves or each other in such vast numbers. Moreover, the organic life forms that used to eat these missing millions of insects must either be eating something else for nutrition (N) or what is more likely – simply dying off. The dominant reasons why this insect species loss is occurring and its implications will be considered later in the section on humanity. Meanwhile we need to continue to consider the ecological role of animals in their own particular quests to metabolise the organic and inorganic materials they need for their own individual lives and their species life on earth. Of course, there are a few plant species such as wheat, barley, rice and maize, which achieve pollination by the action of wind blowing pollen across fields, however there are many more plants and fruits which are dependent upon insects or small animals.

Without the pollinating insects, for example visiting the flowering and fruiting plants that other animals (including humans) rely upon for a healthy varied diet, would simply die off as an individual organism, or the species be reduced or die off. The many vegetables, fruits and nuts which are available to eat (for those who can currently afford to buy or grow them) would die off and disappear. Therefore, humanity as a whole, needs to mature and cease regarding microorganisms, plants and insects as 'pests' but regard them as they actually are in the interconnected web of life on earth; as the solid biomass foundation upon which the rest of the planet's organic life is built. The human species cannot eat, work, clothe, reproduce or breathe without the interconnected life-cycles of insects and their habitats being maintained and sustained. Without this integrated biomass foundation, everything else would collapse just as our houses would collapse if their solid foundations were carelessly or deliberately undermined beneath them. Finally;

"Bugs are a vital part of the recycling of nutrients, without which we cannot survive. The soil in which we grow most of our food is created largely by the guts and jaws of worms, mites, springtails, termites, beetles and many more. They mash up the leaf litter and the dead bodies, so we don't have to, releasing some nutrients and making plant material more easily decomposed by fungi and microbes, which then releases more vital nutrients like sugars, nitrates and phosphates for plants to absorb and grow." ('Rebugging the Planet' by Vicki Hird.)

Meanwhile, I hope it can be reasonably asserted that enough evidence has been provided within the chapters so far presented, to establish the following three general observations. 1, that all the insect species of life on earth are linked in various ways for their nutritional (N) requirements and, 2, are utterly dependent in one way or another upon the contribution which plants provide to the environment, the ecological system and the atmosphere of the entire planet. 3. As is the case with plants, insects are not just self-assembled from a single cell, but are dependent upon a prior organism plus many other contributing microorganisms, environmental and organic factors. In the next chapter we will consider to what extent and how the lives of animals are also intertwined and inter-dependent upon the previously considered species of life on earth.

Chapter 5 Summary.

It is estimated that insects make up 75% of all the multicellular animal life forms on planet earth and have existed for at least 500,000 years. During this long period, they have maintained essentially the same body shape of head, body and limbs, with some limbs developing into specialised purposes, such as for grasping, crawling, stinging and flying. Throughout their existence insects have had a close and functional relationship with plants using them as sources of nutrition (N) and materials needed for their existence. In doing so many have become the unintentional carriers of plant pollen, thus directly assisting in the mass reproduction of plants and extending the rate and range of plant growth on earth. Large scale pollination of plant species can only be achieved by wind, animal or insect dispersal, and of the three, insects are the most numerous and most reliable means. Insect life-cycles, (often short), include the same (N-M-G-R + A-D) processes as other life forms.

It is also within the insect form of life on earth that the form of sexual reproduction in which the female of the species embodies the function of producing (by grubs or eggs) the next generation of the species, becomes clearly evident. Moreover, many insects are unique among life on earth by having extended (metamorphic) reproduction (R) processes. The additional level of complexity in this regard involves intermediate 'larval' stages between initial and final reproductive forms of some insect species. The specialised cells within insects also produce substances such as sweet liquids (honey), strong fibrous material (silks) and other materials such as shellac. Many insect forms also consume dead material and others (bees, wasps, ants and termites) form vast communities with community functions distributed among them. It is only since the creation and extension of large agricultural communities that any insect species has been regarded as permanent pests rather than occasional irritants. Vast sources of nutrition attract vast swarms of insects.

CHAPTER 6

ANIMAL ORGANISMS.
To repeat again from a Gaia perspective of life on earth, it is important to recognise that despite their many differences, animals, like plants, microorganisms, and insects, are all made up of multicellular associations of life on earth, generally specified as individual organisms which are structured around the common (N-M-G-R + A-D) bio-chemical processes. Therefore, with the exception of most plants, they all get their energy and materials to move, grow and reproduce mainly by absorbing and metabolising material from other inorganic materials and other organisms such as plants and other animated life forms. The multi-cellular compositions of animals also contain some cells that have evolved somewhat differently from the cells in other species of life on earth. These are called 'Epitherial' cells and they have particular properties and important functions. Thus;

"These are brick-shaped cells, lacking the rigid cell walls found in plants. Epitherial cells are arranged into flexible sheets with specialised proteins holding neighbouring cells together and other proteins sealing the gaps between cells to make a waterproof layer." ('The Animal Kingdom'. Peter Holland. Oxford. Chapter 1)

These sheets of cells are not only extremely strong for their size and membrane dimensions, but also very flexible allowing the sheets of cells to bend and fold which gives an extra degree of suppleness which occurs within animal bodies. These modified cells are particularly crucial with regard to the muscle tissues and internal organ structures of animals. The main focus of this chapter will be with regard to those animals who are closest in terms of their (N-M-G-R +A-D) to the human species and are classed as mammals. The mammal species among the animals are known as warm blooded animals or endotherms ('endo' meaning *inside* and 'therm' meaning *warm*). The function of keeping the insides warm when the environment outside the body is cold requires a lot of energy hence warm blooded animals require a lot of carbohydrates in their nutritional (N) sources.

Carbohydrate compounds are a mixture of carbon, hydrogen, and oxygen, the latter two integrated in the form of water and the carbon contains sugars in three different types. These inorganic substances along with other materials are absorbed in mammals across the intestine wall and thus into the bloodstream. The cells having metabolised the carbohydrates thus release the needed energy throughout the blood circulation process of animals which combined with the energy absorbed from fats and proteins allows animal multi-cellular organs and bodies to function in their varying temperature fluctuating environments. The combined result of this energy metabolism and transfer keeps the blood of mammals rich with energy containing material which is transported around the body and its organs.

From the information contained in the chapters so far, life on earth, despite its amazing variety of forms, seems to have evolved a few basic structures and persisted with these, but with manifold modifications. For example it has been already noted that cells have two basic models - Prokaryotic and Eukaryotic - but with innumerable nuanced variations in both these forms. As noted earlier, the majority of plants comprise of roots, stems and foliage, but again in almost countless variations. Also insects mostly take the form of head, thorax and body with legs, but yet again with multiple variations. In the case of animal species most of those which have become species on land or in water have a) a skeleton consisting of a backbone with head, ribs and limbs attached to the skeleton; b) flesh surrounding these and organs suspended within the inside of the skeleton and the skin. In some cases the limbs have been modified into wings or their aeronautical equivalents, as in birds and bats, in others as flippers and fins in sea adapted mammals, others in the form of legs, arms and feet. So again in the case of the large numbers of different animals, the multiplicity of basic forms are still retained and supported by essentially the same fundamental skeletal form. Moreover, in addition, despite many animal differences, their life forms are still produced and sustained by the same (N-M-G-R + A-D) life cycle process that all other forms of life on earth undergo. For some the (N) source is absolutely or predominantly vegetable matter but among the animal species there are many more forms which have become adapted to live on the flesh of other animals, whether currently dead (obtained by scavenging) or alive (obtained by active predation).

Thus from huge whales and elephants, down to pygmy shrews and tiny humming birds, the basic skeletal structure has persisted along with the two organic animal or plant based nutritional (N) sources. In the case of animal life on earth the bio-chemical functions noted within cells and plants, also seems so far to adhere to an evolutionary process of; *'if the cellular combination and process of (N-M-G-R +A-D) actually functions well, this biological process keeps reproducing it and it is only occasionally or accidentally that the cells produce something different'*. Since at the cellular level there is no prior intention and no feedback mechanisms to indicate that mutations might be successful in the long term, survival of a species depends upon the successful completion of the (N-M-G-R + A- D) processes by sufficient numbers of normal or non-adverse mutated organisms. Consequently the success or failure of any random mutations or cellular adjustments within animals may well alter part or all of an organism's form or function positively, negatively or not at all. In this regard, the two main sub-variants of this vertebrate multi-cellular reproductive form of life on earth have been with regard to how to deliver the reproduced offspring into the external world. Some animal species eject the next generation within a shell (or eggs) containing initial nutrients inside which provide the initial independent (N) nourishment (as is similar to the case with plant seeds); other species deliver live offspring by means of muscular contractions within the birth parents womb membrane to produce live organisms. In the latter case this only occurs after the offspring has been through a growth period attached to a placenta within an internal amniotic membrane. Although involving different processes, both these reproductive results are clearly those based upon the success of the overall evolutionary method of foetus development and nurture in the mammal womb by the female half of such species.

The amniotic nurturing process of mammals has also evolved another long lasting tweak to animal life on earth which has persisted for multiple thousands of years. This involves the bio-chemical process of providing initial after-birth nutrition via modified blood of the female partner produced in the form commonly known as milk, through organs of lactation. This process functions via the system of hormone distribution contained within the female reproductive biology of each species. Therefore, biological femaleness is not a social life-style choice, as some 21st century misguided people seem to suggest, but a long established, deeply rooted, fact of biological reproduction in animals and mammals. This pattern of reproductive process in essence started with the sexual based reproductive mechanism of ancient multi-cellular forms of life on earth. The fact is that any cellular species of life on earth not capable of asexual reproduction or self-replicating internal mitosis, (excluding artificial manipulation), is now bound by a non-reversible biological necessity. One of each sexually reproducing species (the one we class as female) must from birth store, eventually release and internally locate a large cell (ovum), which once naturally or artificially impregnated by a male sperm to fertilise it, begins to grow (G) within a functioning exclusively female cavity (the womb) which is an internal structure specific to the female gender. The only partial exception to this pattern I could locate is in the case of the male sea horse which has an internal body cavity in which the young are kept until they are able to become independent. In other species, the female half of the live birth species internally and traditionally externally nourishes (N) until it is either independently able, or is socially assisted to commence, the necessary individual and social (N-M-G-R + A-D) processes of life on earth.

The estimated evolutionary span of animals.

The periods of time (or earth orbits) which have elapsed since life began on planet earth have been given sequential labels known as Era's. In one system the earliest known Era is the Palaeozoic, which stands for 'ancient life'. The next one is known as the Mesozoic Era, meaning 'middle life' and the third and present one is the Cenozoic Era, representing 'new life'. Each Era is further sub-divided up into periods, such as the three more commonly known periods of the Mesozoic Era, the Triassic, the Jurassic and the Cretaceous. There are usually bands of years given to each of these eras but again as previously noted, these time-frames are estimates and given that the evidence for such long periods of existence, dating is not always reliable or conclusive, (even among scientists) not everyone agrees on them. Again for most things as well as this study it does not matter if there is a lack of exact dating or disagreement, because accurate dating is unnecessary for a generally accurate understanding of how life functions. I suggest it is only essential that the reader comprehends that the lengths of time that animal life on earth has been in existence and evolving within its species produced biosphere are immensely long. During all those periods we can be confident enough to assert that the process of (N-M-G-R + A-D) existed and continued to exist within each of the species, however much the individual phases have been modified.

Life on earth in the form of 'animals' comprises of a huge group and with the exception of plants and fungi everything else such as molluscs, jellyfish, starfish, worms, fish, birds, arthropods, reptiles, marsupials, mammals and primates have been placed in different sub-groups within the category of animals. As noted animals also differ from most other multi-cellular species in that their cells also include a complex protein structure of collagen which helps hold their cells together. Moreover, apart from a few of the most basic forms, the rest have muscle and nerve systems enabling them both to move and to intensely and accurately sense their surroundings. Thus most animals, as with insects, considerably extend their range of biosphere activity by seeking out their sources of nourishment (N). Many animal species, complex or simple, also feed on other organisms that are either alive or were recently alive. Sponges, for example, although anchored to rocks, are among the simplest forms of animal life, and lack the mobility of many other life forms, yet they have evolved some intricate and varied pro-active forms of obtaining nutrition. They feed upon other forms of organic life and often resemble plants. Although existing in integrated colonies, their cells have not become permanently specialised and each cell remains capable of recreating the whole organism of which it is part. Some of these cells also retain the flagella and cilia that other cells also have but these are not used to move the sponge cells about but function to agitate a current in the water which draws the suspended particles of organic matter toward the part where the sponge can absorb them.

Having briefly introduced such variety, the remaining focus for this chapter will be land-based mammals. Nevertheless, by not including many of the sea based animals and mammals in this chapter, I will nevertheless assert, until otherwise persuaded by convincing evidence, that all the animals not covered in this or other chapters can be considered as adhering to the life cycle phases of (N-M-G-R+ A-D) in some lengthened or shortened form or other. Furthermore, their nutritional (N) sources also contain inorganic material and organic material from life forms either living or once living. Therefore, I shall assume the full range of reproductive life cycles, apply to species within the sea as well as those on land. Some, of course, reproduce small numbers of live offspring, others larger numbers, yet others produce many spawn type or egg type offspring and others produce them in even larger quantities such as occur in bacterial blooms and krill concentrations. So what is covered with regard to land-based animals, I suggest, will also generally apply to life in the ocean. Even in the deep ocean trenches animals exist on the (N) of organic debris which continually sinks from above or in the form of complete or dismembered animals that have died and sunk to the bottom. Deep down in the even darker ocean depths and under immense pressure, there are also ambush and hunter predators securing their (N) from engulfing live animals. Of course predatory animals also defecate and in doing so release organic and inorganic material which becomes the nutritional (N) source of the life-cycles of other life forms. In a number of places it is now common knowledge that there are also deep-sea thermal vents (known as smokers) that through their chemical content (metal acidic sulphides) and heat energy sources (350 – 400 degrees C) from magma sources also support chemosynthetic bacterial microorganisms. Thus;

"Life in the smokers doesn't just endure these infernal conditions, it cannot live without them. It thrives on them......Sulphur bacteria can extract hydrogen from this mix and attach it to carbon dioxide to form organic matter." ('Life Ascending' Nick Lane. Chapter 1)

On the basis of their metabolic (M) capability of extracting inorganic sources of energy, known as Chemosynthesis, these life forms have become part of the basis of a deep ocean based localised food chain up to the level of crustacean animals and beyond. However, since it is generally accepted that mammalian life initially developed on land and humans evolved from within that group of life forms, as noted earlier, it is the land based animal species which will remain the focus for this chapter. In this regard, the organic nourishment sources (N) for land based animals comprise of three main categories; plant based, insect based and animal based. For animals, plant based nourishment is relatively easy to obtain because unlike animals, insects and birds, plants are rooted and cannot move away. Their chemical and structural defences (poisons, tough bark and spike-like barbs) are also not insurmountable either and can often be easily overcome. More importantly, the rapid and prolific reproductive (R) and growth (G) phases of their (N-M-G-R) living cycle favours the use of plant seed and sprouting seed as nutrition for many animals including mammals. Seeds passing through insect, reptile, bird and mammal digestive tracts and landing in a warm bed of ready-made organic rich fertiliser, has obviously been essential for the evolutionary success of the many inter-dependent and integrated species of life on earth. The evolution of their sweet tastes and high energy concentrations has played an obvious role in that regard.

If we pass over the lush vegetation of the Jurassic period of the mega era and the as yet unproven causes (!) of mass extinctions, which took out the now popularised dinosaur species, then vegetation either remained or returned prolifically during the later new life (Cenozoic) era of life on earth. Certainly by then plant-life had largely recovered its old and new levels of abundance. Prairie grasses and other vegetation eventually developed and for hundreds of thousands of years, the habitable terrestrial part of the planet was covered with Forest, Jungle or by the relatively quick reproducing grasses of the Savannah or Prairie regions. The latter regions' grasses eventually supported herds of million and more different ruminant animals, in various parts of the planet, as well as elephants, cows, horses, gorillas and monkeys. However, the relatively low concentration of proteins in plants means that large size for plant eating animals often requires continual grazing and practically a whole day's activity in order to maintain their size, their energy and to continue their (N-M-G-R + A-D) based life cycles.

Clearly, the proliferation of such vegetarian based animal life, I suggest, is what created the conditions for some animals (as with insects) to develop into carnivore species, rather than the opposite. I find it unlikely that carnivorous animals gave rise to vegetarian animals. The purposeful selection by predatory carnivores of the young, the old and the injured among the vast herbivore herds etc., as the easiest prey, may seem callous to our human sensibilities, but as noted previously, prey animals do not have such moral sensibilities and are just obtaining nutrition in the way their species adaptations have evolved. In terms of understanding life on earth, it is crucial to recognise that from the last extinction until approximately ten thousand years ago all the myriads of species then, whether existing in Jungle, Forest or Savannah, had already existed for hundreds of thousands of years without failing to find sufficient nourishment (N) to complete their (N-M-G-R + A-D) cycles. Furthermore, to recognise they did so without any species causing the mass extinction of any species available as prey. In the case of animal life on earth, if we inquire and find where the nutrition (N) comes from and where the (D) dead organic materials ultimately go to, the answer will point to the crucial inter-connected circle of life on earth. It will also indicate how the ecological balance and other balances between species are retained and maintained on planet earth, by the integrated self-regulated cyclical processes of life itself. Consideration of how the complex interconnected (N-M-G-R) phases are completed in each species is undoubtedly fascinating and bewildering, but it is wise for the purpose of this study not to focus on the detail and cause the focus be directed away from the common biosphere (N-M-G-R + A-D) processes. That is because life on earth - at the Gaia level - depends upon the whole interconnected and integrated evolutionary cycle of the life and death process of its millions/billions of inter-dependent organisms. Throughout that whole evolutionary development, stretching across millions of years, animal reproduction (R) was continuing, energised by organic nutrition and motivated in the case of sexually reproducing animal life on earth, by the tactile attraction of male/female copulation.

Furthermore, evidence and logic suggests that for at least hundreds of thousands of years if not millions, the millions of species of life, that survived were able to find enough nourishment and safe resting space to fulfil their (N-M-G-R + A-D) process without exhausting the supply of nourishment or the places available to rest or nest. It is worth pointing out in this particular regard that mammals were still an immensely successful species despite the need for far more sources of energy rich nourishment - ten or more times the quantity of nutrition (N) - than non-warm blooded animals. Furthermore, despite this extra nutritional requirement and apart from life in certain restricted locations, there is also little or no real evidence within the animal world to support the Malthusian and Darwinian anthropocentric derived concept that all species are constantly at war with each over available resources of nutrition or reproductive partners, and therefore it is not this imaginary war which has determined evolutionary developments. The corollary false assumption being that species die out because another species or variant has monopolised limited sources of (N), is likewise devoid of evidence to support it. There is also no evidence that any of these myriads of organic species, by their own individual or collective efforts, have ever eliminated another entire species of life, whether plant, insect, fungi or animal, by predation or grazing.

So in reality, for many hundreds of thousands of years, land based herbivore animals have been finding their sources of nourishment from sun, air, water and plants, the latter in the form of grasses, mosses, leaves, fruits, nuts, tubers and roots. These plant based life form resources have been exponentially reproducing themselves, by their prolific reproductive activity between their respective (plant-based) sexes. They have done so in such vast quantities and at such a rate as to sustain huge herds of animals. Bison, Wilde-beast, Reindeer; moderately large groups of Zebra, Elephant, Rhinoceros, Deer, Goats, and Merekats; troops of Apes, Monkeys, Gibbons, and Gorillas etc. These are all examples of animal groups living entirely from species of vegetation. To this list of animals and eventually the human species we can add the huge flocks of seed and fruit eating birds and bats. Alongside the vast mass of vegetation consuming animals are the lower numbers of carnivore and omnivore, birds, reptiles and animal species which also eat live and dead organisms, but which these prey have in turn mostly survived on vegetation. Given that in the authors life-time vegetarianism has been perceived negatively and often ridiculed, it is interesting and informative to understand that vegetation by producing oxygen, base-line nutrition, and other essential raw materials has been the foundation of all species existence, including the human species which produced those jaundiced view of vegetarianism.

The existence of life on earth over billions of years, suggests to me that organisms, utilising plants as nourishment have always reproduced faster than those organisms that directly consume animals! Moreover, nourishment (N) for all life on earth has consisted of the organic material resulting from the (N-M-G-R + A-D) cycle of one or other of the species of life on earth. Even after digestion, the residue of the N-M-G phases of organism metabolism, in the form of excrement, continues to provide sustenance for a vast range of beetles and micro-organisms on land and animals in the sea. Those proto or potential organisms not surviving beyond egg or seed stage have also become either the source of nourishment for a whole ecosystem of species such as bacteria, microorganisms, plants, insects, some animals and fungi, or as residue building up like limestone from animal shells, or concentrated carbon such as coal and oil. It is obviously crucial for the survival of life on earth that the energy contained in the cellular structures of active and inactive organisms survives when the organism itself ceases to be active as such, for this condensed energy once released by digestion and metabolism in species using this as nourishment revives the organism that successfully metabolise it. The sheer number of land based microorganisms, plants, insects and animals, living and dying and thus sustaining life on earth over the millennia is remarkable. It also provides evidence why life on earth - when allowed to create its own natural rhythm and balance - has been eminently sustainable and ecologically balanced.

Animals viewed from an Anthropocene perspective.

Perhaps here is a good place to alert the reader again to the often distorted description of life on earth depicted by the frequent anthropocentric focus and bias of much of the past and present research and study. The phenomenon of confirmation bias within human opinion making, if not yet universally understood, is now considered to be a frequently occurring problem, yet it is not always guarded against, particularly within animal studies. The fact that the vast majority of those professionals who have studied one or more of the areas of life on earth, over a generation or more, were males, is perhaps significant in this regard. The overwhelming majority of those professionals had been socialised into human societies which were rigidly patriarchal, and which by their ideological production and anthropocentrically based assumptions could not have ensured sufficient objectivity and it clearly didn't. On the one hand, behaviour observed in animals which confirmed what was expected of male or female humans, was invariably viewed as typical for many animals and thus confirmed what had been imagined and thus expected. On the other hand behaviour which contradicted the observer's expectations was ignored or invariably viewed as untypical exceptions. Thus in view of human male attitudes to females, aggressive sexual behaviour by male animals was assumed to be typical and thus was assumed to make male animals and mammals dominant in all aspects of animal life. Yet the undoubted resistance and subversion of this male domination and aggression, by alliances of females and less strong males was ignored or viewed as marginal. This anthropomorphic tendency extended to the actual terms and language originally applied to some species of animals (and retained in the 21st century) reveals this confirmation bias blatantly and extensively.

The so-called, 'Kings of the Jungle', such as Lions, vividly demonstrate this anthropomorphic distortion of reality, because more often than not, it is not the males, but female alliances that ensure the hunt for a supply of food is successful. Similarly in a number of other animal species males fighting amongst themselves, is assumed this is in order to be the ones to have the 'right' to exert control and mate with the females. However, this assumption misses the obvious fact that even in the most violent cases, male animals are often fighting each other not for the right to mate at all, but for the right to be available to be 'chosen' or to be allowed to mate by a female of the species. It is obvious that if sexual reception was not being restricted by female denial or resistance, there would be no reason for males to fight and damage each other, whilst waiting for permission to copulate. Moreover, in the animal species, this female acceptance of male penetration only ever occurs when the female is ready and willing for it to happen! This same pattern has been observed in many animal species such as Lions, Wolves, Hyenas, Apes, Monkeys, Gibbons, Buffalo, and of course Birds. Males in the latter category frequently need to display elaborate behaviours and body markings to even gain some sustained female attention let alone to gain access to sexual intimacy. Even then the most spectacular and strenuous efforts of 'display' by male birds are not always successful in bringing about copulation, if the female is not ready to do so, they just walk, run, fly or swim away.

Yet in numerous televised wildlife documentaries the narrative commentaries invariably accompanying the programmes are still loaded with male anthropocentric assumptions and prejudices. Some of the most popular 'front men' of nature programmes in the 20th and 21st centuries are arguably the worst offenders in tailoring their observations of nature to coincide with their own inherited male ideological anthropocentric bias. Observer bias has also often failed to record or register other more less obvious instances of gentle and tactile comforting behaviour between animals of all genders and even examples of gentleness between different species. The only frequent exception to commenting on male species gentleness is in the case of instances between male parent and offspring and of course among those animals domesticated as pets. The patriarchal shadow cast over two or more generations of uncritical disciples of Malthus and Darwin's anthropocentric *'survival of favoured species'* ideological construct, ensures these commentaries muddy and in some cases drown out any potential serious discourse on the 'origin' and beneficial inter-connected relationships of all species of life on earth. Thankfully this 'blinkered' approach has started to change a little in recent decades, but it is still rare to come across research which establishes a more complex and female-centred reality than the long dominated male centred one depicted by previous and current generations of professional male observers.

More on Mammals.
"The key to understanding how mammals have adapted to such a variety of life styles in such a wide range of habitats is in their metabolic rate. This is a measure of how rapidly the chemical process in their cells can produce the energy needed for the animals activities." ('Mammals: a very short introduction. T.S. Kemp.)

It should be noted that the number of functioning mitochondria cells in mammal bodies tend to be increased so that the volume of energy producing cells assists the processing speeds and quantities needed from the individual mammalian cells. It is common knowledge that many animals, birds and fish consume insects as part of their metabolic intake. Indeed, it has already been noted that the consumption of insects as grubs, caterpillars or fully developed insects is so prolific that it forms crucial parts of the chain of nutritional resources for life on earth in general. Furthermore, some insects have absorbed enough poisonous or irritating substances to ensure they are avoided by many other life form seekers of nutrition. With these exceptions aside many animals add a wide range of insects to their diets of vegetation, fruits and other animals.

Here again with regard to animal species we have the general observation that animals - in their natural existence - invariably exist in social groups even though as adults they also invariably eat (i.e. consume organic and inorganic material) as individuals – within a socially congregating and socially inter-dependent collective of individuals. A similar pattern exists for birds, fish, reptiles and sea based animals. A social existence in herds, flocks, schools, pods, and groups still allows more or less unrestricted access to the sources of their metabolic requirements which they consume as individual organisms. I leave aside for this particular section, the fact that humanity when it developed animal pastoralism and agriculture, placed artificial barriers in the way of animal foraging and hunting, both by restricting animal movements (by fencing, netting and hobbling them) and by the full domestication of some species, thus making domesticated animals almost entirely dependent upon human actions for much of their lives and any protection, nutrition and welfare they became limited to.

We have seen that for land and sea based microorganisms, viruses, bacteria, plants, insects, and animals in the natural world, their efforts as a species to metabolise the planetary materials they need for existence and reproduction have not been and are not seriously impeded or denied by any other species. Those predatory animals, like pre-agricultural humans (as we shall consider in another chapter), only kill to obtain nutrition (N) not for other reasons or simply because they can. When not hungry even predatory animals do not deliberately kill, not even when testosterone levels in predatory males rise to a fever pitch. This is invariably the case, even though as individual organisms, some may become prey to the nutritional appetites of other individual life forms. Again, while animals are alive in nature, the results of their nutritional acquisition activity are directly theirs to consume. Within the animal species, as with insect species, there are therefore, only direct, 'natural' relationships between individual organisms and the things they need to survive. With the exception of mating rituals and the nurturing of new offspring, nothing is gathered or hunted to supply to, or to exchange with, other individuals of their species. The gathering or hunting of food by individual social animals, insects and microorganisms, is simply the small-scale direct appropriation and absorption of the products of nature by individual organisms living within a specific form of beneficial social grouping. And of course;

"Mammals, along with the biologically remarkably similar birds, are the vertebrates that are most completely adapted to the physiological rigours of the terrestrial environment.." ('The Origin and Evolution of Mammals'.T.S Kemp. Chapter 3)

Whilst giving and sharing between animals as with parent and off-spring (and as also with group defence) are perhaps the early stirrings of conscious social awareness, within animal species, their social origin and development has remained a natural one. The 'bonds' between individuals in beneficial social groups are naturally developed ones, not socially constructed intellectual ones. We can include in this natural/social development, the amazingly sophisticated facial muscles of the primate section of animal life on earth. That gradual physical alteration and subsequent modification of basic facial muscle structures, along with vocal forms of articulation, for social communication purposes, was also a socially reinforced natural development. Monkeys, apes and gorillas all have a full suite of facial muscles which can indicate a variety of socially recognised emotions and indications of possible actions. Although often filtered through the preconceptions and biases of those who carry them out, anthropological studies of such primate species indicate a lot about how animals act and feel individually, socially and how they interact collectively.

The patriarchal view of Alpha males as being the animal equivalents of human kings or patriarchs but 'ruling' in the domain of the jungle or savannah, rather than a nation or country, needs to be increasingly challenged by a new generation and be reflected in future field observations. It increasingly seems that in monkey and gibbon troops what were once considered to be absolutely dominated by established alpha males - when studied without prior bias - are not so dominated. Modern observational evidence is recording that, in many cases, large and strong males can be defied or even permanently ousted from the troop by an amalgamation of female and/or junior male troop members. The assumed control of females by males for sexual activity involving reproduction (R) also needs to be challenged as the same social dynamic operates. Female receptivity and even female initiation of intimacy and copulation are observable in animal studies and female animals equipped with the means to resist unwanted predator interference in any form are obviously capable of doing so over unwanted sexual intimacy. In a well-documented lengthy case study of the frequently bullied members of one gibbon troop the rest of the troop simply left the Alpha male asleep during one night and re-located elsewhere taking their group members and offspring with them.

Routine, bullying and oppression by those who are stronger than others in a group or community is not a development with fully natural origins, not even in animals who lack the advantage of language and higher cortical reasoning. Successful and attempted domination is a socially derived attribute stemming from a strong individual animal taking advantage of general group amiability and tolerance. This becomes obvious when any dominant animal consistently oversteps the mark and a revolt takes place by some or all of the rest of the pack, troop or band. Moving away or rising up and overthrowing or driving off the dominant one, is only as frequent as the symptom of bullying. Acceptable social behaviour in such cases is re-established by welcoming or promoting a gentler alpha male, or a sub-group moving away to form or join another group. Evidence within modern animal studies is revealing that the longer lasting so-called alpha males in primate animal groups, tend to be those strong enough to help defend and help the troop in difficulties or emergencies, but are otherwise moderate or even gentle towards their troop members who of course are often also their immediate family members.

In all the categories of life considered in this short study, we can reliably conclude that, beyond an initial stage of growth, all adult life forms orientate directly towards what they need to exist nutritionally and what they need for safety and that they engage in intimacy and copulation at their own discretion. This is such a universal phenomenon within life on earth, that when the need is for sunshine, air, nutrients or water, even plants with roots fixed in the ground or rocks will endeavour to move petals or extend leaves, or roots to obtain what they directly need. As noted in an earlier chapter, even the tiniest cells of algae and sperm, have evolved cilia or flagellation tails which flex repeatedly and move them through the liquid medium they are situated in. When we consider insects, animals and fish, we immediately note the advantage that organic life has when it develops wings, legs, tails, fins and flexible spines. All these appendages serve the function of allowing them to move toward and obtain the materials and environments they need or to move away from situations inhospitable or dangerous to them.

Bio-chemical nature in its organic forms, has evolved not only to enable movement, but has evolved the means to move toward what has been beneficial and away from what is sensed or experienced as non-beneficial. In each of the species considered so far they have all evolved this ability and thus the action of directly interacting metabolically with the nutritional parts of nature is universal. Furthermore, apart from humanity, no other species has been able, or willing, to prevent any other species, as a species, from directly satisfying those bio-chemical needs arising from their essential conditioned processes as organic life forms. Life forms are all products of what we classify as nature, they are all evolved and descended from nature and they all feed off nature and in death they all return to the general biosphere condition we abstractly call nature.

The young of many animal species are the exception to this general rule of independently finding a source of nutrition and consuming it as an individual organism. In these mammal cases the growing young are provided with a balanced variety of organic and inorganic material in a liquid form through the medium of blood from females delivered via the placenta before birth and by glandular breast lactation after birth. In other cases, for a short time, the adult animals will also bring suitable masticated or pre-digested organic material to the young for their consumption. Many insects, birds and mammals will play such a role in providing the early material for the metabolic processes of energy, cell renewal and growth. With the exception of humanity, there is no other species of life which forces or encourages some particular members of its own species (or any other species) to supply nutrition needs to a privileged section of the species. The existence of servants and those they 'serve' are a phenomenon unique to the human species. The issue of exceptional differences of humanity within the entire spectrum of species of life and its consequences will be dealt with in the next chapter. Therefore, for the moment, let it be recognised - as an established fact - that the norm for all other forms of life on planet earth - is that individual metabolic requirements are generally satisfied by direct individual relationships to the organic and inorganic materials needed by each species for their own evolved (N-M-G-R + A-D) processes.

It should also be recognised that it is the case that for all other species - with the exception of modern humanity - that their waste materials after their metabolic activity has been fulfilled, (and their bodies after death) if not appropriated by another organism, are actually delivered back to the source of their inorganic nutrition, the soil or the lake, river or sea bed to be absorbed or not by other organic life forms. In short, there is in what we commonly designate as 'nature', (i.e. 'life on earth' as a whole) within its biosphere a continually completed recycled circuit in the life cycles of all organic life forms. It is a continuous circuit, in which their reproductive processes, their births, their consumption and expulsion of material and their deaths during their (N-M-G-R + A-D) processes, are such that this begins (in my choice of sequencing) with one organism's (N) and the consuming organism ends back itself as the (N) or potential (N) for another organisms life's circuit.

Despite huge differences in size, shape, and location, if our attention moves from the predatory carnivores such as lions, tigers, leopards, wolves, etc., to the massive prairie herds of vegetarian bison, wildebeests, reindeer, roe deer, sheep and goats etc., we invariably find an inevitable social character to their behaviour. Apart from short duration skirmishes and disputes among males for access to mating opportunities, individual organisms of herd species become socialised to be tolerant of and even tactile with other herd members and often with other non-threatening lifeforms. Even when young, many animal forms engage in activities which are interactive and non-confrontational, which resemble what human observers often classify as play. All animals, including mammals, have short or long periods of a social existence, with almost unrestricted access, uninterrupted by other herd members to the food or foods of their choice. It has also been observed by many researchers that many prairie, forest and river dwelling species associate beneficially with animals of other species again, apart from sexual access disputes, without confrontation and aggression over space to rest or nourishment to consume. When one patch of nourishment is exhausted, such social animals simply move on to a new patch and in extreme cases migrate or fly across huge distances to another whole area of vegetable or sea life growth.

Furthermore, a generation ago it was considered by many 'experts' that the human animal was the only life form that manufactured tools. Tool manufacture in order to facilitate the extraction, softening up or breaking up of materials containing the minerals and organic proteins needed for nutritional (N) purposes was considered a defining characteristic of humanity. However, in the space of one generation that type of male centred anthropocentric prejudice within most knowledge based disciplines has altered somewhat. In the case of tool making and via evidence provided by investigators with a less blinkered approach, observations have uncovered the one-sided bias involved in most of them. It turns out that many animals make improvised tools and not only that but female animals are among the ones that do the most improvised tool making from stones, twigs, branches, leaves, shells and water for cleaning and then the skill is learned by their immediate offspring by watching and copying. Birds, fish, dolphins, insects, apes and monkeys are among the species so far identified as having worked out how to make their essential nutritional (N) gathering easier by utilising available materials. So if tool making, intelligence, biological reproduction, the requirement of metabolic interaction with nature, and living in social groups does not really distinguish humanity from the rest of the life forms produced by nature we shall in a later chapter need to consider what, apart from language, does distinguish humanity from the rest of life on earth.

Mammal interactions.

It is here that we should remind ourselves that among the social animal species, a phenomenon analogous to empathy in humans is often noted by those who study them. Not just the nuzzling of a young animal by an adult and vice versa, but also between adults of the same pack or group. This indicates a continuum from the natural tactile exchanges at birth which then becomes socially reinforced and in this way perpetuates and cements a natural bond or affinity between them. The frantic call of a lost or abandoned baby animal will quickly focus adult animal attention and elicit support from most other associated adult animals, where this is possible. This phenomenon extends to birds and land based social mammals in general, but also to aquatic species such as dolphins, whales, otters, seals etc. The interesting thing is that such attention is not always the result of an emergency response to problems but is often triggered by a form of mutual animal interaction based on an animal form of response frequently resembling what is often classed as altruism within human communities. For example, in primates, an injured or distressed animal within a group will be comforted by others, whether these are immediate family members or not. Thus;

"A typical example is how chimpanzees console distressed parties, hugging and kissing them, which is so predictable that we have documented literally thousands of cases. Mammals are sensitive to each other's emotions and react to those in need. The whole reason people fill their homes with furry carnivores, and not with say, iguanas and turtles, is that mammals offer something no reptile ever will. They give affection, they want affection, and they respond to our emotions the way we do to theirs." ('The Bonobo and the Atheist' Frans de Waal.)

An amazing dog called Gryff, owned by friends I know, confirms and exemplifies this assertion as fact even in non-primate animals. Gryff displays eager sustained eye contact to judge whether play is an option from the family members or from any visitors that he is comfortable with. After play, he doesn't just sit next to someone he has interacted with and trusts to rest, he leans on them or places a paw on them to maintain or establish contact. It is here that we should perhaps comment upon the extended repertoire of animal inter-species relationships that occur when animals have been thoroughly domesticated. Mammals are highly socialised animals and particularly those retained as pets, become even further socialised into human societies. In these latter cases, the sources of nutrition and safety are invariably provided by the human species and thus highly domesticated mammals need to focus less on securing nutrition and therefore have far more opportunity to extend their repertoire of social interactions with other species, by imitation or by forms of social conditioning or by more intensive forms of training. In this way they can come close to replicating some forms of purposeful behaviour exhibited by human beings. However, I again suggest, as with the observation of all animal behaviour, we should hesitate before assuming that all their behavioural responses are motivated by the same (or even similar) 'purposeful' social and intellectual processes as those occurring within human interactions. Since animals cannot be asked whether any human interpretation of any purposeful behaviour or emotional states is accurate or not, we should not assume we know. Conjecture may be interesting but is in no way conclusive and is frequently wrong.

Although the earlier noted and quoted book is focussed upon the Bonobo species of chimpanzee, who are invariably led by a female member, the research team producing that particular evidence consistently did the same observations with other species of chimpanzee. They found, as will be considered below, that even in apparently bossy alpha male-dominated chimp societies, not all was as it seemed on the surface. Twentieth century evidence based upon Bonobo primate social groupings has also challenged the long-held male-centred view that alpha males always rule a social group and primatologists have catalogued many cases in which female primates have played active roles in social harmony and in controlling any aggressive behaviour of males by female and non-alpha male alliances and by calming them down. In fact within many primate groups the females play a leading role in most group dynamics and welfare. The Bonobo primates, in particular, indicate that the possibility of group solidarity based upon non-aggression and male deference to female members is not only theoretically possible but has arisen naturally and has been a stable characteristic for the evolutionary existence of some species. This role of female influence within primate societies generally, is eloquently revealed in a study of Chimpanzee group interactions focussing upon a female chimpanzee who the observers had named Mama.

"Mama went so far as to punish females who dared to side with males she did not approve of, acting like a party whip...The result is a reduced power gap between the sexes. Since all females are present all the time, actively supporting each other, it is impossible for any male to get around the female power block." (ibid)

Among social animals, some life experiences gained both positive and negative, produce actions which resemble those classed in human intellectual terms as compassion and altruism or morality. Since these actions occur in animals we can conclude the actions arise naturally from non-verbal social forms of interacting. It is only an anthropocentric level of self-conscious contemplation of these actions by some humans that give rise to patriarchal type hypotheses and theories about these non-species specific behaviour patterns. Consequently, it needs to be constantly born in mind that these observer contemplations are themselves too often filtered through previously acquired assumptions and opinions residing within the social culture. These are then carried into the research discipline being considered. In the animal primate and canine behaviour experiments, carried out by the above author and his colleagues, the observation was made that rewarding tasks with one kind of treat (cucumber slices) was successful until that group were allowed to see another group being given a nicer, sweeter reward treat (grapes) for exactly the same task. The cucumber group became agitated and ceased cooperating. Leaving aside the dubious morality of caging animals in order to gain a substantial salary for 'pay for view' zoo purposes or for professionally paid experimental activities, these observations indicated that these animal brains processed what they witnessed and like even very young children, judged that some kind of differential system was being practiced. Making such judgemental assessments requires substantial neo-cortical observational and processing power and these are clearly there in other forms of primate and non-primate life. It is possible to write this because a similar experiment, by the same group, with rewarding dogs with nothing or with sausages for executing a learned behavioural trick, yielded similar results. Evidence such as this suggests that life on earth among many social species with processing ability of a brain is able to compare and contrast, without either the benefit of language or formal education.

Such experiments and preferably field observations of natural animal behaviour indicate that what humans' currently judge as socialised moral forms of action arise out of naturally based behavioural norms of social interaction. Since dogs, chimps and many other socially adapted animals and birds do not have intellectual constructs such as religious ideologies, or Teachers, Priests, Iman's, Vicars or Rabbis to tell them how to think and behave, we can conclude that the basis for any actions resembling what we would judge as a pre-human form of multi-cellular species 'morality' is not religion or science, but lived social reality. If the hypothesis and theory of evolutionary development is valid, and in general (but not on particular points) I consider it valid, then this must also be the basis of such actions among early human communities. Before language and verbal communication evolved additional complexity among hominid communities, actions there also spoke louder than words - and in most areas of modern living they still do! It was only much later in evolutionary terms that these socially reinforced or socially sanctioned actions and behaviours were eventually designated as moral and were provided with the anthropocentric gloss of a secular or religious god-given interpretation.

Animals, life and pollution.

But of paramount importance for this particular study of life on earth, is the fact that among all those species of 'life on earth' considered so far, three more things have been established, beyond serious dispute. First, not one species over billions or millions of years of existence has fulfilled its minimal or considerable life cycle needs of Nourishment, Metabolism, Growth, Reproduction, Ageing and Death (N-M-G-R + A-D) to the permanent detriment of the ecological environment it existed within. Rubbish and detritus has not poisoned land or sea from the activities of life on earth, because the activities of life on earth as a whole have been making an excellent recycling use of almost everything organic whether alive or dead. Second, not one species, even those species which have evolved as predating carnivores, have caused the temporary or permanent extinction of any of their prey or non-prey species of life on earth. Third, the interactive, interdependent and integrated collectives of species of life on earth have not left the water and air of the planet permanently polluted and unserviceable for the respective future generations or life in general. Until the modern era, the evolution of 'life on earth' has been a self-re-cycling and self-eco-balancing bio-chemical system.

Throughout the previous chapters covering micro-organisms, plankton, plants, insects and animals, it has become clear that in seeking the nutrition required for their metabolic purposes, all these categories of life have obtained what organic and inorganic material they need, either by foraging, by gathering or by hunting or by all three. Even in the smallest of environments such as in a drop of rain on a leaf, microscopic life is actively engaged in the processes of nourishment, metabolism, growth and reproduction, ageing and death (N-M-G-R + A-D). Moreover, even in these microscopic environments, species reliance upon life as a whole is not relative, but absolute. In such cases, the drop of water and its many inorganic and organic contents is their indispensable world and is a distilled fraction of the larger planetary biosphere. The inter-dependence of species upon the immense interconnected intricacy of nature (life on earth) is not an option for life on earth, but a contingent part and a continuing necessity.

The construction of an evolutionary history of these discrete but integrated species, from bacteria, to plants, to insects and animals is frequently wrongfully based upon how humans evaluate these species have functioned with regard to human cultural assumptions and not how they have functioned at the whole of life bio-chemical level. How species have organised their social existence in the process of extracting the organic and inorganic materials needed to survive and secure a life for themselves, their offspring and each other, is likewise too often fed through an anthropomorphic intellectual filter. From an anthropocentric perspective some species, for a time, *appear* to live as individuals, yet others live in permanent social groups and others *appear* to alternate between group membership and periods of individual hunting or gathering. However, the biological (N-M-G-R + A-D) process when considered fully, indicates that at the organic level no individual organism can survive - even for a short period of time - without the continuous bio-chemical contributions of the myriads of life forms in existence. Furthermore, at the inorganic level no organism or species can exist without consuming and others producing gasses (nitrogen and oxygen etc.) by plant based organisms and by reducing essential inorganic and organic materials to an appropriately absorbable form. And of course, no species can exist without the existence of sunlight, minerals, water and even the gravity supplied by the planet's inorganic mass and its orbital movement around the sun.

Animal Life: Freedom or necessity?

We have seen that all life forms on earth are not only determined by the planet on which they live but also what they eat and by how, when and where they eat and the environments they frequent. No life form is 'free' from the need to consume either relatively passively or actively. The metabolic interchange between organic life forms and between organic and inorganic materials determines to a greater or lesser extent how viable (or healthy) the organism is, but how this metabolic exchange occurs also determines how viable reproductively the organism is. A static form of life which gathers or awaits its nutrition needs to be in a place where nutritional material moves toward it and the organism must have the means to ingest that material, or alternatively, it must develop a means of moving toward the sources of nutrition. The examples given of the first category include animals such as fixed or semi-fixed filter feeders in water based environments and land based plants that attract insects and digest them. The second category includes the microscopic cellular animals that have developed cilia of various forms and levels of oscillation and sophistication to the animals that have the supplementary organs, limbs and muscles to allow them to hunt by agility, sensory awareness and speed.

Despite some partial and singular understandings of life on earth, organic life forms are not entirely determined primarily by their blood or DNA, as is often assumed, but primarily by what they breath, drink and eat. In the dialectics of cellular life the survival of viable multi-cellular DNA strands is as much dependent upon nutrition (N) and reproduction (R) as it is upon the inorganic elements of life on earth. No life form is 'free' from, or independent of, these bio-chemical requirements, nor are they 'free' from maintaining the means to obtain them. The bourgeois concept of 'freedom', as with many other concepts, is frequently misunderstood in everyday common-sense thinking and often this is carried into scientific discourse. The commonplace cliché *'as free as a bird'*, for example, is an anthropocentric nonsense phrase, if this is considered literally. A bird must eat and must move to obtain something to eat by walking, flying or swimming; to exist as a species it was also necessary for each bird that its parents were able to copulate and nurture their young, and likewise the species or the species would cease to exist. Moreover, like most other organic life forms, birds are not free from dependency on oxygen containing air at an adequate level or from the effects of gravity. Sentiments such as 'free as a bird' and the concept of 'freedom' in general belong to the anthropocentric realm of poetry and imagination, not to science or reality.

The whole 'being' of an organic life form, from the simplest to the most sophisticated, including any limited or extended consciousness of each particular entity is dependent upon many interconnected relationships. Each life form depends upon the stability of the planet's orbit, its environmental conditions and by the frequently noted (N-M-G-R + A-D) requirements continuing to function within the relatively stable inorganic conditions of the entire planet. How organisms evolve or fail to evolve in response to any radically changed environment they inhabit is something not yet fully understood. Consequently the anthropocentric abstraction 'freedom' and 'freedom from' in terms of planetary and organic evolution I suggest, is a fairly recent concept. It was developed most emphatically by the bourgeoisie in their struggle to break 'free' from the feudal absolute restrictions of the late middle-ages. The concept of 'freedom' has continued to have a degree of intellectual currency within the thinking classes because due to the extensive division of labour within industrialised capitalist countries the petite bourgeoisie (the small bourgeoisie) have been 'freed' from continuous need to kill, grow or gather nutritional (N) material and thus also 'seem' to have a degree of occupational freedom of choice with regard to the divisions of labour in hierarchical mass societies particularly those based upon the capitalist mode of production. But of course all species – including the human species - have numerous limitations imposed by the bio-chemistry of nature or by the social form they live within. We shall need to bear this in mind when we consider in more detail humans and human societies in the following chapters. How humans think, how humans interact are not just determined by what we eat physically, but how we socially obtain what we eat, this also determines to a greater or lesser extent how we act, the skills we need and therefore also how we think. The socio-economic stratification of modern class-based societies also determines to a greater or lesser degree on how we think about our relative or absolute restrictions within the social systems and the life on earth systems we exist within, as well as how we think about animals as either objects to control and consume or as essential contributors to the biosphere we all inhabit.

Of all the animal forms that have evolved so far, only a relative few species have evolved a highly complex system of sensory and reflective awareness. In some such cases multi-cellular structures in mammals have evolved specialised cells and organic structures and formed a sensory processing organ which is known as a simple brain. By this means, not only are such animals aware of their surroundings and other organisms, but a few are also aware of themselves. Out of these animal forms has evolved a number of species whose systems of sensory awareness have included a central processing organ such as the highly developed human brain and have become consciously aware not only of other organisms, but of themselves as living entities. The human brain has a number of layers of cellular processing material, from the Medulla running upward from the spinal cord; to the Foramen, the Cerebellum and on upward to the large Cerebral hemispheres. Such complexity and size is undoubtedly the evolutionary result of successive stages of development of the animal and primate form of central nervous system. It now provides the human species with an enormous capacity for processing and re-processing external (and internal) impulses from the five sensory systems which we recognise as touch, hearing, sight, smells and taste. Each sensory system also stimulates socially modified emotional states within animals equipped with these systems. As we have read, mammals, in general, show physical and emotional connections to other animals and not only within their own species, but to other species as well. As noted earlier, tactile association of the same and different species is quite extensive and often life-long attachments are often made. In the primate groups of animals such tactile and emotional attachments to others are often exceptionally strong.

However, among the animal species humanity is the only species which has socially developed the potential intellectual capability of understanding the interconnectedness and interdependence of life on earth. However, whether humanity utilises that potential and exercises that capability fully or wisely is another matter. Therefore, humanity is the only species which through reflection and processing relevant information is capable of understanding that the current efforts at saving a single species in the vast web of interconnected dependence, is not the solution to saving life on earth in its past and present form. Humans are the only species capable of understanding what the abbreviation (N-M-G-R + A-D) means and what the full implications of distorting or disrupting its integrated fulfilment will mean to the future of life on earth. However, being capable of understanding and being willing to achieve and act on this level of understanding are two very different processes and levels of commitment. Historically, anthropocentric thinking has always been dominated by its successive modes of production and currently this is the capitalist mode of production. Therefore it is by no means certain that enough people will be willing or able to spend the time to understand the whole situation and be willing and able to respond in the way necessary to stop the continuous drive of essential (N) production of non-essential and superficial additional artifacts, that are currently depleting the species which are necessary to avoid a future catastrophe of even greater proportions than recent ones. Hence, in terms of species depletions, it is the case, even among the successful mammal branch of life on earth, that;

"More than 350 mammals have gone extinct since Homo sapiens came out of the forests and swept across the world, and many species are at high risk of extinction today (think tigers, pandas, black rhinos, blue whales). If things continue at the current pace, half of all mammals might succumb to the same fate as the woolly mammoths and sabre-toothed tigers: dead and gone with only ghostly fossils to remind us of their majesty."
('The Rise and Reign of the Mammals.'. Picador. S. Brusatte. Introduction.)

Species only cease to exist if enough of them can no longer fulfil some or all of the (N-M-G-R) phases of the essential (N-M-G-R + A-D) processes of their species of life on earth. If human production volumes and methods eventually deplete sufficient suitable nutrition (N) for their bodies to metabolise (M) this will affect Growth (G) and the ability to reproduce (R) so that increasingly Ageing (A) and Death (D) will occur before reproduction can take place. Populations will decline, sometimes rapidly as they have done before. Any defect in one or more of the first four of these stages can affect the survival of an organism and its particular reproduction of a further generation. However, for an entire species to die out, it usually requires either a large scale removal of the quantity and quality of the needed source or sources of Nutrition (N), or some general physical or chemical destruction of the external or internal Metabolic processes of most or all of the species. It needs to be remembered that habitat destruction does not simply deprive the most visible species such as plants and animals residing there of their nutrition or shelter, but also all the hidden species underground, in the soil and in the undergrowth. Habitat destruction can affect any of the (N-M-G-R) parts of the life cycle of species, depending on the destructive means wielded against the habitat. Fish in polluted streams and seas may or may not lack suitable food sources, but the attachment of chemical, plastic and metal pollutants to nutrients can affect or alter the M-G-R phases of the reproductive processes they need to survive as a species.

The next chapter on the human species will therefore consider evidence which indicates how similar and how different to other life forms, were the efforts of the various prehistoric and historic hominid and human species in this vitally important necessity of relating directly to the sources needed for metabolic purposes in nature. Given the importance of understanding the negative effects of human production capabilities and methods on the rest of life on earth which in one way or another supports them, the following chapters will of necessity be much longer. It is clear from archaeological and anthropological evidence that despite ancient myths of a superhuman act of creating a single being or single family, that in reality in order to live, pre-humans and later humans actually needed to live in cooperative groups. It was not by magical mystical miracle interventions that they sustained themselves. It was by daily absorbing the essential metabolic organic and inorganic materials supplied by natural species around them and the biosphere they collectively produced which was required in order to sustain their individual and species life cycles of (N-M-G-R + A-D). But considering the (R) phase of life on earth and its links to nutritional (N) needs across life on earth in general reveals an interesting line of inquiry of contemporary relevance to the future survival of all species.

Chapter 6 Summary.

The multifarious animal species, ranging from molluscs to primates, are also multi-cellular organisms sharing the common but varied pattern of (N-M-G-R + A-D) life processes. Animal cells, however, have evolved particularly strong and flexible brick-like cell structures. Some animals have evolved to be warm-blooded and others remain cold-blooded. A consequence of this is that the consumption of nutrition (N) for the former exceeds that of the cold-blooded species. On the basis of the success of animal species in general, some animal species have also been able to evolve as carnivores, predominantly consuming the flesh of other animals. The existence of huge herds of grass and foliage eating species, such as the bovine groups, deer, buffalo, rabbits etc., have allowed some animals to specialise in killing live animals for the nutritional aspects of their existence. However, it is notable that such animal life-terminating activities only extend to the immediate nutritional needs of the predators. Outside of this evolved carnivore nutritional source, even the fiercest animals develop affectionate social bonding among their immediate animal associates and either degrees of empathy or neutral indifference to the other species around them. The need for extra nutrition (N) by mammal species has not by itself led to the extermination of entire prey species by predation. The mammal species by its internal and external reproductive function within and from the female partners body (gestation and lactation) confirms and illustrates the evolutionary pro-female direction multi-cellular life on earth has taken, beyond the cell, the plant or the insect.

Furthermore, there is growing evidence that animals, when not threatened and once nutritionally satisfied, are not aggressive or oppressive with regard to each other or to other animal species. In fact among the billions of species of life on earth, in the research undertaken for this book, only one contrary example has emerged. The existence of a species with random or systematic murderous or genocidal tendencies toward its own species and other species of life on earth is restricted to some members of the human species. Moreover, that 'unnatural' aberration from the evolutionary 'norm' of the rest of life on earth, only applies to a small fraction of the human species. Yet this overwhelming negative evidence drawn from every branch of animal studies has not prevented previous human generations from anthropomorphically presuming that animals replicate all the negative aspects of some of the members of their own hierarchical mass societies. It is becoming evident that once anthropocentric observational bias has been eliminated from serious animal studies, it turns out that male domination of female members of animal species and non-nutritional reasons for killing are so rare as to be negligible. The unnatural conditions created by animal captivity aside, the primate forms of the animal species, in particular, have indeed preserved all the natural social aspects of life on earth in general, with murderous levels of violence either absent, or due to nutritional or other forms of imposed constraint.

CHAPTER 7

The Social Evolution of Hominid Life on Earth.
Introduction
Throughout the previous chapters it has been pointed out that all those forms of life on earth considered so far, have had integrated and inter-dependent relationships with each other, often invisible, but nonetheless maintained in various ways for millions if not billions of years of evolution. From archaeological, biological, genetic and contemporary studies, the evidence suggests the above noted inter-dependent relationships have been the continuously fluctuating patterns within and between all species of life on earth, probably from life's earliest commencement. Therefore, new species and new types have emerged within and merged with some aspects of the (N-M-G-R + A-D) processes of all the other forms of life on earth. Apart from plant life on land and plankton type life in the seas, the former types of inter-dependence species have been the overwhelming nutritional relationship variations for all multi-cellular forms of life on earth. However, as was noted, the contrast between animals and insects and Plants and Plankton has been quantitatively different when it comes to rates of species reproduction (R). The unprecedented reproduction rates of these two particular life forms has been such that it has enabled the embryonic products of such species reproduction to be consumed voraciously as sources of nourishment (N) by many other species from the smallest to the largest; from microscopic single cells to huge animals such as elephants and whales.

The inter-connected and inter-dependent chain of nourishment (N) and thus the chain of metabolised (M) energy for all life on earth is primarily based upon the naturally evolved, unplanned, high reproduction rate of photosynthetic plant life, in one of its numerous forms. It is plant life that has converted solar, gaseous and mineral forms of energy into organic nutritional forms via the amazing photosynthetic and chemosynthetic cells within these organisms. It is plant life and the microorganisms on them and in them that together have supplied the bulk of nutrition as well as base-line nutrition and useful materials to all insects, animals and human food chains. Without sufficient plants, sufficient insects cannot survive, without sufficient insects, enough plants would not be sufficiently pollinated to mature. Without insects, birds and small mammals would no longer find sufficient nutrition (N), etc, etc. Take one species out of the real life chain (or the authors schematic circle) of nutrition - in sufficient numbers - and all those which feed upon them, as well as those who feed on those who feed on them, etc., will decline.

This knock on effect is complex, multifarious and sometimes unpredictable, so it is not always understood at a practical level by human non-specialists and even specialists on just one species, may be unaware of the full extent of the chain. In this regard, I suggest that only understanding partial chains of dependence and interdependence is no longer sufficient to comprehend the interconnectedness of the whole of life on earth. Nevertheless, sooner or later, if or when, the vast chain begins to unravel along the weak and even broken points of its nutritional links, its effects will become apparent. The fact that herd animals vacate a region because of lack of water or because of excessive heat, as currently in regions of Africa and elsewhere, (2024), which in turn means that extensive grasslands ceased to be grazed and as the heat dries out the ungrazed grasslands, wildfires more easily break out. These fires in turn can, and do, spread to trees, which are habitats for animals, insects and micro-organisms. All this ecological disturbance removes nutritional sources (N) from local insects, animals and humans, many of which subsequently die or are displaced locally and cease to pollinate local crops. The loss of pollinators removes the organic nutrition (N) from future plants, insects and animals, the naturally evolved chains of dependence and inter-dependence begin to be severed.

Hopefully, it will have been sufficiently demonstrated in this and previous chapters that the generic abstraction, *'life on earth'*, is no longer sufficient to acknowledge either the bio-chemical complexity of individual organisms or the inter-connected and inter-dependent complexity of the many species – as a whole! The abstractions 'nature' and 'life on earth', as useful as they are as shorthand references, actually blot out more than they reveal. Until humanity begins to consider life on earth as involving complex, detailed and inter-dependent processes of (N-M-G-R +A-D) at both the individual organism level and also at the collective inter-connected species level, far too much of crucial importance has been and will continue to be overlooked or in some cases deliberately ignored. The manifold differences between the many thousands of species of life on earth are only revealed in the particular detailed content, duration and results of the six life-cycle stages (N-M-G-R + A-D) within each species, but not by a different overall bio-chemical life process itself. Life on earth is an inter-connected and inter-dependent whole, not a series of independent species who happen to share a planetary biosphere as most mainstream thinking has been tutored to imagine.

Each species of 'life on earth' may be **N**ourished by some different organic materials; they may **M**etabolise the results in different environmental locations and in different forms or cyclical rhythms; they may **G**row differently according to the evolving bodily parameters for their particular species and nutritional content; they may **R**eproduce in different ways, at different times, with differing frequencies and numerical results. Each species also **A**ge at different rates, and **D**ie after different life spans and in different circumstances. But from the example of the solitary cell to the multi-cellular human, 'life on earth' follows that same recurring (N-M-G-R + A-D) bio-chemical, cyclical process and is dependent on the whole biosphere to complete it. It has also been demonstrated in each chapter that every form of life is utterly dependent for (N) upon the combined collective reproductive (R) contributions of some and in many cases all (plants) the other forms of life on earth. It has been established by ample evidence, that not one species or one individual organism within a species can exist by itself alone. It should be a sobering fact to realise that the cycle of life or death of each individual of each species depends to some extent upon the sequence and timing of life and death of every other species and that the premature or natural life cycle deaths of one or more organisms are essential nutritional sources for the life cycle of many other organisms.

As noted in a previous chapter, it has also been established that within the millions of sexually reproducing species of life on earth, there has been a continuous biological bifurcation of the reproductive role between what are classed as male and female of each of the species. Consequently, throughout the whole extent of this evolutionary period, with a few exceptions, the main bearer of the reproductive development and initial support for animal offspring is shown to have been provided by the species partner that has evolved biologically to be equipped to do so and is designated as the female, within each species. The accumulation of evidence so far considered, has sufficiently established the existence of two important and epoch-spanning characteristics of the evolution of life on earth. First; as already noted, prior to human hierarchical mass societies, there have been no persistently high levels of continuous aggression within species and between different species. Second; the pre-eminent role of the female in reproduction and in nurturing have been both the 'natural' and hence the 'normal' outcomes of the evolution of plant, insect and animal life on earth. Therefore, where the importance of either of these natural evolutionary outcomes has been altered or abandoned by the human species, then any rational curiosity suggests that a sufficiently powerful reason must have been involved and that this reason needs to be identified and the processes which brought this about needs to be understood and altered.

Mammal and human Reproduction. (R)

However, before sufficiently persuasive 'evidence' is explored further, I suggest another distinction needs to be considered with regard to the general and specific reproductive activities of most species. It is common knowledge that most reproductive activity, including sexually determined reproduction, has evolved to coincide with abundant supplies of nutrition (N) both for the female producer of eggs or embryos and therefore for the newly produced offspring. In general seeds are only dispersed from the mature organism when the planet's orbit around the sun has modified the soil temperature and moisture to be capable of nurturing them. Eggs only hatch from animals, grubs from insects, spawn from fish and amphibians when nutritional resources are generally sufficiently available to sustain them. Live births among larger animals and mammals, (including primates) are also frequently timed to occur when other forms of life providing climatic conditions and nutrient sources are producing abundant supplies of organic material. In other words, reproductive activity for most species of life on earth is not independent of the pattern of other forms of life on earth, or independent of environmental and climate patterns. Most forms of life on earth, from plants, insects and animals, are strongly motivated by some internal form of material, tactile and sensual need to reproduce or copulate, but this only successfully occurs at some particular environmentally triggered stage,. The trigger in most reproductive activity seems to be initiated by a seasonally linked pattern of temperature and hormonal changes.

The concept of a 'season' or 'mating season' or in agricultural terms 'flowering' season, derives from this almost universally observed pattern of plant, insect and animal reproduction. Outside of this restricted period most species of life on earth, whether of male or female genders, seem not to be interested or motivated to engage in sexual activity. This is a prime reason why assertive sexual activity by males or females of sexually reproducing species, do not routinely take place outside of such 'seasons' either on land or within the sea. The difficulties universally experienced by captive breeding programmes, in attempting to get species to mate, also indicates that male or female eagerness to copulate - at every opportunity - is not evident in the vast majority of species. Furthermore, even during the mating season a healthy female animal that can – of necessity – outrun or beat back all but a determined specialised predator, and can also easily avoid any unwanted attention from a male of their own species. The only exceptions to such seasonal characteristics of reproductive activity (R) that I can currently identify are two species out of the millions or billions of species of life on earth. One is a species of apes (the Bonobo's) and the other is the human species. In the case of the human species, the ovulation pattern of females is also dependent upon nutritional levels, but in modern agriculturally based human communities this pattern is modified by the high nutritional energy levels that can be obtained within them. However, in the cases of deliberate malnutrition during female slimming activities during the mid 20th century in some advanced countries of Europe and North

America etc., the phenomena of ovulation (period) suspension or delay occurred in considerable numbers of females.

Nevertheless, in the case of the latter two species they engaged naturally in consenting sexual activity not, because they understand its original bio-chemical function as a means of species reproduction (R), but primarily because such intimacy can be socially and mutually pleasurable. The human species only became clearly (or rather accurately) aware of the biological connection between copulation and childbirth relatively recently in its social evolutionary history. Interestingly, the Bonobo social groups, whose communities are not so aware, are all led by female chimps and consequently these primate groups are also matrifocal as well as matrilineal. The females are thus the ones initiating and sustaining tenderness and sexual intimacy on the basis of mutual enjoyment or alternatively as compensation-tenderness for unpleasant things that have happened. On the basis of current evidence from life on earth in general, the continuing aggression, rape and sexual harassment of females by some (but not all) ancient and modern human males is a phenomenon restricted to certain forms of human societies. A consideration of how such an 'unnatural' characteristic of forced sexual and reproductive activity came about within the evolution of humanity will be considered in more detail in one or more later chapters.

From Mammals to Hominids.
So to recap: After the first stages of reproductive activity, animals, mammals, including primates and humans, incubate the fertilised ovum (as a neonate) within the biologically evolved female womb and nourish the unborn with energy and nutrient rich blood through the female-specific placenta. Nevertheless, all life on earth, as impressive and complex as it mostly is, starts off as nothing more superficially impressive than a single undifferentiated and unfertilised cell, released from within the body of an adult female at certain times. As noted in the chapter on cells, the male role in bio-chemical reproduction (R) is merely to provide the fertilising sperm cell containing one form of DNA. Then after leaving the female womb, the newborn is historically further nourished by female modified blood in the form of milk,

until more solid nutritional (N) sources can be processed. With this distinction duly noted, we can say without too much need for further qualification that considered biologically, human beings, like all other sexually reproducing life forms, are not reproduced entirely by the efforts of an individual (or two) and in no way do they exist throughout life as sole individuals. Although ideologically and culturally modern human beings have inherited from past generations the inaccurate notion that humanity exists as a species of independent individuals, who sometimes cooperate together on common projects, this ideologically driven myth is not in fact biologically true. Shocking as it may seem to some people, individual human beings are always social and biological entities entirely made up of and entirely dependent upon, many inputs from many visible and invisible forms of cellular life on earth.

In fact this practical and ideological cultural assertion of the primary existence of human individuality appears to be just a product of the mass society systems of living - imposed by some of our historical ancestors. In reality it is not hard to blow this anciently developed ideology away with a few fresh gusts of observed reality. Every one of us are totally dependent 24/7 upon others of our own species and also on millions of other life forms (large and small) for our initial existence and for our air, food, water, clothes, heating, housing, transport and thousands of other things. Even when we are at our most alone reading and thinking and writing (as I am at this particular moment); we are thinking, reading and writing within a social context and for an anticipated audience, within a socially constructed environment and using a socially learned language and text, devised by previous social generations, taught to us by contemporary social individuals and distributed to us in books or electronic means by other previous social individuals. Therefore, even in our most private and isolated moments of thought and contemplation we may happen to feel emotionally neglected, (or even desperately lonely) but in reality we humans living in communities are never really or entirely alone as individuals. The widespread, and alienating contradiction, of living in mass interconnected and interdependent societies comprising of millions and yet large numbers of us are feeling emotionally neglected is clearly not 'natural' form of evolution, but is a result of the content and form of the current hierarchical, divided and competitive mass societies. This is a contradictory phenomenon which is a result of hierarchical mass society form, a form which will also be considered further in the following chapters.

Bio-social changes.

When we turn to the species of life on earth known as hominids and their evolution into modern humans we are still biologically and conceptually in the realm of the animal species in general and the mammalian species in particular. That is to say humanity is a species of life which like every other species of life on earth still cycles through the earlier described process of Nourishment, Metabolism, Growth, Reproduction, Ageing and Death, abbreviated as (N-M-G-R + A-D). As with other animals, the evolutionary modifications from warm blooded, egg laying species to placental incubation and live-birth hominid species did not radically alter either the skeletal structure, the binary reproductive essence of the male and female sexual dimorphism or the general process of animal life on earth. The exact evolutionary path from the earliest known hominid to the earliest example of *Homo sapiens* is something else that is subject to speculation, is also contested and in its detailed sequence - the 'missing links' are still missing and are uncertain. However, again that uncertainty does not affect the validity of this current study into the relationship between humanity and the rest of life on earth. That there have also been naturally based alterations in form and even function within the arms, legs, head and body posture within the human species is only seriously contested from within a religious fundamentalist and dogmatic perspective. I think from an evolutionary perspective of life on earth, the fact that hominids and humans needed to traverse the stages of (N-M-G-R + A-D) throughout these long stages of existence will also not be seriously contested. Outside of religious fundamentalist dogmatism, there is initial agreement that of all the different hominid and post-early hominid species, that 'modern' humans, probably descended from the pre and post hominid branch of Australopithecines. Furthermore, the teeth found among the fossilised remains of these particular early hominids gave a clue concerning the source of their basic forms of nourishment (N). For example;

> *"The australopithecines' small to moderate-sized incisors and large thick-enamelled, flat molars were adapted for crushing and chewing nuts and other hard, brittle food items, as well as soft, sugary fruits when these were available. This dentition suited the australopithecines to habitats ranging from open savannah to the 'gallery' forests that form as corridors along rivers and wetlands, but it lacked the shearing action required for chewing meat. Without the tools for processing meat, it was assumed that the australopithecines must have been vegetarian."*
> ('Prehistorical Investigations; (Christopher Seddon. Chapter 7)

From this, and many other logical deductions based upon morphological evidence uncovered by archaeology, pre-humans were either fully vegetarian gatherers or mainly gatherers of vegetable sources. Grasping hands that can also be gentle in handling babies are necessary for handling soft fruit and leaf eating and could be used for other purposes such as scavenging from already dead animal bodies. However, in ancient as well as modern times, dead body scavenging is clearly not a reliable source of everyday safe nutrition. Observations of the life processes of some apes, gorillas and monkey primates demonstrate that hunting animals and eating dead animals is not as sufficiently reliable for regular nutrition (N) as roots, fruits, nuts and leaves and therefore probably did not become a general part of securing nourishment until a much later period in hominid evolutionary terms. Indeed, evidence will be presented in the following chapter that even among the later evolutionary developments well beyond *Homo habilis* and Homo erectus there were pockets of Homo sapiens in isolated regions of Africa and South America who retained this basic hunter (20% animal nutrition) gatherer (80% vegetable nutrition) mode of production until the 20th and 21st centuries. Even among most skilled hunters, meat eating was rarely a staple food source. Studies have indicated that even among the most skilled hunter-gatherer communities not every hunt produces sufficient (N) for the hunter-gatherer community, so reliance on non-meat (N) gathered sources, they settle near where these are available, was (and is) the default survival strategy.

It is perhaps here that the term 'mode of production', which will now be used more frequently than the earlier chapters, and therefore should be made a little more explicit for this and the following chapters. In this context my use of 'a mode of production' will be to refer to a way of communal *acting, doing* or *existing* with regard to the whole socio-economic stages of obtaining the organic and inorganic materials necessary for the essential (N-M-G-R + A-D) process of living. It is important from this chapter onward, that the *'mode'* of production should not be confused with *'means'* of production, as it often is. Gathering and hunting techniques, using sticks and containers such tools are *means* of production of (N) as when 'digging' for roots and carrying them in baskets, or preparing them. Therefore, social gathering and hunting contains both a *means* and a *mode* of social living and producing (N). The *means*, therefore, help secure and transport the nutrition (N) but how the community is collectively structured beyond devising *means* to ensure the (N-M-G-R + A-D) processes, as a whole, represent the mode of production. Modes of living among most species along with the means are generationally passed on by example and copying. Pastoralism (or animal herding) is also a 'mode' of social living and production, whilst milking and slaughtering are the *means* of procuring the nutrition from that source in nature. Farming is also a *mode* of social living and producing (N), with its own agricultural *means* of digging, planting, reaping etc. Industrial levels of manufacturing is an industrial *mode* of social production, with its own industrial *means of production,* such as factories, machines, tools etc.

These modes of production terms are also used to refer to the 'dominant' mode of production within a particular period and are not necessarily the only mode and means of production. For example, pastoral herders may also 'gather' and farming communities may also 'hunt' as do some groups and individuals among the modern industrial communities. Modes of production that are dominant are usually the preferred modes of production used by the majority of their communities, but not necessary by all members. Indeed, in relatively recent colonial history, reliable anthropological and ethnological evidence indicates that many non-European historical human communities, in North America and Africa, even shunned bribery and physical force by European colonial forces to persuade them to change from hunting and gathering to pastoral or agricultural modes of production and living. Nevertheless, to sustain any mode, as with many other early hominid developed activities, the mode requires basic 'means' such as tools and the widespread use of these means in turn both require and produce a progressive modification of the upper and lower limbs, hands and even brains of the individuals engaged in it.

Therefore, like other animal species, among early proto-human species, a series of crucial anatomical developments took place in conjunction with human production and the preferred hunter-gatherer (N) source. Clearly bipedalism became routine (as the 3 million year old hominid skeleton known as Lucy indicates); brain development in the neo-cortical (grey matter) and other inner brain areas also accompanied an increased physical and social sophistication and brain size (volume and surface area) along with linguistic communication (languages) increased. (However, size is not everything, even in information processing as my children when young and small could often outsmart me to get what they wanted or avoid what they didn't want.) Manual and facial dexterity improved via the development of an opposable thumb and intricate facial muscle developments. The former, needed for the accurate manipulation of gathering and in the production of tools, containers etc., the latter for non-verbal forms of communication, useful in activities requiring silence or stealth. For over three million years pre-hominid and hominid communities had lived socially together to navigate through the biological process of (N-M-G-R +A-D) as they continued to evolve. The tool making skills needed to secure sources of nourishment (N), therefore, gradually went beyond modifying available rocks, animal horn and repurposing sticks to chipping and shaping rocks and other materials such as bone, hides and logs.

Morphological changes.

A hand and arm that carries delicate things whilst walking and/or accurately delivers spears and throwing sticks at a stationary or moving target requires much more arm and hand dexterity and forethought than simply hurling a stone or piece of wood in a general direction, as many socially frustrated chimpanzees still do. I suggest it is also important to note that modifications to human bones, limbs, hands, facial muscles and brains, was not specific to males of the pre-hominid, hominid and post-hominid species of primates. These significant morphological changes or physical adaptations occurred within the female gender as well as the male. This suggests that with the exception of pregnancy and lactating periods of nurture, the day to day activities of both hominid genders in obtaining nutrition (N) and social interaction did not substantially differ throughout that whole extensive hominid and pre-hominid period. Male and female activities were sufficiently similar not to create huge morphological differences. Indeed, sufficient anthropological evidence exists to suggest that strict male and female hunter-gatherer stereotypes, where men are assumed to be the hunters and women assumed to be the gatherers are frequently inaccurate, speculative or presumptuous assumptions. Pre-hierarchical mass societies, men also frequently gathered and despite any periodic impediments of birthing or breast feeding, women also fished, trapped and even hunted.

Therefore, when we consider our hominid ancestors, before the pre-Homo sapien stage of development, we can reasonably assume (but not know exactly how) that in terms of group behaviour, in all probability for most of their ancient life cycle, they (in a more developed sense) mirrored one or other of the ape-like animal species at the time and subsequently. Where it remains the case that female animals hunt or gather their own materials for nutrition and general use. Just as female chimps and gorillas for example gather their own food and make their own sleeping platforms we can assume by anatomical evidence that so too did the hominid and later humanoid species did. Moreover, wherever they existed, humans had to collectively fulfil the (N-M-G-R) phases of the full process of any living cycle in support of the young, the old and the ill. In short early humans of both genders were moving around, eating, resting/sleeping, procreating and defecating, like all animals do. We can reasonably assume that extremely long periods of time and various physical and social modifications were necessary to eventually produce a fully bipedal, large brained, opposable thumb species of male and female hominid, which then over many further cycles evolved into the species now designated as *Homo-sapien*. From DNA comparisons, if and when those are considered sufficiently accurate, it appears Homo sapiens may have also interbred with other hominid variants such as the one designated as Neanderthal. If this is true then it begins to erode the frequent assumption that early humans have always reproduced on the basis of a rigidly established pattern of inter-group or extended family life, either as family based sub-groups within a larger group (tribe) or in the form of a loosely paired up inter-group family.

The idea that the modern family was the template or basis of everything which followed in human social evolution (such as societies, property, oppressive relationships) was clearly an assumption produced from within much later societies with an existing material or 'sacred' agenda to conserve. That form of retrospective opinion that the nuclear family was the basic social unit is a form of inherited logic that is proving difficult to maintain if humanity did in fact evolve from animal forms of life. No animal species form distinct non-biological grouped families, even when some animals sexually pair for life. Most animals temporarily sexually pair or bond with a member of the same species who happens to be close at hand and available at the time and who are receptive when the urge is strongest. Furthermore, within most, if not all, animal species the female in general is the only consistent and continuity determining social basis of the young individual and their initial social phases of life. The female, her sisters and her male and female children are a natural basic sub-unit of any animal social species aggregation, including the pre-modern human species. To such female-led sub-units the rest of the more extensive hominid gatherer (or hunter-gatherer) band would socialise with and relate too in any number of ways. However, although we know very little of such early probabilities, we can be completely sure they all consistently foraged and gathered as a social unit to secure their metabolic needs from the natural world, even if anatomically and intellectually they had not at that stage evolved to hunt or to hunt effectively or consistently and be sufficiently successful at it.

Furthermore, we can also be reasonably sure that apart from geological and climate based natural disasters, nothing organic (i.e. no other living plant or animal species) prevented them - as a hominid or human species - from completing their natural life cycles (N-M-G-R.), before ageing and death (A-D) which then returned their bodies protected or not, to the soil and a potential status of becoming recyclable organic material. Archaeological evidence has revealed that at some stage the human species (Homo sapien, Neanderthal and Forensis, etc.) became technically competent to ignite fires, make clothing, create shelters, to shape sophisticated flint and bone tools and increasingly to bury their dead, with formerly used artifacts of living. And during this extensive stage they frequently moved to other locations, until the human species - over immensely long periods of time - eventually inhabited most habitable places on earth. These eventually ranged from the hottest desert climates to the coldest artic ones.

The cave drawings discovered on many continents also indicate that their thinking and daytime-determined activities had gone well beyond a focus on their immediate biological, metabolic, nutritional and security needs. Their mode of production (obtaining nutrition and shelter) had become sufficiently productive and nutritionally certain to allow periods for doing other things in between the basic survival necessities of ensuring (N-M-G-R.) + (A-D). Archeological evidence suggests that during those long periods, early humans were evolving into a thinking, communicating, externalising, reflecting and continually inquisitive species, par excellence. Biologically, they still remained a social animal species - and humans always will be - but one which eventually developed sophisticated verbal and visually depicted communications, oral languages and high level dexterous skills among both genders. In the form of humans, the evolution of natural bio-chemical multicellular *'organisms'* had become not only conscious of their selves and surroundings, as with most other life forms, but increasingly self-conscious of their existence as a species and self-consciously aware of themselves as individuals and collectives. Through the development of these attributes, it is not surprising that in comparison with other species, early humanity sooner or later considered themselves as an *'exceptional'* and superior type of *'life on earth'*.

The more socially aware and conscious that humans became, particularly as vocalization evolved into articulate language, the more it became obvious that humans were in a number of ways radically different to other life forms. The difference was not just in physical appearance but in an intellectual and species-aware sense. It must have become obvious to early humans that they were the only living things that could systematically talk and converse with each other on an extended and sophisticated basis. It would have been difficult for them not to conclude from such observations that humans were not just different to other living things but in one or more particular ways - uniquely different. Lacking an understanding of biological evolution but having the ability to make things out of raw materials it would also be hard for them not to conclude (at some later stage), that this uniqueness of humans to think and imagine, had been made possible by some mystical process or entity with such super powers. Imaginative logic would suggest that since humans, in this sense, were unique, perhaps the mystical entities they imagined (i.e. gods or spirits) were also unique and also uniquely similar to themselves' morphologically and intellectually.

If the sophisticated articulation of words was in pre-history (as it is now) a defining characteristic of the uniqueness of humanity then the idea that *'in the beginning was the word'* could during those periods eventually also be considered a logical assumption. Closely following this logic, within later hierarchical large-scale societies, the further assumption by elites with both the time and incentive to imagine that *'and the word was God'*, became an additional logical imaginative assumption. In this primitive framework of thinking - unaware of the biology of cells and the multi-cellular evolution of all life forms - then the pre-scientific logic of humanity might conclude that everything alive and not alive must have been 'created', and that the rest of life on earth had a pattern that this imaginary God had intended. This is a relatively unsophisticated trend of ancient thinking that still survives in all forms of modern religious dogma. It has taken the eventual manufacturing of electron-scanning microscopes and much else to be able to begin to contradict such limited 'inherited' thinking and to now assert that actually; 'life in the beginning - was not created by a god, but evolved from the chemical molecule, the biological organelle and the cell"'s ability to link together with other cells, was the step leading eventually to all animal and mammal species and ones that could read and write these words'.

Nevertheless, by modern 21st century reflection and considering life on earth as an inter-dependent whole, the exceptional uniqueness of humanity (language and writing) is in actual fact a rather marginal asset to life on earth. Indeed, life on earth – as a whole - including human life managed pretty well without languages and writing for billions of years. Indeed, outside of human communities, millions of plant, insect and animal communities have managed perfectly well to exist and evolve without these attributes of advanced consciousness. In fact, these additional human skills contribute hardly anything to the actual and essential bio-chemical (N-M-G-R + A-D) processes of life on the planet earth generally. As noted in previous chapters, compared with plants and algae, which by their bio-chemical functions provide the oxygen and food that all life on earth needs, the ability to gossip, misrepresent, lie and make wild assertions, write books and sing songs, etc., shrinks to miniscule importance. Under the influence of our intellectual abilities, we tend to forget that we cannot write, paint, manufacture or sing ourselves some breathable air, some edible food. We cannot bring some clothes into existence by writing or un-pollute our water. The reality of life on earth once understood beyond the abstractions 'nature' and biosphere, and beyond our anthropocentric fixations, is that on the spectrum of essential pre-requisites for life on earth as a whole, our human abilities lie along a very modest and problematic part of the scale of evolutionary development.

Yet the wilful and egotistical anthropocentric exaggeration of this one ability to speak, write and read words has such a strong hold on human thinking that even scientists familiar with biology, astrophysics and evolution can still anthropocentrically 'believe' in the absolute superiority of humanity over nature in general and constantly act accordingly. Yet not one human being can do what a plant can do, when it photosynthesises gasses using solar energy. In many exaggerated cases a narcissistic self-regard develops in some individuals and collectives that they begin to imagine they are 'exceptionally superior' over all other such similar human individuals or groups'. Yet even individual narcissists (and Olympic medal winners) cannot reproduce themselves, which is what the most basic bacterial cells have been able to do for billions of years without the means to think, run fast, or play chess. I find it hard to imagine that our hominid ancestors would have at any time in their evolution begun to exhibit such colossal human arrogance alongside such wilful ignorance that is currently being witnessed in the 21st century. Believing in the imaginary existence of an invisible, superman creator and controller of the universe, who has 'chosen' a certain community of people over others is only a step once removed from such self-opinionated human arrogance developing into the genocidal tendency of a mass elimination of their own species to increase their possessions.

I also find it astonishing that the complete lack of independently verifiable evidence for the existence of gods or a god seems not to bother people who, in their everyday lives, would require extensive and certifiable proof and guarantees of something's actual existence and utility before actually purchasing it. No well-balanced intellect could be persuaded to believe in an imaginary father, an imaginary house, an imaginary car, and act upon that delusion. No rational individual would rely upon an imaginary fortune or an imaginary cat in a box somewhere in the universe. Yet millions of humans can be convinced of an imaginary heaven. Evidence (and also the lack of it) suggests that monotheistic belief systems, current and past, are based upon and are entirely dependent upon some partially preserved ancient camp fire mythical type narratives and ancient intentionally cobbled together papyrus fragments. Moreover, historical evidence suggests that these ancient mystical musings are the products of certain ancient elite men who had a vested interest in becoming crowd-funded influencers to the ancient gullible. They certainly succeeded in that project. Yet, to my reasoning, the underlying mistake, apart from gullibility then and now, stems from a short-sighted narcissistic exaggeration of the limited intellectual abilities exercised by humans. This ability has at the same time created machinery and power sources which are used to perpetuate myth and magic and are at the same time also degrading and destroying the essential life support materials provided by nature. By consciously trivialising and downgrading the amazing bio-chemical abilities and contributions of all other forms of life on earth, most elites (religious, scientific and political) are undermining the future of their own species.

We shall encounter the eventual results of this narcissistic uniqueness obsession in later chapters and also consider evidence that humanity has become in theory and practice, overly self-indulgent and overly self-obsessed. However, it is clear that humanity, by means of this growing anthropocentrically focussed tendency, has become the means by which our one particular species of life on earth has persistently dominated and interfered with all other species to the increasing detriment of everything else - including their own future existence. To my mind, monotheistic thinking within the human species in many ways parallels the infant stage of individual human beings. Most young children go through a protracted "me, me, me" stage (roughly known in the west as the 'terrible two's') where, because of their actual age-related social circumstances, they can only view themselves as the most important (and needy) centre of all the living entities around them. This, in a metaphorical sense, led by its elites, represents to my mind the modern human species as a whole. At the individual human level that childlike developmental phase lasts until the child matures sufficiently to recognise the actual extent of its dependence upon others within a larger interdependent human social community and begins to socially act and think accordingly.

To continue the analogy, the elites within hierarchical mass societies are still emotionally going through an extensively protracted stage of child-like me, me, me, existence (I want more and more toys) infancy and dragging many others along with them. Indeed, the 'me, me, me demands of elites in the 20th and 21st centuries extend to exorbitant levels of wealth and to the ability to decide that; "If I want to own and control an island" or "If I want to purchase or have manufactured a vehicle to enjoy a trip into space, or go look at the Titanic, and I have the means to do so – I will! Moreover they then go ahead and commandeer the resources necessary, for such self-indulgent follies irrespective of the effects on the human and non-human communities within their societies or outside them. However, unlike a normal spoiled child who will only eat most of the chocolate once after it has made them sick, or only occasionally trash their bedroom, the global elites continually take more wealth than they need, lock the rest away in banks and portfolios. Trashing the environment with their multiple use cars, aircraft, ships and mansions becomes an essential means of ensuring their 'own' retarded infantile individual self-fulfilment. It should be obvious by now that globally there are so many greedy childlike elite adults that their self-indulgent obsessive needs currently geared to capitalist based production, consumption and wealth accumulation, are now seriously endangering life on the entire planet at an accelerating scale.

The social form of hominid life on earth.
Another interesting confusion concerning early humans that many modern commentators have made is that they are often imagined as being 'free' compared to modern mass society populations. A false dualism of 'freedom versus necessity' has long entertained and impeded many a philosophical discourse. Yet if the concept is looked at seriously, life, including pre-historical human life, before the onset of ancient slavery and modern wage slavery, was never 'free' of natural constraints and never can be. Nor are social species ever 'free' from social constraints either negotiated or compulsory, which are dependent upon the form of social organization they are within. As we have witnessed all life on earth was (and is) supported (and therefore constrained) by the imperatives of the already noted bio-chemical processes of Nourishment - Metabolism - Growth - Reproduction plus Ageing and Death (N-M-G-R + A.D). No species of life on earth is free from having to; obtain nourishment, shelter, experience growth, engage in reproductive activity, ageing or death for an individual organism and their species to survive. It is ignorance and nonsense to think otherwise. It just so happens that these original and universal naturally evolved phases and their particular energy requirements are met from within the

existing inorganic material of the planet, the nearest star (the sun) and the rest of organic life on earth.

As already noted and clearly needs repeating that the energy containing nutritional material (N) is consumed by individual organisms (from within social forms of species grouping), but this material is produced directly or indirectly by contributions from the whole, integrated and inter-dependent material/nutrient cycle of life on earth. The relatively individuated forms of organic life on earth are continuously involved in a metabolic interaction with the rest of organic and inorganic nature. Viewing any or all of the 'natural' phases of existence pessimistically as constraints or difficulties, and wanting to be 'free' of them I suggest, is to fail to understand the essential means and evolutionary produced ability to live. Considering any of the natural phases (N-M-G-R + A-D) as inconveniences or impediments to existence, I suggest, is a form of anthropocentric subjectivism arising from the hierarchical mass society form of class and gender based exploitation. I further suggest that such philosophically produced ideas which lack a critical appraisal of the socio-economic system, in essence are oxymoronic deductions. These could only arise among those human individuals and communities that have failed to understand the bio-chemistry of 'life on earth' and the overwhelmingly contradictory role played by human hierarchies and their unnatural enforcements of class inequalities and have merely been intellectually justified by their intellectual producers ever since the emergence of hierarchical mass societies.

Leaving aside the physics of inorganic material entering the biosphere, just as an individual social insect cannot survive without the insect colony, or an individual social species of bee cannot survive without the bee hive colony, any individual member of a fully social species cannot survive long without the holistic support of the society within which it has physically and socially evolved. This applies to the human species also. This fact of existential interdependence of social species introduces the additional natural phenomenon that for the (N-D-G-R + A-D) metabolic requirements of 'life on earth'; in general, the wellbeing of the whole or most of the species community is actually just as important as the wellbeing of any particular individual. This phenomenon also extends to a certain degree among those species which have adapted to a solitary existence for large parts of their life cycle. As isolated individual organisms, members of most species can only find organic Nourishment (N) if it has been already reproduced by another life form. Even then the ability to metabolise and grow from this nourishment has been dependent upon many prior life forms and individuals of sexually reproducing species. Furthermore, no individual organism within a sexually reproducing species can engage in species Reproduction (R), without the cooperation of another compatible organism of the same species.

Moreover, as embryos and new born species members, without prior post birth adult support the next generation of any partially solitary species are unlikely to survive. Returning to the existence of the species of pre-sapien hominid during its 400,000 year hunter-gather mode of existence, I maintain that all the points contained in the last four paragraphs above apply. In particular; 1; the absolute dependence of humanity upon a planet containing millions of contributory life forms ('organic nature') and their products; 2; the absolute human dependence upon inorganic energy, water and gaseous material. 3; a practical understanding that to be successful social organisation needs to ensure the well-being of every social individual within the whole human community is actually integral to the whole. These are the three most important species-based factors in the survival of life on earth. In mass societies the activity of the nutritional suppliers (and other essential workers) are absolutely necessary for the survival of the whole community, whilst the activity of the elite hierarchies are not.

In any social species the colony or community could (and almost exclusively does) exist without a privileged leadership or exploiting elite, but not without a communal workforce. If nutrition (N) is an essential intake for all life on earth, and clearly it is, then those who collect or produce it inside or outside of each species are also essential and more valuable to survival than those who do not. However, in the case of hierarchical mass societies of humans, as we shall see, this importance of (N) work based producers is practically and ideologically reversed and takes on an altogether sinister aspect. In elite controlled manufacturing practices and ideology, the elites are considered far more important than the essential workers and the latter can be deliberately sacrificed in hierarchical mass societies by elite decisions. This occurs even to the detriment of the survival of almost the entire community or nation in some cases. Hence there appears the historical and modern phenomenon of hierarchical warring elites - on all sides - being prepared to sacrifice large numbers of their armies and civilian populations in order to continue to dominate what is left of the hierarchical mass societies after the hostilities have ended.

Therefore in maintaining a 'life on earth' or Gaia focussed perspective, the problem for the ecological future of life on earth is much larger than that of organising the piecemeal protection of a few favoured endangered animal, insect and plant species as they currently edge toward extinction. That form of 'saving the planet' is a partial and superficial knee-jerk reaction by many organisers of campaigns such as 'Save the Whale', 'Save the Tiger' or the 'Snow Leopard', etc. I suggest they are the biological equivalent of what a local history campaign would be to protect an excellent window, a smoothly functioning sink tap or a perfectly hinged oak door in a listed building in which the masonry and timbers are already crumbling from the foundations all the way up to the roof. Such specific species campaigns give an impression of being sensitively concerned with 'something' wonderful but at the same time they are ignoring all the other problems which are causing the whole society and its 'wonderful' ecological support structures to disintegrate and collapse.

For example, in the above highlighted case, in order for Whales and humans etc., something should by now be crystal clear: That to survive, thousands of other essential life forms, such as insects, copepods, dinoflagellates, forests, etc., need to be preserved in sufficient quantities and qualities that they will be able to continue to replenish the air, absorb the carbon and be the foundational organic and inorganic elements in a complex inter-dependent chain of nutrition and other essential materials. It is only these often invisible essential key-stone species and their inter-connections with other species which in turn enable such emotionally 'favoured' species as Panda's, Penguins and

Porcupines to survive. Saving a species, even one key species, is not enough to actually save it - all nature needs saving, from what the current mode of elite led human production is doing to all of it! Even the future of as yet unborn humanity needs saving from the way current elite-led humanity now organises the mass production of (N-M-G-R + A-D.) and in doing so currently undermines the vast interconnected web of the biosphere, which is the foundation of all life on earth and ultimately threatens entire human communities.

But to return to the probable hominid beginnings, rather than the possible end of future humanity we should consider the traces our species ancestors have left as their evolutionary existence. It is estimated that of the four classifications of our early ancestors, Homo *habilis*, were gathering and scavenging or hunting over 2 million years ago. Later still, Homo *erectus* families were lighting fires over 1 million years ago. We can reliably assume that for these millions of years these pre-human hominids and later human beings successfully completed the Nourishment - Metabolism - Growth - Reproduction – Ageing – Death cycle, not as individual mythical Adams or Noah's, but as groups of social individuals who lived through these (N-M-G-R + A-D) sequences in collective female-focussed groups of various and fluctuating sizes. Archaeological evidence, although often sparse, nevertheless establishes the fact that humans, wherever they lived, with the occasional later exception of a hermit or recluse, always did so in groups and never as isolated individuals. Indeed, even to eventually exist as occasional hermits and recluses they had first to be born into communities and learned to grow and survive in communities before being motivated to relocate to a nearby cave, hut, pole or tree house.

Only in fantasy fiction or in religious type myths do we find assertions of individual or two parent families existing entirely on their own. Instances of castaways and marooned sailors do not count as these already originate from communities. We shall note later and comment further, on the fact that these myths of individual 'origin' and 'creation', only fully mature within large, anciently established, hierarchical mass society conurbations. But before considering mass societies, in more detail, we need first to trace the few things we can reliably know from the study of pre-history and the biological principles we have considered. This knowledge includes the fact that wherever a branch of the human species now lives, that branch would not be there if these ancestors had not been sufficiently successful at locating nutrition (N), water, shelter whilst travelling, communicating, reproducing and exploring beyond their original locations. The global existence of our own and other species demonstrates how natural and successful over multiple millions of years the previous generations of plants, insects, animals and humans were at securing and ensuring their own (N-M-G-R + A) processes before becoming nutritional resources before or after dying (D).

Hominids and tool making.

Many early anthropocentric biased commentators on the characteristics of the various species of life also mistakenly classified early humans as being completely distinguished from other animals by the fact that they were 'tool makers' and innovators. Some still cling onto that inherited misconception. To my mind this simplistic assertion was perhaps prompted by a too urgent concern to make a radical, but one-sided distinction between life in the human form and life in any other evolutionary form. Plus this assertion, once made, could only survive on the basis of an almost complete lack of information and knowledge concerning tool use and innovation by birds, apes, monkeys, fish, otters, dolphins and others. Ignorance of reality seems never to have hindered the urge of vested anthropocentric interests to promote fallacies in science as well as politics and religion. In this case, doubtless other species will eventually be 'noticed' using some inanimate extensions of their bodies (extensions such as sticks, stones, shells, water, fire etc.) as 'tools' to break, dig, lever, pull, wash or heat some organic source of nutrition before using it for essential nourishment.

Although the use of tools and innovation, have been taken to the most sophisticated lengths by humanity, it is the sophistication that is the really distinguishing feature between species in their (N-M-G-R) processes of maintaining (and in the case of humans) this sophisticated tool making is now being used by humanity to directly or indirectly exterminate life on earth. Moreover, the use of inanimate tools is only a distinction between the 'means' of obtaining ('N') which each species utilises. Nor are tools the cause of humanity becoming separated from each other and from nature as some so-called 'experts' (recent and old) have claimed. Tools and organisation are a 'means' for social species, which are used to secure the (N) and other phases of life for the species and this includes humanity. Where tool use is shared socially and innovation shared socially by human communities it can bring the users closer to nature and even uncover previously hidden or formerly considered inedible forms of nutrition. However, when serious social and biological contradictions become introduced within human societies, as we shall indicate in the following chapters, tools can also just as easily become weapons and the prototypes for more deadly weapons. Indeed, the earliest human made weapons were in fact modified or unmodified agricultural tools and the later specialised weapons were invariably informed by the kind of tools which could effectively destroy and dismember plants, fruits, animals and of course humans.

It is important to grasp the fact that we cannot actually know in full detail how our ancient ancestors conducted themselves on a daily basis, what they thought and how they made decisions, but we can, with appropriate care, infer quite a lot from various materials and tangible sources. Observations from mammalian studies, from surviving hunter-gatherer artefacts such as stone tools, bones, cave-art and, of course, studies of those hunter gatherer groups, that survived into the 19th and 20th centuries, all provide indications of what was possibly and even in some instances what was probably taking place. But of course, exactly what took place can never be known, it is an anthropocentric conceit to think or state otherwise. The period of European colonialism did much to destroy and eliminate the countless numbers of hunter-gatherer and non-agriculturally based settled groups of humanity that were spread far and wide across all continents, and even that colonial era level of genocidal destruction still left a much restricted, but visible trace of hunter-gatherer communities. These surviving traces, can provide sufficient clues to sketch a probable outline of the wider pre-hierarchical mass society organisational forms of humanity, before the colonialists began their pillaging, patricide and profiting. After the colonial era acquisitive purge was over, the few surviving hunter-gatherer communities became variously influenced and dominated by European capitalist materials, tools, attitudes and aspirations. Undoubtedly, within a short period of first contact with colonial 'explorers' and 'missionaries' who pioneered the colonial expansion of European capitalism, indigenous peoples, whatever mode of production they used to ensure their (N-M-G-R + A-D) processes, their behaviour changed to varying degrees. However, as we shall include later, enough evidence has remained available to establish probable outlines of socio-economic living that was practiced globally before the 17th 18th and 19th centuries and some that continued long after that initial colonial dispossession period had ceased.

As noted in an earlier section; life on earth has evolved as organic parts of nature; and organic nature is a term used which includes all life on earth as it continues to evolve. Furthermore, it is obvious that in no material sense have humans evolved separately from all other life forms in the millions and thousands of years of evolution of life in general and animal life in particular. Therefore, there are not two domains of organic existence; humanity and the rest of organic life as our historical ancestors decided to believe in and was passed down to us so that many still choose to ignore evidence that contradicts those beliefs and perpetuate the myths. So from accumulated evidence, rational thinking strongly concludes that life on earth in general, is one inter-connected domain which has spread across all habitable lands and seas. That is so even though all species of life on earth have evolved at varying rates, whilst constantly interacting with other species and with their local environments. Indeed, in the transition from bipedal, ape-like mammal to the pre-human hominid we can assume our ancestors continued either gathering (as Gorillas and Monkeys in the wild still do); gathering and scavenging (as some baboons still do); and gathering and occasionally hunting, as some observed ape species still do. Consequently, apart from myth and magic, it is now undeniable that humans comprise the same structural body elements and minerals as all other forms of organic life, albeit in different combinations and proportions. The one other pertinent evolutionary distinction, between human and animal life in general, is that some several thousand years ago, some human communities significantly altered their mode of production, from a natural gathering and hunting one, to one based upon socially organized planting, growing and technically producing the nutrition they required.

Hominid modes of production.

For a social species, the method of socially obtaining the organic and inorganic necessities for survival and reproduction, are those we humans now define as the economic foundations upon which everything else socially arises. As noted earlier, that foundation for the human species has earned the modern descriptive terms of 'mode of production' and 'culture'. I have already noted that the use of the term 'mode of production' requires some explanation with regard to the previous 'hunting and gathering' part of human living. So, because the term may not be familiar to some readers, a re-cap may be useful. Although gathering is not actually producing the material used, it is clear that some animals and early humans were already fashioning leaves, twigs, branches and stones to carry, break or retrieve sources of organic nourishment. They were also creating ways to make some food sources more palatable by soaking, scraping, cleaning, burning or sweetening tough or bitter substances. There is also evidence that some early humans were also preserving some foods by immersion in particles of salt and sun-drying fruits and fish. With the invention of reliable means of lighting fires the cooking and 'smoking' of food sources also became possible. This suggests that all prior efforts or subsequent activities to gather and hunt natural production, such as preserving and transporting, can be legitimately included in the term 'mode of production'. Thus the human mode of production of nutrition, to a considerable extent, determines the human 'mode' of living and this was applicable to the way early human hunter-gatherers were obtaining and processing the bio-chemical necessities for their (N-M-G-R) processes.

It is therefore the various modes of production which for humans has delivered the biological necessities of (N-M-G-R) and allowed the development of everything non nutritional erected upon those socio-economic foundations, such as those covered by the term - culture. It is generally accepted that in the case of humanity, there have been several distinct modes of production. As previously noted, they have been characterised as; 1, the 'gatherer' mode of production (in foraging groups); 2, the specialist hunter-gatherer groups (often a fluid division of labour between hunter and gatherer groups); 3, The pastoral mode of production groups (those living within domesticated animal herding groups); 4, the agricultural mode of production (settled farming groups and communities); and 5, the modern industrial mode of production (capitalist mode of mass production) and their social division into economically productive groups producing essentials for life and groups not producing essentials for life. It has often been asserted by some commentators that these 'modes of production' have occurred at discrete historical stages and thus form a linear progression through time from prehistory to the present. I consider this to have been a mistaken and ideologically produced retrospective assumption. Archaeological and Anthropological evidence indicates that these modes of production often existed side by side for generations and that individual sub groups and larger communities often went from one mode to the other. As we shall see in the following chapter, when agricultural mass societies developed in the Fertile Crescent region of the Middle East some 10,000 years ago, those outside those developments and the rest of the global population of humans remained predominantly hunter-gatherers or in various types of non-farming communities. In particular, it should be remembered, as will be considered in the next chapter, the hunter-gatherer mode of production continues to exist in 2025, alongside advanced capitalist modes of production, albeit now only in some fairly isolated enclaves and riverside Amazon villages.

 The impulses to fulfil the four necessary phases of the life process in humans - Nourishment, Metabolism, Growth and Reproduction - are undoubtedly stimulated by physical sensations and the emotional feelings associated with them, and not by ideas about nutrition, the latter knowledge came much later. The desire to obtain Nourishment (N) is stimulated by the bodily sensations of hunger; successful Metabolism, is indicated by the bodily sensation of restored energy balance; Growth by the bodily sensations associated with increasing strength and abilities; and Reproduction initiated by proximity and the sensations of sexual arousal. From observations of wild life we can assume that this pattern of cause and effect occurs in all sexually reproducing life forms in some form or other. The effort involved in securing nourishment by gathering, scavenging or hunting - in all animals (even among humans) predates human ideas and therefore is not motivated by them, but is motivated by the individual bodily or cellular sensations noted above. Outside of habits, the fundamental biological cycle of metabolic process for life on earth to exist is prompted by these bodily sensations of relative comfort or discomfort. Of course, in articulate humans these sensations are associated with particular words. Since these needs are common to all individuals, in the case of a social species, then these needs are also sought and satisfied socially.

The evidence which contradicts the previously mentioned outdated idea of suggesting successive discreet stages in modes of production is not simply derived from a source of contrary intellectual opinion or from a logical deduction, but is clearly revealed by reality itself. Even amid modern industrial modes of production and on their isolated fringes, hunting and gathering is still retained as a leisure pastime for some and actual modes of living for others. Even during their most abundant or restricted seasons of the past, the reality of pastoralists and agricultural modes of production also retained - in one form or another - gathering and hunting as supplementary means of nutritional supply or as 'sport' or pastimes. Furthermore, we need to remember the historical evidence of early colonial settlers in North and South America, Africa, and Oceania which provided numerous examples of immigrant colonising people giving up the European introduced vagaries and uncertainty of isolated farming and cattle rearing to join or return to a friendly hunter gatherer band. Such early settlers 'going native' did so consciously and rationally, many in order to enjoy easier access to varied nutritional sustenance, supportive companionship and to obtain more extensive and enjoyable leisure time. In such cases, they consciously chose a better way of living out their (N-M-G-R + A-D) processes than the precarious individual family based farm based one. Since hunting and gathering in fruitful locations frequently established the labour time necessary to survive as a couple of hours of productive activity, this contrasted favourably with the 8 or more hours of back breaking digging, ploughing, reaping or herding on a few acres of isolated farmland. Going native for some early colonists of North and South America was therefore hardly surprising.

It is reasonable to assume that if some modern humans in the 19th century colonial era could make the choice of changing or alternating the mode of how they produced the (N) they needed from life on earth, then we can hardly rule out the fact that some of our early human ancestors with their large brains and considerable skill sets could exercise the same rational flexibility - either permanently, seasonally or episodically. Indeed, the scant evidence of archaeology, as we shall indicate later, also suggests that this switch between modes also occurred within generations and between generations on a number of occasions in pre-history and occasionally during the same historical times. Therefore hunter-gatherer communities, pastoralist groups of families, agricultural peoples and mixed agricultural/cattle based empires along with modern industrialised modes of production, always need to be considered from a critical and factually based understanding rather than any previously promoted ideological perspective emanating from previous generations. However, since hunting and gathering or gathering and hunting were the earliest identifiable modes of production and indeed ones that lasted in most of the non-European world until the 18th and 19th centuries we shall consider the detail of this mode of production and the social behaviour this engendered more fully in the following chapter.

The (N-M-G-R + A-D) processes of early, hominid and other hunter-gatherer groups whilst being completely different to animals in many respects are nevertheless so similar with regard to life on earth that in dealing with them the following environmental facts were also essential. Whatever location they chose to reside in, needed to have close by, sufficient available resources, close by in order to satisfy the groups needs for water, food, shelter and clothing. Whenever those resources started to become insufficient, the group would be faced with the need to either reduce their numbers by dividing their community and one segment moving elsewhere; or the whole community would need to move on to another sufficiently resource rich location. This gives rise to the historic and pre-historic symptoms of groups moving on or around a particular region or between seasonally abundant areas and also to the phenomenon of large groups dividing and becoming separate but remaining related social and biological entities. Whether, or not early humans understood natural growth cycles partially or fully, it is clear that what was actually occurring in populations continually moving on is that the land (sea or river) based organic resources, roots, nuts, fruits, herbs, grubs, fish etc., having been used for a period, are being given time to replenish the microorganism nutrients and mineral resources they 'grow' in and to reproduce (R) their species. Whether this moving on is planned or unplanned, the effect is to give the natural produce and soil time to recover and thus allows the partly or totally exhausted resource locations to reproduce and commence their (N-M-G-R + A-D) processes and become sufficiently abundant again. In other words, within nomadic hunter-gatherer modes of production, nature was able to self-fertilise and self-reproduce itself with no other systematic and technically organised help from humanity.

Hunting and gathering in arctic regions obviously required different housing, clothing, nutritional sources and methods than those located in the middle of a tropical jungle or those in temperate zones. However, wherever hunting and gathering takes place, the resources need to be sufficient or made sufficient, for the size of the community utilising them and alternative arrangements made for when they are not. In most, if not all hunter-gatherer groups, all healthy adults play an active part in the production of one or other of the food and ancillary resources. Although, as noted previously, many groups had a gender division with men predominantly hunting and women predominantly gathering; also women child rearing and basket weaving whilst men did the heavy building and producing hunting equipment, canoes etc., this was not the whole picture. Indeed, as we shall read, according to colonial occupiers of native lands, among 19th century hunter-gatherer groups there were sufficient examples of women hunting, trapping, making tools and men cooking and child minding, that modern rigid stereotyping retrospectively applied is not necessarily accurate. This suggests it is not necessary and even can be grossly mistaken to make too many definitive assumptions about all prehistoric gender distinctions within hunter gatherer peoples.

Despite the many differences in locations and available resources and despite geographical and cultural differences the hunting and gathering mode of production ensured that the source of nutrition (from nature) was available to all. No one person or group of people within a socio-economic band could effectively monopolise any general or particular section of nature, even had they wanted to. Moving on sooner or later by all or a sub-group was always an option. All adult healthy individuals could participate in obtaining the nutritional needs (N) of the entire group or band. Considered abstractly, the hunting and gathering of food, water and other materials is the appropriation of nature by socialised 'individuals' although it is done through and from within a specific form of social grouping. The hunter-gatherer bands, therefore, provide the material for a distilled essence of the social nature of humanity in its pre-hierarchical mass society forms. The human species, under any mode of production, cannot exist without its absolute dependence upon the rest of life on earth, for its oxygen, its mineral intake, its organic nourishment, its materials for clothing and housing. Plus, like any other social species, the individuals within human groups cannot survive for long without the active support of the entire community. Moreover, it takes the combined efforts of the entire community for each branch of the species to survive.

In certain places there undoubtedly occurred changes from nomadic, tool assisted gathering, scavenging and hunting, to occasionally more settled or seasonally settled tool assisted gathering, scavenging, hunting and then planting. The latter situation, leading to the domestication of plant and animal species, was observed among the North American indigenous peoples and certain African tribal groupings by the 17th and 18th century European settlers on those two continents. In certain advantageous places the sources and processes of obtaining Nourishment, Rest, Growth and Reproduction were gradually improved and a transition to settled, larger - scale group living took place on many different continents around the world. In certain places, domesticated food sources (crops and herds) gradually predominated over wild gathering and hunting and planned agriculture and animal husbandry increasingly became the main source of nutritional nourishment. Consequently, certain phases among the human, plant and animal (N-M-G-R + A –D) processes, particularly the (G-R + A-D) ones were effected and modified.

It should be noted, however, that in most cases, the transition between gathering nature's production and socially planting and herding community sources of Nourishment, a pre-requisite for these mode of production transitions was primarily enabled by the natural forces of the planet being already sufficiently productive to sustain those species who existed. Transitions between one mode of production and another and their consequent cultural adjustments - for any social species - cannot be accomplished on consistently empty stomachs. This suggests that the many river based city state locations in the near and middle east, were chosen for sustained planting and agriculture because of the fact that the rains and snow melts caused by the planets orbits and seasons, consistently flooded valley plains and provided large cultivated and uncultivated resources to feed the transition from planting and waiting to harvest and prepare the food source grown or the herd domesticated. The planets, gravity and waters' fluid characteristic's, enabled the flooding of many valley plains with rain and river water containing fertile, mineral rich silt, which in turn nourished soil micro - organisms and plants along with nurturing abundant fish stocks.

The rivers also watered the herbivore herds and attracted wild animals to it to drink, enabling supplementary hunting and fishing to take place. The rivers also allowed easier means of travel for light and heavy loads. Thus in any transition between settled agricultural and non-agricultural modes of production, the planet's inorganic forces and substances provided four free essential assistance to ancient human communities when changing their mode of production. This natural planetary assistance is why large concentrations of human social groups evolved in places such as the Nile Valley and its Delta, (i.e. enabling the eventual formation of two Egyptian kingdoms) and also between the rivers Tigris and Euphrates (i.e. enabling the formation of the city states of Akkad, Sumer, Babylon, Assyria) and the Indus with its Harappan settlements, and those around the great rivers of China. Of course nature, when not interrupted or disrupted, still provides these free natural resources to all life on earth.

For example a similar transition to more settled economic activity occurred in South America, (via the Incas, Mayans, etc.), in Africa, (Congo Kingdoms), in Asia (China). Some of which we shall consider in more detail later. Meanwhile we should recognise that this transition did not occur rapidly or all at one time or by the same processes. Broadly speaking it is possible to say that there would have been two main means of processing or enabling that transition between the two modes of production. One was possibly voluntary and peaceful, with groups voluntarily coming together to take up farming; the other was by the use of force and violence, in which compulsion was used to force slave-based agricultural communities to live according to a different mode of production. Unfortunately, we have far more evidence of forced violent removal of hunter-gatherer modes of production than peaceful voluntary transitions because historical evidence has recorded this violence more frequently. Furthermore, many of these forced transitions occurred only a few generations ago as by the above noted European colonists in North and South America, Africa, Asia and Oceana. These European invasions invariably drove native people off their naturally productive habitats and eventually imposed a different mode of production upon the conquered territory and the indigenous peoples.

Time lines in history and pre-history.

As indicated, it is usual to divide the history of the human species into two distinct periods or categories, designated as prehistory and history. Prehistory is generally divided into three sub-sections based upon the use of durable materials for the human-made tools of the period, such as stone, bronze and iron, hence; Stone Age; Bronze Age and Iron Age. This designation is not strictly accurate because tools were also made from wood, bone and animal horn, much of which may well have rotted away and left little or no trace. However, the general convention is the above noted demarcation so I will stick with it. The so-called Stone Age is reckoned as lasting from 3.4 million BCE (Before the Common Era) to 3,000 BCE. Three million years of stone-age living by early hominids and humans is an immense stretch of time and indicates that even with limited stone technology human life and evolution was successful in both social individual and species terms. The so-called Bronze age is estimated to have lasted from 3,300 BCE to 1,200 BCE; and the so-called Iron Age was from 1,200 BCE to 400 BCE.

The Common Era refers to the calculation of yearly earth orbits around the sun, from the Christian religions estimated year zero as being the possible birth year of an alleged Jewish dissident named Jesus. Jesus was a popular name during that period of history and one bearing this name had followers who, after his death, claimed he was a Christ (and son of Joseph or in different narratives the son of god) and kick-started the religion of Christianity. This part of history will be considered in a later chapter. Until the 20th century the chosen designation of this period was BC and AD (i.e. Before Christ and Anno Domini - after the death) but the convention was changed to before and after the 'common' era hence (BCE and ACE) so as not to annoy the sensibilities of the millions who were not Christian believers. Generally speaking the dominant source of tangible evidence used for understanding the pre-history of humanity comprises artefacts (such as pots, bones, stones, wood, seeds, cave paintings) found in various places and not in narratives passed down by word of mouth or in written form. The academic discipline which collects and interprets this material source of evidence is, of course, known as archaeology, but it now includes radio carbon dating technology and other technological forms of dating bones and artifacts.

However, in contrast to prehistory, the dominant source of evidence used in the study of the ancient history of humanity are the written records made by those in human communities who had learned to use systems of visual symbols (writing) that had been invented and which were recorded initially upon, stone, clay, pottery shards and later, animal skins and papyrus or paper. It should not be imagined that written records provide exponentially more reliable information than archaeological artefacts, because it needs to be remembered that few people could write until modern capitalist societies were developed and those who wrote in ancient times were few and rarely unbiased in what they recorded and what they did not. Thus there are two main problems faced by reconstructing the transition from a pre-history of human social forms based upon semi-nomadic people who gathered and hunted to social forms based upon people planting crops and herding animals. First, the evidence for understanding pre-history is in the form of physical artefacts which although tangible are often circumstantial. A stone axe is an undeniable artefact when found, but how it got there, how it was used and how and why it was made all too easily made subjects of much imagination and conjecture.

Some conjecture is of course inevitable, but I suggest that too often, too much imaginative gap filling is presented as factual accuracy. Correlation is also too often assumed to be causation. The problems with regard to understanding history is probably quite as bad as understanding pre-history because although frequently there are written records which offer explanations of what was occurring. As will be indicated in the next chapter, elite human beings, the only ones with the ability to write, are notoriously prone to selecting the instances and opinions expressed within what they record in such a way to conform to their own preferred point of view or grand narrative. This preference can exaggerate either positively or negatively what is described and also omit large elements of what occurred, including any conflicting accounts of what occurred. Furthermore, the early methods of gathering information was not always by first-hand experience, so all sorts of first and second hand bias, hearsay, myth, tall stories, fiction and propaganda, from slight to huge will have entered their accounts of the periods considered. Having said this, these sources are all we have and so using them is necessary whilst at the same time being constantly aware of bias, ignorance and undue influence. Keeping a constantly critical dimension to the research material is undoubtedly an onerous task, but it is essential to avoid reproducing ancient misinformation and regurgitating fiction as fact. Unfortunately, it is the case that in the life sciences, this kind of rigour is not always practiced.

Consequently, by concentrating on the 'form', rather than the 'content' of animal, insect and human life as it exists within their various societies, many modern analysts of life on earth have inhabited an ideologically produced and transmitted perspective. Historians and Archaeologists have often constructed virtual realities through analogy and imagination and retrospectively imposed these virtual realities upon ancient societies - both prehistoric and historic. In this way they have tied themselves and their readers up in endless speculation and further (and often deeper) into confusion, which gets further transferred to other readers who perhaps trustingly assume that unequivocal rigour and authenticity has been undertaken, when it has not. Some 'authorities' have even projected back into prehistory their own imaginary peaceful idyllic or war-like savagery periods, others have suggested a long ago golden age, before things changed for the worse. In that latter tradition, the myth of one then two human individuals magically created by an invisible male super-being in a Garden of Eden lies at the root of ancient monotheistic ideology.

An important reminder of humanities bio-chemical origins.

Of course, in modern mass societies humanities daily food and water is no longer gained individually but by a long chain of intermediaries between the sources of field and pasture production, its subsequent manufacture and its eventual distribution, prior to consumption. Individual participation in a collective socio-economic system of hunter-gatherer production, distribution and consumption has been replaced by division of labour classifications such as producers and consumers and occupational categories, in which all members play some vital or less vital part. Citizens of such societies have, therefore, become socially dependent for their existence upon each other and yet still remain biologically dependent upon all the life-forms and inorganic gases, liquids and minerals existing within nature. But of course, humanity's dependency upon life on earth goes even deeper than the world outside the surface of our skins. As already previously stressed, we human beings, as with all other species, are composed of multiple, specialist eukaryotic cells, living within us and cooperating with millions of other cells within our integrated network of cells that make up the body - that while we live – is us. In fact, these discrete cell structures and microorganisms within us, which we think of as our own, are in a sense really only on loan to us from life on earth while we live. As was discussed in the chapter on cells, even these cells *'loaned for the duration of the life of an organism'* that exist within our human bodies have within themselves, borrowed, living reproducing organic units (organelles, mitochondria, ribosome's, DNA etc.) and inorganic material, actively involved within them. So here is a further reminder of our existential dependence upon multiple species of life on earth from another author on cells. As we proceed to consider the history of human life on earth, our focus will tend to move away from considering life on earth as an integrated bio-chemical whole, upon which all life depends, and focus upon the species which now dominates, damages and distorts that billion year evolutionary dynamic. Therefore, before starting the next chapter, it is perhaps worth a short reminder of our human origins in the world of nature and its amazing evolution of cells and multi-cellular organisms.

"At the interior of our cells, driving them, providing the oxidative energy that sends us out for the improvement of each shining day, are the mitochondria, and in a strict sense they are not ours. They turn out to be little separate creatures, the colonial posterity of migrant prokaryotes, probably primitive bacteria that swam into ancestral precursors of our eukaryotic cells and stayed there. Ever since, they have maintained themselves and their ways, replicating in their own fashion, privately, with their own DNA and RNA quite different from ours. They are as much symbionts as the rhizobial bacteria in the roots of beans. Without them, we would not move a muscle, drum a finger, or think a thought." ('The lives of a Cell'. By Lewis Thomas. Penguin. page 3)

This biological fact is evident from their own internal reproduction by the combined efforts of internal organelles within each of their cells; by the production by some organisms of the gases that other organisms need to breathe or imbibe and by land based and aquatic carbon dioxide converting plants. The ecological chain of inter-dependence extends to the breaking down and conversion of inorganic minerals required for internal and external structures; to the organic materials which nourish their lives and provide energy. All these interlocking contributions have evolved allowing life on earth to exist and reproduce. Once it is seriously considered, the evidence is overwhelming in establishing that life on earth has evolved over millions and even billions of years to form an intricate connected web of supportive inter-dependent life forms upon which, in one way or another, every form of life on earth ultimately depends. As demonstrated, this dependency upon other life form's, stretches from the ones humans frequently see around them to those they could not see until sophisticated technologies of detection and magnification were developed. So it is a very recent development that we humans can now know that the whole system of life on earth is one interdependent, inter-connected system, and as such it either survives as a system or it disintegrates as a system. The readers of these chapters are the first generation of the human species that have ever known or understood these evidence based facts in the entire history of the human species. Those of us alive now are the first humans to be able to understand that any individual species of life on earth does not survive as a collection of disconnected parts. Moreover, we are the first generation to have the evidence available to us to understand that when far too many of the essential links in the ecological chain of life on earth become missing by extinctions, whether through neglect, unintended results or deliberate actions, the effects will descend upon all forms of life. Although this was the reality of the world in which the successive stages of hominid lived through and as we shall see did so without substantially endangering the existence of any other species of life on earth, this reality was totally unknown.

In the 21st century it has now become widely known that many species of life on every continent and in every ocean are becoming extinct due to the combined actions of humanity. However, before considering the question of how to prevent or reverse the current progressive decline of the biosphere of planet earth, I suggest it is necessary to question and understand two vitally important things. 1. How and why after billions of years of life on earth, has humanity in the space of a few thousand years, caused such havoc to itself and to other life forms on planet earth? 2. In particular how and why over the last 250 years) has it accelerated its mode of production to suffocate, diffuse and pollute the atmosphere, the seas and the land in every corner of this once amazing, life-supporting planetary network of living things? Of particular concern is the trajectory of the last 75 plus years in pushing the biosphere to the brink of climate dislocation and collapse in one area after another.

Late in the literary research for this book I was reminded of the game Jenga, that I played with my young children when they were young. It consisted of a wooden tower, made of separate blocks which once assembled each player carefully pulled out one at a time. The tower remained standing whilst many blocks were removed, until it took the removal of just one more block for the whole tower to collapse - and the game was over. To me that game now stands as a physical metaphor for the game hierarchical mass society humans have made out of living by continually extracting material from nature, without knowing which species it will extract from the biosphere that will eventually cause the whole or much of the biosphere structure to sufficiently collapse to endanger all the more developed biological forms to become extinct. The dinosaur[n] species didn't cause their own extinction by their own way of living, but it is possible that if humanity does not modify its mode of production, it could be the only species that will. To address those two earlier - much ignored - questions is the purpose of these next chapters and to do so we will need to start with a little of the history and prehistory of humanity as illuminated by our own species, social and individual attempts to uncover it.

Chapter 7 Summary.

The early hominid species clearly evolved from the primate species, with all the limbs, hands, brains and facial muscles that had evolved on the basis of primate evolution. The hominids, like the primates, were predominantly gatherers of vegetation, fruits and roots. Like the chimpanzees that occasionally predate upon a monkey, the lack of specialised body parts (claws) and tools, early hominids would have no other choice than to rely upon what grew around them or had died by other means. Tools, which improved hunting, defence and the lighting of fire's, must have been later developments. The social form must have also remained the same, with the primary social unit being voluntarily formed around the females, their off-spring and siblings. Just like the social life of chimpanzees, (Bonobos in particular) with no incest taboos, it is likely that this primary female-led unit was the social basis for obtaining nutritional production and biological reproduction for countless generations. That social system, with occasional recruitment of other acceptable members from passing or nearby hominid groups, was clearly sufficient for evolutionary viability.

In any social group communication and familiarity are engendered and cooperation in tasks becomes routine. It should not be surprising, therefore, to conclude that a largish group of adult, pre-sapien hominids, armed with digging sticks would not need to be afraid of any attacks from predatory animals – even the fiercest. It is still the case in the 21st century that three or four African Kung San tribal members, armed only with long poles, can move a full pride of lions away from their current kill and take half a deer carcass away for their own use, before leaving safely. If over thousands of years, herds of elephants, deer, and wild cattle of various numbers, could (and can still) obtain sufficient nutrition, then groups of hominids would have no undue problems in surviving. Therefore, logic suggests that apart from natural inorganic disasters things would be essentially the same during hominid evolution. Speech, dexterity, tools, and nutrition would all have had time and opportunity for continuous refinement and sophistication. Ideas of extreme levels of general hardship for hominids, based upon imaginative speculation should be rejected, for there is no factual evidence to support these 20th and 21st horror stories concerning our hominid ancestors constantly living in fear.

CHAPTER 8

The social evolution of Homo sapiens.
Gatherers & Hunters in more detail.

There has long been an erroneous level of historic and contemporary prejudice and disrespect for our ancient hominid and human ancestors. This prejudice has been reflected in both religious texts, academic literature and in popular cultural narratives. On the basis of largely ignorant and prejudiced imagination rather than fact, these tendencies have characterised human pre-history as being non-existent apart from a single god made man (within religion), a period of ignorance, barbarism and hardship among humanity from mythical secularism, in popular culture. Even as recently as a few centuries ago, ancient pre-agricultural hominids and humanity were often considered as *'little better than animals',* which was not only anthropocentrically prejudiced, but ignorant and disrespectful of animals as well as early humans. Giants were imagined to have built the many stone circles and artificial mounds throughout Europe before humanity built cities with walls and buildings.

This negative, retrospective scenario of a condition of backwardness, ignorance and ruthless aggression was imagined to have lasted until the arrival of 'civilisation' in the form of agricultural settlements and animal rearing. Such prejudice was clearly utter nonsense and based upon little or no material evidence. This chapter seeks to outline sufficient evidence to not only challenge this prejudiced anthropocentric view but to hopefully end it among those who may still hold it and to begin to overcome that kind of ill-informed prejudice. During the 20th century, the pre-history of early humanity finally became more than a matter of religious speculation or of occasional secular curiosity, and became a specialist academic subject. Since that time the discipline has sprouted into different viewpoints and motives for the continued research concerning human evolution. This division is reflected in the changing terms used to define the previous human way of life, to the now dominant hierarchical mass society formations. *'Foraging', 'gathering' 'scavenging' and 'hunter-gathering'* have been some of the terms most commonly used.

Whatever term is actually used, the usual meaning covered by them is a study; '*of those human groups who obviously obtained at least a subsistence level of nourishment and living, in the absence of the large-scale domestication of plants and animals*'. My own preferred term to cover the defining characteristics noted in italics, is gatherer-hunter or hunter-gatherer; but I would also include the following activities to fall within the term; a) obtaining subsistence levels of nourishment by fishing in seas, rivers and lakes – I treat this activity as an additional form of hunting live animals for nutrition (N); and b) also by collecting shoreline seafood – I treat that as an additional form of '*gathering*'. Within the academic field, the wide range of global hunter-gatherer variability has created the usual disagreements concerning whether the different cultural, spiritual, linguistic, and geographical features should be those which are used to characterise these peoples. For example;

"*Archaeologists often focus on the points at which people stop being hunter-gatherers and become farmers. We have spent much less time asking, when did we start to live in the kinds of hunter-gatherer societies observed ethnographically? This is especially important in the long term of human evolution which may include different species of humans: ('Diversity of Hunter Gatherer Pasts'. B. Finlayson & G. Warren. Chapter 1)*

In my assessment, the final three words in the above quote should read 'species of hominid', since there is now a general agreement that there is only one species of humans. The Neanderthal branch of the hominid species was once considered a completely different species, but as noted previously, DNA evidence now suggests that the bio-chemical essence of their hominid form did not actually become extinct, but was successfully incorporated into the lineage of more modern humanity by interbreeding within early Homo sapiens groups. Thus it would have been a process which of course, would also indicate a general social and reproductive compatibility. Such questions and focuses, whilst perhaps interesting, are too convoluted for this study to pursue and would dilute the essential points I feel have now become more urgent concerns to consider.

Therefore, the approach I have taken to this study is to avoid being drawn into such comparative studies. Instead my focus is upon the common fundamental (N-M-G-R + A-D) biochemical roots and phases of all life on earth and in particular on how those human orchestrated activities effected and eventually which threaten some or all of these phases.

This approach will, therefore, still enable perhaps the original 'natural' common foundation of hunter-gatherer experience to be compared and contrasted with that of other life forms and with other human modes of production. Of course, when reading the above quotation, if we consider life on earth evolves, then what social forms started (or more accurately evolved) within hominids and the various pre-Homo *sapien* species hundreds of thousands or even millions of years ago is not necessarily exactly the same as those that current ethnographic studies actually describe. Also, the observation in the above quote, that different species of humans (such as Homo Neanderthalensis, or Homo Floresiensis), *'may'* have been hunters or gatherers', to my mind utterly fails to understand an essential point about the bio-chemical cycling and re-cycling of inorganic and organic material necessary for the existence of all life on earth. Hominids, human and pre-human - just as all animal species - could not have existed at all without being hunters and/or gatherers of organic and inorganic sources of nutrition. Consequently there is no 'may' about it - all life on earth needs organic and inorganic sources of nutrition (N) – so before some humans lived in hierarchical mass societies, all must have either hunted or gathered them or engaged in both strategies.

An additional reason for not venturing down the esoteric rabbit hole of cultural, spiritual, ethnographic, geographical or contemporary comparisons is that hunting and/or gathering - as defined above - is exactly what all forms of life on earth, (apart from some extremophile bacteria and some modern humans) do naturally. They directly obtain subsistence levels of nourishment (N, and more) from the land based or sea based forms of inorganic and organic material of the planet to fulfil and complete their essential (N-M-G-R + A-D) phases of living. As emphasised throughout this study, this is the case whether the life form is a single bacterial type cell, a multicellular plant, insect or a four or two legged or winged animal. In a very broad sense, as we have seen through the previous chapters, life on earth seeks both organic and inorganic nourishment in whatever way its biochemical morphological structure has evolved to obtain and absorb them. For billions of years, 'life on earth' has done so – within a natural organic and inorganic environment - and by utilising organs or appendages, whether in the form of limbs, mouths, roots, leaves or petals. This observation therefore confirms that hominid and human hunter-gatherers were, and are, a natural part and original form of human existence as well as an evolutionary extension of all animal existence. Therefore the biochemical and social relationships developed within such 'natural' modes of production are also the ones directly emanating from, and corresponding to, the evolution of all the organisms included within the definition of the natural world. The human species as it evolved and spread across the world, is no different in this regard. Thus it is considered that;

"The earliest members of the Homo genus, including Homo habilis and Homo erectus, emerged in Africa around 2-3 million years ago. These early humans had larger brains than their ancestors and developed increasingly sophisticated tool making abilities. Over time, this led to the emergence of Homo sapiens, a species with an even larger brain and advanced cognitive abilities." ('From Hunter- Gatherers to Global Citizens: The Story of Humanity'. Brandon Dutra. Introduction)

Of course size is not everything and even small brains can be incredibly sophisticated and large brains can be frequently used to produce stupid, self-defeating results - as any observation of an extended workplace or political discourse still frequently demonstrates. It is not the physical size of a brain that matters fundamentally but the experiences it has processed and how this experience is subsequently used, individually and socially. Two or three million years is a long time for cumulative experiences to be processed and reflected upon, but among the human species, clearly knowledge of history and pre-history does not always bring wisdom to all those individuals and groups within the latest iterations of 21st century humanity. As noted in previous chapters, the origins of life on earth undoubtedly occurred on the basis of natural inorganic elements combining and becoming self-replicating, bio-chemical organisms. Life on earth has continued on this basis for all species, from whenever they evolved from their first definitive forms, until now. As has been described, no matter how many cells a particular species form contains, or how, when and where it evolved, the bio-chemical physical essence of all life forms is maintained by a cycle of (N-M-G-R + A-D), in part and as a species by the contributions from the whole spectrum of life on earth.

In order to counter the anthropocentric obsession with individual and community exceptionalism, I again stress that the human species is not qualitatively different to other species in this regard. Without the oxygenated air, water and balanced gut bacteria provided by life on earth - in all its plant, insect and microorganism forms - the human species could not have evolved and would no longer be able to survive without these essential contributions continuing. The essential phases (N-M-G-R + A-D) and their requirements have had to be met during the biological and social evolution of humanity no matter what climatic environment each individual organism or species encountered or the social form their groups have taken. Whether by gathering, scavenging, hunting, herding, in small groups or in more settled groups for planting and herding, or for large groups, it has been the securing of the first four life cycle phases (N - M - G - R), that has determined the continuity, well-being and adaptations occurring among humanities individual and collective members. Late 20th century archaeological excavation in North America, has retrieved evidence that, as in South America, Africa and Asia, the integrated network of life on earth by its processes has created some nutritionally abundant locations, which depending upon group numbers, removed the need for hunter-gatherer groups to frequently move around to ensure adequate or better levels of nutrition, comfort and safety. For example;

"The Nebo Hill phase represents a pottery equipped hunting and gathering population, centred in the lower Missouri Valley between Bethany Falls and Oread Escarpments. Available dates place it at the second millennium B.C.........Food remains show that deer and smaller game were hunted, and that oily nuts and starchy seeds were gathered. No evidence for Nebo Hill cultigens

has yet been recovered, but tree-felling tools, hoe bits and site location regularities may point to supplementary gardening at the large upland settlements in the river hills." ('Archaic Hunters and Gatherers in the American Mid-West'. J..L.Phillips & J.A. Brown. Chapter 3)

Such evidence suggests that for over ten thousand years in that area, pottery did not appear among the usual remains left by the previous inhabitants in these particular locations. It was not until just over two thousand years ago that pottery appeared widely among such human communities. These artefacts in themselves may not necessarily indicate changes in human technical abilities but may well indicate a transition from more nomadic to more sedentary existences. Because pottery is easily broken, it rarely features in nomadic communities even where the knowledge and skills required to produce pottery is available. More durable and robust baskets of woven reeds and containers made from animal skins were and are frequently the preferred tools of carrying and containment for nomadic peoples. Moreover, a pre-requisite of becoming a settled community, was the local abundance and rate of reproduction (R) of suitable sources of available nutrition (N) and although these resources were partly domesticated by early humanity they were originally provided by the naturally evolved, inter-connected and inter-dependent network of life on earth, not simply by human ingenuity.

Securing (N-M-G-R + A-D) by Hunting and Gathering.

Furthermore, from the mid-19th century onward, those who have seriously considered pollution and ecological destruction have known that the modern method of obtaining materials in order to traverse these six phases, by humanity, has implications with regard to negative effects upon the planet's life forms and climatic cycles. In any given area, when consumption of natural resources exceeds the reproduction (R) of these natural resources, then 'nature' or 'life on earth' as a whole, is no longer in a dynamic ecological balance. We shall see in this and the following chapter how the satisfaction of the life cycle phases of sections of humanity in various places and at various stages of history has been modified and transformed and not always with unproblematic consequences. The original and natural mode of nutritional production, (hunting and gathering based upon eating, sleeping, wearing and utilising what nature provides, and which was minimally altered by human efforts) will be considered in this chapter was changed in some favourable places to a hierarchical mass society form. This alternative and parallel mode of production form was created by human communities securing their (N-M-G-R + A-D) processes on the basis of the settled mass production of agricultural and animal produce along with the development of craft production of various artefacts. However, it is important to understand that there is no reliable evidence to suggest this change was motivated by a general relative or absolute nutritional poverty in hunter-gatherer communities, as many 19th century commentators have asserted. In places of abundance, where all life gravitates, large surplus nutritional production of essentials and extras could always be obtained, by relatively small communities. If they were not communities just re-located. However, outside of special occasions, an excess of surplus to hoard was not normally necessary or desirable as everything that was needed for nutrition, clothing and shelter was continually growing (G) and reproducing (R). Writing of the Cuiva people in a region of South America stretching between Colombia and Venezuela, a 20th century researcher in the 1970s reported that;

"on average, each person eats 400-500 g of meat daily and a roughly similar weight in vegetables. The work effort does not exceed fifteen to twenty hours a week; the majority spend fifteen to sixteen hours a day in their hammocks. Men hunt and produce meat, most often from the rivers and riverbank. Women gather vegetables from the edge between savanna and forest. Typically, the products are shared; some of the food is offered to every person in camp. Four or five food sources are available at any time of the year at different locations; diet, in the group, becomes a matter of choice, discussion, and consensus. Contrary to another common belief, hunting is not risky: the environment is minutely known and reliable; hunters tend to appropriate exactly what they intended." (The Cambridge Encyclopedia of Hunters and Gatherers. Bernard Arcand; South American Section. Page 98.)

An immediate quantitative contrast becomes obvious between the time spent by human hunter-gatherers and those other animal species who simply gather. Many, if not most, non-predatory animals spend long hours per day eating plant based nourishment such as grass, lichen, leaves or fruits, whereas humans even with frequently erratic hunting results actually needed to spend relatively short periods of time gathering food. This suggests that, as with many other primates, the diet of humans, from the earliest times was probably selectively chosen by them so that their (N) intake was sufficient to sustain them without spending long hours obtaining it. It is likely that this dietary selection, along with other social factors, such as time for chatting and exploration, was both a cause and effect of the growing intelligence of the human species. This chapter will therefore consider in much more specific detail the human forms of securing (N-M-G-R + A-D) that existed during the hominid form of primate evolution and which continued until the emergence of the Homo sapiens species and long after that emergence. As already noted, this early mode of production is commonly referred to as Hunter-Gathering, but again this generic term should not be used to stereotype or obscure the fact that diversity and fluidity in securing nutrition and safety existed regionally and globally. The balance of hunter-gatherer nourishment (N) on the African continent differed from North to South and from East to West and these differences also occurred between Cold climates and temperate ones. What was gathered, utilised and hunted depended very much upon what was available generally and also seasonally. Each general location also resulted in different cultural forms, customs and even different skin colours. However, these were all variations on one particular hominid or human species and on variations to one basic type of hunter-gatherer mode of production.

Although humanity has in one sense traversed a seamless biological continuity through generation after generation between ancient and modern times, it is necessary to take account of certain paradigm shifts or relatively rapid changes in how the processes of (N-M-G-R + A-D) have been modified by humans and how that in turn has modified humanity. There is an obvious difference between 'gathering' and 'hunting' in obtaining what 'life on earth' in general has produced by natural means. Natural seed and foot dispersal of nutritional plants and animal reproduction, was a (N-M-G-R + A-D, process unassisted by early hominids and only minimally assisted by later humanity. This was a radically different mode and process than a later method of harvesting what humanity had previously planted or previously bred domestically. For example, if we consider a typical gathering day for an average hunter-gatherer group camped reasonably close to the source of water and nutrition, (as most did), it will comprise of the following six stages. 1) Walk to the food and water source. 2) Pick or dig the vegetation, fruit or roots; collect some water. Check and reset any traps. 3) Carry everything back to camp. 4. Temporarily store it somewhere safe. 5) Prepare it for eating. 6) Decide what to do with the rest of the day. The first 4 stages, in well-resourced locations were often extremely short (approximately 30 minutes in fish rich locations such as in former British Columbia) therefore nutritional effort may only take a few hours or less to obtain. Each of these six stages would normally involve groups of people if not the whole community so practically everything that occurred 24/7 for hunter-gatherer communities was a visible social event, and it still is among contemporary hunter-gatherers.

In many cases certain hunter-gatherer groups have been observed to choose to separate into a 'hunting' party and a 'gathering' party, but both groups are still involved in social activities. That is to say there is a marked difference between the efforts of social hunting and gathering and eventually consuming (N) and with more numbers involved, than with the delayed gratification efforts required to engage in settled agricultural communities. The latter requires planting, waiting and reaping or in rearing stock, protecting and slaughtering them. This difference will be explored more fully in the next chapter. Moreover, between both modes of production, there is also an identifiable difference in the social relationships between humans and between humans and the rest of life on earth. However, it is the general inter-relationships within human hunter-gatherer communities, together with those between hunter-gatherer communities and the rest of life on earth, which will be the focus of this chapter. Since the literature on the subject of hunter-gatherers as a global phenomenon is immense, for this short study I will restrict the examples used to some North American hunter-gatherer first peoples and a few random examples from other continents. In a long running study of the Hadza group of African hunter-gatherers one researcher commented that;

"The Hadza move for a variety of reasons: to be near berries when they come into season, or move away from a location once a patch of tubers have been depleted. One important reason for moving camp is that the drinking water is drying up." ('THE HADZA; Hunter-gatherers of Tanzania'. F.W. Marlow. Chapter 3)

With so little property to carry, hunter-gatherers could always move elsewhere easily, either temporarily or semi-permanently. The relationships which held hunter-gatherer communities together were also primarily voluntary ones. As will be later demonstrated, no individual or sub-group within human hunter-gatherer communities studied in the $18^{th}, 19^{th}$ and 20th centuries was compelled by external or internal compulsion to stay within their original groups if they continually felt denied something essential, such as nutrition or if they felt physically threatened or unwelcome. They and their supporters could leave to become an independent group or join another community. An earlier chapter provided sufficient field research evidence to verify this fact in the case of animal social groups and primate troops as well as in hunter-gatherer communities of humans. This characteristic was true whether these groups were resident in North America, Africa and Oceania before the modern era. Evidence from a variety of studies indicates that any rare cases of unresolved community friction, persistent oppression or denial, hunter gatherer groups split up into sub-groups or whole groups just moved on elsewhere. This initial and fully natural mode of social production consequently produced the concept and practice of everyone being able to obtain and thus entitled to sufficient food, shelter, safety and social support, which in its modern form now assumes the form of a set of basic human rights, although now those are increasingly denied. .

Despite the many differences in locations and available resources and despite geographical and cultural differences the hunting and gathering mode of production ensured that the source of nutrition (provided by the breadth and reproduction rates of nature's species) was available to all – as a natural right. During the following survey, it will become clear that no one person or group of people within a socio-economic hunter - gatherer community would or could monopolise any general or particular section of nature. All adult healthy individuals (and even juveniles) could participate in obtaining the nutritional needs of the entire group or band. Hunting and gathering of food, water and other materials was also, as with animal species, the **direct appropriation** of nature by social individuals through and from within this specific form of social grouping. And in many places the resources provided by the rest of organic nature available to humans could even be considered luxurious. For example, in a number of historic documents concerning the Northern parts of North America, we read the following with regard to the natural hunter-gatherer habitat at the pre-agricultural period of time;

"The surrounding region is healthy, and amazingly fruitful. The grape, the plum, the gooseberry, and various other native fruits abound; the wild honeysuckle gives its perfume to the air, and a thousand indigenous flowers mingle their diversified hues with the verdure of the plain. These prairies were formerly covered with immense herds of buffalo and abounded in game of every description. The rivers furnished excellent fish and the whole region, in every respect so rich in the bounties of nature, must have formed that kind of paradise of which alone the Indian has any conception. If ever there was a spot on earth where scenic beauty, united with fecundity of soil and salubrity of climate, could exert a refining influence upon the human mind, it was here." ('History of the Indian Tribes of North America', Kenny and Hall. Volume 2. Page 23)

From these and numerous other similar reports from both ethnographic and archaeological sources of observational evidence, for many hunter-gather groups nature was, metaphorically speaking, providing the equivalent of a widely available, free access, local housing accommodation and a constantly re-stocked local freely available fresh food-store. Moreover, life on earth (nature) had supplied large, medium and small areas of such abundant resources scattered across most continents and islands, which were further located in forests, jungles, valleys, as well as along rivers and sea shores. This meant that wherever human and other species chose to roam, there was nearly always the equivalent of a fully or partially stocked free food and free resource bank within easy walking distance, of where they camped or rested. Still metaphorically speaking, nature for life in general was a sort of universal egalitarian 'super-market' without the downsides of modern checkouts, tins, plastic containers and the transport fumes and toxic liquid spills associated with getting the nourishment fresh to every local depot every day or week. Perhaps it will come as no surprise to learn that with such a prolific and free source of (N), that such hunter-gatherer internal and external social relationships were far more benign than social relationships often are in modernity.

Hunter-gatherer social relationships.

Even though many geographical locations differed in flora and fauna, early humans normally only located themselves in regions where a varied and sustained source of nutrition and useful material already existed. Since there is frequently an assumption among modern humans that our early ancestors were primitive and crude (as mentioned already, describing them as 'savages' was a common disparaging term applied to them), it will be necessary to provide ample evidence that such arrogant modern patriarchal assumptions are misplaced. For example one notable 19th century traveller among hunter-gatherer and pastoralists, Alfred, Russell Wallace, who along with Charles Darwin pioneered some aspects of the idea of evolution albeit by *'natural selection'*, wrote the following;

"I have lived with communities of savages in South America and in the East, who have no laws or law courts but the public opinion of the village freely expressed. Each man scrupulously respects the rights of his fellow, and any infraction of those rights rarely or never takes place. In such a community, all are nearly equal. There are none of those wide distinctions, of education and ignorance, wealth and poverty, master and servant, which are the product of our civilisation; there is none of that wide-

spread division of labour, which while it increases wealth, produces also conflicting interests; there is not that severe competition and struggle for existence, or for wealth, which the dense population of civilised countries inevitably creates. All incitements to great crimes are thus wanting, and petty ones are repressed, partly by the influence of public opinion, but chiefly by that natural sense of justice and of his neighbour's right, which seems to be, in some degree, inherent in every race of man." (A.F. Wallace. 'The Malay Archipelago'. 1869)

Despite the frequent prejudiced Victorian terms even used by 'educated' observers (Savages, Primitives, Inferior Races etc.), Wallace here clearly articulates a common experience expressed by many of those travellers and explorers. At least those who took the trouble to study and even befriend the native hunter-gatherer and pastoralist peoples of the various colonised continents of the 17th, 18th, 19th and 20th centuries. My purpose in utilising the above quotation and those which will follow in this section is not to create a fictitious 'golden past' for humanity in which all was perfect and without problems. It certainly wasn't. My purpose is merely to repeatedly demonstrate the crucially important point made above by Wallace (and myself) throughout this book, concerning hunter-gatherer social relationships that were both natural ones and also predominantly benign and supportive ones. Clearly, the consumption of (N) species that serve as nutrition and other useful material for other species, did not exceed the reproduction (R) of such species that function as such. It is this fact plus livable climatic conditions, which has allowed species of life to survive for millions and sometimes billions of years. An additional purpose of presenting these examples is to stress that the nature of internal and external community behaviour and conduct between individuals is linked directly or indirectly to the fundamental relationships established between nature and the particular mode of production. The form (or mode) of ensuring how the (N-M-G-R + A-D) requirements are met for each individual organism and grouping within species, is crucial. Thi is so because these are essential prerequisites to enable biological existence. Furthermore, how these are secured determines much else.

It is important to remember that the 17th, 18th and 19th century documents, used in this study, were compiled and written by members of the visiting and invading European settlers, consequently they contain frequently biased and contradictory observations. We need to keep in mind that the early settlers and observers were after all products of European bourgeois culture and were undertaking perilous sea journeys in order, in some way, to carve out a new and improved life for themselves. They were either running away from something (European poverty and religious oppression?) or running toward something (obtaining colonial wealth and freedom from oppression?). Both of these colonialist motives involved appropriating living organisms existing on fertile land and by seizing control of these exploitable resources and frequently denying them to local indigenous inhabitants. However, occasionally the overwhelming negative bias these settler motives created were dropped in favour of more balanced descriptions. Nevertheless, assumptions concerning the 'savage' nature of the Indians are continually contrasted in colonial era studies to the so-called 'civilised' condition of the invading Europeans and as such, those 'loaded' terms abound in such documents. Nevertheless, despite such violent and ignorant prejudice as the European settler trope in North America, *'the only good Indian is a dead one'*, a different picture can frequently emerge. It appears that until repeatedly cheated, dispossessed and provoked by aggressive settlers, native Indians we're generally dignified, peaceful and extremely helpful to the newcomers from Europe and elsewhere. For example;

"Every person who is well acquainted with the true character of the Indians will admit that they are peaceable, sociable, obliging, charitable and hospitable among themselves, and that those virtues are, as it were, a part of their nature. In their ordinary intercourse they are studious to oblige each other. They neither wrangle nor fight; they live, I believe, as peaceably together as any people on earth, and treat one another with the greatest respect...I do not mean to speak of those whose manners have been corrupted by long intercourse with the worst class of white men." ('History, Manners and Customs of the Indian Nations....' J. Heckwelder and W.C. Reichel. Pub Maids on & Adams Press. Chapter 44.)

It should be understood that the authors of the above book were evangelical Christians whose purpose as missionaries was to convert what they considered were native 'heathens' to their own particular 'enlightened' (and dogmatic!) form of Christianity. However, the fact that to do so they needed to understand and recognise the manners and customs of North America hunter-gatherer characters, prior to and post the main European invasion of that continent, has been of considerable historic value. It allows us to understand the general character of hunter-gatherer humanity prior to the 'planting' of hierarchical mass societies based on settled agriculture in the Americas, Africa, Australia and elsewhere. Indeed, such views are supported by other non - denominational, government sourced evidence and experience, so we can be sure they are founded on an extensively experienced reality rather than on a benign or hostile imagination. For example, a research group from the Bureau of Ethnology in Washington in a later century candidly declared;

"We have taken their land, blotted out their faith and despoiled their philosophy. It has been the utter extinction of a whole type of humanity." ('The Vanishing Race'. J. K. Dixon.)

It tends to be forgotten that savagely taking land and mass exterminating indigenous humanity existed before the 20th century hierarchical mass societies led by Hitler and Stalin, and which was also perpetrated in the 18th century by people led by Pilgrim Fathers, Catholic Priests, Protestant Pastors as well as capitalist funded private 'company' groups from European countries. (incidentally it was recorded in historical documents that the Quaker followers of William Penn deliberately gave disease infected blankets to local Indians to reduce their numbers by spreading European sourced diseases.). However, from the title of the above book and from much of its content, these authors had thoroughly (and uncritically) absorbed the European fiction that humanity was divided into distinct 'races' but at least some of them had not allowed this European inspired cultural distortion of the human species to completely blind themselves to observations of the everyday life of the indigenous hunter-gatherer peoples. Thus some went on to reason that;

"There are many cogent reasons for the belief that before the coming of the white man there were no general or long-continued wars among the Indians. There was no motive for war. Quarrels ensued when predatory tribes sought to filch women or horses. Strife was engendered on account of the distribution of buffalo, but these disturbances could not be dignified with the name of war. The country was large and the tribes widely separated." (ibid)

We need to note that in regard to the prior lack of motive for quarrels, the horse (and guns) were only introduced into the Americas by French and Spanish Europeans in the 17th century, so several centuries prior to that, given the vastness of the territory, there were even less reasons for indigenous inter tribal disputes to arise. It is also doubtful that 'filching' women by men was a normal hunter-gatherer characteristic because as a later sub-section of this chapter will indicate, adult females in most North American hunter-gatherer communities had an independent status in this regard and were able to choose who to personally and intimately relate to. Originally Indian women were free to choose who they teamed up with as the much later consensual partnership career of Pocahontas with a European colonial immigrant demonstrated. Furthermore, as will be also demonstrated, their peaceful and non-acquisitive way of life was a natural expression of their hunter-gatherer mode of existence. In a land of bountiful nutritious provisions and boundless territories, there was no need to steal or store what could be picked fresh or easily obtained every morning of each day, by anyone who was hungry or so inclined.

With no one owning land and the use of it freely available to all individuals and communities, even more extensive than the mediaeval 'commons' in European countries, there was no such thing as trespassing, just a mutual sharing of the vast available resources when they were required or needed. The very early contacts between Europeans and North American Native Peoples produced some interesting observations of European settlers by the indigenous hunter-gatherer peoples of North America. The few Europeans who bothered to listen and understand them frequently had their previous negative prejudices undermined by the example of North (and South) American Tribes and recorded the opinions of the particular tribe they had contact with. For example Father Pierre Biard in the early 17th century (who had been assigned to evangelise among a North American tribe in 1608) reported that a native spokesperson for the Mi'kmaq tribe in Nova Scotia said of the French occupiers;

"..*you are always fighting and quarrelling among yourselves; we live peaceably. You are envious and are all the time, slandering each other; you are thieves and deceivers; you are covetous, and are neither generous, nor kind; as for us, if we have a morsel of bread we share it with our neighbour.' (Quoted in 'The Dawn of Everything'; by D. Graeber and D. Wengrow. In the section on New France)*

A decade later than the earlier quoted Mi'kmaq opinion on the colonial settlers, a Friar; Brother Gabriel Sagard, visited a tribe of the Wendat nation and reported that;

'They have no lawsuits and take little pains to acquire the goods of this life, for which we Christians torment ourselves so much, and for our excessive and insatiable greed in acquiring them we are justly and with reason reproved by their quiet life and tranquil dispositions.' (ibid vanishing race.)

Some of the less biased early visitors to the North American continent consistently observed the different and more humane social attitudes of the native peoples to those of the European settlers who had 'settled' there to colonise, dispossess and disrupt the indigenous hunter-gatherer mode of production. Yet another colonialist racist assumption that was politicised and became 'normalised' is that Europeans have white skin, and the Indians red. This is another distortion of reality for in fact the general spectrum of skin tones of the many branches of humanity are pinkish, bronze and brown, not white, brown and black. The initial observation by North American hunter-gatherers, that Europeans were 'pale faces' was far more accurate than the European colonial racist characterisation of themselves as white and others as 'red' or 'black' meaning inferior and 'white' meaning superior races. Those distorted European dualist and racist ideological constructions, insinuated a contrast between 'clean' (white) and 'dirty' (black), or 'bloody' (red), when linked to words such as 'civilised and savage' in order to ignore natural temperature zone based morphological differences and replace them with prejudiced politicized categories.

Such terminology was manufactured precisely to justify the invasion, conquest and control of other lands and territories such as Africa, the Americas, Oceania and Asia. Humanity, of course, is not made up of different races, for humanity is one species with some regional climate based variations. Nor are human skins truly,coloured either black,or white. Human skin cells are of a common type, which produce various different dark and light pigments according to the predominant amount of sunlight to which they and their ancestors have been historically exposed. Because skin cells are comprised of living adaptable organelles, dark pigmented cells can become pale and pale pigmented cells can become dark when subject to different intensities or prolonged exposures to the energy of the sun. However, such knowledge was either unknown, ignored or purposefully suppressed for colonial expansionist reasons. This distortion of humanities species identity into high-status and low-status categories based upon false terminologies is a legacy that has still not been purged from European languages and thinking, which in many ways still reflects that colonialist and imperialist past rather than the actual biological reality.

Hunter- Gatherer; languages and culture.

The practical culture of the North American hunter-gatherer is broadly reflected in their ideas about the earth and the natural resources available from it. Thus, North American hunter-gatherer cultural thinking was recorded by researchers as containing the following views;

"...the earth and all that it contains for the common good of mankind; it was not for the benefit of a few, but of all. Everything was given in common to the sons of men. Whatever liveth on the land, whatsoever groweth out of the earth, and all that is in the rivers and waters flowing through the same, was given jointly to all, and everyone is entitled to his share. From this principle, hospitality flows as from its source. With them it is not a virtue but a strict duty." (History, Manners and Customs of the Indian Nations. etc. Chapter 4.)

The contrast between life on earth being a resource for the 'common good of mankind' and the current privatisation of land and water resources and the modern monopolisation and hoarding of essential materials for private capital gain, could not be more stark. Elite ownership and control of natural resources has become so ingrained within modern hierarchical mass societies that it is often assumed to be an instinctive characteristic within humanity. Nevertheless, the hunter-gatherer communities of the past and the occasional ones still in existence prove that it is not. As already noted, prior to hierarchical mass society formations, hoarding and privatising abundant free sources of nourishment was in many cases impossible and it made no logical or material sense when (N) resources grew rapidly, are widely available and are often also so perishable that if not consumed quickly they will rot. Leaving nourishment where it grew or lived until it was needed was (and is) an obvious and sensible course of action for an intelligent being living directly from nature. Prior to hierarchical mass societies, animal and human life and evolution were not processes based upon private ownership of anything, least of all ownership of natural resources. Usage of nature by all organic beings is an essential condition of life on earth, but ownership and control of natural resources including the multifarious species within the biosphere is purely a relatively recent human social invention and an anthropocentric form of narcissistic self-delusion.

Personal ownership and control of anything can only be exercised for a set number of years, before death, robbery or social confiscation removes the illusion. The idea of owning and controlling a part of the planet or nature is an anthropocentric inversion of reality, turning the real world into a virtual world. Step out of that virtual reality narcissistic paradigm and it is more accurate to consider that nature and the planet controls human individuals. Hurricane's, floods, tsunami's, volcanic eruptions, forest and prairie fires, extra-terrestrial asteroid visitations, mass transportation disasters, viral epidemics and pandemics, render ownership and control of life and property as intellectual self-delusions. They daily and yearly now demonstrate the reality of how fragile and tenuous is the real and intellectual understanding of even the most sophisticated academics and real estate lawyers of our modern hierarchical mass society aggregations. In the area of anthropological studies, evidence rather than prejudiced opinion indicates that it was the direct and beneficial day to day individual and social experience of hunter-gatherer humans with each other and the living organisms of nature that also gave rise to their corresponding cultural norms and ideas of sharing, hospitality, generosity, sociability and peacefulness. In the case of the North American First Peoples, their spoken language reflected a completely different outlook on nature and 'life on earth' than that displayed by the original European colonial invaders. It was recorded by 19th century researchers that;

"In the Indian languages, those discriminating words or inflections which we call genders, are not, as with us, in general, intended to distinguish between male and female beings, but between animate and inanimate things or substances. Trees and plants (annual plants and grasses excepted) are included within the generic class of animated beings." (History, Manners and Customs of the Indian Nations.' Heckweider and Reichel. Appendix ; 'Letters'.)

Evidence from customs and manners of the North American Indian hunter gatherers in general indicate that it was a common understanding that the earth was made for all beings as well as all human beings; that everything was provided in common and everyone was entitled to a share of nature's supply of organic and inorganic nourishment. Consequently, hospitality to other human beings was not simply a virtue signalling gesture but a normal everyday practice and a life-long reciprocal human courtesy or duty. How the Delaware tribal elders viewed their own social history and the effects upon it of the process of European settlement in North America, was recorded by a participant at a 'treaty meeting' in Easton, Northampton County, Pennsylvania in 1756. He recorded the First Nation Indians as saying;

"We and our kindred tribes", they say, "lived in peace and harmony with each other before the white people came into this country; our council house extended far to the north and far to the south. In the middle of it we would meet from all parts to smoke the pipe of peace together. When the white men arrived in the south, we received them as friends; we did the same when they arrived in the east. It was we, it was our forefathers, who

made them welcome, and let them sit down by our side. The land they settled on was ours. We knew not but the Great Spirit had sent them to us for some good purpose, and therefore we thought they must be a good people. We were mistaken; for no sooner had they obtained a footing on our lands, than they began to pull our council house down, first at one end and then at the other....we were compelled to withdraw ourselves beyond the great swamp.....The whites will not rest contented until they shall have destroyed the last of us, and make us disappear entirely from the face of the earth." (ibid Chapter 3.)

It is clear from ample anthropological, oral and written evidence that hunter - gatherer groups operating in locations of abundance did not need to work at producing food and water for more than an hour or two per day. As already noted, gathering enough fruits, leaves, nuts, tubers, water etc., already abundantly produced by nature, if not located too far away, was not a lengthy logistical task. Hunting may or may not have taken much longer depending upon abundance of game or success in trapping, spearing or netting. However, even when hunting or trapping was not successful the vegetable foodstuffs gathered would generally be sufficient to fulfil the nutritional (N) requirements of the entire community. The anthropologically obtained and recorded range of time spent in food production for hunter-gatherers globally, is from under an hour per day for some and up to half a day for others, depending upon distance and community size. It is also clear from research evidence that for this mode of production there need be no exact start or finish times for gathering or hunting. Strict time-keeping and 'clocking on and off' are modern introductions to living based upon an hourly unit of exploitation of human and animal labour. In contrast, invariably hunter-gatherer communities decided by common assent when they were ready to set off to gather and hunt and when to finish.

Consequently, in such communities there was no necessity for regulating or setting aside a rigid time for production or a set time for rest and recreation. In normal periods, the hunter-gatherer life cycle of (N-M-G-R + A-D) generally proceeded at a community determined rhythm and pace. The quantity of food obtained was also decided by the group and determined roughly by the number of members of the group. The adult community also decided or confirmed individual suggestions when, where and whether to move on to another geographical location or food source. In other words, the anticipated needs of the community determined the level of, and what kind of essential production or recreational activities took place. They decided when, how, where, what, how much and how long they gathered or hunted. Furthermore, and this is a crucially important difference from modernity; they all directly touched, saw and engaged daily with what they were gathering and hunting, including observing the effects this food (N) securing process had on the immediate environment and on any other (N) source species. Non-food production and entertainment was similarly, individually or collectively produced and non-standard in its results. In general this way of living around the various regions and continents, in good times as well as bad, was relatively easy going, mutually supportive, flexible and intimately understood. Since hunting and gathering was the foundation of their (N-M-G-R +A-D) existence, 'naturally' the hunter-gatherer way of thinking reflected this relaxed and egalitarian mode of Nutritional (N) production.

In general, with the exceptions of special gatherings and celebrations, there was no form of stockpiling and monopolising nutritional and other useful resources – it made no sense. There was also no need to tolerate any aggressive or controlling behaviour should any individual within the group (or in another group) develop such anti-social attitudes. The remedy to any such persistent negative behaviour that gentle group peer pressure could not alter, was simply to move away. Re-locating elsewhere, singly or as a sub-group, had no official barriers or impediments to overcome and joining other bands or groups of humans was only a matter of appropriate and meaningful negotiation. It was frequently assumed by early researchers that men being predominantly the hunter in these communities would mean that men would always have more status than women because meat was more valued than vegetables, nuts and fruits. However, this assumption was just the general imposition of a later European male sexist and dietary prejudice upon various global hunter-gatherer peoples. This opinion has been thoroughly discredited in more modern times. Thus on dismissing the assumption of modern meat based dietary preferences, we can read that;

"Evidence from hunter-gatherers contradicts these assumptions. The Batek, for example, do not prefer meat over all other foods; they usually mention fruit as the favoured food of both humans and spirit beings. Women's hunting in many hunter-gatherer societies undercuts the idea that men have a monopoly on meat....Even where people admire successful hunters, people usually undermine any hunter's attempt to exert power over others." ('The Cambridge Encyclopedia of Hunters and Gatherers. Carol L Endicott. Page 414.)

Such previous modern patrifocal assumptions also fail to recognise the tremendous social influence given to the human female within human groups due to their reproductive role in bearing offspring and during the process of infant nurturing of the next generation of the community.

Male and female relationships.

I have not yet been able to uncover a great deal of information concerning how Native American Women in general were treated before the revolutionary conflict between the early American colonists and the British Government took place. However, it is noted in Volume 1 of a book already referenced that in one tribe, the Chinooks, that;

"The women are admitted to a greater degree of equality with the men, than among the other American tribes, because in fishing and in managing the canoe, they are equally expert, and as they share all the toils and dangers of the other sex, they naturally become the companions and equals, and in virtue of their superior industry, the better halves, of their lords and masters. In the savage state, where the employments of the men are confined to war and hunting, a certain degree of contempt attaches to the weaker sex, who are unfit for such rude toils and a timid or imbecile man is, in derision, compared to a woman. But a different relation exists between the sexes, where the employments are such that both engage in them alike, and where both contribute equally to the support of their families." ('History, Manners and Customs of the Indian Nations. Heckweider and Reichel. Volume 1 page 238)

Despite their best efforts at recording aspects of indigenous people's reality, the author's patriarchal assumptions and prejudices still filter through these and many other such reports. The terms 'lords and masters'; 'savage state' and 'weaker sex', demonstrate this deeply ingrained European prejudice. And of course, some of these observations were being made after a generation or two of the pernicious influence of the European way of conquering, exploiting, doing business and mistreating indigenous people. However, without such records, the historical glimpses we get of alternative ways of living and being would remain even more limited and distorted, than they are. So we can, from the available evidence, deduce that the general relationships between male and female genders was similarly socially benign across most hunter-gatherer peoples. Indeed, the importance of the female as partner and 'mother' among hunter-gatherer communities is understandable and undeniable and it still lingers on in muted form among modern societies.

There was also a consistent practice among many hunter-gatherer communities (male and female) of gentle ribbing, raising eyebrows, shaking of heads and even a pertinent nicknaming of any individual who was prone to asserting more individual social value than the community thought he or she was entitled to. There is a recorded example in the historical records of an individual community member of one First Nation tribe who had repeatedly violated the normal level of civility when entering a circle of community members to take the opportunity to boast. No one openly objected or caused a fuss but silently members of the community one by one left the circle until the offender was left alone. Such non-violent social 'reproaches' were frequently enough to either reform the behaviour or even prevent it from being copied by others. In relationship to gender interactions the following observer evidence from North American hunter-gatherers is also typical for the hunter-gatherer way of living.

"...women are not obliged to live with their husbands any longer than suits their pleasure or convenience. It cannot be supposed that they would submit to be loaded with unjust or unequal burdens. Marriages among the Indians are not as with us, contracted for life; it is understood on both sides that the parties are not to live together any longer than they be pleased with each other. The husband may put away his wife whenever

he pleases, and the woman may in like manner abandon her husband." (ibid, Manners and Customs. chapter 16.)

In other words individual adults of either gender were free from any external permanent or semi-permanent 'bond' within personal relationships. There was no 'official' marriage contract of any kind socially regulated and enforced by the community. This did not prevent some early European investigators assuming that women in such communities must be bound by some form of marriage contract in order to be allowed to be sexually active and selective about it. Lewis Morgan, so admired by Frederick Engels, invented a fictitious category called 'The Consanguine Family' to discount the fact that sexual relations in such societies were open between generations and even family relatives and were in fact self-determined choices. The bizarre patriarchal conclusion Morgan made was that every generation in such communities, despite geographical and cultural distance, were automatically considered to be in permanent marriage groups to each other. The unacknowledged implication being that all the tribes' (or communities) grandfathers and grandmothers were husbands and wives to each other and that all brothers and sisters (and cousins) are automatically husbands and wives to each other. These patriarchal minded European men could not accept or process the fact that in early human societies, as in many animal and primate species, if two genders were in close contact and both felt so inclined, they could simply get together to cuddle, play chat and even mate.

Like all sexually reproducing animal species it wouldn't necessarily matter what their age difference was or whose family they were biologically part of. Non-domesticated animals then and now and early humans in pre-history and outside of hierarchical mass societies would simply consent to be intimate and mate for reasons of proximity and pleasure. However, such possible and projected levels of 'promiscuity' could not be accepted as part of the natural human evolution by such Christian gentlemen observers as Morgan et al. Therefore general (and non-existent) marriage agreements had to be invented to give the appearance of exercising some 'decent' European religiously informed social 'controls' to intimacy and tactile interactions. This was a widespread assumption. An associate of Karl Marx,

Fredrik Engels went on in his book ('The Origin of the Family etc.) to cite the example of a native Australian aborigine who could travel hundreds of miles into territory of groups who had been so long separated that they spoke a different language, but were also assumed by Engels to be part of a vast marriage group.

The unarticulated assumption being that any long distance travelling male aborigine, therefore may not understand the language or customs of a distant group he encountered, but Engels asserted that sexual activity could be morally pursued by any of the distant tribal women when the stranger arrived. This would occur, not because of mutual attraction and because they clearly had the desire and independent choice to do so, but because they were considered to automatically be his extended group of tribal 'wives'. In this way an entirely fictitious *'marriage'* group was invented to fit in with ancient Abrahamic religious sensibilities. Yet the facts, concerning animal and human mating, (until restrictions are placed upon them), are that they, like all other intra-species interactions, are freely chosen. In fact even 'incestuous' brother and sister and parent and child mating's were once commonplace in North America, Chile, the Caribbean' Islands and Burma. Furthermore, such relationships were known to exist in the time of the Greeks, Romans and also appear in the folk lore of biblical authors and also in ancient Parthia, Persia and Germany.

This non-monogamous practice in regard to gender intimacy and sexual relationships was similar to the ones practised among the hunter-gatherer tribes on the African continent. For example, the Hadza tribe in central Africa had similar informal female/male partner relationships, although in this latter case the Hadza tribe was Matrifocal (women were more socially decisive and influential than men) and also matrilineal (children were identified by their mothers biological connection) rather than Patrifocal and patrilineal following the fathers biological connection. On mutual agreement to partner, Hadza men went to live with their wives and her mother and kin. Furthermore if the male partners did not treat the women respectfully or fulfil their expected nutritional and social contributions they would be told to go and live somewhere else. It is in regard to such pre-agricultural naturally acquired gender and sexual relationships within humanity that we identify in the next chapter, a radical and substantial change in the status of women occurring. It was a change which introduced a lower social status to our female partners both as mothers and as life partners that, as we shall see, occurred along with a radical change in the mode of production.

However, in this chapter we need merely to identify sufficient evidence to establish what the general patterns of social interactions were between members of the hunter-gatherer communities and how they also related to the organic life forms that were part of their nutritional (N) requirements. Relationships were mutually supportive, respectful, and considerate with regard to all community members whether men, women or children, young or old. Indeed, the old were honoured as embodying the accumulated knowledge and wisdom essential to hunter-gatherer life. Children were generally cherished for their actual existence and as the future continuity of the community within which they lived. Once studied, we can begin to understand from the detail of what took place within hunter-gatherer humanity the general human and humane 'essence' of pre-agricultural based communities. Securing Nourishment, Metabolism, Growth and Reproduction, (N-M-G-R + A-D.) was an act of socialized activity and the human relationships between each other and 'nature' was largely determined by the essence of the subsistence level of gathering and hunting by means of the hunter-gatherer social mode of production itself.

From modern genetic understandings, as well as long held historical knowledge it is a fact that every male and female has normally to be incubated in the womb of a female and to have fundamental elements of their DNA passed to them by the male and female of our species. We also know that even outstanding individuals among our modern societies have only become outstanding because they themselves have been supported by and rely upon the past efforts of their families and the many citizens who came before them. No one can become talented at any specialised activity if it were not for the efforts of those who still labour away at the mundane essential everyday tasks of supplying and assuring the modern (N-M-G-R + A-D) necessities of living. Any exceptionally able individual in any one type of activity can also only become so if someone else has initially guided them and if other members of the community are growing their food, making their clothes, building their dwellings, crafting their tools, teaching them etc., This extreme division of labour in mass societies then frees some other privileged people to develop their skills and understanding in a particular direction - beyond what could be achieved without this continual community support. Such social dependence and interdependence may be ignored or rationalised away in favour of gullibly celebrating individual celebrities, within modern societies, but it cannot be dispensed with in reality. Even modern off-the-beaten track, small scale alternative intentional communities, are dependent upon unpolluted air, clean water and food as well as other people for various forms of previous training, tools, artefacts, education, culture and current mutual support.

Hunter-gatherer attitudes to other life forms.

A section of the North American continent once referred to as 'New France' in archive documents along with 'New Amsterdam' etc., indicates in one or two words what was really going on in terms of permanently taking away the source of nourishment etc., from all those life forms already living on these North American continental tracts of land. Such European sourced place names grafted onto the places and spaces on the North American continent denote the absolute scale of the dispossession of the North American hunter-gatherer peoples by the European colonial powers of that period. It is now common knowledge that not only were native peoples massacred and later herded onto 'reservations' like animals, but that million strong Buffalo herds of vital hunter-gatherer nutrition needed for the Plains Indians (N-M-G-R + A-D) processes, were wiped out by the paid 'per-head' or paid 'per-scalp' for native Indians, by itinerant 'Buffalo Bills' employed by the invading colonists. In terms of the nutrition (N) of many plains Indians at the time, it is recorded that;

"The animal furnished food and clothing, and many parts of the stalwart frame they counted as sacred;......"Within the nine years between 1874 and 1883 over eight millions of buffalo were ruthlessly slain" (The vanishing etc.)

At this point we can consider the question of how hunter-gatherers viewed other life forms they encountered on a daily basis. Evidence suggests that hunter-gatherer groups kept lots of animal pets and that in some cases lactating females even allowed some motherless animals to suckle at their own breasts so the animal would survive. Even those native peoples, who consistently hunted and killed animals did not kill them in huge numbers even if technically this was possible for them. As with the gathering of nutrition, hunting for it was done predominantly for immediate or short term subsistence nutrition. The historical record also indicates that they did not hunt or kill without according to the animals some dignity and indeed, the species they routinely hunted frequently held a special place in their understanding of nature. Where hunter-gatherer groups adopted animals as their group identity badges or totems, that animal was not simply respected as were all other animals, but revered and thus was not to be deliberately harmed in any way. Even among very skilful hunter-gatherers, the simple fact of not being able to carry or effectively preserve lots of dead animals ensured that a limited number of animal lives were actually ended daily in this way. Such 'natural' frugality was the general case whether hunter-gatherer groups were following and hunting wild herds such as Bison, Wildebeest or Reindeer, etc., or trapping other animals.

Available evidence suggests that hunter-gatherer people viewed themselves and other such groups as just one distinct species in a world consisting of other distinct species each with their own place and importance in the overall cycle of life. Moreover, recognising that they, as with all other species, were at the mercy of natural forces, such as wind, rain, floods and seismic events (volcanoes and earthquakes), they often presumed these other 'animated' beings were also manifestations of some invisible primal life force, common to all living things. Inorganic forces of nature beyond their understanding and their ability to control or often even to resist were still treated with respect if not reverence. For example, in the Northern territories of Australia, the Wik-Mungkan hunter-gatherers believed that spirits frequented certain places, particularly where they suggest the Yams they frequently eat originated, in order to keep these sources of nutrition free from salt water. Such special places were called awa or auwa, and;

"There is always water nearby in the shape of river, creek, lagoon, water-hole, swamp or well at the bottom of which the pulwalya (totemic being) resides and into which the dead of the clan are believed to go. This is perhaps why the killing of an animal or the injuring of a plant near its auwa is not only strictly forbidden but believed to be attended by grave consequences". *('Farmers or Hunter-Gatherers; The Dark Emu Debate.' P. Sutton & K. Walshe. Page 584)*

In contrast to the ideas promoted within settled mass societies, where such natural forces were attributed to gods and spirits on mountains or in heavens, that needed to be placated by prayers and subservience, hunter-gatherers revered the actual life-giving nature of their sources of nourishment directly. This led to the practice of other organic resource 'beings' not being unnecessarily disturbed. Based upon their direct experience of nature in the process of living in direct contact with life on earth in general, the differences between themselves as hunter-gatherers and other species of life, was considered an important, but not a fundamentally opposed difference. In many ways it was not a relationship based upon a subject (the human) and an object (the non-human); but on subject and subject. Thus the commonly encountered language among hunter-gatherers by researchers such as 'river-ing', for describing the active movement of rivers or 'hilling' for the formation of hills. The idea that many inorganic things were not actually static and in their unmovable form, but changing, developing and dependent on other forces or life-activating processes, was something that predated the static dualistic method of thinking which emerged under different more static socio-economic circumstances.

The idea of fixed entities and categories which were separate, static, finished, and opposed to others eventually only emerged in sophisticated philosophical form with the speculations of ancient Middle Eastern intellectuals particularly within the agricultural based hierarchical mass societies of Suma and Greece. As will be described in the next chapter, the use of slave and other unfree labour to produce agricultural and pastoral forms of Nourishment (N) by this period, allowed a section of the elite to not only specialise in warfare and conquest, but another section was enabled to sit, think and discuss their understanding of the meaning of life, while others (often slaves) planted, reaped, baked their bread, cleaned elite clothes and homes. A study of ancient philosophical history suggests that it was the intermingling of such economically 'unburdened' elite groups which pioneered philosophy, literature, drama and history and other such predominantly intellectual pastimes and pursuits. A shared ideological elite perspective concerning mass society formations quickly followed. This radically new milieu produced particularly short-sighted, self-serving anthropocentric methods of thinking about the world and its contents. It started a trend among a class unburdened by the need to provide their own basic essentials to keep themselves alive and so were able to pursue whatever interested them, including thinking about thinking (i.e. philosophy). It is an elite phenomenon which continued and continues to dominate elite thinking within the modern bourgeois mode of production. With all of the basic survival necessities, of water, food, shelter, protection provided for these classes 24/7, by slaves, bondsmen. or later wage-slaves. Those supported in this way, can become 'expert' at practically anything - including making imaginative conclusions sound like truths and dress fictions up as carefully considered facts.

Consequently, it is clear that such types of dualistic and hierarchical assumptions about life on earth did not emerge from within a hunter-gatherer mode of existence. Furthermore, it should not be imagined that such hunter-gatherer communities were completely isolated from each other. The Australian aborigine concept of going 'walk about' also existed in North America and probably Asia from evidence found among archaeological excavations. And again, as noted from an earlier quote, there is ample evidence that a separation and then amalgamation of large numbers of individuals for any number of reasons occurred frequently and even routinely at larger tribal gatherings. Indeed, among some North American plains Indians, treks of hundreds of miles and absences of years for individuals and sub-groups before either returning or staying away and permanently joining another group. The hunter-gatherer mode of production had no fixed economic or territorial barriers within it or between groups, and the skills needed were in most cases sufficiently transferable from one region to another. Since all group members except the ill, the very young and the very old, had direct capacity and direct responsibility for their own contribution to socially acquired nutritional needs, the loss of group members to another group may have had an emotional or social element of loss to it, but no serious reduction of vital economic production of (N) for metabolic purposes occurred, by tribal fluctuations.

Hunter-gatherer representation.

With regard to decision making which involved the group or tribe, decisions were generally made by consensus and not by individuals or a minority. They would hold consultations and;

"These consultations are conducted with great decorum, yet are characterised by the utmost freedom of debate; every individual, whose age and standing are such as to allow him, with propriety, to speak in public, giving his opinion. A sagacious head man, however, is careful to preserve his popularity by respecting the opinion of the tribe at large, or, as we should term it, the people; and for that purpose, ascertains beforehand, the wishes of the mass of his followers." (ibid Volume 1 page 189)

The case of Little Bow and a small band which left the Omaha's tribe because of the cruelty and despotism of the chief Washinggusaba, exemplifies the humane avoidance of serious conflict, as this was entirely possible. Simply moving away met no restrictions. A record of this protracted situation is also provided by the authors in the above noted Volume 1 of History and Manners. Little Bow only returned to his original tribe after Washinggusaba had died. This was not the only instance of such low level internal problems and their non-violent solutions. The case of how Shingaba W' Ossin of the Chippewa tribe became accepted as a chief after much community dissension over who should become chief, is described as follows.

"He secured the respect and confidence of his band and was at last acknowledged as the Nittum, or first man. His band became more and more attached to him, until, on all hands, the choice was admitted to be well ordered, and that he upon whom it had fallen, merited the distinction. Having secured the general

confidence, he counselled his charge in all their trials, and enabled them to overcome many difficulties, whilst by his kindness and general benevolence of character, he made himself beloved." ('History, Manners and Customs of the Indian Nations'. *Heckweider and Reichel. Volume 1 page 230)*

The above extract, and many other examples, indicates that the frequent categorising of hunter-gatherer Indian Chiefs, as being the equivalent of 'kings', 'military commanders' or 'hereditary princes', was utterly false in general. This frequent retrospective habit of applying later categories to earlier periods also occurs with regard to long dead human groups. It assumes that what was prevalent in medieval or modern history was also prevalent in the ancient past. In actual fact within the broad spectrum of hunter-gatherer societies there is no evidence of a separation between the (N-M-G-R + A-D) processes of living and the decision-making process for any aspect of tribal affairs. The community consulting collectively decided what to do and the community did it. The modern, now taken for granted separation between those involved in economic activity (i.e. every practical thing to do with fulfilling N-M-G-R + A-D processes) and political activity (controlling when, where and how that economic activity took place), did not exist in the form of two or more classes, within hunter-gatherer communities. These pre-agricultural settled and nomadic communities were generally self-governing, egalitarian communities, for many thousands of years of human evolution.

Consequently, at this point it is worth mentioning and dismissing what I call the 'Great Man' view of history. Until the 20th century, the view that humanity always has had and always needed 'great' men to guide or rescue it, dominated history. This view was largely unchallenged in my youth and adulthood and still remains dominant within all disciplines of science, history, technology, literature, philosophy, politics and art. For a short period, the 20th century wave of western Feminism, made something of an impact upon the male-centred view of the world and its patriarchal assumptions concerning human history. However, it was not enough of an impact to topple the idea of the continuing necessity for elites and for male governance from its own self-congratulatory and largely imaginary pedestal.

However, the flaws and dangers of this 'great man' perspective where it is adopted, if not obvious enough in the 21st century by the actions of Boris Johnson, Donald Trump, Elon Musk and Joe Biden, even more examples will be revealed and considered in the following chapter.

Ideas, which arise from the mediated experience of certain periods, can take root in cultures to such an extent that they become accepted by members of these cultures as general 'laws' existing 'naturally' or as established truths inherited from ancient origins. Such is the idea of male aggression and social domination along with the associated idea that humanity needs 'Great Men" as leaders, so the best the rest of us can do is to simply become loyal and obedient followers. Once critically examined the historical outcome of following Alexander, Fredrick or Catherine the 'great', was far from great and was never beneficial for ordinary people or 'their' soldiers, they frequently recklessly and carelessly deployed. It didn't do a lot of good for the majority of the ordinary followers of the 'Great men; Napoleon Bonaparte, Mussolini, Hitler and Stalin either. More recent political and social research indicates that ordinary people have rarely benefited substantially from the leadership of Putin, Trump, Boris Johnson or Rishi Sunak in the 21st century either. In the UK giving working people some of their tax payments back in the form of Covid assistance grants did not alter the fact that money (or value) was provided by them in the first place. Moreover, the value of the national product was used by politicians to pay themselves as much as they personally thought was appropriate. Hopefully, this study will assist in undermining such patriarchal narratives and wean more people off this debilitating and self-defeating ideology that we need a great man (or even an occasional great woman) to lead us out of the perennial mess that other so-called 'great' (or lesser) men and women have led humanity into.

We have already noted, from previous chapters, that the entire evolutionary existence of life on earth along with the human species has rested not upon 'Great Men' or Great Women, for that matter, but upon a vast foundation of minute cellular life forms, micro-biota, photo-synthetic organisms and multiple organic life forms. As much as it irritates or embarrasses some people to be reminded of their absolute reliance upon the ordinary microscopic organisms of life on earth - including the absolute reliance of everyone in every hierarchical mass society upon slaves and wage-slave working people since the formation of hierarchical mass society formations – this reliance is a fact which can be ignored but not denied. The efforts of the masses of organisms, whether in the form of cells, trees, grasses, leaves, insects, animals or working people, have underwritten all the individual and collective practical and intellectual efforts of humanity since the human species evolved from a distant hominid form.

There certainly were individuals among the 17th, 18th, 19th and 20th century hunter-gatherer peoples, who played significant roles, but they never forgot and were never allowed to forget their absolute reliance upon the community and upon nature as a whole. Moreover, if they ever did forget it, as noted earlier, they were quickly reminded of their actual place. Consequently, it would seem from the evidence gathered so far that the first human hunter-gatherer communities nominated individual members of their group with specific skill sets and/or abilities to facilitate particular aspects of communal life or events, but only for the duration of these particular aspects and only for as long as these aspects needed to have particular attention. Thus important events such as; formal negotiations with other groups; the seasonal moving of camp; the organisation of large projects; the settlement of internal disputes; defence of the community if threatened or attacked. The roles these chiefs or heads etc., that they fulfilled could be combined and even change hands. Some leadership roles occasionally did indeed become hereditary but usually only if the abilities of the sons or daughters were sufficiently similar to their parents to maintain confidence in them. Enough evidence exists in the case of North American native peoples, that a leader was merely an effective 'facilitator' of specific or general group activities and was only tolerated as long as the community were satisfied with the results and the manner of achieving them. They did not control the community, as modern elites do, they could only influence the community by the validity of their reasoning.

Within Hunter-Gatherer communities both evidence and logic suggests that a person chosen for a leadership role (whatever title was used) would not be chosen if they were incompetent or would be demoted immediately if they became so. Furthermore, the community as a whole determined - by consensus - the social norms and practices of the band or tribe. The Chiefs role was therefore to uphold these collectively agreed norms in pursuit of the particular activities or events being sustained or developed. Even in the 18th and 19th centuries the contact between European settlers and preachers confirmed this pattern of Hunter-Gatherer economic and social life. Very few examples deviated from that norm. The idea of permanent chiefs who make laws and/or enforce them ruthlessly only began to occur in North America after Europeans invaded and disrupted the natural hunter-gatherer process of (N-M-G-R + A-D). In the US archives there is documentary evidence that once tribes had been subdued by the American armed forces, the American government officials would decide to only negotiate with members of the tribe they personally chose, not with the ones chosen by the tribe. In such cases, the tribal self-determination over who would speak for them was ended alongside the loss of their self-determination over the land and resources they had lived upon for generations.

It needs to be remembered that during the first phase of colonisation, the French, British and Spanish governments supported home grown Merchant company enterprises which were initiated in Europe and became active in the North and South American continents as well as in Africa. Once established in these New Worlds, British, French and Spanish representatives recruited many Indian and African fighters to fight on their side of the 'European' conquest of the 'Dark Continent' or of the 'New World' as the two continents were often called. By conquest and displacement, they disturbed indigenous ways of living and influenced them in many ways, particularly clearing them away from useful resources and diverting them with the distractions of religion and alcohol consumption. They also influenced and encouraged them to adopt the most savage behaviour to those they fought against. All that influencing and controlling behavior occurred before the colonists eventually turned against the indigenous hunter-gatherer societies on both continents. In reflecting upon the socio-economic realities of modernity and even the contemporary compromised versions of hunter-gatherer societies, one modern researcher had been clearly impressed by his experiences in studying existing hunter-gatherer communities. Despite the unhistorical use of a judgemental collective 'we' this researcher felt sufficiently moved to write the following:

"What we left behind when we abandoned our evolutionary heritage to form chiefdoms, city states, nations and empires was a situation in which you had total equality and an equal right to life for everyone and, paradoxically, a profound respect for the individual and his or her merits." ('The Reality of Hunter-Gatherers' J.A. Hefferman. Introduction)

However, there is archaeological evidence that two forms of mass societies existed around the period in which the hierarchical ones began their careers of genocide against other communities. There is also evidence that in the northern region of Mesopotamian area small and large egalitarian settlements, such as Brak prevailed, whilst in the southern region communities based in Uruk, for example, were distinctly hierarchical. Elsewhere, the Indus valley settlements of the Harappan peoples considered by CK Maisals (in 'Early civilisations of the Old World') revealed no evidence of individual dominance or extremes of wealth and power. As yet I think there is insufficient evidence to accurately consider the numerous possibilities of intermediate or transitional forms between egalitarian hunter-gatherer and pastoral communities and the eventual agriculturally based hierarchical mass society forms which began eventually to dominate the entire Middle East region by utilising the force of arms and then eventually the entire world. The following chapter will therefore consider historical evidence on the early establishment of the above-mentioned city states, empires and nations in the middle east or as I prefer to call them - hierarchical mass societies. This will be done in order to understand how this latter mode of social production radically affected the (N-M-G-R + A-D) processes of humanity. In particular it will describe what effect this change had on the relations between human community members and between communities and the rest of life on earth. The evidence presented there will be in the form of written extracts from the records of many individuals who had both direct and indirect experience of living within them.

Chapter 8 Summary.

It was established in the 48 paragraphs and 20 quotations within this chapter that securing the necessary human (N-M-G-R + A-D) processes by Hunting and Gathering, was rarely a serious problem for human communities as they moved across the habitable world. During those thousands of years, human languages and cultures became more sophisticated and varied, until they could not be immediately or fully understood by anyone, who had not been born or become integrated into each separate language community. For a similar length of time the relationships between male and female were definitely not patriarchal. Men did not dominate women, either, socially, economically or sexually and women were not dependent upon men for nutrition (N) or habitation. Within human groups relationships were characterised as being various forms of matrifocal and matrilineal associations, with males and all offspring relating to the female group for their biological and social identity. Pairing was invariably a voluntary relationship and could be easily dissolved by either partner.

The anthropological evidence considered for this study, suggested that left to their own devices, hunter-gatherer communities rarely had anything to seriously fight about and any disputes were settled by reconciliation or if this failed by individuals or sub-groups simply moving elsewhere. This intrinsic respect for the other human being and for each other, whether known or unknown, was replicated with regard to other species of life also. A living and growing entity had active significance and was highly regarded because of that fact. Even the regular 'hunters' among the 'gatherers' only hunted and killed what they needed, whilst recognising and respecting the importance of the animated status of the life they sought to kill. This respect amongst themselves was reflected in the fact that their representatives in social or other affairs were chosen by adult group consensus on the basis of competence for the task required and the individual removed if competence proved lacking.

CHAPTER 9

HIERARCHICAL MASS SOCIETIES.
Their structure and function.
This chapter will consider the structure and function of hierarchical mass societies as they originated in the early centuries 'Before the Common Era' (BCE). It will also provide evidence to show that despite huge changes in the modern technology of production and transport, in essence the modern versions of hierarchical mass societies retain the same basic socio-economic structure, purpose and function in the 21st century as they did when they were first established in settled social forms of human living. Despite their complexity and diversity, that primary purpose and function is to ensure the production of sufficient sources of nutrition (N) are available to satisfy the immediate (N-M-G-R + A-D) biological process needs of all (or at least a sizable majority) of members of them. In addition to that requirement, they are intended to function in such a way that they provide the extra material incentives and desires that are required and demanded by the hierarchical elite strata. Furthermore, the growing climatic and ecological awareness of many people in the 20th and 21st centuries and the desire by others to avoid linking the implications of relative poverty, negative climate changes, increasing species losses and growing ecological imbalance, to the so-called progress of 'civilisation', I consider it is necessary to produce a considerable amount of documented evidence. A large amount of evidence will be necessary in order to substantiate a negative appraisal of the entire history of the hierarchical mass society form of human aggregation, not just its latest manifestation under the domination of capitalism. As a consequence of this need to demonstrate the self-destructive and eco-destructive essence of all hierarchical mass society forms, this chapter of necessity will be a very long one. However, I have also split it into several sections so that the reader can tackle each section separately.

A. Introduction.

The first part of this chapter will deal with the general social structure of hierarchical mass society modes of production. It is important in this regard, to understand their basic occupational divisions of labour and also their class or caste divisions of social control, influence and also of differential affluence. Secondly, this chapter will address the self-interested nature of the bourgeois inclined perspective regarding the modern history of hierarchical mass society formations. Although a relatively recent development, the bourgeois capitalist era and their perspective on history is one that links ancient history to the 19th century socio-economic structure, based upon the modern capitalist mode of production.The technical mode of production has changed radically over time, but the class based hierarchical social structure of a ruling class, an administrative class and a large laboring or working class has been retained, throughout such technical changes The intellectual link between ancient and modern settled societies is made by means of two dubious concepts. The first is the anthropocentric concept of 'civilisation', which is positively contrasted to everything human that came before it, the latter being classed as barbaric. The second anthropocentric concept is that of 'progress'. Thus the bourgeois form of hierarchical mass society is conceived by its supporters as the continuity and logical progression of ancient hierarchical mass societies (designated as early 'civilisations') that having passed through the supposedly medieval 'dark ages', have moved on into the so-called modern 'enlightenment' civilisation's. Bourgeois era historians, looking back from the alleged heights of industrialised capitalism with its world market and nation-state organised societies, European elites along with 'their' paid educators and academics have looked for and found many links between the classical states of Greece and Rome and those of modern cities and countries. For example, the anciently formed mass society elites and their modern bourgeois counterparts had the following shared characteristics; a high social status, considerable power, wealth, ambition. They also had the means to dominate and exploit their own communities as well as other smaller and weaker societies. Thus the British, the German, the French, the Spanish, and the Russian feudal and post-feudal 18th

and 19th century empire-building projects, all had the ancient Greek and Roman Empires, as reference points for ambitious and flattering comparisons with themselves. Stealing (or copying), Greek and Roman statues, artwork, literature and large parts of their crumbling civic buildings, became something of an obsession and collectors hobby for 18th and 19th century European elites.

Most, if not all bourgeois and petite-bourgeois situated historians, had concluded that these earlier Greek and Roman forms of city-states and subsequent 'empires' were the true beginnings of what they invariably portrayed as an evolutionary struggle of 'enlightened' elites who were leading humanity forward out of ancient 'backwardness' and 'darkness' into 'modernity' or what became termed as the 'the enlightenment'. The process was what they have flatteringly and retrospectively referred to as the 'progress' of 'civilisation'. They convinced themselves they were continuing a noble historic tradition and many important civic buildings commissioned by ruling elites in European cities replicated the Greek and Roman styles in art and architecture as both homage to and an ambition to rival such ancient 'splendour'. The human species, in the form of its elites, like ancient elites were imagined, by the developing bourgeoisie intellectual classes, to be a superior species to all others. A species, that in imagination, had been created by their God's will, and had ascended with some degree of practical and intellectual difficulty from a pathetic state of primitive backwardness and ignorance to what they considered were the magnificent achievements of Greek and Roman power. The task that the European bourgeois elites set themselves, by this self-flattering, but as we shall indicate, largely false narrative, was to continue this 'civilising' mission. They did so by introducing a revolutionary political, industrial and commercial period of production into the main hierarchical mass society structures, and they did so by means of civil wars, between the aristocratic ruling elites and the rising bourgeois elites. These new methods they confidently predicted (and projected into the future) would no longer be guided by tradition, but by science and technology. This they confidently predicted, would introduce enlightened methods of industrialised social production for the benefit of **all** humanity. Therefore, that period of bourgeois development maintained and built upon the broad spectrum of anthropocentric religious exceptionalism first inaugurated in the ancient period of Babylonian, Persian, Egyptian, Greek, Roman and Islamic Empires of the near and middle east.

This imaginary 'upward' (!) 5,000 year historical journey of humanity was traced from an imagined early Fertile Crescent (near eastern) form of granite and marble excellence to a European led regional steel and concrete 'excellence' and beyond. This imaginary 'journey', reconstructed by the bourgeois elites, they imagined would continue and lead toward an eventual glorious, global 'civilisation' of peace and plenty. This future was contrasted to an imagined pre-historic period of stagnation in, (or in some opinions a descent into), a condition of primitive localised 'barbarism and savagery'. According to this religiously infused secular based, hierarchical mass society intellectual conceit, before 'civilisation' emerged, life on earth was composed solely of human beings who resembled 'beasts'. Early humans were often depicted as wallowing in ignorance and filth and were also frequently described as mostly being hungry. Thus by this bourgeois informed dis-information process, our ancient ancestors were not intellectually and physically much better than the rest of the animal species and in some respects worse. Such embellished and repeated false narratives tended to seduce many among the self-interested elites into accepting these distorted illusions as being based upon some ancient reality and therefore, that modern humanity led by its educated elites was therefore fulfilling some kind of 'enlightened' destiny. However, in contrast to such one-sided distortions, this current chapter will also consider the much 'neglected' but very well documented, dark and ruthless side of the hierarchical mass society journey from its inception in Egypt, Babylon and Sumer, to its later imperial stage in Rome and beyond. But having briefly considered our human origins during the period of hunter-gatherer communities, we should now consider and contrast the essential economic structure of settled hierarchical mass societies,. based as they were upon securing the essential (N-M-G-R + A-D) processes of life on earth, by means of organised agriculture and animal husbandry.

B. The economic structure of hierarchical mass societies.

It needs to be remembered that the global pattern of human hunter-gatherer socio-economic activity, described and considered in the previous chapter, was not abandoned everywhere and all at once, but only in certain places. Hunter-gatherer communities continued around the globe almost everywhere outside of Europe until the 16th and later centuries. In contrast, to a world of hunting and gathering, a few permanent agricultural settlements were established within the near east and those human groups living in them became more or less attached to a specific geographical location and to a different mode of obtaining their nutrition (N). This change also involved a different, more intensive way of obtaining and experiencing all their essential (N-M-G-R + A-D) biological life process needs as a whole. Consequently, what was primarily abandoned by individuals in such settled agricultural communities, was their personal daily direct and collective relationship to nature - the actual source of their evolutionary (N-M-G-R + A-D) life cycle processes. Furthermore, alongside that loss of direct contact with nature also came the severing of integrated egalitarian human relationships with each other. Members of this new mode of production, via an occupational division of labour, became primarily attached to specific socio-economic roles and classes within a hierarchical social system of production. They were no longer directly and economically attached personally to their community and to nature as one fully integrated group.

Due to the logic of a social hierarchy and a strict division of labour, important and essential natural resources for nutrition (N), such as land, water, animals, plants and humans, became managed and controlled by the elite within the social hierarchy and eventually control of essential resources morphed into direct ownership by elites either military or religious. In the fully settled agriculturally based community, a division of manual labour slowly evolved or was introduced in which some people specialised in growing crops, others specialised in herding and rearing animals, others, specialised in making a plethora of useful tools and/or decorative objects. In this way indirect occupational relationships began to mediate, and in many cases dominate, personal relationships within hierarchical mass societies. Instead of personal relationships being the primary attachments of social individuals with the whole community thus ensuring a share in socially (gathered) or produced food, shelter and protection, an alienating change occurred.

In the transition between the two modes of production, the validating attachment within the hierarchically structured community became based upon a socially constructed and therefore unnatural division of labour. From then on, In order to secure a share of nutritional (N) and other essentials from within an agricultural community, what an individual did, within that division of labour, became more important than the fact that he or she existed as a member of the human community. This change in validating status of who was considered a worthy human being and thus entitled to food, water and shelter, still survives with us in the 21st century. One of the first greetings between strangers in bourgeois societies, after; 'What is your name'?, is; 'What is your job'? Moreover, in most modern societies, anyone lacking official birth documents, passports and official employment, are not considered completely human. Incredibly, a biological member of the human species is not considered an official member of any modern human society, unless they have the correct pieces of official paper. They are considered stateless, subject to arrest, imprisonment and even deportation. Thus, even without being a criminal, the biological fact of being a member of the human species is routinely ignored (and individuals punished) by the social systems created by human beings to ensure that they are treated as human beings should be.

This early creation of a division of labour also introduced a further division in relative social status. A relatively small number of privileged individuals began to specialise in social organisation and social control, thus eventually creating in hierarchical mass societies a three (or sometimes more) tiered socio-economic system. Early hierarchical mass societies eventually became those who controlled the main means of production (the elite), those who managed the system (the middle ranks) and those who worked to produce all the various articles of food and material consumption (the labouring classes). At some point, control became identical with kingship and ownership. We can only speculate on how and why in certain places the transition between the two modes of production, (between nomadic hunter-gatherer and permanently settled agriculture) was accomplished but we can say quite a lot about how hierarchical mass societies functioned once they were developed as such.

Although exactly how, when and why they started is not clear, however, it is clear that these settled societies began to involve ever greater numbers who needed to be fed, clothed and housed, not by their own direct efforts, but by means of the socio-economic system. Mass agricultural and horticultural social production does not require everyone to work the fields. Nor in the case of large-scale animal husbandry is everyone required to herd the cattle, shepherd the goats, or sheep, but some have to do it. Therefore, a substantial socio-economic difference occurred between that settled mode of production and hunter-gathering. The differences occurred both in terms of the social relationships and in terms of the quality and quantity of tasks members are required to complete. In these cases of planned, settled production of nutritional (N) resources, those who were (are) directly involved in agricultural or animal herding production in general must work longer and often with more intensity and concentration, than individuals did under hunting and gathering modes of production. They also needed to develop different, one-sided, forms of knowledge and skills than was the case with those collectively involved in hunting and gathering.

For example, the following is clearly obvious, but its full implications are less so. Obtaining the source of nutrition (N) from an agriculturally based mode of production does not have an immediate nutritional result, but is extensively deferred. For example, the first initial stage of large-scale agriculturally based production at any time in history, is to; 1. clear the ground of impediments to planting (I.e. bushes, trees, weeds and large rocks); after that workers needed to; 2, create field boundaries, lay out planting patterns or sequences such as rows; then next, and for every subsequent season, 3, they need to plant roots, seeds or seedlings, graft on cuttings or dig in sprouting plants and cover them over; then 4, in the absence of rain or flooding rivers, water them appropriately; next 5, they need to protect the seedlings and plants from birds, insects, rodents, fungal and other air-borne pathogens, at least until the plants were sufficiently mature or ripe. Then task 6 has to be actioned; harvest or pick the desired nutritional growth, when ready and store them; 7, winnow them if grain or de-stalk them if fruit; it then becomes essential in the case of grains to; 8, grind the seeds to make flour; and protect the remaining fruit and seeds from decay or wild life consumption. Then the same or another group of workers would need to implement a further stage 9, in the case of grains and bread as a staple (N), mixing the dough and preparing the ovens needs to be done; 10, then baking the dough; then 11, distributing the bread or cakes daily for social consumption. So within early agricultural communities, the four basic, closely linked hunter-gatherer stages of social gathering, *foraging*, *collecting*, *preparing* and *eating* nutrition (N) were extended to at least nine or ten. So between preparing the ground and eating the production from it (N), there are at least 9, sometimes 11 variously protracted (seasonal) and labour intensive processes. Moreover, as such communities grew in numbers, or as initial soil fertility became degraded, the full eleven stages of creating new fields, etc., would need to be repeated on a recurring basis.

This agricultural process, even at its most basic, would involve for each of the eleven stages (and any possible intermediate stages) undoubtedly a much longer and more exhausting period of physical effort by fewer individuals than would be expended if the whole community were simply daily gathering and hunting on a foraging basis. In the latter case obtaining natural sources of nutrition (N) from hunting and gathering, the naturally evolved growing cycle takes care of 7 of the above 11 stages. Large-scale agricultural modes of production with further divisions of labour between and within these eleven stages also require the producers and consumers to have a more detailed and shared language, common measurements of time and volumes, an extensive and uniform form of social knowledge along with a communicated, systematic organisation of the system of production. Such socio-economic communities also required a more disciplined approach to food production and distribution because control of the correct sequencing, timing and duration of each of the dozen or so stages of producing (N) can no longer be left entirely to nature. A socially constructed process, of necessity, needs to be managed and controlled.

Thus, the changed mode of production needed to function not as negotiable group activity but as a disciplined 'system', which was sufficiently efficient and effective to deliver regular supplies of food to everybody located within the various levels of the hierarchical mass society. It cannot be surprising then that this mode of production could not be initiated or completed in part of a morning or afternoon, as hunting and gathering did, or in a relatively short period of time. Nor can it be surprising that some task allocations were not always undertaken enthusiastically. Therefore, the so-called ancient Agriculture Revolution may not have been achieved in a rapid revolutionary fashion at all, as some retrospective imaginations seem to have assumed. It most likely to have occurred over an extended process of socially and biologically determined and interrupted transformations. Humans, animals and crops had to be trained and disciplined over significant periods of their life times and modified over generations to accept the disciplined social, working and socio-biological conditions required by this new mode of obtaining the (N-M-G-R + A-D) biological processes of human living. Changes in modes of production are gradual, incremental and evolutionary rather than revolutionary.

Furthermore, it is obvious that in the early stages of this transition to a mass society agricultural system large numbers of people had to either volunteer to be subject to the intense and exacting discipline of settled agriculture, animal husbandry and the other spin-off crafts around it, or be compelled to adopt it (or a mixture of both). Relatively spontaneous and easy going people socially adjusted to generations of informal hunter-gatherer relaxed social rhythms had to become transformed into disciplined subjects of the new system of obtaining and ensuring the (N) etc., of the now altered human (N-M-G-R + A-D) cycles of living. There is a recurring modern retrospective myth that settled hierarchical mass societies (sometimes classed as civilisations) grew rapidly in ancient times because this mode of production was attractive to be part of, or because it guaranteed an ample supply of nutrition and other products. But I contend that this was clearly never true historically, nor could it have logically occurred in this way. We have read in the previous chapter that most continents and even islands supported extensive hunter-gatherer communities whose mode of production and living was far from impoverished, culturally deprived or overburdened by excessive labour.

Furthermore the historical record indicates that the outbreak of plagues, crop failures, the consequences of adverse rainfall and frequent raiding parties often created large-scale famines, for early ancient and even for later medieval agriculturalists. Furthermore, with much smaller communities, such outbreaks and mass collapses of pre-agricultural, natural plant production did not occur as often, if at all, to hunter-gatherers. Even if some hunter-gatherer bands occasionally fell on hard times, fresh abundant locations were never more than a day's travel away. Hominids and early humans at the earliest stages of their evolution, like animals and many insects had become astute enough to move location, before, or during any potential or actual depletion of local sources of nutrition. Bovine herds, thousands strong often migrate long distances to find fresh pasture, even before existing grasses are depleted completely. It is logical to assume that early hominids and humans were no less astute with regard to the limits of local resources. It is often assumed by some writers that these ancient city state hierarchical mass societies were so attractive to rural hunter-gatherer and pastoralist communities that they simply flocked to them in droves. However, I have found no reliable evidence or evidence based logical deductions that would substantiate such opinions. I therefore conclude this is an example of wishful or uncritical superficial thinking, undertaken to bolster up the idea that modern preferred social structures are always superior to ancient ones. This chapter as it unfolds will suggest why I think that this is the case.

In fact, the sheer discipline and amount of labour power intensity required for such onerous agricultural and associated activities, are probably why slave labour so frequently became the mass labour basis of practically all early hierarchical mass society formations, particularly within the ancient near and middle east empires that arose. The ubiquitous existence of slavery throughout the ancient period of hierarchical mass society 'civilised' development deserves more than a passing banal assumption that they didn't know any better. They certainly did. Slavery for the enslaved no matter their level of education or cultural development was a source of extreme resentment and is reflected as such in many ancient philosophical discussions within and between ancient peoples. No matter how hard some historians try to suggest that the ancient world of hierarchical mass society because it was considered 'civilisation', was not built on the backs of brutal levels of male and female slavery, the effort logically and historically fails. Their efforts at white-washing certain historical periods are no more than wishful thinking to overcome embarrassment or to ignore the barbarity of the historical civilisations they otherwise esteem. The idea I heard articulated by several Egyptian archaeologists interviewed on a number of 21st century TV documentaries, that the pyramids of ancient Egypt were built by employing free paid labour, is similarly unhistorical and also illogical. Such reasoning does not have any real historic evidence or logic to substantiate it. The economic and financial basis for the employment of large-scale paid labour was lacking throughout the ancient period of Mediterranean and near east area empire building and that general lack lasted until the bourgeois era. In the ancient world of humanity, (as with every other species) money in some form or other was not necessary to ensure that the (N-M-G-R + A-D) processes of existence continued. Until the modern era of the capitalist mode of production, money was only developed to enable the occasional exchange of trading imbalances to be adjusted in frequent commercial transactions between distant communities, and not always then.

Furthermore, the rest of hominid and homo sapien humanity managed perfectly well without money as they had for hundreds of thousands of years. It is logically obvious that if several thousand paid-workers were employed in ancient Egypt and elsewhere on mass or in multiple work groups to build pyramids, dig complex canal systems or erect temples and city walls, over decades, would need a sophisticated system of mass coinage, or at least payment mechanisms along with a plethora of supply shops and establishments for the purchase of what the paid workers would need to daily and weekly live on - food, clothing, shelter etc. In other words, the physical infrastructure that goes with a token or cash-based economic system, would be needed, but has left no material trace. Coins became used in some armies of the later Roman Empire period but even then entire marching armies at that early period existed primarily on growing, sequestering (stealing) livestock, crops, clothing and equipment as they moved across regions often like human locusts through territory they were passing through. Any social system employing paid labour needs to be able to exchange those labour services provided for a token which can then be exchanged for food, clothing or shelter etc.

Even in later Roman Empire periods, coinage was only used among some of the Roman legions who might accept it because they could use it in certain places. In the ancient world, mass labour and even small scale labour was slave or semi-slave labour. There was no such thing as wage or salaried labour for the huge masses of working people until the bourgeois era. I suggest that slave-labour in the ancient world was an absolute necessity to force people to engage with arduous and dangerous tasks that people who were free to voluntarily reside in hunter-gatherer communities, would shun like the plague. That includes shunning the eleven step process of agriculture noted above to enable large-scale agriculture and building to take place in the first place. The same logic applies to the intense and dangerous occupation of human beings working down mines. Even during the long middle ages, slave and semi-slave labour continued as the basis of obtaining and producing nutritional production (N) for the aristocracy before any more modern hierarchical mass societies developed the kind of infrastructure needed for the general employment of paid field or craft labour.

Furthermore, it is logically obvious that the capture, chaining and compulsion of human as well as animal based labour power to do certain tasks was absolutely necessary. This is because most draft animals and human beings would not generally volunteer or stay around for such life-long arduous and extended work schedules, unless compelled. Bullocks by nature were disinclined to pull ploughs or go round and round in circles to raise water or unless chained to a pole to grind corn and so too were human beings. Asses clearly did not immediately leave their groups or herds to volunteer to carry overweight owners or crushing loads on their backs. Camels were not at a loss of what to do until humans forced them to become long distance desert transport vehicles. The fact is that create hierarchical mass societies, large numbers of many species of life on earth (including humans) had to be both, chained, tamed and trained by repeated doses of painful discipline and severe punishment, to carry out tasks, that were not to their liking or which were not of their own volition. Logic would also suggest that as long as there was an easier alternative to obtain nourishment (N) and needed materials, (and there often was) human beings as well as animals would also have to be forced to work the fields, to shepherd the hill-grazing flocks, to dig for long hours in the various mines and to become domestic servants or artisans slaving away from, dawn to dusk. Clearly it would be hard, if not impossible, to find enough volunteers for such lengthy back-breaking drudgery - if there was a viable alternative, like hunting, gathering or small scale herding or locally abundant fishing resources. Furthermore, once seriously considered, paying people wages, in money or kind could only develop much later, when the mass society economic and finance systems had advanced sufficiently to fulfil all the numerous inputs and outputs required for a deferred satisfaction or a token or money-based economic system. However, it could clearly only function that way when eventually all the land was owned or controlled by an elite and therefore during a period when there were no longer sufficient alternative ways to obtain (N) etc., for yourself and other like-minded social individuals.

It is therefore obvious that compulsion (and control) of any kind within a developed social form of human existence, requires a dominant and/or ruling section and a managerial section (or classes) within the community to enforce the essential tasks and manage/control the associated rigour allocated to the rest of the population. It should be recalled from earlier chapters on various species that despite intensive research, no other social species of life on earth has indicated that one sub-group of a species has enslaved or forced the rest of the colony, flock, school or troop to continue to do what they are able to do but to then do it for the benefit of the elite sub-group - in addition to securing their own particular (N-M-G-R + A-D) phases of existence. Life on earth, over billions of years and the primate, hominid and *Homo sapien* species during their millennia of evolutionary existence, also did not evolve to organise the forcible compulsion of individuals of the same (or other) species organisms to secure any phase of their own (N-M-G-R + A-D) life cycles. Even those species with extensive divisions of functions and attributes of natural evolution, did not introduce hierarchy and compulsion into their ranks. On the basis of available evidence concerning the evolution of all forms of life on earth, the formation of hierarchical mass societies with slaves and semi-slaves by some sections of humanity some thousands of years ago (out of millions of years evolution) was a unique, unnatural and unhealthy mode of living and remains so. It also has had long term negative consequences. Thus;

"There were trade-offs to the rise in reliance on cereals and to rising densities of habitation - not least the impact on health. For one thing, work involving heavier tools for grinding and processing grain placed greater demands on the human body, resulting in cases of osteoarthritis rising as crop cultivation became more widespread; for another, the sugars in cereal carbohydrates brought about degradations in teeth enamel, with resulting high incidence of dental cavities. An even bigger biological price to pay came from the costs of living close together. These included faecal pollution and poor sanitation that could cause bacterial disease and conditions that favoured the spread of viruses and parasites from person to person. (P. Frankopan. 'The Earth Transformed') Chapter 3)

In addition to the above, the requirements to redirect and re-fashion 'nature' caused by the new hierarchical mode of settled production were simultaneously biological and physiological constraints imposed upon the lives of humans, animals and plants transitioning to this change in the mode of production orchestrated by some groups of sedentary communities. The constraints on leisure and social integration created by serial, ploughing, planting, watering, weeding, reaping, gathering, drying, grinding, baking and serving, along with herding, shepherding and large-scale slaughtering were totally new chores and tasks requiring a high degree of animal and human control by means of forced 'training' or additionally in the case of humans, cultural forms of 'domestication'. These constraints on what time people got up, how long they worked, when they could rest or play, when and what kind of labour was needed at any particular time, were not the only ones.

How attentive and narrowly focussed the working populations needed to be in the fields, and how much time was left for socialising, were also considerable alterations to the 'natural' (N-M-G-R +A-D) evolutionary processes of plant, animal, insect and human life. Once it was instituted, the sequencing of these elements of production needed to be tightly controlled and if not by a highly unlikely voluntary commitment, then by actual physical enforcement. Consequently, for the elite enforcers of ancient hierarchically organised societies with divisions of labour, slavery for them was not only a moral issue but a practical socio-economic problem to be solved by this particular loathsome means. This is also how it was viewed by elites in 18th and 19th century American sugar, tobacco and cotton plantations and again in 20th century in Stalinist controlled Russia gulags and Nazi controlled German work camps, where torture and brutal punishments for disobedience by inmates were routine and frequent.

Furthermore, a similar increase of socially imposed constraints were involved for those engaged in horticulture and animal husbandry. Skills for such activities went far beyond choosing what to gather or hunt and extended to care and management of animal and plant welfare. Furthermore new tools and implements became essential so the learning and perfection of the means to manufacture tools and crafts also needed to expand. All these skill sets were additional requirements to enable large-scale agriculture and animal husbandry to become sufficient to feed and supply hierarchical mass societies. These specific occupations also needed long hours of disciplined activity and managerial or bureaucratic type control. Any getting up late, having a laugh or messing around which was inevitable whilst gathering or hunting; or just disappearing from the group on an extended adventure by some or all of a community of hunter-gatherers could no longer be tolerated. For hunter-gathering communities, nature needed no continuous management or protection, and likewise animals moved to new pastures without being prompted or constrained by human whips, sticks or fences. So until settled hierarchical mass societies were developed, life on earth just biologically and ecologically sorted itself out, by the moment, by the day or by the season, as it had done for billions or millions of years.

Yet in settled agricultural communities, drying soil needed constant irrigating and/or resting (lying fallow), once soil microbiota or grass fecundity had been exhausted, and of course crops needed regular weeding and protecting. There is of course, as some 'experts' say, the possibility that in a few places the impetus to change from hunting and gathering to farming came from some extra-terrestrial catastrophe. Large asteroids have been known to destroy the natural habitat to such a widespread degree that for those people surviving it with such a catastrophe, hunting and gathering could have become impossible. However, even to start agriculture at that disaster point, the knowledge of how and when to grow crops would need to have already existed within such communities, because as noted, agricultural production of sufficient (N) for even a village community is not something that can be achieved on an overnight basis or on a by next week scale. Starvation time only takes a few days or week, whereas crop reproduction time to harvesting is a several month or seasonal affair. Besides, in such cases, moving away from a disaster zone to a non-disaster hunter-gatherer zone would have been more likely than staying put and attempting to create an agricultural mode of production when there was already insufficient to eat locally.

Wherever, and whenever it occurred, the transition to agriculture communities and herding undoubtedly had a dramatic effect on those entering and enduring them, which for these people served also to reverse the whole relationship between their individual humanity and the rest of life on earth. Suddenly life on earth (i.e. nature), despite its millions of years of natural fecundity - was considered by the elite as no longer good enough on its own – nature needed controlling, 'forcing', intensifying and 'managing'. What is often missed out in most studies of human history in the transition from hunter-gatherer bands to agricultural based hierarchical mass societies, is the drastic effect of this change upon human personal and social relationships. Human beings and other life forms ceased to be viewed personally and subjectively. They were no longer primarily viewed as 'subjects' having a naturally based autonomy and function, in the total web of life on their part of the earth. They had become valuable 'objects' of labour to be owned, possessed, controlled, exploited and even consumed, primarily, but not exclusively, by male elites. The objectification of every form of natural subject (including humans) is also most emphatically demonstrated in the visual arts of ancient societies. It was there that everything natural living or otherwise, was first rendered into a static and perfected object (by drawing, painting, sculpting) becoming an image devoid of any intrinsic quality, agency, movement, feeling or consent and this 'object' existed to be visually consumed by the observer. This objectification of every organic or inorganic subject or object was particularly pernicious with regard to its extension to the human form and relationships.

Thus we find that the language of ancient hierarchical societies commences to include a new concept of possession unknown to hunter-gatherer peoples, the use of the prefix 'my' which continues to this day. My slaves, my wife, my children, my horse, my land, my property, my house, my army, my kingdom etc. These terms become not humane verbal references to merely describe close personal relationships, but to publicly signal relationships of proprietary ownership and control. The logical social corollary then becomes *'what is mine is not yours'*, whatever 'it' is. This concept, unknown to hunter-gatherer communities, became a founding principle of hierarchical mass societies, well before modernity took it to extremes in bourgeois concepts of the cash purchase of personal property, including human slaves. From developed hierarchical mass society formations forward, everything in nature became viewed as an actual or potential object of proprietary ownership and control and this change was enforced by armed elites and embodied in authorised legal statues. Some people not only began to own and control the organic and inorganic substance of the many objects of their desire including large tracts of nature, but also to control the actual bodily functions and actions, including their continued existence. Within human male/female relationships this extended to control of the most intimate and personal relationships of reproduction (R), and tactile and emotional feelings, that a human being can express.

Within hierarchical mass society formations, patriarchal forms of sexual control became transformed into acts of objectification, fixation, possession and control, of the female members of the human species. Harems became a regular elite feature of this new hierarchical mass society form. This objectification and fixation of the female form became a recurring cultural theme within the visual arts and was scrutinised primarily by males. This scrutiny was never pure artistic observation, it was always catering to male sexual arousal who by becoming stimulated by artistic visual perfections of females were socialised to expect or demand such perfection and convenient availability by real female subjects/objects. This socialisation, objectification and fixation upon a constantly available, always willing 'virtual' or slave female object, geared to male sexual desire remains a blight upon humanity and results in many modern sexual assaults, rapes and murders of females by males.

The fact that such objectification, fixation, aggressive sexual possession and control of females by males is now highly available as internet porn, demonstrates that the objectification of femininity (and thus the de-humanisation of female humanity) remains a continuing and serious problem, within modern hierarchical mass society formations. The fact that in some countries, particularly in the west, women no longer have to hide their bodies or their sexual feelings and have established the right to initiate and consent to intimate activity is being marginalised by the continued socialised objectification of them in pornography. More often than not, women are depicted in porn as virtual 'objects' to be possessed rather than as autonomous subjects to be respected, valued equally and understood as essential human partners in the lives of our species. In other countries, their situation is even worse, and this also remains a testament to the loss of humanity that occurred in the wake of the so-called agricultural revolution and the advent of patriarchal 'civilisation', and its ideological reflection in the Abrahamic religions.

But what was also crucially lost by humanity in this transfer to agriculture (and remains lost to working people) was the amount of discretionary time available for the remaining (M-G-R + A-D) phases of human living. This 'free' time beyond working to 'earn' nutrition (N) instead of simply freely gathering it, then had to be squeezed into a much reduced non-work time. A further significant additional change in human relationships to nature also developed upon the basis of this changed mode of production. Prior to settled, hierarchical mass societies, no other species of life on earth had put fences around natural resources and demanded something (work, products or rent) in return for their use. Unlike human landlords, soil does not extract a percentage return from things that grow in it; plants do not extract payment in exchange for their photosynthetic production of oxygen or for their nutritious leaves, seeds, nuts and fruits; tamed animals, unlike their owners, do not insist on a percentage return for any services they provide: the sun does not send out bills for the energy it freely supplies. This rather banal observation may seem somewhat trite, but we often take the integrated contribution of organic and inorganic nature to life on earth for granted. With the onset of hierarchical mass society structures, for the first time in billions of years of evolution, cruelty, torture, and enslavement of humans and animals and payment in kind or cash for monopolised land and nature became dominant and distorting features of just one new and unique group of the human species of life on earth. Some sections of a talented and humane *Homo, sapien* species had evolved into a *Homo percentage extractus* with a weapon in hand to enforce it.

Consequently, moving from one mode of production to another was not so much the loss of a (freedom!) that humans never actually possessed, and never will possess, but the imposition of a set of additional 'unnatural' social controls and requirements on the time spent producing (N). It has long been known that working long exhausting hours and living on a narrowly restricted diet would inevitably have had some effect, however small, upon body Metabolism, Growth, Reproduction, Ageing and Death. Like all life forms, the metabolising organelles within human cells, can only metabolise what material is contained within the source of nourishment (N) absorbed and processed in their own particular way. Moreover, growth (G) can be stunted or deformed by nutritionally poor material, or one-dimensional occupational exertion. Furthermore, the rates or quality of reproduction (R) can be affected by creating or replicating relative weaknesses or by gender birth preferences based upon the altered occupational need for physical strength or endurance. The phenomena of the process of female ovulation being altered by the consistent level of nutrition being increased or decreased due to higher or lower levels of nutrition available may explain why female participation in obtaining nutrition (N) has affected their socio-economic status, within certain modes of production. Having fewer or more babies to care for would alter their ability to focus and commit to anything other than child-care and infant rearing. The resulting dependency of females on other adult members, particularly men, for obtaining nutrition, whilst lactating and caring for multiple infants would significantly alter female socio-economic status in the transition between hunter-gatherer modes of production and pastoral herding and high yield agricultural production.

Female infanticide did become an established tendency where female contributions to agricultural production in particular or society in general were less needed or desired and therefore undervalued and led to them being seen as a burden rather than an asset. In the case of some of the new occupations, such as sustained mining, metalworking, baking, textile manufacture and pottery, the negative effects of the hazards attached to such intensely focussed occupations on the (N-M-G-R + A-D) phases of settled agricultural living would have undoubtedly been substantial. Compared to the varied diet, the less repeatedly strenuous activities and open air living of the hunter-gatherer process of maintaining human life on earth, sustained employment in agriculture and craft production, was not something to be envied. This certainly was the case with regard to the slaves on the plantations of the Americas and with the peasants and workers of European agriculture and industry, whose lives were dramatically shortened during the Industrial

Revolution, the colonial era and beyond it to the 20th and 21st centuries.

Therefore, the means by which agriculturally based elites controlled mass societies and collectively chose to secure the nutritional production (N) necessary to metabolise (M) in their bodies in sufficient amounts to individually grow (G) and reproduce (R), not only affected the individual physical and mental health of its members but also altered almost all human relationships profoundly. This new mode of production necessarily impacted upon when and how they could do other non-productive things such as resting, recuperating, socialising, playing and reproducing. Regular agricultural field or pasture labour is not only more time and energy demanding but simultaneously appears as a considerable loss of free time and a loss of individual and collective decision making. It therefore becomes an additional form of human alienation, alienation from humanity's natural evolutionary essence. It becomes inevitable that, an element of compulsion in hierarchical mass societies, replaces an easy going pattern of hunter-gatherer living, with something more regimented and disciplined. Self-alienation by agreement to sell yourself into slavery, is still alienation and the reason and motivation for selling oneself or ones children into the ownership of another human being cannot be a naturally evolved process, but a socially constructed one.

The introduction of slavery into modes of production, for example, alienates the entire (N-M-G-R + A-D) processes of those enslaved from the victim and places them almost entirely in the hands of the slave owners or their agents. However, even for those volunteering and thus not forced into this new mode of production, it involved a choice of taking on additional burdens and restrictions for a definite individual or collective purpose. No matter how this whole system transition was initially facilitated or managed the above tasks and sequences are those involved in transferring from unforced voluntary social gathering and hunting to the enforced or voluntary membership of settled socialised agriculture. From all the evidence covered so far, there emerges an obvious clear and onerous distinction between being a member of an ancient egalitarian, chief-choosing gatherer-hunter band or being subjected to the disciplining and controlling instructions of a warrior chief, an elite warrior priest, or a king within an ancient agriculturally based city state. This transition and distinctions (enforced or reluctantly accepted) eventually occurred both in parts of the Middle-east, the Americas and Africa.

Another rarely considered, but outstanding feature of hierarchical mass societies, is the generally alienating effect of the division of labour within these societies. In the creation of divisions of labour or occupational diversity, the efficiency gained by this measure is offset by the constant repetitive character of these divisions resulting in a varying degree of alienation from and conflict over the implications of these occupational divisions. Individual personal functions and interests become the dominant concern and primary focus of individualised social existence. Therefore, the common interests of the whole community are frequently relegated by individuals to a secondary level of importance. Where these divisions of labour also cluster into and on to class divisions, the shared concerns within the classes can also become more important than the interests which are common to the whole community. Class interests and opinions, particularly those of the ruling classes, thus become dominant within the hierarchical form of society. Individual and class-based conflicts thus become the constantly abrasive interactions within such mass societies. The class and occupational based conflicts are muted at times and flare up at others, but are endemic and so are never entirely subdued. Thus the interests of the wealthy classes to increase their wealth at the expense of the interests of the other classes, will invariably be resented by the majority, but may not always flare up in the form of open conflict or as civil wars, rebellions or more modern general strikes, until tensions reach an explosive level. Furthermore these internal group alliances within mass societies rarely cohere around a single policy idea or around a single person representing one. Instead, opposition tends to orbit around a cluster of personal or class interests and are occasionally intensified by splits in the ruling elites.

Thus, the following historical and contemporary facts also emerge. The interests of a powerfully placed elite individual, within a ruling dynasty, oligarchy or faction, (e.g. Alexander,

Xerxes, Nero, Charlemagne, Hitler, Stalin, Mao or Putin etc.) who desire more power and control, could (and did) drag their whole societies into wars in which the common interests of the majority were (and in modern cases, still are) exponentially compromised and often physically sacrificed. It should not be a surprise that many decisions taken by elites in power (university educated or not) are also not entirely rationally based. Furthermore, this conflict between individual interests, class interests and the common interests of all society members frequently penalises the least powerful individuals and groups. Their reduced status and welfare is routinely ignored until they eventually combine their efforts and take action. Slave Revolts and Peasant Uprisings are therefore as old as the hierarchical mass society form itself. In the modern age, working class strikes are the equivalent of the earlier slave and feudal rebellions by victims of exploitation and social neglect.

The interesting twist to such socio-economic struggles in modern times is that working class victims of class perpetrated exploitation and indifference are blamed and pilloried when they strike. The accusation levelled at them is that they ignore the common interests of the other classes. It rarely occurs to the middle and upper classes, who do most of the complaining, that it is the common interests and wellbeing of those individuals who have been consigned to the lowest classes, which has been repeatedly neglected or ignored to the point where collective rebellion becomes possible, if not inevitable. The conflicts between the individual interests, class interests and the common interests are exponentially elevated within hierarchical mass societies and remain the underlying sources of personal depressions and anxieties as well as the emergence of sectarian religious and political struggles. Mental health and addiction issues are merely the modern general manifestations of the unnatural human relationships occurring within all hierarchical mass societies. Furthermore, symptoms of climate change, pollution and ecological destruction are the modern general manifestation of the unnatural relationships hierarchical mass societies created between humanity and nature.

Clearly, the written and archaeological evidence uncovered so far is that some sections of the human species, several thousands of years ago, made a transition from obtaining nourishment by the original hunter-gatherer way of living on earth to a settled agricultural farming mode of production. I have suggested that this must have involved considerable social upheaval for those making such a transition. Staying in one place, rather than moving around; growing food, storing it and processing it, rather than picking or digging it up daily, we're radical, and certainly potentially revolutionary changes in a different mode of social living. As noted earlier, this different pattern of social living involved not only a change in what was done, to obtain (N-M-G-R + A-D) processes, but how it was done and when it was done. The detail of when and how this transition was made in pre-historical and/or historical periods and which different geographical regions pioneered it, is not actually well understood, even though many authors can be found who think it can be. However, because of the scarcity of solid evidence, it was not possible in the previous chapter, to construct a fairly accurate representation of the general social and economic relations within and between hunter-gatherer communities and nature. Therefore, at this point I suggest we need to consider in more detail how these relationships changed during and after the settled agricultural farming communities had properly established themselves. Even though each case of actual transition will have had its own particular geographical, ecological and climatic differences, this does not alter the fact that the general elements and order of production for living were changed significantly and these can be established in general.

Physical and intellectual growth (G) which in humanity has always included extensive inter-generational learning and communication also had to be adjusted to the new mode of production. Reproduction (R) clearly continued in forms suited to their different ways of life, but there is also clear historical evidence that the development of hierarchical mass societies coincided with a change from human communities being Matrifocal and Matrilineal to Patrifocal and Patrilineal; Social life changed from having a female focus and female offspring identity to having a male focus and male offspring identity. It is obvious from the historical evidence that in the transition from hunter-gatherer modes of living to agricultural modes, women and children ceased to be fully accepted as equal social individuals and as having their own elements of social agency. Thus this suggests that some aspects of the change in the mode of production functioned to lead to the eventual subjection of women and children to the oppressive and exploitative rule of a male or males.

Quite how this transition came about in detail is not clear, but the fact is that in hierarchical mass societies the natural biological/social links between the social production of (N) and biological reproduction (R) and the female of the species was significantly altered. It is undoubtedly the case that Patrilineality replaced Matrilineality and children became the property of the male parent. Voluntary emotional partnership between female and male genders became altered in favour of male preferences and male determined compulsions, both in the initiation and termination of relationships. This was a change that affected all the classes whose individuals engaged in reproductive activity. This gender bias became firmly established both within the ranks of the hierarchy itself, but also within the rest of the mass society citizens. Whether this social demotion of the female gender was fully consolidated before, during or after the establishment of agricultural settlements is unclear, but the fact that it was consolidated is undeniable. Nevertheless, the same altered gender balance took place in the area of animal rearing, herding, milking, killing; and fruit and in vegetable planting, harvesting, and processing. Within the agriculturally based settlement area, practically all life on earth had one or more of its (N-M-G-R +A-D) phases significantly modified or effectively altered by this change.

Furthermore, since the production of (N) determines to a greater or lesser extent the rest of (N-M-G-R + A-D) processes, it seems logical that the removal of any human being or animal from the activity of obtaining its own nutrition (N), the system makes them less independent and therefore more dependent upon others. The removal of women from the ability to directly produce and obtain their own nutrition (N) by gathering, and by organised agriculture or herding, would make them more dependent upon the men who could. Therefore, such gender changes in occupational divisions of labour for women would tend to make them more dependent and therefore organisationally subordinate to men than under the hunter-gatherer mode of production. Those females bearing more children would face conditions which would also tend to exclude them from the more intense realms of nutritional (N) production. In this regard, there is also considerable body of biological, anthropological and medical evidence that the natural pattern of ovulation in women can be altered by increasing or decreasing the level of nutrition received. The phenomena of 20th century female slimmer's eating so little that their periods ceased indicates that this natural biological survival pattern has long existed within the female half of human species. Extra children or fewer children within agricultural and pastoral based food producing communities, therefore, may also have had an additional bearing on how the social status of women was both perceived and altered within hierarchical mass society formations. There was an interesting retention and partial elevation of the status of 'mother' alongside a demotion in the status of simply being 'female', during the transition to agricultural and pastoral modes of production. Logistically, individually looking after and nurturing two or three or more children, removes a female from the possibility of taking part in many other areas of social life which extend beyond the immediate family location.

With the exception of the elite, in a system of extended divisions of labour and patriarchal hierarchy, (whether rigidly enforced or not) having more or less babies, affects among other things, the amount of discretionary time available for the female. Precisely how the overall changes in obtaining Nourishment (N) took place during the transition from pre-history to the historical period is largely a case of cautiously filling in the blank spaces between certain material finds from pre-history. However, even then of course, many such conclusions concerning female status remain mostly speculative. What can be reasonably established by archaeology plus the written records contained in ancient historical documents, and in 17th, 18th and 19th century documentation, is the following. That hierarchical mass society settlements, in the near and middle east eventually emerged and became established in and around the 'fertile crescent' region of the middle east with a consequent elevation of some individuals into elite status and a reduction in social status for female members of these societies. Within those same societies, in that particular region, written records were eventually made that indicate significant negative changes took place between 'settled' human communities and between human beings and the rest of life on earth.

C. Hierarchical Mass Society in Anthropocentric consciousness..

In this section I have used a selection of quotations drawn from historical documents in the English language. They have been chosen to illustrate the retrospective admiration, euphoria and a general under-representation of the actual bloody history recorded during the formation of hierarchical mass societies as understood by most modern elites. The European historians of the 18th, 19th and 20th centuries seemed to be mostly impressed by size. As noted earlier, the size of buildings, Monuments, Stele and Pyramids in particular were the constant focus of their attention. Anything monumental in Egypt, Greece or Rome was considered seriously impressive and found worthy of admiration. Few questions were ever asked about the health and safety of the actual human beings who laboured upon them (slaves?). For many armchair historians, the seven wonders of the world (and many others), were never considered problematic with regard to the lives and welfare of those who actually built them. Consequently, the conditions of everyday living that the workforce were forced to endure, were largely ignored. Yet a consistent attempt to intellectually airbrush or gloss over the rapid rise of early cities such as Uruk, in ancient Sumer, occurs. We can therefore, read that;

"Improved irrigation and land reclamation created more land; intensive cultivation produced more food; larger walled settlements brought more security; more land more food, and better security encouraged people to leave the countryside and live in the cities, moving from the uplands into the southern plain. The inexorable pull of the cities markets with their necessities and luxuries must have made them additionally attractive, as

cities have been throughout history." (The First Civilisations;. M. Wood. Chapter 1)

As was noted earlier, this extract provides a practical example of some authors constructing a 20th century myth of positive progress within cities and then intellectually applying it to the ancient world. There is no mention of whips, torture, displacements, beatings, rapes, enslavements or deaths at work, none of these are given a place in such glowing retrospective accounts. It clearly hasn't occurred to the author of these and other such similar eulogies that the very amenities he mentions to explain the sudden rise in ancient city numbers, actually presumes the prior need for massive amounts of unpaid labour to be expended before and during their construction. In his imagination the above author of the 'First Civilisations' typically inverts reality or he has put the cart before the horse so to speak. We need to ask what might 'encourage' a rise in such city-building numbers before those amenities and luxuries existed in finished form? Particularly when, before their existence, there was plenty of other vacant land, containing food, shelter and security located nearby or elsewhere? It could hardly be the attraction of long hours of back-breaking work needed to clear forests and fields, to till the ground, plant and reap, build the city walls, and all this to first and foremost feed and protect an elite controlled system. Is it not the case that most people would rather choose to go elsewhere and focus on feeding themselves and their families. Perhaps the above author has made the frequent confirmation biased mistake of projecting a more modern myth back onto ancient history and has assumed his preferred explanation 'must' have been operating then. Yet even in modern times, this bourgeois myth is somewhat tattered and full of holes.

Most 20th century modern cities only receive large numbers (which are invariably concentrated in slums and shanty towns) when people can no longer obtain satisfactory levels of (N-M-G-R + A-D) elsewhere. Or perhaps when their mode of living from natural resources has been curtailed or destroyed outside of the city. For example, towns and cities only swelled during the pre-industrial stage of the UK and Europe after the 'common' fields and woods had been 'enclosed' by landowners. Indeed, to get rural people to leave the countryside in the UK and Ireland, countless villages had to be torn down and cottages demolished by landowners, who desired sole use of large tracts of land, for sheep, cattle or for other reasons. Otherwise rural inhabitants born and bred for generations in hamlets and villages by and large stayed away from the cities or just visited their monthly or annual markets and town fairs before returning to their homes. Like the above author I have no definitive evidence to ascertain why (or if) cities suddenly grew in those ancient times. However, from the little evidence I do have (and which is included in the next section) I think it more likely that in the middle and near east people were captured, enslaved and forced to settle into activities designed to 'irrigate' and 'reclaim' the land, 'cultivate' more food, build 'settlement walls' and 'manufacture' necessities and luxuries. If early hierarchical mass societies grew rapidly it would be more likely to be through the conquest of free or previously enslaved labour. And this enslavement of the 'other' was clearly not for their own benefit, but mainly for the benefit and enjoyment of ruthless elites and their armed supporters. I suggest it is more likely that the only 'inexorable pull', felt by the early labour force recruits to hierarchical mass society cities, was more likely to be from the chain or chains around their necks or ankles.

There is so much gloss and one-sided spin in the extracts which follow that as we proceed with this study the reader needs to bear in mind the evidence provided in the previous chapter, concerning the positive social and ecological balance of pre-hierarchical mass society modes of hunter-gatherer production. It was that mode of production, which had enabled the (N-M-G-R + A-D) process to be so successful that over millennia sections of humanity continually left Africa and repeatedly moved about and populated the entire planet, from east to west and from north to south. Only the two polar caps defied (for a time) the ingenuity and persistence of our ancestral hominid and homo sapien species. In the case of mainly gatherer-hunters and mainly hunter-gatherers on every continent the probability was established that their lives were rarely dire due to the vicissitudes of organic and inorganic nature except in the prejudiced imaginations of many sections of the Victorian middle and upper classes. In a typical mid-20th century bourgeois inspired eulogy of the benefits of mass society civilisations, the American scholar JH Breasted summarised much bourgeois opinion on the Near Eastern contribution to such hierarchical mass society developments in the following way.

"...the Ancient Near East domesticated the wild animals, especially cattle, sheep and goats, which served as food in the form of dairy products. It domesticated likewise the wild grasses, the seeds of which became our wheat, barley and other cereal grains, which could be cultivated in large quantities...It invented the Plough, and by substituting animal power for man power in agriculture it greatly increased the cultivated area....the peoples of the Near East gave the world. ...the first highly developed practical arts, such as the potter's wheel, the potters furnace, the loom and highly elaborate weaving, the earliest metal work...glass making, paper making...sea going ships.." (Ancient Times, James Henry Breasted. Second edition page 279.)

Domestication sounds so positive but deliberately omits the process of initial animal taming, by cruel application of force and pain and the later hobbling and corralling of draft animals. What is missing in this brief summary, but partly (and insufficiently) covered in the text, of this otherwise amply illustrated early 20th century volume of almost 1,000 pages about the Ancient Near East, is a serious questioning of the total domination of ordinary people and slave communities by armed war lords and their military subordinates. Missing too from such rose-tinted reminiscences are the known negative effects of mono-cultural domination and live-stock over-grazing of top-soil land mass, wherever this was practiced. The few exceptions to premature soil exhaustion were in places where the bi-annual valley bottom floods, such as along the Nile, the Tigris and Euphrates, etc. In the absence of major river valley flooding, it was well known even in those ancient days that years of mono-cultural plant growth or long term single animal species grazing in one primary location often exhausted the local soil for many decades. In other words this new mode of living frequently turned healthy productive natural flora and fauna, supporting a comprehensive range of nutritional life forms, and nutrition seekers into close to sterile conditions that supported hardly anything. Furthermore, it needs to be remembered that even for a hierarchical mass society community with zero population growth new land was always needed sooner or later.

It is now generally known, as was considered in the chapter on soil, that soil degradation is not just a question of water supply for degradation also occurs by destroying and unbalancing the range of natural decaying organic matter on which the many crucial micro-organisms and fungi survive and contribute to the fertility of soils. Once exhausted, soils have to be left for considerable lengths of time to recover, even when they can. So new land for agricultural use and other resources becomes a recurring necessity. For settled agricultural mass societies that do experience rapid population growth, the need for new land to cultivate or pasture to graze, the recurrent need for new land is even greater. The additional desire for ancient elites to accumulate wealth in the form of palaces, precious metals, gems, silks and other rare materials, which are surplus to essential nutritional production, has also, throughout history placed existential and ecological pressures upon the inorganic and organic resources of the region in which they first developed. Elite needs and desires have always placed excessive local demands upon production and consumption of the natural resources of the local sections and areas of the planet in which they were located. Understanding this basic bio-economic fact provides clues to the early origins of the rise of military elites and the unending wars between hierarchical mass societies, for ever more land and resources that only commenced when the era producing such societies began.

Undoubtedly, psychological factors of greed and aggression quickly become motivational components of wars within hierarchical mass societies, but it is necessary to look further than these secondary symptoms to explain this ancient systematic and persistent characteristic. Serious consideration needs to be given to the inevitable ongoing consequences of settled agricultural and animal rearing communities upon the fertility of the soil micro-organisms, even among those settled communities which are intentionally and consistently peaceful. The clearance of forests, for mass building material or fuel uses and to gain extra fields for cultivation, is a process almost without end even in sparsely inhabited areas. If the material produced by nature in any location is consistently consumed faster by any life-form (plant, insect, animal, or human) than its evolutionary reproduction rate can replace them as potential or actual resources, then that life form is in existential danger. In the era of hierarchical mass society development, commencing in the near and middle east, the depletion of natural resources in order to secure regular and consistent mass produced sources of nutrition (N) required the continual clearance of forest land and the eventual expulsion of existing peoples from access to all types of naturally fertile land. Therefore, hierarchical mass societies, even at their most primitive and limited in numbers, have always been excessively extractivist and expansionist with regard to the earth's natural resources.

Lacking the assistance of machinery, ancient agriculture consequently required relatively greater numbers of people to work the fields etc., than modern societies. Hence, it was the armed elites of hierarchical mass societies and the conscripts they employed, who in between the pillage and asset raiding of other communities for their own satisfaction, also conducted the territorial expansions required by their governing elites and central administrators, particularly when faced with increased birth rates or immigrant inflows. Military expedition forces were the social means the elites within hierarchical city states used to extend their power to govern the Near Eastern Cities and their later development into the Empires of Egypt, Persia, Greece and Rome. As we shall read in the following section, the most brutal and ruthless atrocities were regularly conducted by specialist trained and armed men from many cities perpetrated against the ordinary people of other near eastern, villages, towns and walled cities. They did so in order to enforce slave labour, 'rent in kind' and frequent tribute from them and primarily to acquire access to or control of new tracts of crop or other resource bearing land. Nevertheless, despite this brutal historical record, a one-sided positive view of the 'achievements' of past hierarchical mass societies is almost universal among the literate bourgeois historians of the 18th, 19th and 20th centuries. This tendency is revealed in the following extracts, where it will become clear yet again that vivid imagination and rampant prejudice has triumphed over carefully considered critical research.

"For sixty known centuries, this planet we call earth has been inhabited by human beings not much different than ourselves....But down through the ages, most human beings have gone hungry, and many have even starved.....Down through the ages, countless millions, struggling unsuccessfully to keep bare life in wretched bodies, have died young in misery and squalor...then suddenly in one place on earth there is abundance... " ('The Mainspring of Human Achievement.' H. G. Weaver. Part 1)

This is obviously not so much a logical or an ethnologically considered description as a prejudiced contrast between a completely imaginary '*dire*' past projection and a '*dazzling*' rose-tinted projection manufactured in modernity. Such opinions offer no evidence for their assertions, because there cannot be any evidence given the lack of accurate ancient prehistorical records - down through the ages. However, there were contemporary field studies of hunter-gatherer peoples accessible in America to the above quoted American Author. I know because I consulted those records myself in researching for the previous chapter. Nevertheless, according to H.G Weaver, hunter-gatherers and their ancestors were consistently 'hungry' and had 'wretched' bodies. He clearly lacked the motivation to visit existing hunter-gatherer groups or to even read the abundant anthropological literature about them produced in the 18th, 19th and 20th centuries before expressing his unfounded academic prejudices as 'facts'. The amazing thing to me is that many, if not most of such highly opinionated academics, were being paid handsome stipends and book receipts to express these feckless historical fancies. This particular author's ignorance was even compounded further, because the 'one place on earth', the above author had in mind was his country of birth, the United States of America. It is well known that the industrial 'abundance' of capitalist dominated North America was at the 'protracted' practice of a genocidal level of human and animal extermination of the previous natural 'abundance' of 'indigenous' human and animal life on the North American continent.

It was then, as later when the expression was coined, that the 'only good Indian was a dead one'. And of course much of the abundance grown in Plantation America "suddenly" came from the decades-long brutal exploitation of slave labour captured by the millions and exported from the coasts of West Africa to the American South. But of course the above author was not alone in such cultural myopia and national narcissistic vainglory. American exceptionalism was merely a New World variation of exceptionalist themes rooted in the 18th, 19th and 20th century anthropocentric consciousness of Spanish, French, Italian, German and British elites and carried by their colonialist representatives. In fact the constant glorification of certain people and nations (or even religions) became the basis for the phenomenon of collective forms of group-centred exaggerated exceptionalism. This in turn led to individual as well as collective forms of rampant narcissism. It gave rise to the phenomenon during the 16th centuries on of whole peoples or groups of rival peoples so in love with an idealised 'idea' of themselves, (such as the ancient Greek and Roman elites at certain periods), that they had a constant need to flaunt wealth, power, elicit admiration and assert that they were chosen by a god of one monotheistic version or another. These are elite sponsored symptoms which develop on the basis of the socio-economic practices of settled hierarchical mass society systems in conjunction with a persistent lack of empathy for all other less privileged groups of their own species.

In the 17th, 18th and 19th century this symptom of collective narcissism was also manifest among the British, Spanish, French and German elites during their 'empire' building stages. The typical lack of empathy for others being extended to each other when seriously competing for resources, as well as a lack for the indigenous peoples they were busily dispossessing and enthusiastically eliminating. In this context, the appearance in ancient Greek literature of the myth of Narcissus and Echo is worthy of a more detailed analysis, than it receives in Freudian type anthropocentric psychology. It can also be interpreted as a literary form of ancient metaphorical reflection of this phenomenon of exaggerated group exceptionalism within near eastern hierarchical mass society empire building. Excessive love of one's own community is rarely a single symptom, but a multiple one. It also invariably leads to a complete denigration (even hatred) of other communities, who then tend to reciprocate.

In the UK, for example, German based human beings were denigrated as 'Huns'; French human beings as 'Froggies'; Chinese human beings as 'Chinks', etc. Meanwhile, from the bourgeois historical perspective of most anthropocentrically and class biased authors who looked back to earlier times, the consolidation of hierarchical mass societies several thousand years ago has been constantly glorified by intellectually biased hyperbole. The naked process of elite orchestrated slavery, pillage, massacre and debt bondage is frequently personified by dressing its elites in ermine and gold and giving themselves the impressive title of 'heads of state'. Thus completing the orchestrated pomp and circumstance theatre of 'civilisation', to camouflage an elite form of ruthless conquering civil power and much else. One of the most concise, influential and original bourgeois views on human pre-history and such forms of elite devised "Civil Power" was provided by Thomas Hobbes who asserted in 1650 that;

"Hereby it is manifest that during the time men lived without a common Power to keep them in awe, they are in that condition which is called Warre; and such a warre, as is of every man, against every man." ('Leviathan'. Thomas Hobbes. Chapter 13.)

To Thomas Hobbes it was clear (or as he put it *'manifest'*) that before the formation of hierarchical mass societies, with their law and order institutions (i.e. 'Common Power'), that humans - presumably he meant on every continent - were constantly at war with each other! As was covered in the previous chapter this is an almost total imaginary retrospective fabrication concerning relationships between hunter-gatherer humanity on any of the continents, including the continent of Europe. Nevertheless, despite its nonsense, the idea of the superiority of bourgeois culture over all others was so seductive to elite sensibility that it continued as part of the dominant ideology and still lingers on among European prejudiced elites and those they effectively influence. Incredibly, the idea of keeping war in check by means of wielding superior military power has also not entirely exhausted its hold on many modern traditionally educated brains.

Power, wielding military power, is the source of wars not the prevention or elimination of this unnatural characteristic to have arisen among only one species of life on earth.

Although there have been archaeological sites dating back millions of years containing large numbers of animal bones, there have been none which have indicated a mass weaponised killing of human communities. The technological means as well as the social motive and whole idea of continual war upon war between human communities did not make an appearance within our species until hierarchical mass societies began to dominate the other previous modes of production. Then in multiple different forms this idea of historic or 'heroic' warfare to obtain 'natural resources' has continued to reappear centuries later, without anything other than elite assertion to back it up. Indeed, as we shall note later, this idea that continual 'war' is somehow 'natural' was at the core of the ideas of Malthus and Darwin and spilled over into their theories of evolutionary development of all life on earth (imagined as a constant war for species survival) and among all species of life on earth in general.

Around the core of the dualistic intellectual class based anthropocentric threads spun by Hobbes and others, has been woven intricate narrative tapestries which have produced much textual variety and many complex juxtapositions but these have rarely ever depicted anything other than a virtually constructed and flattering self-image of hierarchical mass society reality. However, at the same time the authors of most of these so-called ancient his-stories (vestiges of facts coated with layers of patriarchal fiction and male fantasy) have helped to shield and protect the bourgeois ideological presumption that war was something of an occasional aberration and not something directly and systemically related to the hierarchical mass society system of living and producing. The dualistic framing of the issue of human on human violence amongst some intellectual historians, was such that there were often only two forms of human societies, provided as examples. These were; hierarchical mass societies dressed up in fancy dress as 'civilisation' or 'primitive barbarism' dressed up in ragged furs with unkempt hair. This self-flattering bourgeois self-image, dualistic juxtaposed to an imagined pre-history, manages to avoid confronting the fundamental contradictions within hierarchical mass societies. As we shall see later, even those modestly recognising in the 20th and 21st centuries that all was not well with so-called 'civilisation', seem not to be able to free themselves of the inherited juxtaposed dualistic fantasies of 'civilisation' versus 'barbarism'. The assumption of an automatic link between the concept of 'progress' and the concept of 'civilisation' and an imaginary opposite condition to both - 'barbarism' and 'regression' – was even echoed in 2023 and 2024 by the leadership of colonialist-led Israel when they authorised the saturation bombing of Gaza. This 21st century use indicates the concept is still well entrenched in elite minds. Meanwhile, here is a slightly more honest definition of 'civilisation' written in the 20th century.

"The definition of civilisation commonly used by anthropologists and archaeologists is a material one. For them civilisation means literally 'life in cities'. We speak of the 'rise of civilisation' or the first civilisations on this basis....their common markers in material terms are virtually universal: cities, bronze technology, writing, great ceremonial buildings, temples, monumental art, hierarchies and class division, all sanctioned by some form of law, and held together by organised military force." (In Search of the First Civilisations'. Michael Wood. Preface.)

The author providing the above description acknowledges in the last sentence that everything in hierarchical mass societies, whether the word civilisation is used to label them or not, is based upon class divisions and *'held together by organised military force'*. This characteristic as much as anything establishes a fundamental difference between hierarchical mass societies of humans and the rest of biological and social life on earth since it began billions of years ago. In all other social aggregations, individual forms on reaching adulthood, including those human beings in hunter-gatherer societies, are overwhelmingly voluntary associations of organisms within each species. There is not a shred of evidence that any other life form, out of the millions of species noted in chapters 2, 3, 4, 5 or 6 are compelled by any internal or external force to remain within a particular social species community against their will. Furthermore, I have not come across one recorded instance in history where any species, other than the human species, has caused the complete existential extermination of any other species of life on earth, either plant, insect, or animal. Not one! Being held together and even being held apart - by force - is a completely unnatural state of biological evolution for any species of life which has evolved on earth. Furthermore, it is a uniquely late post-hunter-gatherer human occurrence of hierarchical system rule within the millions of species which have evolved over the billions of years of evolution. Considered against the whole spectrum of species in the evolution of life on earth, hierarchical mass societies are indeed a different and clearly an unnatural stage in the biological organisation of social life on earth. Yet it is still possible to read about early city states, that;

"These city states represented a new stage in social organisation.....The land was made abundantly fertile by the river born mud. Before this fertility could be effectively exploited, the rivers had to be controlled, and the large-scale systems of irrigation that was developed to meet this need involved a complex social organisation....some part of the population was freed from devoting all it's time and energies to the unremitting task of providing food....some men were able to function as specialists. Foremost among these were the Priests and Rulers...Below them were other classes...spinners and weavers, who are usually slaves." ('Lost Worlds'. Chapter 5 'The Dawn of Civilisation'. L. Cotterell.)

The author of the above and of an otherwise comprehensive and detailed resume of ancient history from written and archaeological sources, had clearly not done enough homework on the time spent by typical hunter-gatherer communities in securing the (N) of the (N-M-G-R + A - D) process of living, growing and reproducing. Indeed, abundant evidence was provided in chapter 8, of the same author's book, that the opposite was predominantly the case. The land was abundantly fertile before rivers were controlled by settled humans and the systems of irrigation, merely mimicked what the planet (by land collapses) and other animals (such as beavers) had done previously to change the direction of rivers. Perhaps I should repeat here again that I am not trying to depict a 'golden age' of humanity where human life on earth prior to hierarchical mass society formations was perfect or without any serious challenges. I am not! I am merely making the often neglected case that it was far more natural, far less stressful, certainly more egalitarian and far less ecologically destructive and polluting than later mass society modes of living and producing.

Plus I am making the case that our pre-historic ancestors were probably far more intelligent and skilful than they are given credit for by many modern scholars and commentators. Indeed, even many of our modern insect and animal species are equipped with enough sensory organs not to struggle to survive in places where there is little to eat or no means to protect themselves. Most living things - even those with the most minimal of central nervous systems- but with legs, wings or fins - just move away from any temporary or permanent barrenness and hardship. They migrate! Sometimes over great distances. To even consider that our ancient hominid and human ancestors, who were capable of hunting, gathering, making fire, fashioning flint tools, drawing on cave walls and no doubt banging out percussive rhythms on logs or skins, if short of anything they needed would simply stay where they were and die out, is nonsense. The modern implication that even early hominids were not equipped with enough sense to anticipate shortages and seek out places of plenty and safety, says more about the level of intelligence of those suggesting or implying that deficiency rather than that of early humanity.

Given the prolific production of organic nutritional matter of all kinds, the modern idea of unremitting struggles for all life forms to find it and utilise it, suggests those who came up with this idea were also the ones with a deficit in experience of field research and accumulating observational knowledge and local indigenous intelligence. Furthermore, compared with hunter-gatherer work/leisure balance, it can be rationally and convincingly argued that it was mass society, based upon agricultural work that introduced dawn to dusk unremitting labour, for some, particularly during harvest time. Note also in the above quote, the importance attached to the progress of reforming (civilising) the natural world by controlling rivers and large-scale irrigation. The idea that some men and women were supposedly 'freed, from the unremitting task of providing food!'

by being forced to dig ditches and construct containing banks in cloying clay and heavy sub-soil to alter the previous 'natural' waterways, can only have come from someone who hasn't used a spade for day after day to dig out ditches.

Even with modern machinery and tools, very little in hierarchical mass societies for the ordinary masses is easy. Practically everything is a drudge when done involuntary and is shunned when possible. Furthermore, dividing communities into leisured rulers, subordinate classes or castes, slaves and eventually a chattering and an academically performing middle class is hardly freeing any of them. No matter how well or ill they are treated, all of them are then trapped in the routines and class roles of the social system they are located within, but do not control. Even with super-efficient modern machinery, working people still have to toil by hand or by brain for 8 or more hours per day, five or six days a week for years on end. It is only necessary to watch TV or listen to the radio in the 20th and 21st centuries, to understand that it is now the role of the intellectual classes that are elevated above the working classes, and with awareness of their need to conform to the elites perspectives, are paid to do little more than endlessly talk, think, entertain each other and continually write opinions like the extract above and the one that follows;

"Of course, civilisation requires a modicum of material prosperity - enough to provide a little leisure. But far more, it requires confidence - confidence in the society in which one lives, belief in its philosophy, belief in its laws, and confidence in one's own mental powers....Vigour, energy, vitality: all the great civilisations - or civilising epochs - have had a weight of energy behind them. People sometimes think that civilisation consists in fine sensibilities and good conversation and all that. These can be among the agreeable results of civilisation, but they are not what makes a civilisation, and a society can have these amenities and yet be dead and rigid." (Civilisation. Kenneth Clark. Chapter 1)

Note the sloppy use of words in this extract. Note that the term *'weight of energy'* has no basis in reality. Energy as an abstraction or in reality has no weight. The word, 'society' is a verbal abstraction and therefore cannot be *dead and rigid*. Only the life forms living within 'societies' can eventually be dead and rigid. Yet the above author was paid for such opinions and given authority to deliver them by those above him. Indeed, most hierarchical mass society-based intellectual descriptions are layered over with many such convenient abstract rationalisations and one-sided appraisals. The achievements made during some outstanding bursts of productive energy, by living populations, are presented as the best thing ever - until the next thing. Moreover, the bourgeois concept of civilisation is still generally rooted in the city-state form of hierarchical mass societies first developed in and around the area in the Middle-East known as the Fertile Crescent. Yet even in the 21st century, the complexity of modern versions of hierarchical mass societies successive iteration's, is so taken for granted that the fundamental alienation from and alteration to the naturally developed (N-M-G-R+A-D) processes of all life is constantly overlooked.

As previously noted, it is obvious that any agricultural based hierarchical mass society, dependent upon farming, relies upon organised, forward planning in food production for its viability and success. Food production and food acquisition in this pre-planned form therefore underscores and overwhelmingly dominates all other forms of social activity with two important social differences. The first difference is that instead of a couple of collective hunter-gatherer hours spent securing food and shelter, specialist working sections of citizens now have to work all day to (not always) guarantee their daily food and shelter. The second difference is that those in the hierarchy who control the means of food production (on land or in rivers or sea), by that very fact, have a privileged and exploitative controlling role within any mass community based upon hierarchical class systems. It matters not whatever the particular mode of production is used to realise those (N-M-G-R + A - D) processes, it is the form and content of those modes which determine the exploitation and privilege.

Unlike among hunter-gatherer societies, differences in status within the hierarchical community arise not on a temporary and individual skills/aptitude basis, but on who effectively (and eventually permanently) controls access to the main means of production and the main means of physical coercion. Since the main means of production in a settled agricultural or pastoral community is the land for the planting of crops or for animal grazing purposes, it is therefore those who control the land through ownership (or control by delegation) who are the most influential or powerful. In hierarchical mass societies, the original social equality of human beings before nature is replaced by inequality before an individual land owner or their agents. And this indicates another change in the relationship between permanently settled humanity and nature and one radically different than the one between nomadic hunter-gatherer humanity and nature. From the commencement of settled agriculturally based hierarchies on, land and water are not only owned (or controlled) by a relative few but this control can only be transferred between elites by armed force and eventually under capitalism, by being bought and sold for profit (or profitable use), backed up by force. But even the latter (purchase and sale) is frequently determined by armed warfare. The purpose this elite control can be put to is determined by them, irrespective of the wider, ecological and climatological effects of its use on nature, life on earth in general and working humanity in particular. Once the intellect is freed from its self-obsession and seriously considered, the fact that under hierarchical mass society formations the choicest pieces of an entire planet can be monopolized by a relative few individuals and its local and regional resources utilised to undermine the very foundations of life on earth is a form of species madness. Yet the underlying rational economic essence behind this biological madness is frequently ignored and then it becomes possible to read;

"The growth of civilisation is essentially about the flourishing of human potential which has occurred during the course of history, and this has involved the steady growth of order, not only in self-control, social control and political organisation, but the imposition of order on the natural world through technology and science, and the life of the intellect through the development of systems of philosophy and religion." (Savagery and Civilisation'. C.R. Hallpike. Section 4)

It is interesting to ponder on how such intellectual champions of hierarchical mass society civilisation can seriously write that the growth of hierarchical mass societies is essentially about *"the flourishing of human potential"*. They must know about the ancient and modern history of slavery, the numerous genocides, the burning of female herbalists and midwives as witches in the middle and later ages, and of course the all-out killing and raping of females during countless wars spread over the last four or five thousand years of hierarchical mass society existence. Yet even more recent critics of modern capitalism can look back at the early formation of hierarchical mass societies and conclude as one author has done that if such societies were to survive and flourish; *"...humans would need not only to dominate nature, but bend it to their will."* In the sense used in such cases, the phrase 'dominating nature' for capital accumulation, actually means destroying or totally depleting large swathes of nature's organic and inorganic resources.

So in fact 'dominating' life on earth (i.e. nature), amounts to humans destroying and using up much of their own (and the rest of organic life's) only means of sustaining their own and other species' existence. That is precisely what modern capitalist based, hierarchical mass societies have been animated to do and with such devastatingly negative and accelerated outcomes. Based upon the abundant climate and ecological evidence, that is the opposite of the conclusions any clear thinking person would seriously arrive at. It matters little that some individuals have exaggerated the speed and extent of this depletion of natural resources and are thus easily contradicted by the supporters of hierarchy and capital domination. It is not the logic of the hierarchical mass society systems economic functioning, which determines the exact year, or month of an eventual cascading biological system collapse. For example, the logic underlying the so-called game of Russian roulette does not predict which bullet will destroy a particular player at a particular moment in time, it merely acknowledges the fact that if the game continues the 'end' will come for some player. Meanwhile, any uncertainty of when a catastrophic outcome might occur should not be used as reasons to carry on treating species of life as if they were commodities, to be bought and sold or consumed as raw materials with no connection with the cycle of life on earth. The latter treatment is what the powerful have been trying to do for generations and have almost succeeded in the case of some species. It is undeniable that the form and shape of the natural world has been radically changed in the past and is still being tragically deformed - everywhere. The forest and sea photosynthetic species which function as the oxygen regenerating species of the planet are now being cut down or clogged up with pollutants. So it is somewhat surprising that past eulogies of 'progress' by the philosophical intelligentsia about the wonders of hierarchical mass societies are still being regurgitated in the 21st century. Here is one from a generation previous to my own.

"The history of the world is none other than the progress of the consciousness of Freedom; a progress whose development according to the necessity of its nature, it is our business to investigate....the Eastern nations knew only that 'one' is free; the Greek and Roman world only that 'some' are free; while we know that all men absolutely (man as man) are free..." ('The Philosophy of History'. Hegel Georg. Introduction.)

It is perhaps not surprising that Hegel, probably the most profound idealist philosopher that 19th century Europe has ever produced, should view German and World history in terms of abstract ideas such as God, Freedom and Consciousness and not on food and reproduction or (N-M-G-R + A-D), bio-diversity. But this quote also illustrates the point made earlier, that bourgeois ideology in Europe saw world history anthropocentrically in terms of the 'progress' of elite based human societies, emerging from the East, traversing through Greece and Rome and on to the advanced countries of Europe. This anthropocentric viewpoint was projected whether the 'progress' being considered was in the realms of the practical arts, crafts and industries or in the creative arts of literature, drama, sculpture, theatre or philosophy. So despite ample evidence to the contrary, (i.e. human and animal massacres, deforestation, water/sea/air pollution, soil degradation, ecological balance destruction and climate change etc.) the celebration of the supposed benefits of hierarchical mass society forms over the last two centuries has continued and is almost universal. The absorption of the dominant ideology of bourgeois mass society culture seems to have blinded some intellectuals to what should be blindingly obvious. The glaringly obvious problems created by hierarchical mass society formations which other, more critically aware people can see, is why the abstraction 'civilisation' has long had difficulty in being fully accepted and has often needed an intellectual stimulant or 'sweetener' to help flavour the bitter medicine of reality dished out by hierarchical mass society alienation and exploitation. The harsh reality of 'civilisation' was thus provided with a linguistic sedative to partner it in the social crime of brain-fogging the population. The intellectual sedative took the form of the 'Idea of Progress'.

"The idea of human Progress then is a theory which involves a synthesis of the past and a prophecy of the future. It is based on an interpretation of history which regards men as slowly advancing -'pedetemtim' 'progredientes'- in a definite and desirable direction, and infers that this progress will continue indefinitely....which will justify the whole process of civilisation." ('The Idea of Progress': An Inquiry into its Origin and Growth'. J.B.Bury. Introduction.)

In this case of promoting a retrospective 'defence for the hierarchical mass society form of living', a sprinkle of Latin has been added to perhaps tickle the intellectual taste buds of those invited to swallow and internalise these twin ersatz concepts of 'desirable directions' and 'progress'. In the above extract the abstraction 'Progress' has also been given the status of a theory and has been miraculously given its own source of internal energy and motion so in imagination it can - continue indefinitely. And it is not hard to figure out, given 'civilisations' track record, that it will be elite opinions (as long as they continue to dominate) that continue to determine and 'justify' what a "definite and desirable direction" might be. So despite wars, conquests and poverty along with increasing evidence of global warming, climate change, sea, air and land pollution, ecological destruction and key species loss, the justification of hierarchical mass society living as 'civilisation' continues its long history. Even alongside the advance of scientific understanding during the last century, there has remained a dearth of critical thinking across whole sections of modern societies. Hence it is possible to also come across many extracts like the following:

"Human civilisation has extraordinary powers of recovery; and, since its original appearance long ago, civilisation has always been preferable to barbarism or anarchy. Renewal is

possible even after a long interval, as is shown, for example, by the revival of Europe after the collapse of the Roman Empire, or the ebb and flow of civilisation in China despite repeated foreign conquest." ('In Defence of Civilisation: How our Past can renew our Present'. M.R.J. Bonner. Introduction.)

I am generally supportive of optimism but such one-sided distortion needs to be called out, particularly if there is overwhelming evidence to suggest it is being used to inculcate or perpetuate naivety, complacency, vainglory and gullibility in the reader. Civilisation in the form of at least 13 of the 'empires' of the historical past have brutally wiped themselves out and hierarchical mass societies have not always been preferable to non-hierarchical and non-mass societies as the study of anthropological and archaeological evidence have demonstrated. A re-constitution of the same system by a similar ruling elite system within past hierarchical mass societies has never removed the contradictions within them and would not be the equivalent of a transformation led by groups of citizens who were dedicated to re-fashioning how they relate to each other or to nature. The amount of reverence extended to the pre BCE agricultural mass society re-shapers of life on earth by practically all the 19th and 20th century bourgeois historians is immense and almost overwhelming. The sheer volume, quantity and unanimity of this ideology of 'progress' as a process of so-called benign domestication and alteration of nature, makes it hard for most people not to be swept along by it. Resistance to being swept along or swept away by torrents of such propaganda however, can be strengthened by constantly keeping in mind what was (and is) actually happening to the status of most humans, many animals and many plants. The (N-M-G-R+A-D) processes of life for all forms of domesticated species were being progressively altered and chained (yes often literally) to this alternative mode of production based upon a hierarchical mass society structure. Here is another example of an author's abstract optimism on steroids.

"We are on the cusp of the fastest, deepest, most consequential transformation of human civilisation in history, a transformation every bit as significant as the move from foraging to cities and agriculture 10,000 years ago.....We have the opportunity to move

from a world of extraction to one of creation, a world of scarcity to one of plenitude, a world of inequity and predatory competition, to one of shared prosperity and collaboration." *('Rethinking Humanity'. J. Arbib. & T. Sebastian. 'Executive Summary'.)*

Note the exclusive anthropocentric focus in this extract and its total divorce from the class based reality of the capitalist mode of production. The future of life on earth is seen purely through the prism of human self-centered narcissism. Not only that, the above authors have not even understood that the abstractions 'extraction' and 'creation' they have used are not two alternative modes of human social existence, they represent two tightly bound inter-dependent connected parts of a socio-economic process. Extraction and creation are not parts of separate worlds. It's impossible to have one without the other. In order to create something tangible, material must be extracted from somewhere and processed (i.e. created) into an alternative material form in some way. As was demonstrated in previous chapters, within the realms of organic life on earth, from the microscopic cell to the largest whale in order to create the most sophisticated forms of organic (biological) growth and reproduction, organic and inorganic material must be extracted, from the environment, internally metabolised by the organism's cell processing structures and waste material extruded.

To create a non-organic object of utility or decoration, additional energy rich raw material must also be extracted; to produce motive powers for propelling extractive technologies needing machine manufactured movements. Sources of energy must be extracted from the material containing it. Hierarchical mass societies have been mass extracting in order to mass create nutritional and other utilitarian products since their ancient origin, albeit within a restricted area of the planet until the late 20th century. Moreover, the capitalist mode of production, in the form of industry and automation has now turbo-charged both extraction and so-called productive creation of commodities and technologies with life-destroying and planet damaging consequences. This next particular quote is from a book by an author who recognises the many problems that modern hierarchical societies have created and acknowledges the current crisis situation embracing the entire world. However, by the book's title ('The Ascent of Humanity') and with following introductory remarks the author also cannot help but focus on and emphasise a positive side to the massive and fatal anthropocentric contradictions at the heart of hierarchical mass society forms of living. He writes;

*"Accumulating over thousands of years, culture and technology have brought us into a **separate human realm**. We live, more than any animal, surrounded by our own artefacts. Among these are works of **surpassing beauty**, complexity, and power, human creations that could not have existed - could not even have been conceived-in the times of our forebears....We have created a realm of **magic and miracles**."* ('The Ascent of Humanity' C. Eisenstein. Introduction. Emphasis added. RR.)

A 'separate human realm'? Really! Can the human species live outside of an oxygenated, nutrient abundant, and microorganism prolific realm of the earth's biosphere? We need to question just how such forms of Doctor Pangloss anthropocentric type reality denial, such as the above, can arise in such so-called educated intellects. To even consider that the last century (i.e.the 20th) and this 21st one so far has been a realm of surpassing beauty, magic and miracles! When in fact two World Wars, the trafficking of women and displaced people, several organised genocides of various branches of humanity, mass extinctions of various key life forms, (Insects, Forests, Birds, Fish), a number of lethally circulated pandemics, devastating levels of air, sea, river, lake and land pollution by plastics, metals, oils, pharmaceutical chemicals and Nuclear waste dumping; are hardly invisible or fail to exhibit known characteristics. Despite a few isolated things of artificial manufactured beauty and complexity, the former natural beauty and complexity of pre-industrial life on substantial parts of earth has at the same time been overwhelmingly and repeatedly degraded. In the 20th century and now in the 21st, the so-called ascent of humanity can far more relevantly be described as more of a descent into a dark polluted and polluting abyss for humanity that has also taken many other living things down with it. Despite the many modern existential problems caused by hierarchical mass societies, the flow of euphoric hyperbole still gushes forth. Observe also the use of the collective 'we' in the above quote, for proposed changes which will actually be controlled not by 'us' but by a relatively few elites. Note also that the sentiments expressed are firmly in the tradition of bourgeois anthropocentric ideas of continual (even infinite) material 'progress' and of course any form of material progress means extracting, processing and consuming more and more organic and inorganic material and at a faster rate than it can reproduce itself or be replaced.

Essentially the same sentiments were uttered by similar bourgeois idealists at the outset of the 17th century Industrial Revolution. Mass production, they preached, would make things cheaper and more available so everyone would have a drip down share in the future prosperity of the bourgeois elite. In reality the rich got richer, the poor stayed relatively or absolutely poor and the bombs, shells and pollution got larger and more widespread. The ideological purpose of pro-capitalist 'pushing' or 'spinning' of such fantasy futures is to convince people that without hierarchical mass societies and state power wielded by an elite, then humanity will inevitably return back to the imaginary state of warlike barbarism. But we have seen that previous to ancient hierarchical mass societies humanity existed without elites dominating and ruling human communities. The elite also have an additional rational fear, that given a choice, the majority might in future decide to dispense with them and move on to establish some form of egalitarian and ecologically-sound social organisation. Consequently the use of the dualistic construct of 'civilisation' versus 'barbarism' has been chosen to remove any serious discussions of other possible forms of future living and to cast a benign glow over the dark progress of hierarchical mass society formats. And there is good reason for such one-sided perspectives as we shall read in the following section on the dark side of hierarchical mass society evolution. Finally, to close this section's review of a cross section of the pro-hierarchical mass society lobby, I include a more jaundiced view of civilisation that hints at - another world might be possible.

"When people imagine civilisation breaking down, they often imagine a brutal world where food is scarce and we have to fight to survive - something between what they imagine 'cavemen' to be like and a Mad Max film. But if we consider that contemporary

hunter-gatherer people regard the incursion of Western industry, working practices, technologies and ideologies into their worlds as savage and destructive, the picture switches. We can look at things differently." (Veneer of Civilisation'. Will Black. Chapter 1.)

It is to be hoped that this random selection of extracts supportive of hierarchical mass society settlements, has been sufficient to convince the reader that among modern elite 'influencers' these were, and still are, typical of many such pro-capitalist views. They can be replicated from within most technically 'advanced' countries of Europe and the world. Although these above are unevenly spread, both geographically and historically, these and similar comments have appeared during three centuries of supposedly considered judgement, by many industrialists, historians, educators, politicians and even military elites. Moreover they can be found in far more than one or two countries. Furthermore, even though I am really trying, I have failed to find one seriously critical, modern appraisal of the concept and practice of hierarchical mass society living. Still less have I found a few links that have , made to the socio-economic sources of the continuing 20th and 21st century alienation suffered and diagnosed as mental and physical disorders, by human and animal species. One of the few exceptions is with regard to psychiatrist J. Moncrieff, who argues that 'Blaming the Brain' (the title of a book by, psychologist Elliot Valenstein) for socially created class based alienations and prescribing drugs such as Prozac, Zoloft, Paxil, Celexa and Lexapro, conveniently diverts attention away from the social system in which people are living amid socially constructed personal contradictions. She writes;

"The medical approach doesn't help people find solutions to their problems, It substitutes a careful understanding of each individual's predicament with a diagnostic label. And rather than providing the social support and community that most people need, it discourages people from understanding the social implications of their feelings and hinders them from reaching out to others to find collective solutions. . . . ultimately, mental health problems like depression and anxiety are social and political problems. If we wish to tackle them, we need as a society to

prioritise addressing the circumstances that give rise to them."
(Chemically Imbalanced' J. Moncrieff.)

This anthropocentric obsession with avoiding critical appraisal of elite humanities negative relationships within its own species due to its mode of production, is the other side of the coin to the elites negative relationship to nature. Nature reflected in the anthropocentric elite mind-set is merely present as an interesting and useful backdrop to so-called 'civilised' human activity rather than the absolute foundation of everything that exists on planet earth and everything that lives within its biosphere. This absence of a serious and thorough large-scale criticism of hierarchical mass society formations, suggests that for all practical purposes there are none. The continuing task of criticism, therefore, still remains, to uncover and consider what kind of dehumanisation went on during the formation of these so-called 'civilisations' and to figure out why.

D) Hierarchical civilisations in practice.

It has long been held that the beginnings of what are now given the title 'civilisations' occurred in what is known, from its rough arc of inclusion on a map, as the 'fertile crescent' region of the middle east. The lower arc of this imaginary crescent can be visualised as covering the fertile region inundated by the river Nile and now known as Egypt. This imaginary crescent of fertile land arched upward, through what is now Palestine and Syria and over toward the east covering Babylon, Mesopotamia, Assyria and down to the Persian Gulf. In modern times it covers the countries currently designated as Egypt, Syria, Persia, Arabia and the Gulf States. This fertile crescent area is considered, by those 19th and 20th century European traditions we considered above, to be where an agricultural based mode of production first allowed numerous human groups to settle around places where the (N-M-G-R + A-D) processes based upon domesticated crops, animals and people could be controlled and managed efficiently and effectively. This radical change in the mode of production in turn enabled both the feeding of large numbers of settled people and the segmentation of human groups into hierarchical concentrations (city states) and within them, into social groups referred to as classes and into various occupational strata.

Nevertheless, ancient archaeological evidence has also unearthed similar societies in many other places such as the Island of Crete where a well organised settled form of mass society described as a Minoan civilisation which had links to the Mycenaean mass societies around the Aegean Sea. In the 20th century many hierarchical mass society formations were also discovered or rather re-discovered in Central and South America and on the African continent. However, the dating of these finds has not always been agreed by many of the academics who devoted their time and careers to one or other of the city state and empire formations of settled mass societies. However, since the purpose of this study is primarily to consider the effects of mass society aggregations upon life on earth as a whole - by a representative collection of its main forms of production - then the chronological sequencing of their evolution is less important. What needs to be established in this study is simply the fact of the radical form of the change itself, its social essence, and the ecological effects this human concentration had upon life on earth in general.

Whatever the actual origins and transitions to larger and larger concentrations, I suggest that it is useful to consider that these city-state formations represent a second settled stage that had been reached beyond an original and localised settled transition from hunter-gatherer modes of production. That is a stage when successful settled agricultural communities had become sufficiently spread across a fertile region and classes within them had become firmly established. In these city-state developments, male ruling elites had socially evolved and had elevated some male citizens into a permanent group of armed rulers/warriors, and had made women and many men into actual domestic and/or social slaves, engaged in reproductive, agricultural and occupational craft work. In such cases, the ruling elite, religious or secular, not only controlled vital resource sources but as a class effectively controlled or 'owned' land, water and crops, which were the essential (N) sources needed to continue the whole agriculturally based (N-M-G-R + A-D) mass society process. Moreover, by this middle-eastern stage, the elite also controlled and 'owned' many (and later) most of the people in their communities. Some human beings and animals had ceased to be viewed by the elites as just other examples of life on earth species that shared and sustained the planet. In fact economically speaking, non-elites within hierarchical mass societies had in practice become units of exploited labour and were viewed as such. Their numbers became calculations in a complex economic system devoid of any humane or species considerations or any concepts of 'rights' for those animal and human life-forms then being captured or bred into slavery. In this regard it is useful to consider the period of the Greek author Xenophon's ongoing open concern for developing state ownership of human labour-power assets in the ancient city of Athens Greece. Revealed by this particular author, is the cold and calculating considerations that the typical so-called 'civilised' elite men in ancient hierarchical mass societies, were by then making. He wrote;

"Assume, however, that the total number of slaves to begin with is twelve hundred. By using the revenue derived from these the number might in all probability be raised to six thousand at the least in the course of five or six years. Further, if each man brings in a clear obol a day, the annual revenue derived from that number of men is sixty talents. Out of that sum, if twenty talents are invested in additional slaves, the state will have forty talents available for any other necessary purpose. And when a total of ten thousand men is reached, the revenue will be a hundred talents" (Xenophon. 'Ways and Means'.)

In Xenophon's hierarchical mass society elite consciousness, some human beings have ceased to be fully human beings and have become alienated units of labour for the elite's surplus-labour and surplus-value extraction calculations. Those 'Ways and Means' outlined by Xenophon were essentially the same type of economic calculations that appeared in modified forms during the North Atlantic Slave Trade Plantations hundreds of centuries later. Business as usual in the hierarchical mass societies of the ancient middle-east was practiced on less scientific but a similar calculated commodity-type trading basis as modern capitalist industrial societies. Life forms of many shapes and sizes could then be owned or controlled on a regular basis, thus sources of labour power became dehumanised or domesticated elite-owned units of economic enrichment and development. One set of human beings, the elites, could, if they choose, become cold calculating exploiters of plant and animal nature whilst another section of humanity, the permanently enslaved or 'bonded' masses, became servants to the elite. On the basis of this socio-economic social structure, all animal organisms could be compelled to become life-long beasts of burden or labour-power instruments of anthropocentric production and wealth accumulation for the elites in control of them. This ancient fact illustrates, that the problem for the bulk of humanity and other life forms is not primarily the most recent capitalist mode of alienated production, but all modes of production based upon the hierarchical mass society, divisions of labour, as directed by an elite whose motive became the exploitation of life on earth to accumulate wealth. Hence, the naive and simplistic ahistorical concept articulated by many people in the 20th and 21st centuries, that capitalism was the only and central problem for working people and for life on the planet in general. Hence also the mistaken naive 'socialist' conception that slightly different forms of hierarchical mass societies (with less ruthless or greedy elites) could solve the problem of slavery, exploitation, oppression, alienation and wars of conquest and annexation. As we shall read, such inhuman practices and attitudes to other human beings and other species, are not optional, but are structurally built into all forms of hierarchical mass societies - no matter what political labels or modes of production are attached to them. It matters not what fantasies about themselves, (sadistic or humane) the different elites and their citizens have swirling around in their heads, the hierarchical mass society system functions according to a logic of over-exploitation and over consumption of natural resources. Hierarchical control of the essential (N-M-G-R + A-D) biological processes grinds out its own class-determined levels of de-humanised logic.

Thus in the ancient period, when other such successful settled hierarchical mass communities became established within a day or two's march of a pre-existing one, the possibility of recruiting and using the warrior class to conquer them and exact tribute and slaves from them became a possibility, a probability and then an eventuality. This outcome stemmed not primarily from a 'wicked' human trait but from the necessity to control ever more resources in order to satisfy a growing number of labouring mouths to feed and a growing number of governing elites to keep in luxury. Therefore, the march to and conquest of, foreign land was just waiting for a sufficiently motivating cause for it to be triggered into actuality. Eventually when excessive wealth became viewed by ruling elites as a logical elite *entitlement* for them, then war and conquest became both a lifestyle choice and a necessity for some, particularly when the ruling elite expanded, via its own reproductive (R) activity with or without their enslaved women gathered in harems. The resulting elite male offspring invariably wanted a piece of the hierarchical entitlement to wealth, power and foreign pillaging 'action'. The hierarchical mass society form had, by successive increments of growth and military technique, then arrived at a stage of development which allowed the empire building activities which over many centuries took place in Sumer, Babylon, Egypt, Assyria, Persia, Greece and Rome, before the more modern feudal and bourgeois 'empires' essentially followed the same basic pattern.

It should be noted that the pre-dynastic mass society city-states prior to all these named ancient empires were already interconnected and influencing each other, through trade and other forms of communication. However, in this case again the precise developments and interactions of each were rarely recorded in detail and therefore can only be approximately estimated. The more definitive records of interactions between hierarchical mass society formations are those celebrating victories in wars and battles. For example a large carving discovered in 1898 in Upper Egypt depicted an Egyptian king wearing a crown in the style of Upper Egypt. In one hand he holds a mace and with his other hand he is grasping the hair of a kneeling figure. Clearly this represents a conquest of somewhere and of some human resources; possibly (if not probably) the conquest of upper Egypt by lower Egypt. A further, much later event inscribed on a stele (stone tablet or column) reads;

"I fared downstream in might to overthrow the Asiatics by the command of Amen, the just of counsels; my brave army in front of me like a breath of fire, troops of Medja-Nubians (mercenary soldiers) aloft on our cabins to spy out the Setyu and to destroy their places." *(Quoted in Cottrell 'Lost Worlds'. Part 4.)*

Note that this is an unwitting record of the actions by a particular hierarchical mass society elite before the invention of the modern term 'civilisation' which was then retrospectively applied to everything and anything that could be remotely connected to the current forms of hierarchical mass societies. Yet another inscription on an Egyptian chapel wall records "clubbing", "striking down", "trampling", and "enslaving" people within the territory of an invaded region. This type of public acknowledgement and celebration of aggression and brutality in hierarchical mass society Egypt, indicates that these particular social formations had long before the event depicted had trained human beings to be not only indifferent to others of their own species but to be absolutely hostile to them. The military forces of such hierarchical mass societies, were by that period, fully prepared (socialised) not only to brutally kill and maim, but, as we shall read, to torture, rape and enslave other members of their own species. By this period of history, the naturally evolved humanity of much of pre-hierarchical mass society human species had been deformed into its inhumane opposite, by the complete immersion of some human beings in the alienating structures of hierarchical mass society living.

It is clear from the studies of early Egypt from the Upper and Lower mass society communities/kingdoms, that in all cases, intensive and extensive divisions of labour had already been imposed along with class divided and enforced social structures. In Egypt, a relative few at the top of the social hierarchies in the middle east, were then living in absolute luxury, whilst in the middle strata's, considerable numbers lived in various stages of administrative wealth and relative affluence and the mixed occupational non-elite masses at the bottom of these hierarchical mass-societies lived by means of exchanging their relative levels of daily labour drudgery and servitude for just enough to keep them usefully alive. Occupations such as digging ditches, working in quarries and down mines or initially conveying buckets of water all day from the river Nile to irrigate the crops in adjacent fields. These occupations became an exhausting, and intellectually numbing 24/7 routine for months on end for those human beings relegated to the status of the working classes of ancient hierarchical mass societies.

Moreover, digging and clearing irrigation channels and canals had to be done routinely and continually by physical immersion in them. For others, as previously noted, sowing, reaping, threshing, storing, grinding and baking also became one-dimensional daily and life-time occupations. Moreover, as noted above the products of the labour that all this intensive and extensive process created in Upper and Lower Egypt became both a reason and a means for the leading elites in these (kingdoms) to employ violent armed men to conquer, control and exploit more and more resource and labour rich territory. And not only human slave labour but also, the animal, vegetable and human tribute resources already extensively domesticated there. Twice this military conquest 'unification' of the two kingdoms of Egypt occurred and as we shall see, this process of invasion, conquest, pillage, tribute, rape and slavery, became the template for all future settled, hierarchical, regional mass society 'civilisations' controlled by armed elites. Historically, this pattern of hierarchical mass society formation began first in the Near East, then centuries later, was spread to Europe and eventually in the 18th, 19th and 20th centuries to the entire globe, with similar consequences. Here is another example of modern historians in retrospective admiration of the power and splendour of previous ruling elites, but failing to recognise the brutal reality and the contradictions in (and beyond) what they write. This time again writing on early Egypt and imaginatively fantasising about the ordinary people's mystical regard for their kings;

"The prosperity of the land, the fertility of the soil, the survival of his people depended ultimately upon the king. In their eyes, he was divinity incarnate, and after his earthly death he would continue to watch over Egypt's welfare as he had done in life." ('Lost World's. Chapter 2)

In the mind of the above author, the transition of humans to hierarchical mass society labouring has been accompanied by an ideological transference of agency for obtaining the human (N-M-G-R + A-D) processes. The agency of collective living has been intellectually projected onto a single privileged individual – the king. These two sentences are clear evidence of deliberate fabrications and myopic prejudice being applied to the historical past. Only extreme modern prejudice could imagine that ordinary people of ancient Egypt would of their own volition actually believe such hocus-pocus written in the above quote. With regard to the first sentence: A) the prosperity and fertility of any land based upon agricultural production, then or now, depends upon people tilling, manuring, planting, watering the land and working on the production of essential foods and non-foods - and the masses from daily experience certainly knew that! Those who worked the land know that no way does producing crops depend upon some privileged male wearing a specially constructed gown and ridiculous hat who potters about or is carried around the palace halls in a litter on the shoulders of slaves, and stopping off for shade in the palace gardens.

And B) It was also well known at the ordinary agricultural folk level that the fertility of the soil in the Nile valley depended upon the seasonal floods. Some even guessed that rains and snow melts in east Africa, and the effect of gravity bringing water, rich in minerals and organic material, down the two Nile rivers, the White and the Blue, and depositing it on the flood plains. The ordinary people at the time certainly knew the crops depended upon the Nile Floods, even if they did not know what caused them, or how far the water had travelled. Even the most uneducated agricultural slave, if they knew nothing else, would know that fertility ultimately depended upon themselves working the flooded fields during the seasonal floodings of the Nile. Apart from impressionistic imagination and gullibility, even thousands of years ago it was known that the seasons and water flowing down rivers and over hills had nothing to do with a king but everything to do with the rains, the climate, the planet's orbit, and gravitational attraction. Their working people were already building walled gardens, temples and Pyramids. Moreover, they also knew that many of these natural events occurred freely without the expenditure of any labour! C), Even without the benefits of such detailed modern scientific research most ancient peoples knew that their survival depended upon the inorganic and organic material provided by nature the latter by this time being planted, tended, grown to maturity and harvested by efforts of the people, not on this or that pronouncement or incantation by a king or priest. It is just perpetuating sycophantic mystical nonsense to describe economic success as the result of some real or imaginary elite being, and suggesting otherwise demonstrates a total disrespect for previous generations of human beings. .

Moreover, it should be overwhelmingly obvious that after an interval of 3,000 years, the author of the above lines had no way of knowing the details of what ordinary people thought about the king. Let alone that *"in their eyes"* the king was *'divine'* or that they thought "prosperity, soil and survival" depended entirely upon him. The above author has just made up this whole make believe narrative or has uncritically borrowed the idea from some other privileged spinner of royalist fables and fantasies. It is this modern author whose understanding of humanity is probably more backward than the people he is imaginatively denigrating whilst describing. However, making things up to fill any gaps in knowledge or to suit a particular ideological position was (and is) not solely a matter of class prejudice by historians, for there is an abundance of that within all forms of ancient and modern literature. However, the sparsity of accurate and reliable historical evidence from the 'lower orders' has also invited the use of make believe narratives by middle class intellectuals to pad out what might otherwise have led to incredibly thin historical volumes. The line between fiction and non-fiction literature is far too often extremely difficult to untangle. Very few historians, particularly European based ones, trapped in Abraham anthropocentric patriarchal religious beliefs with their 'kingdoms of god' from childhood, can resist the temptation to supply snippets of myth and legend drawn from one monotheistic narrative source assumption or another and stretch it and weave it into or onto another selected source in order to engage or flatter the dispenser of modern stipends for exercising the skill of writing. One of the few 19th century historians to even recognise what was typically happening in the creation of history was George Grote, who in 1846, included in his history of Greece, the following;

"I begin the real history of Greece with the first recorded Olympiad (776 BCE). For the truth is, that ***the historical records, properly, so called, do not begin until long after this date;*** *nor will any man (!) who candidly considers the extreme paucity of attested facts for two centuries after 776 BCE be astonished to learn that the state of Greece in 900, 1000, 1100, 1200, 1300,*

1400 BCE, - or any earlier century which it may please chronologies to include in their computed genealogies - cannot be described to him (!) upon anything like decent evidence."
(Grote: Quoted in 'Lost Worlds'. Emphasis added. RR)

Indeed, in the weaving of Greek mythic literature there are assumptions that the Greek island and peninsular habitations were founded by colonising expeditions from Egypt (allegedly founding Athens), from the Caucuses (led by Prometheus), from Phoenicia (allegedly led by Cadmus) and fortress walls (allegedly built by the mythical Cyclopes). However, this mythology can only be considered indicative of the influx of ambitious groups into the Fertile Crescent region in general. It cannot be used to authenticate chronological, geographical or historical accuracy. This lack of reliable historical record in the case of Greece is no less valid than is the case with city states and empires prior to the period of Greek domination of the Middle East by the mythical 'greatness' of Alexander of Macedon. Whilst it is true that since the early 19th century archaeological evidence in the form of artefacts and their dating has exponentially increased, sufficient caution in interpreting them in order not to confirm ideas and opinions already formed is still not regularly practiced.

In fact the previously noted author (Cottrell) should know that despite this warning by Grote, and others, he was still connecting sparse factual things together by manufacturing myth-based links and embroidered speculations. This is revealed later in the same chapter when he describes wall scenes painted in tombs showing farm hands sowing and harvesting crops; drivers of cattle moving herds and butchers cutting up carcasses. His own evidence based, wall painting observation, of what was depicted there contradicts what he actually wrote earlier. This contradiction does not negate Grote's earlier warning for the author above then proves the opposite of what he had previously written, but does not even bother to correct his false facts or his own unsubstantiated opinions. In fact only five pages later in the same chapter the above author presents evidence which should have cautioned him against making such sweeping assertions. In commenting on the condition of the kings bodies in eighty or so known pyramids, large and small, built for the various kings and Pharaohs of Egypt, he writes;

"Every one of these bodies was stripped, destroyed and robbed of its precious equipment thousands of years ago. All that survives are the empty shells of the sacred tombs. The bodies of the royal dead have disappeared, as have those of the countless hordes who laboured to build these eternal homes for the great ones." (ibid)

In other words these supposedly 'revered' kingly bodies and funeral relics had already been fully disrespected and trashed, long before modern European collectors followed this disrespectful pattern and as agents of their own professional advancement, and agents of museums and wealthy collectors plundered them yet again. This time the relics and valuables were transported to stately homes and museums in the UK and Europe. Whilst this fact of endemic tomb robbing within a short period of death in Egypt is not itself sufficient evidence to conjecture that most people in ancient Egypt had considerable contempt for the king or his so-called divine status, it does suggest that even respect for authority in Egypt was not as universal as some deferential modern 'experts' on Egypt would have us believe. Furthermore, lacking long distance transport, the fact that ordinary ancient tomb robbers were possibly (or probably) part of the local community and the stolen grave goods would circulate among and between such communities' obviously means one thing. It means that the circle of disrespect was far wider than just the ones who got their hands and knees dirty digging away the dirt and carrying out the actual tomb raiding and recycling any valuable contents.

Plus it is obvious that the ancient Egyptian elite already knew that official precautions and complex strategies of hiding tombs and entrances were absolutely necessary in order to try to avoid or minimise future tomb raiding. It was clearly common knowledge in ancient Egypt that ordinary people considered it fair game to rob, strip and destroy royal tombs as soon as it was safe to do so. I point this possibility out not to suggest that I have sufficient evidence to confirm what people actually thought of a king who lived in luxury and ordered thousands of slaves to build massive tombs for themselves and their queens. I clearly do not have such evidence. No one can really know how ordinary people felt or what they thought even a few hundred years ago let alone a few thousand. I am merely pointing out such illogical academic projections and assumptions and imaginative interpretations to alert the reader to the function of widespread historical academic self-serving 'spin' and to urge caution against accepting uncritically what people who present themselves as historical experts claim to know. This is particularly relevant when those ordinary working people have already been contemptuously described by the writer as "hordes", not as ordinary working people.

With respect to the previously noted whole period of initial developments into city states and kingdoms, the earlier noted Thucydides, in his 'History of the Peloponnesian War' notes that during part of this period, cities in Hellas, were just a collection of villages with no surrounding walls, no magnificent temples or public edifices. This suggests that small-scale subsistence agriculture during the early development period of settled agriculture made it difficult to even contemplate let alone sustain large-scale warfare. At the same time such village based agriculture would have contained very little surplus production which would have been totally inadequate for a large army to pillage. However, beyond a certain point in the history of hierarchical mass societies, the leading elites of certain expanded tribes or city states had become physically numerous and strong enough and organisationally united enough to conquer and enslave other successful settled economic communities. In some instances such subdued communities eventually became strong enough to also rebel against their own earlier enslavement. Thus Thucydides being aware of this writes;

"But as the power of Hellas grew and the acquisition of wealth became more an object, the revenues of the states increasing, tyrannies were by their means established almost everywhere - the old form of government being hereditary monarchy with definite prerogatives - and Hellas began to fit out fleets and apply herself to the sea." ('The history of the Peloponnesian War' Thucydides. Chapter 1.)

The Mediterranean Sea was the early means of obtaining the quickest form of communication along with the rapid transportation of articles of trade but also of obtaining wealth by piracy, raiding and pillage. It was also the means of ensuring the adherence of reluctant peoples to conform to the exacting tribute conditions imposed upon the conquered peoples. Such navies once formed were a means of reducing many island communities to subservience and extracting regular tribute or in some cases of displacing them and taking over their houses and plots of land. But this intermediate stage did not venture far beyond local conquests and pillaging or continue for more than a few hundreds of years. Only later did defensive confederations of city states emerge and then in some cases became the basis for establishing centrally controlled, pro-active empires, bent on increasing the tribute in products, metals, money and slaves. But, as with other cases, the result of hostilities between city-states such as Athens and Lacedaemon went beyond occasional pillaging excursions and led to extended periods of warfare.

"Never had so many cities been taken and laid desolate, here by the barbarians, here by the parties contending (the old inhabitants being sometimes removed to make room for others); never was there so much banishing and blood-shedding, now in the strife of faction." (ibid)

Banishing and bloodshed, inhabitants removed, cities laid desolate'; how depressingly modern this sounds as I write this section in 2024. It appears almost inevitable that once successfully established, hierarchical mass society elites repeatedly indulged (and in the 21st century continue to indulge in) such conquests to such an extent that these armed incursions and conquests became the new norm. In some places this led to the transformation of temporary armies of slaves and agricultural workers organised for defence purposes into permanent armies of highly trained soldiers and mercenaries. A principle of internal mass society citizen submission was established and enforced at each social layer of the people by the hierarchical elite. These permanent armed bodies of men would then become a definite military class used by elites to conquer new territory, garrison conquered cities of importance and enforce the terms of tribute from these and from any surrounding towns and villages. In this way the interests of each sector (or class) of hierarchical mass societies had interests which both overlapped and diverged.

The interests of the elite ruling would differ in some respects to the military class, hence military uprisings, but would often coincide over invasions, conquests and tribute sharing.

In most cases with well established ruling elites, these would tend to be interested in long term, regular yearly or seasonal amounts of tribute whilst in most cases the general rank and file soldiers would be interested short term sacking, pillaging and as we will read from the records - murder, torture and rape. Consequently, many ruling elites would for a short period of time, allow, or turn a blind eye to any military excesses in pillaging and rapine. But in all these cases, the character and morality of the men who were ready and willing to perpetrate such outrages had to be moulded from late childhood to adulthood. It is obvious that each generation of children are not born as heartless, merciless, obedient genocidal killers (or racists and misogynists for that matter); they have to be socialised and trained to be so. This training was administered during their physical growth from adolescence to adulthood. A detailed account of how this was achieved within the Homeric world of ancient Greece is provided once again by the author Xenophon with regard to the contrast in the training of the Lacedaemonian youth of Sparta, (training devised by Lycurgus) as compared with other Greek city states.

"When a boy ceases to be a child, and begins to be a lad, others release him from his moral tutor and his schoolmaster; he is then no longer under a ruler and is allowed to go his own way. Here again Lycurgus introduced a wholly different system. For he observed that at this time of life self-will makes a strong root in a boy's mind, a tendency to insolence manifests itself, and a keen appetite for pleasure in different forms takes possession of him. At this stage, therefore, he imposed on him a ceaseless round of work, and contrived a constant round of occupation. The penalty for shirking the duties was exclusion from all future honours. He thus caused not only the public authorities, but the relations also to take pains that the lads did not incur the contempt of their fellow citizens by flinching from their tasks. (Xenophon. 'Constitution of the Lacedaemonians'.)

Xenophon considered that such extremely rigorous training/socialisation and submission to authority was the military basis for Sparta being the most powerful and celebrated city in Greece at the time. Nevertheless, whether severe or mild, achieving the means to obtain military obedience and subservience to the ruling elite and their chosen methods and 'system' was essential to the economic survival of hierarchical mass societies. However, given the intellectual capacity of the human species, domestication was also extended to the conceptual training and functioning of the brain. Thus the schooling and training of thought patterns as well as the physically productive motor skill activities of stabbing and clubbing by those humans becoming militarily accustomed to obedient submission, quickly moved from being a desirable outcome to an absolute necessity within these increasingly ruthless hierarchical mass societies.

It has already been noted that for those masses captured as slaves or employed later as serfs, any previous relatively short sustenance work of gathering or hunting for immediate personal nutrition, had for them become transformed into day long labour to produce various products for others in exchange for a set allocation of nourishment (N) and a place to live. In some instances, a payment in 'kind' was met via giving away a percentage (a tithe or tenth) of what they had produced. The prior holistic variety and variability of living on earth for the majority of those humans living in the near and middle east during that period, was being transformed into unremitting repetitive labour directed from dawn to dusk and from childhood to shortly before death by the owners of land or controllers of the surrounding enclosed cities and lands. We need to remember that these were lands that for millions of years had been a common-stock of organic and inorganic resources available to all forms of species life on earth. On the other hand, for the ruling elites of such settled agricultural mass societies, any previous joint community activities they may have undertaken to obtain sufficient nutrition was transformed into a future of permanent leisure and luxury from dawn to dusk and also from childhood to death. Their forcibly achieved freedom from continuous productive labour and even from useful community work allowed them to do more or less as they pleased; and knowledge of what pleased them frequently continued to be what had already become the permanent dark side of hierarchical mass societies. For example, one celebrated ruler, Ashurnacirpal, (approximately 860 BCE) even openly advertised his brutality in the subjugation of those who rebelled after having been previously conquered and subjected to his rule by his loyal troops. Thus he boasted;

"I drew near to the city of Tela. The city was very strong; three walls surrounded it. The inhabitants trusted to their strong walls and numerous soldiers; they did not come down or embrace my feet. With battle and slaughter I assaulted and took the city. Three thousand warriors I slew in battle. Their booty and possessions, cattle, sheep, I carried away; many captives I burned with fire. Many of their soldiers I took alive; of some I cut off their hands and limbs; of others the noses, ears and arms; of many soldiers I put out the eyes. I reared a column of the living and a column of heads. I hung up on high their heads on trees in the vicinity of their city. Their boys and girls I burned up in the flame. I devastated the city, dug it up, in fire burned it; I annihilated it. (Standard Inc., col. I. 113 - 118./ quoted in 'A History of Babylonian and Assyrians'. By George Stephen Goodspeed. Section 168.)

Such examples were made and broadcast as widely as possible in order to strike terror into those elsewhere who might refuse to submit to the new elite and the hierarchical mass societies they now totally controlled. Nevertheless, at least a part of this horrific personal boast is obviously wrong since Ashurnacirpal clearly had an army whose soldiers did the majority of the brutal things recorded on his orders. Incidentally this relationship would allow the now almost universal retrospective defence of the rank and file killers of other members of their species; *'I was only following orders'*. From ancient to more modern times this has become the defensive mantra of all those deliberately choosing to be trained as brutal killers on command of the military section of the various hierarchical mass society formations. And these openly admitted and documented facts are an undeclared testament to the transformation taking place within certain sections of humanity due to the adoption of the hierarchical mass society structures based upon settled agriculture and animal herding. In particular the evidence suggests that the socio-economic changes led to transformations within the morality and psychology of many human beings dragged into the project of hierarchical mass society living. Moreover, these changes occurred in Sumerian, Babylonian, Egyptian, Persian, Greek, Roman and Islamic forms of hierarchical mass societies. This fact clearly indicates that the origin of the symptoms came from the socio-economic form and not because of any particular ideological expression or regional expression of the hierarchical form. Merciless aggression and ruthless exploitation of everything organic and inorganic became (and remains to this day) a universal feature within all hierarchical mass society systems, from the ancient middle east through to the modern nation states situated around the entire globe.

The brutality and ruthless disregard for others of their own human species, by the elite during the period of consolidation of city states, was not only a personally acquired psychology, but also increasingly class based and thus structurally systemic development. Such excesses were not only the occasional idiosyncratic symptoms of deranged individuals (of which there were many) but symptomatic of the entire hierarchical mass society system. Any individual derangements simply echoed and amplified the base line function and purpose of the economic resource imperatives of such societies which routinely led to conquests, sackings, capture and booty. The economic imperatives would also mean that a moderately inclined elite would sooner or later still want more wealth than their own slaves could produce and sooner or later the exhaustion of the local available soil, forests, mineral seams, fish resources would require expansion into areas already occupied by other peoples. If such resources would not be voluntarily given up (surrendered) by a neighbouring hierarchical elite, then force of varying magnitudes would inevitably follow.

The establishment of actual empires may have been the desire of some of the unhinged megalomaniac elites, (in ancient as in modern times) but it was the founding and subsequent 'existential class needs' that hierarchical mass society 'systems created that (real or imagined) actually motivated and enabled the ruthless or moderate desire for expansion to be supported. By this early period of ancient history, natural relationships between human beings had been so distorted by mass society living that mass genocide and brutality could be perpetrated not by a deranged few individuals but by a rationally planned and trained cohort of men carrying out a thought out, rehearsed and practiced strategy of large-scale annihilation. These perpetrators were born as ordinary human beings whose initial humanity had been diluted or driven out by the three elite imposed strategies of 'fear', 'propaganda' and 'self-interest'. As infants their emotions and socio-psychological reflexes had been gradually re-programmed by the process of hierarchical mass society living until for some nothing brutal or inhuman was considered off-limits. Hannah Arendt's 'banality of evil' was a reality endemic long before it was used by her to describe the 20th century phenomenon of German based Fascism and its mass killings of Jews, Gypsies, Communists and Slavs.

Each 'empire', although different in a great many ways (some initially were relatively small city-state combinations) was nevertheless induced, compelled or forced by its internal social structure and the class-based socio-economic circumstances of essential and non-essential production, into following a common pattern of invasion, sequestration, exploitation and forced (enslaved) labour. After any conquest not involving or followed by genocidal elimination, those that survived the battle would be made slaves and a vassal chief imposed or retained over them to administer any newly conquered territory for the benefit of the conquerors . The remaining survivors would be also subject to the authority of the leader or leading oligarchy of the conquering elite. In recounting what is known of the development of Athens in the city-state and empire building maelstrom of that period (and later) the following author points out the changing nature of elite governance in this part of Greece.

"Cimon was also the last leader of his party, who led it as a soldier rather than as a statesman. Those who came after him had other views, and other means of carrying them out. The soldier and the politician began to diverge." ('Pericles and the Golden age of Athens'. Evelyn Abbott. Chapter 9.)

As each city-state based empire grew in size and extent, trade and agriculture in certain places would flourish and decline in others. In some cases, after divergent expansion, the armed forces would be able to demand a greater share of essential and non-essential production and thus become a drain on the resources extracted from the mass of productive slave workers. In mass societies, those such as soldiers and ruling elites, who did not directly produce products for essential consumption and/or exchange, must nonetheless, still consume them. Consequently they are a drain on the annual or seasonal wealth produced by the productive workers and appropriated by the elite. In this recurrent mode of regional expansion the necessary element of a permanent class of armed men for defence against invasion or for external conquest, eventually became a source of internal socio-economic weakness. They take from the essential social food, clothing and lodging production, but do not add to it.

An excessive unproductive elite and an unproductive administrative bureaucracy remains a common factor still operating in the 20th and 21st centuries capitalist based economic systems. Furthermore, the more resources needed to equip an army, the less resources are proportionally available for the rest of the nation's citizens and the elites will ensure that any consequent product or financial reductions or restrictions do not fall on their elite shoulders – so in some form austerity for the masses follows. The cost of a modern army, navy and air force and the equipment they require and demand, also means a relative restriction on the available resources going to other types of modern public services. The continued existence of too many unproductive citizens in general inevitably drains resources further away from productive citizens and places greater burdens on the latter to increase production. In the historical development of hierarchical mass societies, resentments, desertions and rebellions of armed forces could - and according to the historical record - did follow. Such patterns of uneven and excessive development within such societies would invariably create other associated weaknesses and strengths, as Gibbons depicted much later in his 'The Decline and Fall of the Roman Empire'.

By these inbuilt processes of internal social and economic contradiction, the Egypt 'empires' declined, so too did the Assyria, Babylonia, Persia, Greece, Rome and of course much later the Dutch, Spanish, French, Russian and the vast British Empire, became too costly to administer and control. The ancient

Assyrian empire also provides considerable evidence of this relatively early process of empire spreading, declining and then falling, clues of which are contained in the many cuneiform tablets uncovered by archaeologists and later deciphered. Some of these Assyrian tablets also contained stories and myths which were later to resurface in the allegedly 'holy' ideologies of the three Abrahamic monotheistic religions of Judaism, Christianity and Islam. For example, the coincidence of the later empire building period and the establishment of the basic monotheistic myths contained in the Abrahamic religions of Judaism, Christianity and Islam is revealed in ancient stone and clay tablets. An earlier version of the biblical myth of the 'Flood', for example, is to be found on one such cuneiform tablet. Similarly, the myth of a human and godly resurrection clearly originates from a stele found in ancient Egypt. These and other examples indicate that the thousands of years of empire spreading had created a common middle - eastern core of actual and mythical based characters, ideas and beliefs which were later taken up and adopted within monotheistic ideology in either a largely modified or less modified form. At this early mass society stage in the study of humanity's departure from direct personal relationship with nature and from each other as citizens to ones mediated by hierarchical, class-based, mass societies. Consequently it is worth considering some further origins of the historical record. One useful source is that set down by one of the earliest historians, from 5th century BCE Greece - Herodotus. For example he notes the early development of the patriarchal male inheritance of military force to obtain tribute and writes;

"This Croesus, first of the barbarians of whom we have knowledge, subdued certain of the Helens and forced them to pay tribute."......He made war with those of Miletos, having received this war as an inheritance from his father: for he used to invade their land and besiege Milton." (Herodotus. 'The Histories'. Book 1 Clio section 6 and 17.)

This particular ancient Greek historian, Herodotus, frequently acknowledges that the information he is recording is often in the nature of hearsay obtained from the memories of people he interviewed and information that he, or no one else could corroborate. He frequently acknowledges that some of his evidence is in the form of 'tall-tales', but nonetheless, despite this inconsistency and subjective inaccuracy, there are many preserved instances of economic, political and military warfare involving savage treatment of men, women, children, animals and buildings, which confirm these 'horror stories' were indeed common practices. Therefore, if only a small percentage of what Herodotus records is based upon actual fact, then the oral testimony he collected contains enough glimpses of actual probabilities and some cases of actually occurring realities, that it has considerable value as evidence for this human section of the study of life on earth. Moreover, as will be demonstrated further in this section, such traits were also recorded by other Greek, Roman and even biblical authors. For example;

"The large-scale plundering expedition launched by the Aeolian into Laconic around 240 BC (see Wallbank, HCP I. 483; cf Will, HPMH I.305) which according to Polybius caused the enslavement of the perioeic villages, is said by Plutarch to have resulted in the carrying off of 50, 000 slaves.." ('The Class Struggle in the Ancient Greek World' by GEM de Ste. Croix. Page 507)

50, 000 slaves, however divided up, is the basis of a mass labour force, of domestic slaves, agricultural slaves, slaves in quarries, wood and household slaves. Once seriously studied, this long era of early hierarchical mass society building often prejudicially described as the spread of 'civilisation', was already steeped in the blood of repeated violent patriarchal mass killings and the savage acquisition and treatment of human labour in the form of women and slaves. Tribute followed the plunder and pillage of foreign based wealth (i.e. in the form of products of other people's human labour) along with the most brutal forms of human oppression imaginable. To confirm the above instances within ancient Greek societies are not one off isolated cases; Herodotus again informs us that;

".. those of them who set forth to their settlements from the City Hall of Athens and who esteem themselves the most noble by descent of the Ionians, these I say, brought no women with them to their settlement, but took Carina women, whose parents they slew.." "Now when the king (of the Scythians) puts anyone to death, he does not leave alive their sons either, but puts to death

all the males.." (Herodotus, Histories book 1 section 146 and Book 4 section 69.)

Just how distorted the social essence of humanity had become amongst the allegedly 'noble' civilised elites who killed all the males and prostituted the women as concubines, is revealed in the hundreds of pages of notes and comments by

Herodotus in his 'Histories', relates a couple more horrific examples that are worth considering with regard to how humanity had become divided into hostile camps by the implementation of hierarchical mass societies.. First, following a request to a Persian king in the build-up to a planned invasion, a prominent warrior requested that one of his four sons be allowed to stay behind to preserve the family line, in case of excessive deaths during the intended war. To the 'noble' warriors' relief the Persian king responded by suggesting that all the four sons should be permitted to stay behind. After dismissing the now very relieved father, the king ordered his associates to kill all the four sons. Thus in this narrative, the king had deceitfully kept his word - for all four now dead sons would now clearly all stay behind, but would no longer preserve the family line. The question immediately arises what kind of human beings would do such a thing or invent such an act and what process had made so many of them into such flawed examples of the human species? The second example, involves the eventual revenge taken by an adult Eunuch named Hermotimos, whose genitals had been severed as a young adult on the orders of an elite character named Panionios. Herodotus records that Hermotimos, the Eunuch, had survived this mutilation (not all deformed in this way did survive) and much later this victim had gained sufficient official authority within his hierarchical mass society regime to be able to obtain revenge against Panionios who had instigated his earlier castration. Herodotus writes that on his capture;

"Panionios was compelled to make eunuchs of his own sons who were four in number, and being compelled he did so; and then when he had so done, the sons were compelled to do the same thing to him. Thus the vengeance by the hands of Hermotimus overtook Panionios." (Herodotus Histories. Book 8, section 106)

In one sense it does not matter if this particular event is exaggerated or even if it was completely invented by some informant of his, because Herodotus and his readers at the time knew the story was sufficiently plausible to be recorded precisely because horrific things like these were not at all untypical during this period of Assyrian, Chaldean, Persian and Greek so-called 'civilisations'. Enslavement, extreme forms of torture, brutal gang rapes and death were standard operating procedures by all the so-called well known elite heroes and lesser known champions of hierarchical mass society civilisation in the Near and Middle East. Killing their own brothers, fathers and mothers within elite family ranks in order to advance one individual's status or access to wealth and power, was not unknown. Indeed, by this period of so-called 'civilisation', such inhumanity was normalised and rampant among the elite classes. Herodotus was not alone in recording such behaviour by so-called 'civilised' people for a further example is provided by Thucydides, who informs us that;

"First the Athenians besieged and captured Eion on the Strymon from the Medes, and made slaves of the inhabitants, being under the command of Cimon, son of Mitigates. Next they enslaved Scyros, the island in the Aegean, containing a Dolopian population, and colonised it themselves." (Thucydides. 'The History of the Peloponnesian War'. Chapter 4.)

The audience in Greece and elsewhere, whom Herodotus, Thucydides and others were primarily aware of at the time of writing or orally recording and transmitting it to their students or readers, were literate and would be reasonably familiar with Homer, Hesiod and Aeschylus etc. The themes and narratives of Greek literature, drama and philosophy has amply recorded, mythologised, fictionalised, dramatized and romanticized, such odysseys, battles and conquests. In doing so, the elite intellectuals then and subsequently, often avoided mentioning the real substantive economic and political causes for conquests and wars. Instead, they often chose to focus on or create other secondary or purely personal issues such as slights or sexual misconduct and dishonour in various forms. However, the economic motives and benefits of conquests and subjection of other human communities were clearly at the basis of the power and wealth of the rising city state elites and prominent in the motives for Imperial type conquests. This is made crystal clear in occasional lists of tribute. For example;

"From the lists of the tribute paid by members of the league which have been preserved in inscriptions, we find that in the assessment of the year 446 BC (BCE) the amount of tribute is considerably reduced; a large number of cities either withdrew from the alliance or did not pay tribute. In the period 450-447 the number of contributing cities may be put at 190 - 200; in 446-440 the average is 170, and the total amount of contributions only reached 434 talents, of which not more than 400 talents were really paid." ('Pericles and the Golden Age of Athens'. Chapter 9.)

An important point for this study on the evolution of life on earth and the socio-economic forms some among the human species implemented, are the numbers of city-states subdued and or colonised by Athens and persuaded by threats of further force to 'join' its 'league'. The number is approximately 200 and even at a 'low point', the Athenian elite were still extracting annual or bi-annual surplus-product (use values extracted from natural organic or inorganic resources) or labour-power value from the peasants, slaves or workers within 170 other settled mass societies as well as from their own slaves. We also know similar violent invasions and associated individual and collective atrocities and conquests occurred throughout history. For example, it occurred during the later period of Roman hierarchical mass society civilisation; the Medieval period of hierarchical mass society building; the numerous European Christian wars and the infamous European Medieval Crusades to the Near East. Furthermore, violence and wealth extraction from other communities occurred during the centuries of Muslim mass society Empire building also in the Middle East, but also in North Africa and southern Spain. The extraction of natural species wealth in the form of extracted organic species products, slaves or valuable inorganic raw materials was always **a** deciding factor if not **the** deciding factor in the territorial expansion of hierarchical mass societies throughout hierarchical mass society history and those of the present day.

From many different documentary sources, it would seem that in the whole region from the Near East through the Middle East and to the Far East, humanity for a period covering several thousands' of years - was in periodic and regular violent turmoil. City states arose and fell, arose again and conquered other city states or were themselves conquered by rivals. Some successful ones even became consolidated into empires of different sizes and durations which nevertheless also arose and fell. At each stage of this long gestation of agricultural based hierarchical mass society living and expansion, ordinary people when not killed during invasions were in peacetime also subjected to paying tribute/tithes/taxes to elites and/or providing unrewarded labour by becoming indirect or direct slaves. In many cases defeated ruling elites became slaves themselves or in some cases were allowed to become local proxy Governors of a conquered region. It is not surprising therefore that the general monotheistic tendencies which gradually gained popularity throughout that region, (religious elements of which were clearly evident in Egypt, Persia and Greece) embodied not just a common stock of mythical Gods, mystical (Osirus type resurrections), and great flood devastation myths, but also the extreme social 'lamentations' and pessimism which arose generally; such as the biblical type theme of 'All my troubles Lord; soon be over'.

The ancient myth of a battle between the Babylonian god Marduk (supposedly signifying order) and the Babylonian goddess Tiamat (supposedly signifying chaos) was presumed to have occurred before the creation of the world, perhaps indicating at least two things. First a prevalent ignorant belief at the time that life on earth was a 'creation' by the efforts of a male supernatural force (as with a powerful male god); and second, a reassignment of reproductive and biological 'belonging' roles of newborns away from its natural basis in the biology of female and male genders to that of the male. The once widely common wood or pottery fertility icons and models of pregnant females were also abandoned and women's role and well-being became dependent not on their own extensive female family line and their own productive efforts but on a single male, who in future would be chosen for them. The female gender from then on became designated as secondary in social status and women declared eternally problematic. As with the myth of Adam and Eve in the Abrahamic version of monotheism, the stabilising and continuity role of women in the (N) and (R) phases of hunter-gatherer (N-M-G-R + A-D) life cycle, had been progressively distorted or denied and re-assigned to males. In all probability, this is a reflection in religious ideology, of the practical subordination of women to men occurring in the transition to settled, agricultural male dominated mode of production. It is certainly an indicator of the ascendency of Patrifocality and Patrilineality over Matrifocality and Matrilineality within agriculturally based hierarchical mass societies. Staying with the period of Assyrian ascendancy for evidence, a little longer, an Assyrian inscription on a wall relief boasted of the brutality the King had inflicted upon one town. The inscription reads;

"*My officers...put to the sword the inhabitants, young and old, of the town....they did not spare anybody among them. They hung their corpses from stakes, flayed their skins and covered with them the wall of the town.*" *(quoted in 'Lost Worlds' L. Cotterell. Horizon. Chapter 7.)*

That such inhumane brutality became a built in facet of the new mode of production based upon hierarchical mass society living, is undeniable. From before the common era period (now abbreviated as BCE) to well after the common era (now abbreviated as ACE) period until the sacking of Rome by the Barbarian invasions the same pattern continued repeatedly. Furthermore, we know that after the decline and fall of the Roman Empire, this hierarchical model of agricultural societies and their pessimistic doom-orientated religions continued throughout the long middle ages of the numerous Feudal European dynasties. Consequently, so too did the pattern of war and conquest. Predictably, the post-Roman Empire period of Czarist, Kingly and Priestly elites throughout medieval Europe also regularly engaged in wars of territorial conquest and human extermination in order to increase the control of wealth and power shared among their religious and secular elites. It is not hard to deduce from historical evidence that 'life on earth' for a majority of the human species in the hierarchical mass societies of North, East, South and West European continents, remained generally alienated from nature and almost universally socially alienated from each other. Many individuals and communities in these societies became increasingly diseased, emotionally disturbed and bodily deformed by the repetitive forms of occupational living in these hierarchical forms of mass society aggregations. To illustrate the extent of the reciprocal inhumanity which had developed among human communities organised under the so-called civilising hierarchical mass societies of the near and middle east, I have not yet come across anything more clearly formulated than the following quote from Thucydides. He suggests that the following views were spoken by Nicias to his troops.

"The fortune of our greatest enemies having thus betrayed itself, and their disorder being what I have described let us engage in anger, convinced that, as between adversaries, nothing is more legitimate than to claim to sate the whole wrath of one's soul in punishing the aggressor, and nothing more sweet, as the proverb has it, than the vengeance upon an enemy, which it will now be ours to take. That enemies they are and mortal enemies you all know, since they came here to enslave our country, and if successful had in reserve for our men all that is most dreadful and for our children and wives all that is most dishonourable, and for the whole city the name which conveys the greatest reproach. None should therefore relent or think it gain if they go away without further danger to us." ('The History of the Peloponnesian War'. Thucydides. Chapter 23.)

Alexander 'the great' of Macedon (my research suggests in reality, rather than hyperbole, he was not so 'great') had previously conquered much of central Asia Minor to exact tribute, and long after his death (after a period of autonomous self-rule) the Romans also conquered much of that entire near and middle-eastern territory. It was during the turbulent times of revolts and re-conquests by Rome that the following incident took place in the area of Athens in Greece. A Roman General, Sulla had been appointed to restore order and tribute in the near east and in the area surrounding Athens which contained a population determined not to be subjected to Rome any longer. Sulla undertook a siege against the city of these rebellious Greek people. After a time the Roman legions managed to break into the city and the author Appian informs the reader that;

"Sulla ordered an indiscriminate massacre, not sparing women or children. He was angry that they had so suddenly joined the barbarians without cause, and had displayed such violent animosity to himself." ('The Foreign Wars'; the 'The Mithridatic Wars'. Appian. Chapter 6.)

From all this historical evidence so far, and more yet to be presented, we can understand that this pattern of ruthless lack of concern for other human beings emanates consistently from hierarchical mass society formations. No other human social formations could create such armed mass assaults, on other communities or process and utilise the amount of tribute gained from such savage conquests. These aggressive and brutal processes could only be practiced and sustained by hierarchical mass society aggregations, and these aggregations could only arise on the basis of the mass production of suitable nutrition and habitation. Moreover, this socio-economic process spread across the centuries and formed the basis of the Egyptian Empire, the Persian Empire, the Greek and the Roman Empires and was perpetrated not only against their enemies, but also against allies who were considered unreliable. Details of the numerous medieval Crusades and the First and Second World Wars in the 20th century, reveal that since the development of hierarchical mass societies, the mass of ordinary human beings have not been valued for themselves but only for what they could contribute to the welfare and wealth of numerically small numbers of elites situated at the pinnacle of their hierarchical societies. For example during the same Roman Empire period, a local king opposed to Rome's rule, named Mithridates, thinking that certain people would turn against him to support the Roman's, is said to have taken the following precautions;

"....he arrested all suspects, before the war should become sharper. First he put to death the tetrarchs of Galicia with their wives and children, not only those who were united with him as friends, but those who were not his subjects-all except three who escaped." (ibid.. Chapter 7.)

On the murder of the Roman Emperor, Alexander Severus, by his own troops, Edward Gibbon, records that once betrayed and deserted by his troops Alexander;

"....withdrew into his tent, desirous at least to conceal his approaching fate from the insults of the multitude. He was soon followed by a tribune and some centurions, the ministers of death; but instead of receiving with manly resolution the inevitable stroke, his unavailing cries and entreaties disgraced the last moments of his life...His mother, Mamaea.....perished with her son. The most faithful of his friends were sacrificed to the first fury of the soldiers." ('History of the Decline and Fall of the Roman Empire' Edward Gibbons. Volume 1. Chapter 7.)

It would appear from even this abbreviated array of examples of elite male behaviour and their armed supporters over several hundred years that the behaviour and thinking of some human beings, contrasted with the hunter-gatherer communities quoted in chapter 8, had maintained or undergone significantly negative changes. The transformation from a naturally evolved social mode of production based upon subsistence hunting and gathering, to ones based upon socially organised, hierarchical settled, agricultural mass extraction societies, had changed nearly everything. The different experiences of living in hierarchically socialised existence within a different mode of production had clearly modified the way certain people routinely and habitually behaved and also how they thought. It had done so sufficiently and so thoroughly that an entirely new type (or variety) of humanity had become socially adapted to be selectively both inhumane and brutally aggressive. Hierarchical mass society living had socialised men in particular into becoming almost a different sub-species of *Homo sapien*.

In the social process of creating a different mode of production, the multi-million year natural biological evolution of *Homo naturalis* and Homo sapiens had been put on hold by the elite social enforcers and practitioners of hierarchical mass society living. Within a few hundred years many had of course remained biologically Homo sapien, but had been socialised partly or wholly into being *Homo unnaturalis*. This assertion is more than a fanciful invention of my own, because in the 21st century, often hidden away from public view, is a widespread recognition that much of modern living is unnatural in a number of ways. It is unnatural in a direct practical biological and economic sense. Hunger and homelessness is not natural; they are not a product of natural evolution, they are clearly socially created symptoms. In an emotional sense, extreme loneliness, isolation and mental health breakdowns are not natural either. Furthermore, in an ecological sense (large-scale air, water and land pollution and essential species loss) are not naturally occurring symptoms either. Natural waste and debris from dying and decaying organisms is normally consumed as nutrition (N) in the (N-M-G-R + A - D) process by some other species among the integrated cycles of species life on earth. It is only the human manufacture of non-organic or excessively toxic waste materials and the excessive extraction and destruction of natural organic species which causes pollution, ecological destruction and knock-on imbalances in temperature and climate changes. None of these exclusively human-species factors and symptoms are a result of the integrated, inter-dependent function of 'nature' but are of human social construction and determination. For example, a survey on mental health in Europe in 2023 concluded that 38% of ordinary European people had mental health problems in adjusting to the conditions of working and living in modern hierarchical mass societies. The very description of these types of illnesses as 'mental health' problems is a case of 'blaming the biology of the brain', for what are predominantly socially created dis-eases and dysfunctions.

To return to the historical perspective, it would also appear from the historical evidence that the first individuals who did the controlling and withholding of unrestricted access to land and its natural resources, were specialists in fighting and killing (i.e. full-time warriors). Later this 'gatekeeping' of control over 'class based private property' was shared by, or delegated to, specialists in governance and/or specialists in religion (i.e. hereditary kings, aristocrats, bureaucrats and/or priests). This hierarchical mass society system lasted throughout the long ages between the ancient hierarchical mass societies of Egypt, Assyria, Persia, Greece and Rome and the bourgeois revolutions of the 17th century. Essentially the same social structure, template was maintained throughout that entire period. It consisted of a hierarchical class who controlled most things, a middle sector who administered most things and a large class of slaves or eventually wage-slaves who produced most essential and useful things. The latter were forcibly employed to ensure the biochemical essential (N-M-G-R + A-D) processes of living were produced for all social classes and luxuries for the elites. Then by degrees and revolutions during the 17th, 18th and 19th centuries, the bourgeois owners of capital and their governments became the ones who by monetary purchases took over the owning, controlling and withholding of land and means of production from human and other species often defined as trespassers or pests.. From that point on, fencing off and withholding human (and often animal) access to the natural (N-M-G-R + A-D) sources of human and animal metabolic processes, encompassed increasingly huge areas, until practically the whole world, including the two polar regions, was fenced off or had access restricted by order of one section of the hierarchical elite or another.

As was covered in Chapter 3 (on Soil), and noted earlier, it is a fact that intensive and extensive mono-cultural agriculture rapidly degrades the (N-M-G-R + A-D) life processes of the micro-biology and mineral content of the soil. Over successive generations, particularly since the 20th century, this degradation has led to large areas of micro-organism depleted, tree-less, insect-deficient, bird-scarce tracts of land and via excessive excrement (plus later chemical) run-off, fish-depleted seas. This continuous problem of excessive extraction brings with it the need for hierarchical mass society elites (the main beneficiaries of the system) to keep seizing new fertile and resource rich land, whether it is already being utilised by life on earth in general or by human communities. Existential social conflicts, leading to wars of asset/resource seizure and extermination become almost inevitable for wealth focussed elite governed communities. This elite determined, unnatural form of human hierarchical living created and maintained an unnatural need for human resource acquisition, wealth accumulation and killing. It is this motive which has led to wars and to genocidal levels of destruction of life on earth, in all its forms; micro-organisms, insects, plant varieties, animals and humans who previously lived on it. We have seen that hierarchical mass society agriculture by the evidence generated by those who lived through its own historically determined process, is a one-sided, cancerous type distortion of the long-term, evolutionary balance of land and water based nutrition (N) produced by nature - or life on earth as a whole.

It is not difficult to conclude from the evidence so far considered that hierarchical mass society agricultural and animal rearing is a system in recurring existential crisis, needing ever more resources from a planetary biosphere which is limited in size and limited in its reproductive capacity to keep up with humanities ability to consume them and pollute it. Unless human societies are radically deconstructed and reconstructed on a different basis its current processes must continue destroying life on earth in its naturally evolved form. It has no means not to continue in its socially evolved unnatural and distorted form. Yet we never hear from any branch of the elite or academic disciplines that the hierarchical mass society form based upon agriculture and industry that the current system is so unnatural that it is destroying the natural foundations (air, water, soil, trees, insects, and animals) of life on earth. Yet it clearly does. It not only creates intra-species conflict within humanity itself, but pits humanity against its own natural species supporting biosphere foundations within the inter-connected web of life as a whole. Yet the elites continue to uphold and champion the current system and claim that this still represents progress.

The most extreme and relatively recent cases of this 'privatising of nature' in the bourgeois era occurred in the 'new world' territories of North and South America, Africa and Australia. In such places only a few generations ago, hunter-gatherer peoples were cleared off the land and ranches and land holdings of huge areas of potential metabolic nourishment the size of English counties became the exclusive domain of individuals or boards of private companies. Nature, in such private holdings, whether ranches, plantations or private game reserves for hunting, ceased to be entirely 'natural' or sustainable and to a greater or lesser extent, became artificial mono-crop mutations alongside the inhuman characteristics of their owners and controllers. Land having been previously privatised in Europe, this exclusive ownership and use of colonised new world continents and islands by private individuals, governments and companies etc., became a second stage in the slow, or in some cases the rapid, changing of the natural species rich balance of the biosphere in the Americas and Africa.

On a global scale, Prairie, Forest, Jungle and Woodland have been transformed from multiple, high-intensity life-form habitats for millions of 'wild' species, into resources for exploitation and habitat degradation by domesticated species. De-forested regions, open cast and deep mining areas, monoculture crop plantations or single species cattle rearing became the *nuevo environmental scenario* of vast swathes of previously naturally evolved planet. In numerous cases, in South America, for example huge tracts were simply fenced off and left empty by absentee land owners. The planet's dynamic evolutionary balance of natural growth, natural species integration, natural recycling, natural adaptations of inter-dependent species, established over millions (or even billions) of years was steadily unbalanced by continuous micro-organism and macro-species exhaustion or environmental deterioration and pollution. This unbalancing occurred in soil, reductions in plant variety, insect population densities and seasonal disturbances, animal species extinctions and fungal root system changes.

From evidence provided by the participants, advocates and historians of this so-called 'progress' of mass society 'civilisation' it has been revealed that at the same time this hierarchical mass system has institutionalised and globalised cruelty, torture, genocide and slavery of animals and people. To control and plan the agricultural growth of domesticated grasses as crops and animals as domesticated herds, their life-cycles of Nutrition - Rest - Growth - Reproduction (N.M.G.R.) needed to be seriously de-naturalised or in modern biological based language - genetically modified. Crops and animals were selected and the territory they occupied limited to certain specific areas bounded by natural or artificial fences. Artificially constructed fields or ranges replaced natural expanses of land. To accomplish the large-scale activity of mass farming (i.e. physically 'taming', 'controlling', restricting and limiting the natural species within habitats), it was necessary to create settled mass societies based upon agriculture and herding, and now industry. Thus drastic measures were taken to interfere with biological processes and evolutionary patterns of development, and now climate predictability.

Throughout the history of hierarchical mass society development, not only were certain animals selected for domestication (and frequently tamed by beating, removing their organs of sexual reproduction and shackling,) but many human beings were selected for exactly the same form of treatment for their 'domestication' as slaves by ruthless elites. At this point I suggest it is essential to contrast the two sets of practices denoted by the concepts of natural socialisation and authoritarian domestication. The first; natural socialisation, originates naturally, is voluntary and is developed initially within all social life forms, whether plant, insect, animal or human. The second, selection and domestication, is exclusively a coercive product of human interference in the natural (N-M-G-R + A-D) processes of life on earth. It is these repeated interferences with natural evolution, which have now accumulated exponentially to the point where they are destroying the organic and inorganic foundations upon which life on earth as a whole has been developed. Air doesn't self-replicate; it needs the process of gas exchange by photosynthetic plants as aided by soil microbiome and by sea based algae. Food doesn't just grow. It 'lives' at its own evolutionary reproductive rate (R) and by the same interconnected and inter-dependent bio-chemical (N-M-G-R + A-D) processes as every other form of life on earth. Everything that lives does so through an inter-connected web of (N-M-G-R + A-D) processes.

Chapter 9; Summary.

In section A), the economic structure of agriculturally based hierarchical mass societies was described as involving at least twelve, arduous, day-long, backbreaking, agricultural activities by a restricted proportion of the community, even before any nutrition (N) could be extracted by the community from the resources eventually produced. This lengthy process was contrasted with the few hours required by the hunter-gatherer community whose nutritional labour generally produced the bulk of their nutrition (N) as a whole group, male and female, young and old. There was no distinction between the general community *and the general labour force, except in circumstances of danger. Logic (and evidence from the 19th century colonial period) suggests that those communities located in favourable places were reluctant to transfer to the agricultural or pastoral modes of production for precisely this reason. Hence, agricultural based hierarchical mass societies, almost from their inception in ancient Sumer, Babylon and Egypt required a new form of enforced labour - large-scale slavery.*

In section B), the 'modern' theory of the ancient establishment of hierarchical mass societies, enthusiastically and retrospectively given the title of 'civilisation' was considered. Numerous extracts were presented from the historical records of the modern bourgeois era indicating the one-sided representation of these ancient societies as progressive, liberating, desirable and inevitable for all members of society. The dark-side, the oppression, the exploitation, the aggression, the continuous crimes against humanity, the slavery, the persistent misogyny were almost never referenced as structural elements of these societies.

In section C) the omission of the dark-side was rectified and the literature of the ancient near east was introduced. This indicated that pillage, conquest, enslavement and genocidal levels of crimes against humanity, were almost yearly or bi-yearly events. Within such recorded history, the most horrible forms of torture and agonising deaths were openly and regularly admitted, and inflicted upon young, old, and male and female non-combatants. Examples are provided which are almost too graphic and horrible to relate in a book on life on earth, but have been included so that more of us can face up to the fact that these kinds of acts are still being conducted by the same hierarchical mass society form in the 21st century.

CHAPTER 10

HIERARCHICAL MASS SOCIETY IN ANTHROPOCENTRIC IDEOLOGY.

Throughout this book numerous and varied opinions on the history of the planet and its many life forms have been considered from a revolutionary-humanist and Gaia-centric perspective. However, as noted throughout this book too often mainstream opinions are of course often based entirely upon pre-formed anthropocentric ideas. Furthermore, these ideas are also frequently based on very little reliable and independently verifiable evidence. Most of us, if we are completely honest with ourselves, would admit that many of our opinions, expressed as 'facts' are often based upon what we want to be true or valid either for convenience or for preference. Since we cannot independently research in detail the vast amount of information we come across in daily life, we frequently make assumptions. This is why it makes sense to assign a provisional assessment to our general understanding and be prepared to consider further evidence if it proves to be both This is not always easy since much information in our modern info-tech society is offered as being relevant and reliable when it is actually a product of selection and bias even when it is not the result of careless misinformation or deliberate disinformation. Consequently, there is very often a sliding scale of difficulty accepting that what we (or anyone else) have wanted to be valid may not be valid at all. Being self-critical and facing up to being wrong is a challenge that not everyone can privately face up to never mind publicly admitting. I for one have had my previous understanding of many things challenged and seriously altered during the research for this book.

I have concluded, however, that it has been better to admit that many of my previous assumptions were based on trust in so-called professional 'authorities', my own inadequately cross referenced fact-checking and insufficient personal research. In my quest to understand the logic of human activities and motivations, from a perspective of life on earth, I have found it better to admit previous inadequacies, reject accumulated intellectual errors, test and abandon any flawed borrowed assumptions and be persuaded by the weight of evidence rather than the weight of general or 'expert' opinion. Continuing to be a mistaken advocate or a misguided activist on the crucial question of what happens to life on earth – as a whole - is to risk our children and grandchildren being taken down by even more false practical and intellectual dead ends; literally as well as metaphorically. Not doing anything or doing insufficient to correct our own and others past false ideas and our own present negligent practices, is to risk allowing those who have no intention to be self-critical or critical of our current parasitical destruction of our own species and the rest of the millions of species inhabiting the biosphere we describe as nature.

From all the evidence presented in the previous chapters we should definitely not assume that the ideas and opinions swirling around the relatively large human processing organ known as the professionally trained political, scientific and religious brain and reproduced in written documents, always accurately reflects their reality, let alone the reality of other forms of life on earth. In hopelessly divided societies, despite any pious rhetoric, there is undoubtedly a tendency to motivationally orientate around what we consider to be our own short term, class, gender, national or religious self-interest. However, most readers will have children and even grandchildren and possibly great grandchildren who they love and care deeply about (as I do) and that means there should be sufficient generational self-interest to motivate many more individuals than the most self-centred narcissists, to change or increase what they are doing in order to become part of a campaign to stop and reverse what collectively is being done to disfigure and destroy the wonderful sophisticated integrated species network of life we live with on earth.

Furthermore throughout the chapters I hope I have made the case that whenever our ideas concern serious matters or issues, the evidence we use to arrive at them should be based upon the most extensive, reliable and verifiable evidence that we can obtain. This is why I have used numerous quotations in varying quantities, from many various sources, within the chapters of this book so that the reader can themselves consult and verify the accuracy and relevance of the evidence sources I have used throughout. Of course, as the author of this book I have openly demonstrated considerable bias throughout its chapters, but I insist it is not bias motivated by a perspective of any form of personal preference, prejudice or gain. I neither hope for or intend any advantage to accrue to myself or my family and loved ones. My bias is with regard to the facts I have discovered and the relationships I have uncovered concerning the amazing spectrum of varied and integrated life on earth and its naturally based evolution. Whilst I hold that in the real world there is no such thing as absolute truth about anything, I also hold that somethings when studied seriously and accurately can come very close to being sufficiently valid to allow us to reliably act upon the conclusions drawn and which can be (and should be) confirmed and if necessary 'modified' as a result of any subsequent evaluation of reliable and verifiable evidence, knowledge and understanding.

The inorganic elements briefly covered in chapter 1 and the main organic structures of life in the form of cells, micro-organisms, plants, insects and animals, in more detail in chapters 2, 3, 4, 5 and 6, were the most relevant and reliable conclusions that I could obtain with my limited working class research resources. Within those chapters, it was noted that life on earth has evolved over immensely long periods of the current solar system based concept of 'time', before the understanding of the human species, evolved to a point beyond that of differentiating between night and day. It seems reasonable to assume, with regard to the origin of the concept of 'time', therefore, that an evolutionary point was reached, when humans began to use the movement of the sun and the shadows cast by the sun, during the earth's axial rotation to differentiate between periods occurring between the sun rising and setting. Eventually, some innovations meant the human species were able to then segment these shadow movements into hours and on a longer duration to count them as days, then weeks and the earth's orbits around the sun as years. Mentioning this evolving process of knowledge gained from experience emphasises an important distinction, made throughout this study, of the importance of starting from the observed reality rather than starting from ideas about reality.

Starting from the idea that time is not a human invented measurement, but something that has always existed, leads to even more imaginative nonsense..

So I also consider that the starting reference point and concluding remarks in any serious study should always be reality and not the ideas handed down to us from previous generations. Evidence suggests that contemporary Ideas about reality and unreality are often simply inherited opinions and ill-considered abstractions which are frequently misguided and are often just plain wrong. All ideas, both ancient and modern, need to be tested as thoroughly as possible against reality. For example, the conviction, reached from simple monitored visual perception, that the earth was flat and that the sun went round the earth are just two further clear examples of what may have seemed obvious to the visual perception of previous generations, but were ideas that were absolutely wrong. In some cases mistaken ideas have had no serious consequences, but it needs to be remembered that powerful people making decisions based on mistaken ideas can and do inflict severe consequences on those whose lives are rooted in reality. Astronomers in the middle ages who challenged the earth centred religiously constructed astronomical system were curtailed and severely punished by the all-powerful Catholic hierarchy, who believed the ideas they were told and relied on inherited mystical assumptions that had hardened into inflexible dogma. However, these ideas and many others, were entirely wrong. Privilege and power combined with a little bit or even a moderate bit of knowledge can definitely be a very dangerous combination.

Yet there are many such inherited assumptions in all walks of life and in all academic disciplines, which are just factually wrong. Starting with the already mentioned idea of 'time', for example, this concept has led to the confusion that the idea and word 'time' is not simply an exclusively human thought entity, operating in conjunction with other thought entities, but exists independently throughout the universe. Therefore, some of those who thought that the idea of 'time' was an independent real world entity, rather than understanding what it really was, came up with the oxymoronic idea of time travel. Things can travel through space but not through time. But even some scientists have not bothered to think about this thought entity 'time' through to its origins. The number of occasions you hear the crass expression 'since the beginning of time' from those classing themselves as 'scientists' referring to the origin of the universe, and repeated by supposedly educated commentators with university degrees, is incredible. The 'beginning of time' was when people started measuring planetary and celestial movements that were quite regular and consistent. The idea of specific units of 'time' and the instruments which are used to measure those movements and units, didn't exist until then. The movement of the planets and stars existed, of course, and still do, but time is purely a product of human intellectual effort assisted by human constructed complex movement measuring mechanisms. These movements and the instruments which are used to measure and record them are real but the concept and the divisions used within them are entirely dependent on human decisions and agreements. Time is just the agreed measurement and recording of the solar based planetary material movement by various instruments.

So although planetary objects and their motions do exist as external realities and exist independently from biology and humanity, but as already noted 'time' is purely a human concept and was entirely dependent upon the earth's material movement around the sun. This continuous orbital type movement of inorganic material is the natural rhythm not only of the planet, but from repeated and confirmed observations, also that (at different rates) of the entire solar system and the universe. However, the fact is that the millions of planets in the Milky Way galaxy are orbiting around their own stars, and very few will be orbiting at the same speed or over the same orbital distances of any other orbiting bodies. This obvious fact has practical implications which also logically reveal that time is not a universal 'thing', but that movement is. As noted, the concept of our notion of time is dependent upon the orbital tempo of the planet earth and of those human devised instruments determining and measuring that movement. The implications of these anthropocentric derived limitations could not be clearer. Any measurement of time based upon orbital transits within a universe of galaxies would be different on each planet and within each galaxy, where this particular observational method was used as a template. The speeds and distances of all celestial bodies are also variable and not constant and so a unit of time is not and could never be a universal constant or even a universal concept.

I have risked boring or patronising the reader with this level of detailed reflection on time to demonstrate a crucially important consideration for all areas covered by this and other such studies. It is that although the scientific method in general intends to be as exact as possible, even the approximate realisation of that intention is entirely dependent upon the quality of the accuracy and reliability of evidence and the socio-economic motivation of the scientist conducting the measurement. It should be remembered that many scientists believe in God and 'chosen people' without there being a shred of material evidence of these concepts' actual existence. All scientists are still human beings with emotions, impatience, grants to secure and a range of ideas and beliefs not necessarily all of them being based upon sound, irrefutable evidence. The frequently used sceptical paraphrase 'trust me I'm a doctor', can also be usefully applied to scientists, politicians, popes, vicars and many other authority figures. In the case of the estimated time of the existence of the Planetary, Solar System and Galactic bodies, the evidence, upon which it is based, is actually largely based upon estimated guess work. The conclusion from this level of understanding is inescapable. The quality and reliability of Galactic evidence in regard to dating accuracy and much else, is not reliable, not confirmable nor is it absolutely necessary.

Therefore, in general any assertion of 'scientific' exactness without sufficient reliable supportive evidence, is not emanating from science but from pseudo-science or to put it more politely, from varying mixtures of fiction interspersed with fact or fact interspersed with fiction, often with no clear distinction between either. Nevertheless, the current 'estimates' of the exceptionally high number of orbital circuits do serve to indicate that life on earth, prior to human hierarchical mass society formations, has been both robust and enduring. In chapters 7 and 8, a selection of the available evidence of the pre-history of hominid category of species was introduced and this included an estimate of the long period in which the mode of production known as hunter-gathering was practiced by the Homo *habilis* variant and the later

Homo sapien variant of the hominid species group we appear (as yet) to be descended from. It has also been established during this study that among all the multifarious categories of life on earth, each organism within each species, has evolved its own particular nuanced variation of a common bio-chemical life process that nevertheless conforms to an abbreviated (N-M-G-R + A-D) form and sequence. In addition, the unique sequence of each species has been shown to be intimately connected with the bio-chemical sequences of all other life forms. For example, the organic material of each life form, whether living or dead, is both the result of and the source for, the nutritional input (N) of organic and inorganic material utilised in the maintenance of one or more other forms of life on earth.

Hierarchical reality reflected in ancient records.

Once the basic three-class social framework of ancient hierarchical mass societies, noted previously, had become sufficiently established, the individuals socialised within these societies had their own material socio-economic process for meeting their bio-chemical processes provided for them. The division of such societies into a) a ruling strata; b) a middle administrative strata; and c) a labouring strata was achieved on the basis of the labouring strata being forced (by the imposition of various levels and types of slavery) to produce the essential food, water, clothing and housing supplies for the individual (N-M-G-R + A–D) purposes for all three classes. This division freed the ruling classes to concentrate on the practical tasks of ruling; and (with some interaction and oversight by them) allowed the administrative classes to focus on the intellectual and practical tasks of social organisation and administration. One section of the administrative class was trained as a special military enforcement section often on a sworn condition of loyalty to the dominant oligarchy within the ruling class.

Another section of the administrative middle class was required to become literate and numerate and this section laid the social basis for an eventual sub-division of this class into full or part-time, educators, musicians, philosophers, poets, playwrights, and religious officials. It is these intellectual strata's that became the recorders of events (historians) the intellectual rationalisers of events (philosophers), the recreational diverters from mundane events (entertainers) of the increasingly alienated populations of hierarchical mass societies, dating from, if not before the ancient Sumerian peoples. Whether individuals within these class systems liked it or not (and not all did) they all those becoming members of such societies had to play the socio-economic roles they were allocated to. Rulers' had to rule, administrators had to administer and slave labour was forced to labour at numerous, mostly difficult, repetitive and harsh routine tasks. The recording of the multiple alienations, from non-negotiated occupational choice have become 'the sighs of the oppressed' (in religion), the intellectual justifications or rationalisations (in philosophy), and the subversive counter-narratives (in histories, poetry and drama) that have been variously preserved in historical documents. It will be extracts from religious, historical and philosophical records that will be considered in the following sections.

In chapter 9 extracts from the ancient history of hierarchical mass societies was introduced along with a huge litany of outrages and inhuman acts of torture, rape, conquest and genocide. Clearly, since the fundamental bio-chemical functions of the evolution of life on earth are dependent upon each species securing the (N-M-G-R + A-D) processes necessary for them, these essential processes and functions were necessarily retained within hierarchical mass society formations. However, as is amply recorded in historical documents, these were practiced and retained with distorting and disturbing modifications. The documentary evidence presented in chapter 9 indicated that within such formations, the fundamental (and natural) direct means of securing the (N) of this essential biological and social process was considerably altered and for some classes completely eliminated. Throughout the Middle and Near East, elite classes emerged which consumed nutritional and essential production along with luxury production in huge quantities, but did not produce anything biologically essential themselves and therefore whose relationship to nature and other human beings was no longer complimentary but parasitic, oppressive, exploitative and often indirect.

This mode of production opened the way for a) the dehumanising of large sections of the human species (by reducing them and certain other animals to forms of slavery and semi-slavery) and b) the removal of self- selection for the reproduction of those plant and animal life forms on earth which became the prime resources intended for mass society nutrition (N). This pattern was repeated among those humans enslaved to produce it. This de-humanising and de-naturing of intimacy was initially achieved by containment (shackles and fences) and by the application of controlled breeding processes for plants, animals and humans. Many of the socio-economic results of this change are recorded in the opinions and incidents contained in the extracts reproduced in previous chapters. However, it needs to be remembered that throughout history, all these varied opinions emanated one-sidedly from within educated and literate sections of the elite classes within human societies. So these perspectives only represent the often biased views of a tiny minority of the articulate and literate members of the human species. Yet the horror described was also experienced first-hand by thousands and by second-hand, word of mouth by hundreds of thousands of others. Therefore, it is possible, if not probable, that the anger and disgust at such treatment of ordinary people would have been widespread and considerable at the time, but of course, remained largely unreported.

This suggests that the views of the millions or perhaps billions of the masses who had directly or indirectly experienced living through pre-history and the later successive iterations of hierarchical mass society formations, have had no independent voice. Therefore with regard to pre-history and history their stories remain fundamentally untold, their voices virtually unrecorded. The masses had no independent literature and very few among the respective literate elites bothered to accurately record the views of their slaves and semi-slave workers. Occasional accounts of ancient citizen uprisings in Greece, (Athens) and slave revolts (Spartacus) and various city revolts (Hannibal) during the Roman Empire period, percolate through some elite accounts, but very little of the breadth and depth of everyday experiences endured by the plebeians and slaves during the formation and consolidation of hierarchical mass societies, are available for modern humans to consider. For a rare example, in a discussion of the ancient Mediterranean slave trade conducted by the ancient Phoenecians, one author commenting upon the history of slave rebellions noted that;

"The scanty and comparatively insignificant fragments of her history which now exist are filled with accounts of such revolts, generally ending as most fearful tragedies. An uprising of this kind occurred in Tyre about ten centuries BC; and history records, that at that time the king, the aristocracy, all masters, and even great numbers of non-slave owning freemen were slaughtered. The women, however, were saved and married by the slaves;" (The History of Slavery From Egypt and the Roman's, to Christian Slavery. A. Gurowski. Chapter 2.)

Despite a scarcity of direct historical evidence, nevertheless a strong trace or dark shadow of popular feelings have been left imprinted in the cultural and religious myths which have been handed down to later generations. We do not need to simply imagine how the inhabitants experienced hierarchical mass society existence, because it was occasionally recorded so we can now read it. This chapter will therefore give an outline of some of these cultural and religious traces of the views of the 'captured', 'enslaved', 'oppressed' and 'exploited' masses whether restrained physically in chains or trapped economically within hierarchical mass societies. Some of the sharpest shadows thrown by the distress and alienation of the masses to living in the hierarchical mass societies of the ancient middle and near east were cast onto and into the oral narratives and then written onto the scrolls and parchment of the various monotheistic eastern religions.

The origin and development of institutionalised and codified local religions could only begin alongside the origin and development of hierarchical mass societies, because organised and top-down regulated religions require an organised and top-down regulated society. In contrast, hunter-gatherer nomadic and semi-nomadic bands were not constrained by location or by a fixed authority or orthodoxy. A previous amalgam of hunter-gatherer, earth mother (pagan) practices were undoubtedly carried into the very early mass society formations and survived until a later period. However, fixed temple buildings and specialised occupational individuals (priests) only become possible in settled hierarchical mass society settings, which also eventually produced a huge surplus of (N) and other supplementary acquired needs. Moreover, during those long periods of hierarchical mass society gestations, the changes in how people lived affected how people thought about life on earth and these changes were reflected in those myths.

It is important to recognise that the religions of Sumer, Babylon, Egypt and Persia all commenced in the form of oral narratives until writing was developed far beyond the period of being occasionally chiselled onto steles, walls, monuments and on palace tablets. The myths of 'creation out of chaos', the 'flood' or 'deluge' and the construction of a large boat to save examples of humanity and animals from a flood, were regional verbal narratives until recorded on clay tablets and eventually onto parchment or paper. They more or less all feature the same basic mythic story lines, albeit with different character names, extra additions and changed emphasis from Egypt in the south of the 'fertile crescent' to Assyria in the north. The region became not only the melting pot of trade and exploitation interspersed with inter-city wars, regional conquests, capture of booty, tribute taking, killing and enslavement, noted in the previous chapter, but also of the borrowing, copying and swapping of religious ideas. These ideas included concerns over the different circumstances and status of humanity, the origin of life on earth and the creation of the planet earth. Across the entire middle-east region there was a common pool of varied creation myths with local and regional historical additions or omissions. The common elements experienced by all usually involved the nature of the sky, earth and water. In this regard, it has been suggested that the ancient Sumerian version of the common pool of 'creation', 'deluge' and 'fall' myths probably dates back to the earliest hierarchical mass society times. Those authors who have examined these particular documents report that;

"The bulk of our material is furnished by some early texts, written towards the close of the third millennium BC (BCE). They incorporate traditions which extend in an unbroken outline from their own period into the remote ages of the past and claim to trace the history of man back to his creation." ('Legends of

Babylon and Egypt in relation to Hebrew Tradition'. L.W.King. Introduction)

For the purposes of this study I shall disregard criticising the myth of material and biological 'creation' apart from noting the fact that the existence of microscopic bacterial cells, fungi, viruses and soil micro-organisms, essential to all life on earth, are obviously completely missing from these creation myths. Furthermore, this early part of monotheistic myth largely based upon ignorance is obviously meant to draw a vaguely understood contrast between **before** and **after** life within hierarchical mass societies. The commonly spread imaginary ideas of 'creation' were that in the beginning, the skies and the earth (the inorganic material of the galaxy) were yet unnamed and all the waters of the world mingled. In the Abrahamic trio of monotheistic religions, Judaism, Christianity and Islam, the anthropocentric and patriarchal myths spun around ancient hierarchical mass society reality, reached their ultimate expression. The authors of creation myths, lacking knowledge of the slow evolution of species, were primarily concerned with the creation of organic life and in particular humanity and its uniqueness. Monotheistic religions are ancient, anthropocentric, patriarchal obsessions which were first expressed orally before becoming written up as religious ideology. The written evidence contained in monotheistic religions indicates that the originators of them had no understanding that life on earth as a whole evolved over billions of years and during that evolution, humanity was only one of the many varied species that emerged from the bio-chemical interactions of the earliest forms of organic cells. Nor do these scriptures indicate an accurate knowledge of the fact that humanity was totally dependent - not upon an imagined god or gods - but upon the whole of nature, not just the parts it consumed. This general ignorance is hardly surprising because many of these relationships were unknown until the 20th and 21st centuries.

However, such was the anthropocentric arrogance and understandable ignorance of the originators of the various monotheistic narratives, that they used themselves and their imagination to invert the reality of the life they and others lived on earth that unfolded before them and instead invented the idea of an all-powerful, invisible, male God who they asserted created the primal man 'in his own image'. The obvious contradiction of how the gender of an asserted invisible entity could be known, was apparently not considered. In this muddled Abrahamic monotheistic version of life on earth, two versions of the then common middle-eastern myths seem to have got mixed up. In Genesis chapter 1 verse 26 it is written that the head God talks to other gods and decides to make a male and a female. Yet in the next chapter (Genesis 2) the other gods are not included and it is written that God, having made Adam, is imagined to have felt sorry for Adam's loneliness and in Genesis verse 18 makes him a female "helper" (Eve) out of Adam's rib. Clearly the originators of these mythical stories knew about sexual reproduction from their own and animal reproductions, which were constantly occurring, but could not at that point in the religious fictional narrative, acknowledge this fact. To do so would have undermined the idea of the 'creation' of earth and life on earth by God - out of nothing! So possibly the idea of sexual reproduction was only allowed into the 'story' after the cobbled together version of a six-day creation by an invisible male super being, had become an accepted part of this male produced religious ideology.

Another part of the common myth also accepted by the authors of the original Abrahamic version was that in the beginning there was nothing but chaos. It is only when the myths of gardens of Edens and original sin appear in the mythical narrative that chaos leading to 'god given' social order, removes (through sin) the ease of living 'naturally' and gives way to god-imposed hard and monotonous labour in field and pasture. So even according to religious myth there is a dim literary shadow of recognition that there was a previous alternative to the labour intensive agricultural- based, hierarchical mass societies beginning in Sumer and Babylon. It was these social forms that consolidated a different mode of production based upon hard labour divisions for the toiling masses. Consequently, the dark shadows cast by alienation and oppression under the hierarchical mass societies developed in Sumer and Babylon were recorded and are still retained and discernible in the monotheistic literature preserved by its adherents. This suggests that known hunter-gatherer modes of production, in areas of natural abundance may, with some justification, have lived on in hierarchical mass society myth as idyllic pre-historic 'Garden of Eden' type conditions. But of course, myths invariably exaggerate for effect and undoubtedly, the reality of hunter-gatherer life was more mundane and occasionally geologically and climatologically precarious, than depicted in myth. In reality, hunter-gatherer communities, ancient and modern, regularly move on to better locations when one area is depleted. Like all other grazing animals they knew when to move on, locally and regionally as resources became scarce, and did so. Moreover, the myths of a 'Garden of Eden's' original times were not unique to one religion. Such myths were widespread enough to become incorporated into at least three of surviving monotheisms - Judaism, Christianity and Islam. Thus;

"The general dependence of the biblical Versions upon the Babylonian legend as a whole has long been recognised, and needs no further demonstration; and it has already been observed that the parallelisms with the version in the Gilgamesh Epic are on the whole more detailed and striking in the earlier than in the later Hebrew Version." (Ibid Lecture 2.)

In the religious type oral myths common to wide areas of the region at the time, those versions originating in ancient Sumer and Mesopotamia, with regional variations, are the probable prototypes for the subsequent documented three Abrahamic monotheisms and at least part of the Zoroastrian religion of the Persian Empire. It is interesting that in these original 'creation' myth versions, produced in Sumer, the imagined 'creation' out of chaos at the beginning of life produced not one but two original gender differentiated God's. Tiamat, the Goddess who was imagined to be salt water made human and Apsu the God who was imagined to be fresh water made human. Since all religious imaginations extrapolate their material, directly or indirectly from the general human experience, the two gods did what most humans did, they mated and raised a family of gods and goddesses. This narrative, gaining numerous additions, was obviously passed on by word of mouth possibly for generations until writing was invented then it became written down. These were ancient speculative versions of the more modern, imaginary 'big-bang' type imaginative creation myths of the universe. An instantaneous transition from nothing (or the tiniest particle) to 'everything' appears as an 'imaginary event' which leaps across scientific as well as religious neo-cortical dendrite gaps. Lacking exact provable evidence based knowledge, and wanting to avoid admitting ignorance, human imagination often supplies imaginative acts of creation. Such speculative hypotheses have remained a common theme and have been rationalized as plausible 'theories' ever since. Consequently, the creation of life on earth by speculative gods (or speculative big-bang type explosions), is a closely allied part of the common mystical creationist view of life on earth, within, but not exclusive to, the Abrahamic religions.

An interesting intellectual fossil found residing in this particular version of ancient myth is that the Goddess Tiamat is imagined to be the equal of her male partner and when their children become too noisy the male God Apsu decides to kill them. However, one of the sons hears of this and preempts this outcome and kills his father - the primal God. This imaginary act of patricide, we are informed, makes the imaginary Tiamat sick to her stomach, but this part of the narrative implies that in the religious imaginary world 'she', not 'he' is suddenly the most powerful creator being. The early anthropocentric myths, for a period of time, allowed a female creator to legitimately exist. Meanwhile monsters and serpents enter the common mythical theme and the Goddess Tiamat, with a view to waging war (another common religious theme reflecting hierarchical mass society reality) against these monsters, delegates her other son Kingu to be consort. She then gives him the imaginary 'Tablet of Destinies', (no doubt based of course on 'tablets' commissioned by human elites) and increases his imaginary powers. She then declares that in future **he** (Kingu) will rule everything. In this world of earth based anthropocentric imagination, it is hardly surprising that rules appearing on tablets of stone (Moses), provided by Gods are another common religious theme during that period, since tablets (or stele) were the common means elite rulers had of informing the literate sections of their own and conquered peoples of how they were expected to conduct themselves. In this imaginary fictional scenario, the powerful female god, having become the highest power in the world, immediately delegates that power to her male son - not to her female daughter. I suggest that this myth provides a clue to how ancient anthropocentric imagination dealt with the real practical subordination and cultural humiliation of women, within early hierarchical mass societies. This myth highlights yet another common element of this period in the gradual or sudden replacement of Goddesses who for a time, represented practically everything in the world, by Gods representing practically everything, until the monotheistic idea of one all-powerful god representing everything was promoted and the other gods gradually demoted (as appears in Greek mount Olympus myth) until mythical powerful female deities were completely removed.

So in this middle-eastern mythical tradition we encounter a mythical explanation of how the original nurturing and creative role of the female principle - established by the bio-chemical evolution of all sexual forms of reproduction - had been replaced intellectually and socially by the male creating and also destroying (war) principle, which had become hierarchical mass society reality. This suggests an intellectualised mythical oral (then written) reflection of something that they imagined had happened previously in reality but was by then no longer accurately or favourably remembered and no longer valued by the patriarchal religious elites. It certainly occurs to me that the authors of this ancient myth have created a retrospective mythical explanation for the actual change in female matrilineal and female focussed status established within the hunter-gatherer egalitarian modes of production. Settled agricultural production seems to have produced social conditions that severely disturbed and then overturned the previous 'natural' based biological relationships and gender balance within humanity and thus altered their respective ideas about each other. The religious myths of this transitional period are perhaps responsible for casting a similar intellectual trace onto the written inscriptions on what is known as the Palermo Stele. It has been noted and suggested in this regard, that since early humanity gave high status to women and to female mother goddesses, a transition was obviously occurring and the traces in this case had not been entirely erased, for there it is in at least this one ancient script;

"..the Palermo Stele's inclusion of the mother's and omission of the father's name in its record of the early dynastic Pharaohs. This suggestion does not exclude the possibility of the prevalence of matrilineal (and perhaps originally also of matrilocal and matripotestal) conditions among the earliest inhabitants of Egypt." (ibid.)

Indeed, this historical remnant certainly does not exclude the previous female lineage or social status, but emphatically records it. Herodotus in his pre-biblical 'histories' also makes reference to groups of people who in his time reckoned the family line through the female gender and of course this continued to be the case within some Jewish family traditions that have lasted into the 21st century. It is also perhaps revealing that important city names and crucial day names, which have been habitually used and have tended to resist changes over long periods of time, still record an indelible record of previous female gender importance. A number of cities in the middle and near east still bear female names (e.g. Athens) derived from the goddess Athena. The case is similar with regard to days such as (Friday) from the goddess Frida. The planets in the solar system also retain a share of goddess names. Prior to the agricultural 'tillers of ground' and resource conquering armed male dominated societies (settled agricultural modes of production) it is clear that the status of women was fundamentally high with regard to production as well as reproduction and naturally so. It is also interesting to note in this regard, that the later agriculturally based Greeks still had Demeter as the goddess of agriculture and well into the period of the Roman Empire, the goddess of agriculture in their mass society was known as Ceres.

For an extended period of time, practically all the essential Nourishment sources (N) for humanity were attributed to the positive activity of a female derived activity or female focussed process. The economic base of agriculture of at least two ancient hierarchical mass society professionally 'armed' empires was framed as resulting from the original oversight of a feminine deity. But as previously noted, after hierarchical mass societies began to dominate human aggregations locally (but also by promotion, both far and wide), feminine status in practice had been reduced radically and in many cases degradingly so. The question therefore arises; was this because of the division of labour changes that those human societies went through in obtaining the (N-M-G-R + A-D) processes when the hierarchical mass society agricultural and pastoral mode of producing (N) was introduced? The currently available evidence may not answer this question conclusively, but it means this line of questioning is legitimate and needs to be further explored. Meanwhile, it does push the possibility along a path toward establishing the probability that this indeed was (and clearly still is) the multi-causal source of socio-economic inequalities between genders and classes, within hierarchical mass societies. Patriarchal, mass societies continue to exist and so do the lack of equal rights for female and other non-elite humans. Of course, correlation does not always prove causation, but in combination with other factors, in some cases it actually does.

Evidence containing the 'sighs of the oppressed'.

The evidence considered so far suggests that by the time of the Roman occupation of the entire Mediterranean area, hierarchical mass societies had existed for many generations and some had frequently become empires and repeatedly created systematic inhumane conditions for the bulk of settled humanity. In the Mediterranean and near eastern regions of the then known world, humans had made themselves the overwhelmingly dominant and dominating species of life on that part of the earth's surface. Most human beings and all other species of life within that region had sooner or later become subject to the whims and fancies of the ruling elites, in order to obtain sources of food, pleasure, labour or entertainment within and out of these city states and empires. It cannot be entirely surprising then that in this human male-focussed and centred region of the world, an ideological expression of that anthropocentric exceptionalism emerged within monotheistic forms of religious ideology. Indeed, considered from the perspective of life on earth in general, Monotheism, once examined, is merely the ultimate ideological expression of anthropocentric exceptionalism and patriarchy. It was arrogantly imagined and asserted by some of the male elites during that period, against previous practices, that an invisible all-powerful male God had created the world and all its contents and who in appearance looked very much like a middle-aged European human being who had magically created everything they could see in their environment. Moreover this imaginary superman had created the world and everything they knew about - exclusively for humanity to use, or abuse - as they saw fit. These few ancient monotheistic Patriarchs were by various means able to convince others among them that this imaginary scenario was based upon sound evidence and logic, when it was actually based upon myth and imagination. .

And as religious documents often phrase it, eventually *'it came to pass'* that many millions were also prepared to believe this adult anthropocentric and patriarchal fairy story about the 'beginning of life on earth' and along with it, the meaning and purpose of their own existence. Henceforth, the ruling secular and religious elites invariably lived in luxury, whilst the working poor invariably lived in relative or absolute poverty. Or as my generation were taught to sing frequently at school; *"The Rich man in his castle, the poor man at his gate, all things bright and beautiful, the Lord god made it so"*. The literary evidence which follows in a paragraph or two will utterly contradict rather than confirm this centuries old religious "all things bright and beautiful" 'spin' on the state of hierarchical mass society life on earth. Of course, located in between these two Christian *'bright and beautiful'* extremes of rich and poor were the administrative and regulatory middle classes. For the overwhelming majority, there was clearly little or no consolation for living within such hierarchical mass societies and neither was there any realistic hope of an alternative way of living emerging.

Thus a religious cult belief system which offered some form of diluted intellectual consolation in the here and now and a future intellectualised hope of better times (at least after death) for the equally imaginary human soul was bound to have regional appeal. Around that later historical period a group of dissident Abrahamic Jewish monotheist preachers, after pointing out the financial corruption and socio-economic collaboration of Judaic religious elites with the Roman occupiers, gave up trying to reform mainstream Judaism and tried a new strategy. According to their oral history, eventually some of these reform minded itinerant Jewish oppositionists, formed an alternative religious cult and declared themselves Christians. It was then that the new strategy they devised involved presenting a modified version of the Jewish monotheistic belief system, with the imaginary addition of a human connection to the invisible god. An alternative narrative was conveniently adjusted concerning a long dead preacher (Jesus) whose parentage was transferred from his being a son of Joseph the carpenter, to being a son of god. This competitive, and now alternative version of monotheism, could then be offered to everyone who would accept their 'good news' creed.

It is at this point that it is worth considering the essence of many of the formal and informal cults which blossomed in the early hierarchical mass society formations and which continued to emerge within modern hierarchical mass societies. The essence of a cult, whether religiously formed or politically constructed, is both to critique and attempt to mitigate (or negate) the worst effects of competitive and alienated forms of living within these early and later versions of the hierarchical mass society form of human aggregation. Alongside the tensions and anxieties arising from occupations, plus the restricted personal relationships and uncertainties experienced within alienating and competitive social forms, cults offer a temporary physical and intellectual sedative. This comes in the form of cooperative fellowships, with an extended form of community belonging, which include forms of emotional support and a shared purpose with a progressive aim for enhanced personal and collective support for life within the rampant social contradictions. These characteristics, 'belonging', 'acceptance', 'validation' and 'support', are all important social needs, especially (but not only) within the human species and are almost completely missing for the masses within the so-called civilisations formed by hierarchical mass societies. All the current institutionally based mass religions, political parties and occupational associations have developed from such ancient cult beginnings and have retained some of the essence of their earlier forms, although in many cases this essence quickly became distorted by the cultish tendency to emulate the hierarchical mass society form, by instituting a hierarchy within the cult.

Cults as well as mass societies tend to have 'charismatic' leaders, a middle level tier of trusted believer's (aids or disciples) and the rank and file dog's-body activists or workers (the members or congregation). The latter are essential, for it is these - as in their hierarchical mass society form - enliven and support the cult's social pyramid emotionally, intellectually and financially. Authority, power, influence and control descends form the top to the bottom of the political party, religious denomination, personality cult, revolutionary sect, fan club or trade association etc. Whilst the benefits of the collective enterprise (power, influence, money, prestige, admiration and even adoration) work their way up from the lower ranks to the top. In other words, cults and consequently any evolutionary developments of them into mass movements, despite any different ideological frameworks and belief systems, actually replicate the hierarchical mass society form. This is so even when they generally promise (and even originally intend) to be revolutionary or radically different from the hierarchical mass society form.

This outcome includes replicating the oppressive and exploitative characteristics of all hierarchical mass societies, such as grooming juvenile males and females for servile or sexually servile activities, engaging in social and economic advantage which comes the way of those with influence and power, and of course siphoning off for personal use any valuable assets whether in money or property. The non-religious cults such as fan clubs and those organising 'followers' of other successful charismatic personalities may or may not offer the same form of cult membership as full blownl cults but for a short period they do also mitigate or numb to some extent the isolation, alienation and ennui endured by the masses in their everyday existence within such societies. That the function of 'fan' based entertainment has long been a secular based intellectual substitute by temporarily blotting out or dampening down the emotional discomfort or even the suicidal inducing pain of hierarchical mass society living was evident by the seating capacity factored into of the huge auditoriums sited around the 'empires' of ancient Greece and Rome. These emotional props are of course replicated in modernity by entertainment and sports centres, because a human based 'meaning' for satisfactory living does not arise directly from the experience of living in hierarchical mass societies and has to be artificially created in the form of spectator events of various kinds.

It is perhaps appropriate at this point, to consider some written evidence concerning the oppressive effects of ancient hierarchical mass society living, that I came across during research for this section. The following comes from the period of the Roman occupation of Egypt and the near east and during the reign of the Emperor Tiberius. At that period Roman regional occupying powers used taxation as a way to extract surplus product from "everyone and everything", particularly the labouring population. Philo of Alexandria writes of an Imperial tax collector who;

"When some who appeared to be defaulting merely through sheer poverty took to flight, in dread of severe punishment, he forcibly carried off their women and children and parents and other relatives, beat them, and subjected them to every kind of outrage. Although they were unable either to reveal the fugitive's whereabouts or (because of their own destitution) to pay what was due from him, he persisted torturing them and putting them to death in a cruel manner. When there were no relatives left, he extended his outrages to neighbours and sometimes to even to villages and towns, which were rapidly deserted by the flight of their inhabitants to places where they hoped to escape detection." (Philo, De spec. leg, 111 158-63. Quoted in, 'The Class Struggle in the Ancient Greek World.' G.E.M. de Ste. Croix. Page 499)

Nothing very bright and beautiful seemed to be occurring for the poor at that particular location at that particular stage. However, the above extract provides an informative snapshot of the way well established hierarchical society elites increase the socio-economic factors which eventually trigger their *'decline and fall'* as Edward Gibbon extensively covered in the case of the Roman Empire. As noted earlier, and it is worth repeating here, in all periods, ancient and modern, the armed elite who help dominate and rule hierarchical mass societies initially create a full-time military cohort to control the inevitable tensions and antagonisms within their own hierarchical system and those regularly occurring between rival hierarchical systems. These militarily equipped forces are systematically increased both to defend the society against attacks from other raiders or conquerors and also to perpetrate such actions against other large-scale mass society formations. By these institutional means two increasingly large unproductive sections (or classes) are created in such societies; a ruling/administrative section and a policing/military section.

Both of the above 'sectors' produce nothing essential for human (N-M-G-R +A-D) processes, they only enforce symptoms of 'order' and 'control' but nothing essential or practical for the bio-chemical maintenance of life itself. Nevertheless these forces still need to be fed, housed and provided with the tools required to do their jobs. Thus economically speaking they are overwhelmingly 'unproductive' and whilst socially active they only 'produce' the conditions that enable the ruling elite to continue to exploit the masses. Therefore, as long as their unproductive existence is required, the essentials for their (N-M-G-R + A-D) processes have to be supplied by the productive working classes, whether these are peasants, serfs, slaves or wage slaves.. Thus the productive workers must agree to, (or be forced to)shoulder the burden of producing, not only for their own (N-M-G-R) needs, but also the burden of producing for the needs of the elite within the hierarchy, along with their armed supporters within the military. And of course, any other non-productive entertainment individuals the elite employ, must also be fed and housed. This double or triple burden on the working classes, whether extracted in the form of tax in goods kind, or tax in money-form, ruins the health and shortens the amount of non-work living for the rural and urban working classes, whilst creating increasing social tensions.

The historical record indicates that these two (or even three) non-producing classes by becoming more numerous, and some by becoming more accustomed and able to demand ever increasing advantages of wealth and status, achieved ever more demands from a productive workforce increasingly exhausted and impoverished. In effect the increasing needs and expectations of the hierarchical systems ruling sectors in all periods of history sooner or later have begun to sap the labour-intensive socio-economic foundations of any settled (N-M-G-R + A-D) society. In short, the historic and contemporary pattern has been that the rich start to get richer and the under-classes as slaves, serfs or wage slaves stay or start to become poorer, more desperate and more discontented. For a long period in the early stages of hierarchical mass society developments the elites of successful City States and young Empires, could offset this tendency and gain additional resources by launching foreign conquests, securing extra taxation, pillaging and tribute.

However, as the hierarchical mass society systems matured, and eventually ran out of places sufficiently near enough to conquer, subdue and exploit, the stagnation and decline of hierarchical mass society systems began. Hence the protracted decline and eventual fall of the empires of Egypt, Persia, Greece and Rome in the ancient world and the Empires of Germany, Holland, Spain, France, Russia, and Britain in early modern age. By these empire collapsing stages, however, even the most far-sighted members of the elite could not imagine or accept their own cancerous role in the contradictions, rippling and tearing through the hierarchical socio-economic system, their ancestors had initially set up. Neither could they imagine living under any other form of human society. This ensured then (and does now) that these elites and intermediate middle-class elites did not even think of doing anything practical to eliminate the massive contradiction they and the original rulers had introduced into the hierarchical mass society forms of living.

Eventually the steady declines became more pronounced, the existing tensions and crises increased and new ones emerged. This type of internal and external tectonic type social turmoil divided and therefore weakened the ruling elites and sooner or later made foreign invasion more likely. For some cities and empires the decline accelerated and was accompanied by civil wars and invasions, which were the earthquake type arbiters of the coming dynastic collapses and failures. Although, the usual recorded histories of hierarchical mass societies are invariably focussed upon individual rulers and their peculiar shortcomings, or imaginary 'brilliance' to explain their successes or downfalls, the above abbreviated outline can be traced in all the rises and collapses of City States and Empires of the Near and Middle East from Sumer, Babylon, Persia, Greece, Rome to the demise of the Islamic Empire. Similar outlines can also be traced in the rises and falls of all modern hierarchical mass societies, such as Britain, France, Spain and Germany.

It is often remarked that an army marches on its stomach and this is metaphorically true in the sense that unless its members are provided with (N) on a regular daily basis, the (N-M-G-R + A-D) essential processes of their life on earth deteriorate and along with them every other skill or aptitude they personify, quickly deteriorates. In this sense an army is no different than any other form of social organisation of life on earth - including the hierarchical mass society cities of humanity. Without an adequate quantity and quality of natural resources to enable the (N-M-G-R + A-D) processes for all its direct members and for all the additional species essential for life-support in general, the hierarchical mass society system will atrophy and disintegrate. Meanwhile, it will now be useful to consider more sources of the long dead 'sighs of the oppressed' as Karl Marx famously depicted them, for these contain the literary echoes of social tremors indicating tectonic shifts occurring in the foundations of hierarchical social pyramids.

All my troubles, Lord, will soon be over.

Anyone who has diligently and extensively read the large body of scriptural texts known as the Torah and Talmud in the Judaic branch of Abrahamic monotheism and in the form known as the Old and New Testament in the Christian Abrahamic branch will know there are many desperate, disturbing and distasteful actions and ideas recorded within them. Similarly, those who diligently read the Qu'ran will also know that the Islamic branch of Abrahamic monotheism is based upon a great deal of the Old Testament characters and assumptions which are part of monotheism and only some parts of the New Testament gospel narratives. However, what such readers may not have fully realised is that what they read in these scriptures is not entirely original or unique to their particular religious branch of myth and mystery. As noted earlier, the basic religious ideology that the modern converts are reading and accepting as sacred texts, started out as wide-spread common oral histories of the peoples and their religious leaders living within those hierarchical mass society formations that were considered in chapter 9. As already noted, it was only much later that these common oral traditions were modified, solidified and set down as distinctive texts after their various dedicated 'holy-men' had added their own tweaks and twists to the common concerns and traditions of the entire region. Consequently religious and philosophic texts from that period also have a shared concern with how individuals can learn to adapt to or tolerate the inhuman conditions or make a success of living in hierarchical mass societies and how to deal with its many brutal downsides.

For example, it is not only that the mythical characters Cain and Abel in the Jewish based Genesis narrative are punished for transgressions by becoming 'tillers of ground' and 'keepers of sheep', that suggests the original oral authors of these scriptures considered that something valuable (and natural) had been abandoned when the main imaginary Garden of Eden source of (N) subsistence had been changed. But much more than that is revealed amid the rampant mysticism and make believe. The religious texts of monotheism reveal and confirm that the whole hierarchical mass society enterprise being created during that period, constantly needed ever more sources of land and labour. Moreover, it did not appear to matter to each hierarchical-led city-state system (and their religious elites) just whose land and labour they 'went forth' and appropriated. For example, according to Genesis 13, Lot and Abram agreed to share the whole land of the previously occupied territory of Jordan and Canaan between them, but that chapter is somewhat vague on how the original people occupying that land were finally removed from their normal pastures. However, this eviction process is known generally because Genesis 34 gives a more detailed example of how such things probably happened. In this case an already locally occupied town was approached by the tribe of Israel (having previously left their own enslavement in Egypt, and now led by Moses), and discussions were held about forming an inter-tribal amalgamation. A negotiated condition of this jointly proposed tribal integration was that the indigenous men of the town should be circumcised so as to be just like the Jewish newcomers who were suggesting they amalgamate. In the scriptural narrative of this particular part of the myth, the regular non-Isaeli town's people agreed to this proposal and all the men of the town voluntarily submitted to the painful cutting of their foreskins and were duly circumcised. Then the religious script informs the reader that;;

"...on the third day when the men were sore, two sons of Jacob, Simon and Levi,....took each man his sword...and slew every male and plundered the town...took sheep and oxen...all their wealth and their little ones and their wives they carried captive.." (Genesis 34 verses 25 to 29.)

The recording in scripture of this oral tradition of tribal hierarchical deceit, ruthless genocidal killing and conquest for plunder and slaves is not an isolated example, for there are 20 other such references to aggressive land possession, killing and securing captives in Genesis alone. In Exodus, there are 13 references to death and killing and 15 on obtaining captives. In Leviticus there are 7 instances of killing and 4 on obtaining land by conquest. Numbers has 10 references to killing and 7 to conquests of land and captives. This already amounts to 70 such references recorded in the first fourteen books of this biblical assembly of allegedly god-given sacred revelations. It is not difficult to conclude that these Abrahamic texts reflect essentially the same pattern of ruthless and inhumane asset seizing as those recorded in the secular historical texts which were quoted in chapter 9. However, one incident recorded in the Abrahamic narrative I think is particularly detailed and informative with regard to the establishment of a highly inhumane phenomenon that in the 20th century is classified as wars against humanity or genocide. Numbers chapter 31 suggests that God and Moses instructed the tribe of Israel to go to war with the Midianites to obtain possession of their land. The biblical narrative records that they did so and slayed all the men and took the women captives. However when the troops returned to camp to report back to Moses, we are informed by this sacred (?) scripture that;

"Moses was wroth with the officers of the army, the commanders of the thousands and...said to them. Why have you let all the women live? ....Now therefore kill every male among the little ones and kill every woman who has known man by lying with him...But all the female children who have not known a man *by lying with him, keep alive for yourself." (Numbers 31 verses 14 to 18.)*

Does any of this ring a bell within modern history? To me this reveals that by the time of the oral origin of this part of the narrative, the de-humanising of the 'other' and the total degrading abuse of the female half of our species was deeply embedded in this region, not only within the practice and mentality of the religious elite, but also those who loyally followed them. Inhumanity had become so universal within hierarchical mass society living during that entire historical period, that sexual abuse of women and young children had become normalised. The Jewish and Christian bible records a number of actions by organised groups of armed men and their leaders, which in the 20th and 21st centuries would have prompted a referral to the International Court of Justice as acts of crimes against humanity and genocide. By that pre-BCE period of hierarchical mass society living, these symptoms of callous and brutal collective punishment conduct were so endemic that they were orally carried into and later written into the documents of the dominant religious belief systems taking root there. The reality of hierarchical mass society (later retrospectively rose-tinted as 'civilisation') building also went to the lengths of deliberately killing male children to prevent future revenge possibilities, when male children became adult men. Those human beings not killed were de-humanised as non-valid 'others' and were treated as economic slaves and infant sexual slaves to their ancient Israeli biblically recorded 'masters'.

This transformation of the previous predominantly 'natural' 'humane' progress of human aggregation presented within previous chapters, had been transformed into a new socialised form of inhumanity and was so thoroughly absorbed and normalised that it not only found its way into mainstream elite versions of mass society thinking, but has remained as spurious justification ever since. However, that was not all. Also finding its way into the Jewish, Christian and Islamic scriptures by this time were deeply held irrational prejudices concerning the natural reproductive processes (R) of their own female half of the human species. The entirely natural menstrual cycle of the female, which is an essential biological process for all new individuals in mammalian species, is given a wholly negative characteristic retained in all three monotheisms. Women are designated as 'unclean' because of the monthly emission of unused nutrient fluids that would otherwise have been utilised to keep human babies (male and female) alive within the female womb. This reactionary attitude cannot simply be dismissed as a result of ancient ignorance or backwardness, because the biologically determined female reproductive menstrual cycle was well known, if not fully understood, in all previous generations of hunter-gatherer and pastoralist peoples but without it causing prejudice or detriment to the social status of the female, within those social formations.

The similarity of many of the more violent examples of these events to some of those noted in the previous chapter is remarkable and indicates that not only the monotheistic mystical elements were common to the entire near and middle east region of hierarchical mass societies, but so too where the common socio-economic practices of all these hierarchical mass societies. The common elements in these socio-economic practices arose not just because they were all based upon mixed agriculture and pastoral modes of economic production, but because at the same time they are all also based upon hierarchical and patriarchal political systems. Deuteronomy, Joshua, Judges, 1 and 2 Samuel; 1 and 2 Kings, and 1 and 2 Chronicles have a similar number of references to killing, captives and conquests as those noted above, whilst Ezra, Nehemiah, Esther, Job reflect other dominant concerns. Indeed, another of these early recorded urges to commit crimes against humanity or to suggest implementing a holocaust comes in the first book of Samuel, as follows. It reads;

"Now go and smite the Amalekites, and utterly destroy all that they have, and spare them not, but slay both men and women, young people and infants, oxen and sheep, camels and oxen." (1 Samuel chapter 15 verse 3.)

It should not be imagined that this urge to kill every human being of another human community, was the exclusive product of the Jewish people of the ancient near east, or of their imaginary god Yahweh, for, as we have indicated, such sentiments and activities were by then a regional product of all elite sections of hierarchical mass societies in general. The Egyptian, Babylonian,

Persian. Greek, Roman and Islamic elites were all operating upon the same socio-economic logic of the hierarchical mass society model and were driven to routine crimes against humanity and frequent genocide by this hierarchical socio-economic logic of needing and desiring ever more natural resources, whether they were inhabited or not. It just so happens that the ancient Jewish elite not only agreed with this model of socio-economic living but also, like Herodotus and other narrators or writers, recorded it within their oral and written records. Similarly, it should not be construed from the above biblical quotation that all the modern Israeli elite were only influenced by this religious quote in their area bombing of Gaza in 2023-25. The area bombing of Gaza, like all other such whole-sale efforts at total civilian destruction, is the logical outcome of the modern hierarchical mass society process of elite survival as well as the ancient.

This socio-economic growth logic operates when its elites are competing for urgently needed (or desired) land and resources and resistance to its conquest is being met by already existing user communities. Hierarchical mass societies, by their design, require the continuous production and consumption of natural resources beyond those ordinarily needed for human communities to subsist and survive. This elite imperative for the 'hierarchical mass system as a whole' to survive leads inexorably to a self-declared exceptional right by the elite to obtain the means for the entire system to survive - no matter what it costs in the lives of one's own community or of any other community. In all hierarchical mass societies, the ordinary working sections of those communities become the non-biologically related pawns in the competitive game of rival elite expansion in order to continue to live in the manner they desire. Instead of any resource shortage leading to the abandonment of a system' of living which is both inhumane and unsustainable, the contradictions within hierarchical mass society systems of living, are directed by elites to institute a premature 'end-of-life' conflict for substantial sections of their own citizens and the citizens of rival elites.

Whilst the first 14 books of the Torah/Old Testament are saturated with examples of aggressive hierarchical mass society killing and building, the Psalms and Lamentations texts also give a feel of what it's like to be on the receiving end of the Fertile

Crescent regions hierarchical mass society building. For example the following list of pleas are written in the forms of; *"Let not mine enemies triumph"*; *"How my oppressors rise up against me."*; *"How long O lord will you forsake me ;* *"Avenge my cause against a merciless people."*; *"Deliver me from my enemies"*; *"Let us break their hands asunder, and let us cast away their yoke from us"*. *"Why have you let me live"*? These are just a few of the over 100 aggrieved desires turned in the Psalms into pleas (89 personal pleas) to be free from control by an elite ruled system of hierarchical mass society living. Sixty seven of the Psalms refer to *oppression, killing, vengeance, destruction or captives.* Here is an extract from an example based upon some individual, personal experience of oppression. :

"5 v 6. I am weary with my groaning; and every night I water my bed and wash my mattress with my tears. 7. My eye is weakened because of my anger; and I am troubled by all my enemies." (Psalm 5; verses 6 and 7)

It is interesting that in these Psalms, Lamentations and other sacred texts such as Isaiah that the concerns, complaints, worries and requests to god for an end to repeated oppression do not record any female calls for ending the very obvious issues of female oppression and exploitation by patriarchal males. When it is understood that these Abrahamic scriptures were assembled from a wide-spread, common stock of experiences and reflections on the progress of hierarchical mass society settlements throughout a whole middle and near eastern region, then something becomes crystal clear. These sentiments were not just the feelings of a particular religious denomination that has retained them to this day, but were large-scale regional expressions of a general human condition of misery as articulated mainly by elite men. Ordinary citizens also found themselves alienated and brutalised at the hands of the city-state systems of enforcement. Furthermore, this hierarchical mode of agricultural and pastoral production created to secure the (N-M-G-R + A-D) processes for 'unfree' humanity was clearly far from attractive to the ordinary people. Indeed, hierarchical mass society formations were clearly so repulsive to basic humanity that the disgust and disappointment in it underwrote and helped fund a number of religions which promised future mystical forms of heavenly peace and well-being with immediate recompense, eventual heavenly redemption and an 'end-time' destruction of these oppressive and exploitative systems.

Having also considered the secular based evidence of organised brutality and ruthlessness in chapter 9 from sources other than religious texts, it is similarly clear that the system of hierarchical mass society living was by then so powerfully established in the entire region that it was practically impossible to escape from its socio-military clutches or change its structure from within. Moving away on foot, across hundreds or thousands of miles - to where? – was an impossibility. The only real hope of escape for most was a mental escape; the nightly (or weekly) prayer to an imaginary powerful creator god who hopefully might turn up one day and force the oppressors to restructure society along more acceptable lines to the ones experienced by the supplicants. The Abrahamic Monotheistic religions of Judaism, Christianity and Islam, along with other religions such as Hinduism, Sikhism, Buddhism, etc., initiated during this period, became either the hope for a different future or became the here and now outlets for the collective congregational 'sighs of the oppressed'. However, the religious mentality itself was so tainted and schizophrenically deformed by hierarchical mass society living and its assumptions that within the Psalms and the rest of the 'religion of the books', alongside pleas for escape from oppression were clear desires for turning the tables on the oppressors and becoming oppressors themselves. Thus;

"37 I will pursue my enemies and overtake them; I will not turn again until they are consumed. 38 I will smite them so they shall not be able to stand; they shall fall under my feet." (Psalm 18 verses 37 and 38.)

To recognise that this statement is no isolated angry individual indiscretion we need only recall the instruction by Moses to kill all women who have known men, which is repeated in Abrahamic scripture more than the once quoted above. The same type of aspiration continues throughout the whole of the 'religion of the book'. The following quotation is just another one of many such threats, this time put into words supposedly uttered by their god in the book of Isaiah.

> *"For the nation and the kingdom that will not serve you shall perish; yes, those nations shall be utterly destroyed by the sword; those who oppose you shall come bowing down to you.; and all those who provoked you shall make obeisance at the soles of your feet....You shall also gain the wealth of the Gentiles, and shall obtain the wealth of kings." (Isaiah 60 verses 12, 14 and 16.)*

This and other such scriptural writings in Isaiah, record a clearly expressed aspiration by the early Israelite narrators and elites, for their own aspiration for colonial conquest, slavery and genocidal levels of extinction. So the frequent sighs of the oppressed we read in these religious tracts are just a one-sided manifestation of a submerged angry desire by some victims of the system to overthrow their own personal oppression not in order to end oppression but to become the oppressors themselves. These two fundamental strands of a) opposition to the systems inhumanity felt by the oppressed and b) the need or desire of some among them to impose submission on other peoples and their resources, are woven inextricably together in Abrahamic religious ideology. Abrahamic religious ideology is fundamentally rooted in this hierarchical mass society form of living with their religious hierarchies playing an active part within those hierarchies and promoting their fundamental beliefs whilst doing so. Those who firmly believe in the essence of any one of the extracts above are likely to believe in them all. The secular hierarchical elite based upon ownership and control of mass agricultural and pastoral production is mirrored by the religious hierarchy who themselves are based upon that mass social exploitation and corresponding discontent. Submission to each paradigm, earth and heaven (King and God), is the unifying motif and the two personifications of elite status are often blended together. It is remarkable that in studying this period, the two fluctuating phases of Narcissism, '*grandiose*' and '*vulnerable*' also seem to continually operate at the elite group level. The exceptional or exaggerated, self-centred social symptom (Narcissism) manifested at the individual level, is being collectively manifested at the hierarchical mass society elite level.

The situation had become no better in the later period of the Roman Empire in the Eastern Mediterranean, where the events recorded are reflected in the production of the Christian New Testament 'gospel' narratives when they were created. The next extract contains the words allegedly spoken by the already mentioned dissident Jewish character known as Jesus, who according to scriptural traditions was initially urging a return to the strict (fundamentalist) Jewish law and more. Thus he is supposed to have said;

"Do not suppose that I have come to bring peace on earth; I have not come to bring peace, but a sword. For I have come to set a man against his father and a daughter against her mother. And a man's enemies will be members of his own household." (Mathew 10 verses 34 -36.)

This extract is repeated almost word for word in Luke chapter 23 verses 51 to 53. It indicates that the idea of religion being used to further divide the oppressed within hierarchical mass societies into warring religious sectarian factions is of long standing. This is indicated by the fact that essentially the same message also appears in Isaiah chapter 19 verse 2, with regard to Egyptian society. There it is declared that 'brother will fight against brother', 'neighbour against neighbour', 'city against city', 'kingdom against kingdom'. Institutional sectarian violence had also become so normalised that these later religious elites who authored the gospels think that their originally nominated son of Joseph and Mary, later to be proclaimed as a son of god, was as bloody minded as Moses and Yahweh or as the previous, Greek, Persian, Roman and Islamic regional occupiers. Incidentally, this religious sectarian characteristic of setting believing family members against non-believing family members is also extant in the more modern Jehovah's Witness cult version of that ancient monotheism.

That particular modern version of Christianity has bettered (in this family splitting regard) what all the other mainstream Christian alternatives have managed in modern times. In contrast, the other monotheistic elites have acted upon these Abrahamic doctrines and made actual enemies out of each other's religions and ever since have backed the wars of expansion, conquest and exploitation initiated by their hierarchical mass society ruling elites. Missionary and Military pacification along with the export of God and Mammon have been the conjoined inhumane twin practices and ideological incentives of hierarchical mass societies ever since. The Jehovah's Witnesses have limited their open opposition to all other denominations of similar fairy-tale believers in 'holy spirits' to frequently ridicule and in some cases have 'enabled' the choosing an invisible, non-existent, male fictional alternative 'father in heaven' over a real family father (or mother) on earth. Leaving aside this inhuman issue of using religious myth to encourage or exacerbate family tensions and divisions, Christian Good News gospels did not try to offer any 'good news' of earthy escape for women and men from economic or domestic slavery. Thus;

"Wives submit yourselves to your husband as your Lord. For the husband is the head of the wife even as Christ is the head of the church...Therefore as the church is subject to Christ, so let the wives be to their own husbands in everything." (Ephesians 5 verses 22, 23 and 24.)

And;

"Servants, be obedient to your masters according to the flesh, with reverence and trembling and with a sincere heart, as to Christ....And serve well with your whole soul, with love, as to our Lord and not to men." (Ephesians 6 verses 5 to 7.)

If any reader should think (or hope) that such ancient forms of inhumanity would be no longer applicable in more modern times should seriously read the history of colonialism from the 16th century to the 19th. Sermons regurgitating essentially the same ancient Christian message of oppression and submission were delivered to congregations to justify the enslaving of African peoples, exterminating North and South American native Indians and later still delivered by the cotton, tobacco and sugar plantation owners to each other and to their African slaves captured and sold to them. The writings of Bartolome de las Casas, a Spanish Friar writing on South America is a good place to start and, 'The History of Slavery by A. Gurowski and 'The Last Slave Market' by A. Hazell are also good sources to consider the long lasting accommodation of monotheistic elite ideology with the practice of brutal slavery and eventually to include wage slavery.

An interesting aspect of the somewhat later evolution of the Islamic branch of Abrahamic monotheism in the region, is that it placed greater emphasis for admission on earthy submission, rather than heavenly redemption as its pre-eminent invocation. The economic model of ensuring the (N-M-G-R + A-D) processes for the Arab pastoralists who rejected Judaism and Christianity as institutional forms to adhere to, was not as city based as Judaism and Christianity and therefore had a slightly different emphasis. Elite Arab pastoralism was predominantly based upon small-scale subsistence production and limited commercial trade which gave rise instead to a version of Abrahamic monotheism not dominated by creating agriculturally based city--state concerns and became known as Islam. However, early Islam came to rely heavily on pillage and taxes rather than mass agricultural production and thus the surplus production of their own tilling and herding, or the manufacture and trade of their own surplus non-food production. Hence the empires built by the Islamic elites and their armed forces were based upon governing and taxing the conquered, hierarchical agriculturally based mass societies rather than becoming direct agricultural producers themselves. This led them to accept the fundamental content and narratives of Jewish monotheism as in the Torah and Tannach (Old Testament) whilst rejecting the Christian emphasis of worshiping an imaginary three-fold holy trinity; the father, the son and the holy ghost.

That 'trinity' compromise reached by different sectarian Christian tendencies of 'God the father, the son and the holy ghost' based upon the Constantine supported version now embodied in the New Testament was an intellectual construction incomprehensible to Muhammad and his subsequent followers - and also to many Christian's at the time it must also be said. Nevertheless, socially Islam does retain a commitment to sustain the alienations arising from hierarchical mass society living whilst also retaining a strand of mystical hope for future release and redemption by submitting and doing Allah's bidding. Consequently, the 114 chapters of the Qu'ran contain 195 references to punishments, 99 to rewards, 48 to the day of judgement, 9 to killing, 33 to fighting and 80 to creation. So although there is a different emphasis in the Islamic version of Abrahamic monotheism there is broadly the same overall perspective. It is that hierarchical mass societies are acceptable

God given (or God blessed) ways of living, but that also contain some serious flaws which need to be tolerated until the "final days". Then the imaginary higher power of an invisible, male super-being is imagined as returning and sorting out the inhumane mess the earthly powered male elites have made of life on earth. Until then;

"Those who recite the book of Allah and attend to their prayers and give alms in private and public may hope for imperishable gain. Allah will give them their rewards and enrich them from his own abundance. He is forgiving and bountiful in His rewards." (Surah 35 v 29. Qu'ran.)

So as with the other two monotheisms, the absolute and relative poverty and alienation created by hierarchical mass society forms of social production, is not to be ended - not even as an aspiration by the Islamic Allah, the Jewish Yahweh or the Christian Jesus/God. Instead, some of hierarchical mass society's worst effects are to be alleviated slightly by voluntary charity from those who are better off. An added incentive for such charitable donation will be the promise that Allah (or God) will reward that giving to the poor by bountiful means of enrichment. Charity to the poor created by hierarchical mass societies in this version is presented as a win-win social investment opportunity. The outlook for female equality and respect for their individual autonomy in the Islamic version of monotheism, however, is not substantially better than either of the other two monotheistic versions.

"Blessed are the believers, who are humble in their prayers; who avoid profane talk, and give alms to the destitute; who restrain their carnal desires (except with their wives and slave-girls, for these are lawful to them) and do not transgress through lusting after other women; (Qu'ran Surah 23 v 1)

Wives and slave girls in Islamic fundamental ideology are again asserted to exist in order to be available to satisfy male carnal desires. In one sense it cannot be surprising that given the level of education and scientific understanding such mystical hopes and fantasies would arise from the socially locked-in horrors of hierarchical mass societies briefly portrayed in this chapter and chapter 9. Within the entire region, slave revolts, civil wars and mass exoduses had failed to produce any substantial change in hierarchical mass society systems. Individual protests and appeals had altered nothing - remember the loyal soldier in chapter 9, who merely asked if one of his sons could avoid the coming war, and all the sons were killed? Whatever practical measures people tried, the 'system' had such a firm hold that it continued to grind out the same, inhumane symptoms and brutal responses generation after generation. What else could people do but pray to an imaginary being they were sincerely told existed and could change things if he wanted? What is more surprising to me is that despite the advance of technological science and forensic tests to replace 'belief' with verifiable evidence for any test of secular validity, that so few people have been able to see behind the spin and deception perpetrated by the religious elite and their paid propagandists. It is obvious that hierarchical mass society forms based upon mass agriculture and mass animal breeding were causing mass alienation for people and mass pollution for the environment. Three thousand years of simply praying – individually or on-mass - to a non-existent super being for much needed changes to the human mode of production, suggests that this option has been a waste of individual or collective energy and time.

It is important to remember that prior to that period of transition to settled hierarchical mass societies, the evolution of life on earth had been an entirely natural process. Each species of life on earth had evolved, with some biological adjustments, within its own rate of growth, adapting to its own preferred habitats, its own preferred source of nutrition and its own cycle of reproduction, ageing and death. And all this occurred whilst remaining within a complex interconnected network of all other forms of life on earth. We have noted that Nutrition (N) itself was part inorganic and part organic and with a few exceptions, other forms of organic life are a substantial part of the nutrition of all living things and remained so within the (N-M-G-R +A-D) process of hierarchical mass society living, but of course with a notable difference. The availability and form of nutrition (N) for domesticated animals and humans was no longer entirely a result of natural processes or of their own choices to extract from nature. Obtaining nutrition (N) had become an elite determined social process. Social inventions such as agricultural tools, fencing, irrigation, treadmills, lifting equipment, wheels, sail powered boats, the taming, cross breeding and teaming of harnessed and whipped animals for agricultural and transporting power, all contributed to the growing domination of social processes over the process of obtaining nutrition (N) from natural sources. The same was true of the phases of growth (G), reproduction (R) along with ageing (A) and death (D). Life on earth had previously been an entirely natural process of evolution over multiples of millions of years during which beneficial associations, symbiosis and endo-symbiosis were the essential bio-chemical processes which are the evolutionary foundations of all living things.

Prior to the full blown agricultural revolution, nature (life on earth in general) had, apart from inorganic planetary and inter-planetary disturbances (earthquakes, volcanic eruptions, meteor bombardments, storms, etc), determined what happened to life on earth in general. Until the advent of hierarchical mass societies, nature had self-regulated for multiple millions of orbital earth years. So to recap; From the onset of settled, hierarchical mass society agricultural modes of production, different human relationships began to dominate and different relationships between mass societies of humans and nature also. The social needs of hierarchical mass society elites began to determine what happened within the (N-M-G-R + A-D) processes of all life - initially within each hierarchical mass society catchment area. It was by sword, shield and spear, that elite-led mass society requirements were first spread throughout the region of the Mediterranean and the Fertile Crescent. But with the development of another social invention – long range water-based heavy transport - hierarchical mass societies began an additional sort of Jeckel and Hyde or Carrot and Stick form of existence. This was done by encouraging peaceful trade of surplus products and then by trade wars the stronger enforcing the terms of trade with weaker communities. This pattern has continued since and as we shall now read this development was noted by the ancient literary and philosophical elite.

Further mass society Inhumanity noted in Greek Literature.

Although the next quote is from a fictional account of an ancient battle between two early Greek states, the following quotation from Homer's, 'Iliad', confirms what previous secular and religious recorded historical evidence has established and was presented in previous chapters. The representatives of the combined war parties in the Iliad are addressed by Agamemnon and urged to complete the sacking of Troy which at that point they had repeatedly failed to do, even though they had ravaged the surrounding villages and townships. However, after Agamemnon had finished speaking a character in Homer's tale called Thersites is said to have voiced the following criticism;

" Agamemnon, he cried, 'What ails you now, and what more do you want? Your tents are filled with Bronze and with fair women, for whenever we take a town we give you the pick of them. Would you have yet more gold, which some Trojan is to give for his son, when I or another Archaean has taken him prisoner? or is it some young girl to hide and lie with?" (The Illiad. Homer. Book 2.)

In the narrative, the fictional character Thersites is soundly beaten for this open criticism by the loyal supporters of Agamemnon. The character Odysseus then enters the debate and argues for continuing with the original intention to conquer and sack Troy. Incidentally, 'sack' in the ancient vocabulary, meant, totally destroy, kill, rape and steal any form of valuables and wealth that could be carried by hand, animal back, or boat. The author has the fictional character Odysseus then suggesting the following;

"Let none make haste to go till he has first lain with the wife of some Trojan, and avenged the toil and sorrow that he has suffered for the sake of Helen." (ibid)

The last two extracts indicate that unlike the authors of Hollywood film scripts, Homer was aware that the main purpose of hierarchical mass society expeditions by military forces during that period, was not primarily to retrieve or rescue damsels in distress or those such as Helen who had possibly willingly eloped or had volunteered to be captured by her preferred lover. The real underlying motivation was to take possession of materials and people to 'use', 'consume' and/or 'exchange' them in the manner and for whatever the conquerors thought fit. Again the author of the narrative fails to mention, imagine or concern himself with the effect such activities had on the lives of the inhabitants of Trojan townships. Instead the author focuses upon the desires and interests of the invading warrior elites. The thousands of rapes of women advocated by Odysseus and the deaths of hundreds of fathers and mothers by aggressive raiding for bronze, gold and the capture of young girls, is not given a mention as problematic human activities. Yet, then as now, these actions were problematic - to the most extreme degree as the scandals around 21st century grooming of young European girls testifies. And it needs to be remembered that although some of these narratives are undoubtedly exaggerated and or fictionalised, in Homer's Iliad and Odyssey, they nevertheless were in such cases fictionalised events that mirrored or were based upon comparable events and atrocities in the actual history of hierarchical mass societies.

It is therefore not surprising that once such societies were established and accepted as excellent vehicles to represent the interests of the elites, that the intellectuals amongst those elites or dependent upon them should actively produce ideas reflecting and rationalising those elite interests. Since it is perceived as a condemnation of 'civilisation' building to have built it on the backs of rape, pillage and slavery along with other forms of non-free or compulsory labour, there have been many modern attempts to play down the use of slaves and other crimes against humanity in the formation of hierarchical mass societies. However, there is abundant evidence, that from very early in the development of hierarchical mass societies, slaves were used extensively for growing grains, fruits, mining, quarrying, felling timber, herding cattle, sheep, goats, and in their extensive use as house servants. By the time the Greek philosopher Aristotle was born it apparently seemed 'natural' to many elites that some people should be rulers and others should be slaves and servants. As the often admired philosopher Aristotle reasoned;

"For he who can foresee with his mind is by nature intended to be lord and master, and he who can work with his body is a subject, and by nature a slave...that some should rule and others

be ruled is a thing, not only necessary, but expedient; from the hour of their birth, some are marked out for subjection, others for rule. (Aristotle; 'Politics' book 1.)

It is in such philosophical works that the alert reader encounters many ideologically created distortions and contradictions in the thinking of such elites and one is illustrated in the above extract. It should be immediately clear that this assertion is based upon prejudice not fact, for many, if not most people, can foresee and anticipate things. Even animals and small children exhibit such forward thinking in order to avoid dangerous or unpleasant encounters or to locate and repeat pleasurable experiences. But Aristotle has also attempted to use the word 'nature' to justify and authorise a prejudice in favour of elites, and a negative prejudice against the exploited. The two words 'nature intended', is a doubly oxymoronic proposition. The concept and word 'nature' is a linguistic abstraction which has no agency to 'intend' anything. Its use here is either a lazy, immature confusion or a deliberate mature distortion, and is being utilised by one of the ancient worlds most celebrated thinkers to influence those with less critical abilities. Only conscious life forms with the ability to contemplate the external world of life on earth sufficiently to process information, to recognise patterns of behaviour and to imagine alternative possibilities can 'intend' anything by their current or future actions. And of course many life-forms, within the insect and animal realms can actually do that despite a lack of intellectual ability or training. A bee or a hummingbird intends to get something from the flowers they visit even though they cannot know exactly what or what biological purpose that action serves.

Using the concept of 'nature' and natural to suggest an intelligent agency for a linguistic abstraction invented by humans is for all intents and purposes, an oxymoronic use of language. A plant seed, by means of its internal cellular structure functions in certain conditions to germinate and sprout on previously stored nourishment (N) before its cells metabolise (M) from externally absorbed gases and minerals to grow (G) to maturity, but does not do any of these functions by intention. A child growing up may acquire the intention to become a functioning lord and master, but that eventuality would be the result of an intentionally acquired social process, not of a pre-programmed natural bio-chemical motivated intention. The term 'nature' is merely the abstract collective noun used to avoid listing all the billions of life forms on earth, many of which do have agency and the means to arrive at intentions either quickly or slowly. Whilst it is true that the basic (N-M-G-R + A-D) bio-chemical processes of life on earth (encompassed by the term nature) have varied and distinct functions, however there is no evidence that inorganic chemicals 'intend' to create new substances or to explode when mixed in quantities and in circumstances that facilitate this result. Nor is there any evidence that bio-chemical organic entities have replaced their evolved bio-chemical cellular functions by contemplative intention. The reader will no doubt note the same linguistic trick being played by Aristotle in his further prejudiced assertions on gender.

"Again, the male is by nature superior, and the female inferior; and the one rules, and the other is ruled; this principle, of necessity, extends to all mankind......And indeed the use made of slaves and of tame animals is not very different; for both with their bodies minister to the needs of life" (ibid)

In this case Aristotle (or his translator) has slipped in the two terms 'principle' and 'necessity', to strengthen the assertion of a blatant social prejudice. It may have been hierarchical mass society practice at the time of Aristotle to obnoxiously discriminate against women, but that does not elevate it to a principle of life on earth or a principle of all human societies. Nor are males ruling females a social or biological necessity. The chapters on insects, animals and hunter-gatherer peoples provided ample evidence of female centrality to food production, offspring raising and social cohesion so that these facts known at the time also undermines this and other such assertions and exposes the linguistic subterfuge being used. What connects the conduct of ancient hierarchical mass society elites with their modern counterparts, however, is not only the existence of misogyny and slavery in their modern form. These characteristics are after all symptoms arising from the hierarchical system not the cause of the hierarchical systems existence. The hierarchical socio-economic system did not spontaneously arise, from natural evolution it developed out of a previous socially organised system of human aggregation within the biologically evolved biosphere of earth.

Once seriously examined, the root cause of human mistreatment and alienation within hierarchical mass societies, ancient and modern, emerges from the constant existential desire for hierarchical mass society elites to forcibly secure and consume surplus production from their own communities and to obtain new land, materials and labour to exploit from external communities and resources. The inhumane treatment of women and those considered as 'the other', (slaves and rivals) follows from these particular hierarchical mass society modes of production, their division of labour and systems of social control. When I came across the second sentence equating animals and slaves in the previous quote, it surprised me. I had already drawn essentially the same conclusion and made essentially the same comparison in the early research for this book. My surprise was intensified by the fact that Aristotle had made this point several thousand years ago and yet so few elite 'experts' on philosophy, ancient history and 'civilisations' had uncovered and seriously explored that comparison further. Not one of my philosophy or history tutors during my four years at college mentioned this comparison. For any reader interested further in regard to the reflections of hierarchical mass societies in Greek Philosophy I have placed more such material elsewhere.

I have dwelt so much on these aspects of the history of hierarchical mass societies because those dark shadows cast upon humanity by this ancient form of social organisation are still with us and have been intensified in the 21st century. Blatant lies and distortions concerning reality have been repeated by elites over generations with the so-called educated elites simply going along with them whilst drawing their salaries and pensions until the unnatural reality of hierarchical mass society living has become normalised. Consequently, religious and philosophical ideologies developed and nurtured in that tumultuous, tormented and savage ancient past are still being used by many people as distinguishing features and guidelines for modern living. These ancient dualistic assumptions of *'chosen people'* and *'alien others'* still blights the process of human evolution and mass society elites still treat life forms on earth, human or otherwise, as disposable assets to be used and abused as they see fit. And this occurs with the full complicity of the educated middle classes. Furthermore, the personifications of the latest capital orientated iterations of this form of hierarchical mass society have now raised their technological levels to the point where its elites not only continue to brutally and callously mass destroy people (by genocidal military bombing) and the environment (by clearances and urbanisation) in pursuit of their own particular interests, but more. Their activities also threaten the very existence of the more developed forms of large and small scale species of life on earth. Based upon the ancient hierarchical mass society systems, the entire planet and its species have been carved up into elite controlled territories and spheres of influence until modern elite competition for available natural resources engenders constant cycles of cold wars followed by hot genocidal ones and even the brief periods of relative peace are turned into military preparations for the next round of hot ones.

So much has changed technologically, in the intervening centuries, but so little has changed socially, economically and therefore ideologically. A few scientists have recognised the limitations of the planet in meeting the demands of modern capitalist society for ever more raw materials both organic and inorganic, to feed ever more production, to enable ever more consumption and cause ever more air, sea and land pollution. However, many scientists are so much a fully socialised part of the established hierarchical mass society system that their only remedies to resource depletions are to try to obtain the hierarchical systems needs from the few places so far untouched on earth. Their brains are currently exercised in exploring the deep ocean valleys or in the ridiculous suggestion of colonising and mining other planets for further inorganic materials. Projects of drilling for oil and gas in places on earth where the ice and permafrost has receded due the burning of oils and gas in the first place, just about sums up the perverse incentives and lack of concern built into the hierarchical mass society system. It also reveals the one-sided intellectual level of the capitalist minded economic, financial, scientific, technological and political elites.

Research projects based upon plans to visit other planets for colonisation and mineral mining is yet another example of the banality emanating from brains educated and trained to focus down on one specific technical area whilst ignoring the wider implications and socio-economic problems, created by their own ideas and activities. This 20th century 'space travel' fantasy has been turned into numerous 21st century research and development projects in departments of universities and within other public and private enterprises. Many of them are funded by decisions of government elites and the mega rich, but who are clearly revealed as morally and intellectually impoverished by the fact that millions of their citizens are currently homeless or starving or both, whilst they create computer models and actual test vehicles and instruments, for their own self-satisfying fantasy futures. The concluding chapter of this book will consider whether the hierarchical mass society form can be revolutionised before its current elite-led progress causes a catastrophic collapse of crucial bio-chemical species networks which are the foundation upon which other species rest. Or alternatively, whether a future collapse of much of so-called 'civilisation' (!) will be the necessary prerequisite for what is left of humanity and what remains of life on earth to begin again by avoiding repeating the hierarchical mass society system and instead reinstate a natural pattern of (N-M-G-R + A-D) living that is sustainable. That will be the only way future generations can admire and enjoy the amazing spectacle of the varied forms of life on earth.

Summary of Chapter 10.

This chapter began with a preamble on the frequent problem of author preferred opinion being presented as substantiated fact, without sufficient evidence to support it. The phenomena of believing that human invented words and abstractions, (such as 'time') actually exist in the real external world and are independent of human thought, was also noted. Then despite the relative scarcity of pre-monotheistic texts, some trace of the transition from Goddesses to Gods was demonstrated as being retained in some of the common ancient middle-eastern religious myths, as well as in other historical narratives of that period. However, the sighs and frustrations of the oppressed only became highly profiled within the early documents of the Abrahamic Monotheistic religion and some Hindu scriptures. It is in these Old Testament narratives that the brutalised condition of humanity within hierarchical mass societies along with the accumulated sighs of the oppressed are most graphically recorded. Multiple quotations are presented in which Moses, commanded the perpetration of genocide against various tribal affiliations of men, women and children and the character Jesus preached religious sectarianism with the sword and the desire to split families up on the basis of mystical beliefs. The chapter ends with a short resume of the reflections of hierarchical mass society alienation within Greek literature.

CONCLUSION

In chapters 1 to 7, the various forms of inorganic and organic material crucial to life on earth were considered along with the necessary and continuous inter-connected and inter-dependent biological evolutionary links between all forms of life on earth. In the case of the vast array of organic forms of life on earth, for convenience sake, this was condensed into the basic forms of cells, plants, insects, and animals. In each case the life-cycle phases of Nourishment, Metabolism, Growth, Reproduction, Ageing and Death, abbreviated as (N-M-G-R + A-D) were established as common to all forms of life on earth. Also common to all forms of life was the undeniable fact that the Nourishment material (N) essential for each life form comprises inorganic and organic substances, both of which are supplied by one or more of the other life forms in existence. This complex chain of interlinked and interdependent organic production and consumption stretches across all life on earth from the smallest to the largest. Plants, both large and microscopic (algae), energised by the sun's rays, by means of their photosynthetic cells have also long provided the percentage of oxygen needed by almost all other life forms. These particular photosynthetic life forms in the form of plants and algae are also the nutritional (N) foundations for the complex web of food chains required by practically every living entity. By the photosynthetic process of consuming carbon dioxide to produce oxygen, plant life - as a key species - therefore has provided the base-line inorganic material and energy containing organic nourishment needed by every other form of life on earth, on land or water whether this is subsequently obtained by hunting, gathering or socially producing.

A full recognition of this integrated and interdependent process of life on earth renders obsolete and ridiculous all forms of ideologically constructed, anthropocentric exceptionalisms within the various cultural forms emanating from within the human species. Anthropocentric exceptionalism in all its collective and individual expressions is a result of at least two crucially deforming characteristics within the neo-cortical processing organ of the human species. The first deforming characteristic is an ignorance (wilful or otherwise in the 20th century) of the actual inter-dependent reliance of humans upon the myriad other life forms and materials, both visible and invisibly microscopic, for the air they breathe and the food chains they consume. This ignorance also often extends to each individual human's dependence and reliance upon the combined and distilled contributions of all other human beings, past and present, within their current human communities. This dependence of each social individual on society as a whole for their immediate existence extends to whatever high level skills and talents they may have acquired and in whatever form these skills were acquired. The second deforming characteristic, actually flows from the first and comprises an arrogant conceit which is a historically accrued result of the above noted anthropocentric self absorption. This symptom of arrogant conceit most characteristically assumes the form of a variety of 'exceptionalisms', both individual and collective. In the 21st century, these human based exceptionalisms and individualisms can now only arise on the basis of ignoring or downplaying the total and essential contributions of all forms of microscopic and macroscopic organisms to their own individual and collective human existence. This anthropocentric symptom of using the socially evolved skills and intelligence of the whole of humanity to ignore the wider implications of that reality and fabricate intellectually based virtual realities which in effect exclude essential contributions of life on earth as a whole, is now a willful form of ignorance. Ignoring or downplaying the absolute reliance of humanity on the integrated species of life on earth in general, has long been a flaw in human understanding which has now become a fatal one. The abuse of treating the millions of species making up the biosphere as simply hindrances or useless raw materials for the manufacture of inorganic commodities has been enabled by the exaggerated importance attached to the human ability to speak and write, which are then used to depict virtual worlds of imagination - in which anything is possible - except it isn't.

The ability to speak and write is indeed an amazing achievement, but it pales into insignificance when compared with the cellular bio-chemistry of even the most basic forms of biological life itself. The achievement of speaking and writing applied to human collective ingenuity, has led during the 18th, 19th and 20th centuries of capital accumulation, to the rapid development of the sciences and the technologies of destruction, construction, extraction and exploitation of the earth's natural resources. Compared to the complexity and efficiency of the evolution of cellular and multi-cellular life itself, the results of human science and technology are crude and predominantly counter-productive. The invention, construction and deployment of technology, frequently claimed as 'progress' for humanity has enabled and perpetrated a whole range of the means of destroying biological organisms and destroying biological forms of ecological integration. These crude means range from ones instantaneous in their results, to ones which are gradual and numerous categories of destruction in between.

There are now rapid or instant means of biological destruction of plants by chemicals such as Weed Killers, and Mustard Gas; the oxymoronic making of weapons of mass destruction out of biological diseases, and the creation of highly destructive explosives such as TNT, Atomic and Hydrogen devices. None of these are compatible with the long evolutionary development of nature in general, or the continued evolution of hominids and humanity in particular. In addition, there has been an increase in the relentless deployment of slow means of biological destruction, such as metallic, chemical and plastic particle pollutants released in air, in rivers, in lakes, in seas, in soils and in food (N). In between these two extremes of instantaneous and gradual biological mutation and destruction have been aggressively inserted the mid-range placed biological destructions in the form of huge forest clearances, vast strip mining extractions and vast monoculture plantations. All of these human elite instigated actions have contributed to the dislocation and dismemberment of the planet's crucial bio-diversity. It has also served to disrupt the planet's dynamic climatic balance and has ripped aside even more of the planet's ecologically inter-dependent biological relationships. Furthermore, as we have read, in previous chapters, it has distorted much of the natural humanity of the human species and deflected it into the self-destructive paths of personal and collective greed, routine inter-species warfare and recurring episodes of species genocide.

All this recurring destruction has been simultaneously accompanied by the development of cultural distractions and diversions, also based upon speaking and writing. These present distractions from the actual and continual ugly unfolding reality of hierarchical mass society living, and labelled as the progress of 'culture'. Distractions such as the widespread dissemination of fictional 'escape' novels, theatre plays, feel-good films, music, song, and multifarious sports, which not only distract but contribute to the long term ecological problems created by hierarchical mass society living. For a short time these distractions make some producing and many consuming individuals feel better about their own life on earth, and at the same time is making things worse. Emotionally and intellectually escaping the immediate reality of industrial forms of production is only a temporary fix. Moreover, it achieves this effect only by making the long term situation worse. The array of these cultural-based intellectual entertainment, soft and hard drugs of choice, is indeed impressive, but so too is the scale of their negative impact upon the microscopic and macroscopic life-support organisms all life on earth needs to survive. This is not to overlook the insistent and persistent specialist elite type human inspired pseudo philosophical lullabies, spinning their anthropocentric day dreams (and occasional nightmares) of inevitable scientific rescue and technological progress. First, it was industry, then nuclear power, now it is Artificial Intelligence which is being promoted as solving the ills of the system, without any mention of the natural resources polluted or destroyed in the manufacture, production and use of these technologies. Nevertheless, from the perspective of 'life on earth' in general, it is already not too difficult to assess the negative contribution of the human species to life on earth.

Since the creation of hierarchical mass societies several thousand years ago, the impact of humanity upon the adjacent biosphere has been almost completely retrograde. Unsurprisingly, this revolutionary-humanist alternative assessment is the complete opposite of the elites own complacent self-congratulating, narcissistic assessment. Since life on earth in general cannot offer its own perspective on humanity nor is any other species able to expose and confront the human architects of life on earth's progressive destruction, it will be up to a critical-mass of those who can see beyond the system supporters propaganda and then choose to consistently see beyond their own individuality, beyond their own hierarchical mass society elites manipulation and beyond their own inherited group form of national or religious self-centred exceptionalism. In this seeing beyond the immediate, it has been necessary in this book to first introduce how life on earth has evolved in the form of single celled organisms into multicellular organisms and where and how humanity after hundreds of thousands of years, eventually deviated from a natural evolutionary process and embraced an elite, hierarchically-based form of unnatural social evolution.

Indeed, the members of the Potsdam Institute for Climate Impact Research have been monitoring functional biosphere integrity for a considerable period of time in the 21st century. In doing so they have created computer models around nine general indicators of the global socio-biological system. The nine indicators they are tracking are;

1. Stratospheric Ozone Depletion. 2. Atmospheric Aerosol Absorption. 3. Ocean Acidification. 4. Bio-Geo-Chemical Flows. 5. Fresh Water Contamination. 6. Land System Depletion. 7. Biosphere Integrity. 8. Climate Change. 9. Non-evolved Entities.

These nine indicators of the Earth's bio-chemical systems within the biosphere are those in which all life-forms function to maintain the biosphere in a relatively stable condition to support all forms of life on earth. If this stability is disturbed in any of the nine areas, then the whole integrated and inter-connected dynamic balance of the biosphere is potentially unbalanced. The Potsdam Institute have designated 'boundaries' to each of the nine sub-systems and using past and present statistics they have identified in their latest modelling that;

"The model calculation shows that worrying developments began as early as 1600 in the mid-latitudes. By 1900, the proportion of global land area where ecosystem changes went beyond the locally defined safe zone, or were even in the high

risk zone, was 37 and 14 percent respectively, compared to the 60 and 38 percent we see today. Industrialisation was beginning to take its toll; land use affected the state of the Earth system much earlier than climate warming ...At present this biosphere boundary has been transgressed on almost all land surface – primarily in Europe, Asia and North America – that underwent strong land cover conversion , mainly due to agriculture."
('Breaching Planetary Boundaries' published in 'People and Nature' 8/9/25)

Note that the Potsdam Institute characterises the 'worrying' phase of breaching planetary boundaries as occurring during the period of transition from Feudal Agricultural rule to Commercial and Industrial Capitalism, when the capitalist mode of production turbo-charged the method of production by industrialised and mechanised means. But the transgression of local natural biological reproduction rates had begun almost from the beginning of the formation of hierarchical mass society aggregates, as the evidence in chapters nine and ten have indicated. The Potsdam Institute Initiative, represents one of the most advanced anthropocentric concerns in the 21st century, but its members still haven't extricated themselves from the anthropocentric paradigm which currently dominates practically all forms of human thinking.

When the biological process of life on earth is seriously considered from the whole range of species of the biosphere's evolution and comprehensively understood, it then becomes necessary for more people to embrace a consciousness of the need to become part of a movement to change reality. Using our intelligence and imagination to find ways to temporarily cope with it, may be entertaining and distracting but is not changing the external reality. From that eureka understanding (Landslide) moment on, the task will be to speak out, write and act in accordance with the perspective of life on earth in general and advocate a revolutionary transformation of the way humanity secures its own (N-M-G-R + A-D) bio-chemical phases of living, in particular. First 'do no harm', needs to become a Gaia-centric maxim as well as a human medical one. It needs to be a transformation that allows the space and resources necessary for the diversity of life on earth in general to recover and secure their own particular species (N-M-G-R + A-D) phases of living on planet earth. The details of the abstract phases N-M-G-R + A-D are 'life on earth's' integrated, self-perpetuating, bio-chemical, inter-species linked evolutionary process and needs to be respected and protected as such.

Consequently, I suggest that from a biological perspective of life on earth, there are no exceptional nations, religions, peoples, cultures or individuals, all such ideological expressions are human cultivated and accumulated, short-sighted anthropocentric conceits. From the perspective of life on earth, there is only one exceptional process in our solar system (and Galaxy) and that is the Earth's evolutionary bio-chemical process of biologically integrated species securing their (N-M-G-R + A-D) linked processes in their own particular species form. To repeat, it is this process which all life has in common, from the minute single cell, to the largest multi-cellular organisms on earth. I suggest it is necessary to re-direct our process of living, speaking and writing into being located firmly, intellectually and practically within the context and evolutionary perspective of life on earth in general. For example, life on earth for billions of years did not depend upon humans and their speaking and writing ability to exist in order to evolve in the most varied, intricate and amazingly complex ways. Life on earth does not need speaking, writing and technology (or artificial intelligence) to be beautiful, picturesque, musical, amusing, informative and creative.

And as useful and creative as speaking and writing are to human societies these skills are utterly dependent upon the unspoken (non-AI) contributions of millions of life forms creating the biospheric conditions upon which these biological and socially acquired abilities have arisen and upon which these abilities are uniquely sustained. From the perspective of life on earth, therefore, if speaking and writing does not assist in the maintenance of all life processes on earth, but instead, through their use in the pursuit of individual greed and power, assist in continuous environmental and ecological destruction, the verdict should be clear. Speaking, writing and all its associated cultural forms will continue to have no evolutionary value at all to life on earth in general. This also applies to human life, including the accumulated economic value accruing to privileged elites. Their current function is exclusively internal to the anthropocentric self-centred paradigm of a humanity that flatters (and fools itself) that the arrogance and conceit of certain elite humans is the equivalent of wisdom.

In this study of life on earth, from a revolutionary-humanist standpoint, something I have stressed throughout, has been to understand the six interconnected and intersecting linked life cycles of all living things, abbreviated as (N-M-G-R + A-D). We are not separate from nature – we are nature! Simply admiring nature from afar, intellectually or physically as a glorified garden we can take pleasure from or neglect, according to our moods or whims, is no longer an option for a species that considers itself consciously intelligent. I have concluded that this conceptual framework is so different and unfamiliar to our traditional way of viewing life on earth, that I have repeated it almost ad nauseam throughout this book. I have remained conscious at the risk of irritating some readers, by this repetition, but it nevertheless has been my deliberate intention to emphasise those common biological phases by this means. Although (N-M-G-R + A-D) it is still an abstraction, I consider it a rational one, in that each capitalised letter itself indicates an essential process within each life process which can be further considered and which is a process common to all forms of life on earth. Since a pleasant musical melody risks nothing by frequent repetition, I shall hope that this notation can become something of a harmony in reader's lives that can be hummed and sung to an ever wider audience. Humanity with its current mode of hierarchical mass society production is undermining the whole biosphere which sustains and enables life on earth to survive in its most varied and ecologically fitted forms. In considering each individual organism it is essential to be conscious of the fact that each organism's nutritional source (N) is a mix of inorganic and organic material absorbed or engulfed within the outer layers and membranes of each cell in all individual and multi-cellular organisms. Once absorbed, the nutritional source is metabolised (M) and moved around the cells organelles and between cells to enable the appropriate homeostasis, growth and reproduction of that species to proceed. Using this six stage sequence to consider any particular organism, will reveal that life on earth is not a case of 'being' but of 'becoming' and will indicate just how much life on earth is a complex integrated system. Based upon the evidence provided in previous chapters, that six stage sequence has been established as the universal and basic cyclical process of all the species of life on earth. It is applicable to all the various manifest forms and functions of organic forms, from bacteria, through plants, insects and animals. Whatever the form of life on earth is to our unaided visual perception, the biological essence is a physical expression of (N-M-G-R + A-D). Each phase and the phases of species in general are amazingly complex and fascinating to study and can easily take attention away from the broader picture of life on earth. However, for the purposes of this study it has been essential to keep our attention returning to the whole 'life on earth' linked and dependent processes because it is only the 'whole' processes that both enables and explains the success (or otherwise) of each individual or separate species of life on earth.

Although, throughout the study, the cyclical process has been laid out in linear form starting with nourishment or nutrition (N) this has been mainly for convenience and consistency. In fact since the whole process is circular or cyclical and interconnected, the initial starting point could possibly have been the Reproduction or (R) phase and thus a pattern of (R-N-M-G) could represent the intermediate 'living' phases with (R-N-M-G + A-D) for the living to ageing and death cycle. This would have emphasised the point that the results of the reproduction (R) phase of some species organisms, commences the (N) phase for many other species of organisms. However, I have chosen to commence the cycle with the nourishment (N) phase of each organism, since that is consistent with the fundamental economic origins of the concept of a mode of production.

I suggest that it is only by recognising and understanding the detail of this interconnected cyclical pattern that makes it clear that organic life on earth has evolved to transform the amazingly intricate and hugely important metabolic qualities of individual and collective cells into the equally important quantities of multicellular organic nutrition which then become available to other forms of life on earth. It is crucial to recognise that for the evolution of species to occur the individual organisms that most essential food chain species reproduce are not restricted to just one or two amazing copies, that are capable of completing the (N-M-G-R + A-D) cycle. It has been essential that they produce copies and potential copies of them in far greater numbers than species survival would actually require. In fact some species initially reproduce embryonic undifferentiated copies in dozens, hundreds, thousands and even millions in the forms of seeds, nuts, fruits, eggs, spores, spawn and micro-organism blooms. In most cases, these amazing quantities of truly amazing qualities, are actually many times surplus to the requirements for the survival of the species producing them. However, crucially, for life on earth, this prolific abundance of potential and actual offspring has not only become the means of ensuring that enough essential species will be able to complete their own (N-M-G-R + A-D) survival process, but that this 'natural' abundance ensures the ample nutritional source (N) for the survival of all other species.

Yet this prolific, apparent over-production of reproduced neonate cells appeared at first sight by anthropocentric based science as a current and eventual problem of environmental over-crowding for all such prolific species. This is how it appeared to Malthus and those under his influence such as Darwin.. (See Appendix C.). However, from the view of life on earth in general, this prolific abundance has never been a serious problem, because it has been the solution for the nutritional needs for all forms of life on earth. Once it is understood that life on earth is an interconnected inter-species system not a series of independent species, then such confusions are cleared up. Furthermore, the superfluity of potential new organisms, together with the limited duration of the entire life-cycles of many organisms, increases the availability of (N) for other life forms that gain nutrition (N) from scavenging. Even those life forms which do not enter as (N) into some other species (N-M-G-R) life cycle at the seed, egg, spawn etc., stage, remain available to enter it for some species at the (A) or (D) phase. The volume, rate and timing of the reproductive cycle of species, although fluctuating, has through cellular and multi-cellular adaptation become crucial to all the species of life on earth; albeit immediately crucial to some more than others. Therefore any human negative or positive interference with the volume, the rate and the timing of any species reproduction (R) by an excess of crude chemical, or mechanical ingenuity over detailed knowledge, this interference can be seriously detrimental to the whole interconnected species of life on earth.

When humans get rid of insect swarms as pests they also get rid of insect nutrition (N) which is then reduced for other species and of course adequate plant pollination requires adequate insects and animals to transplant pollen. This dependence and inter-dependence of life on earth, and its synchronisation with the planets orbit around the sun is the key to understanding life on earth as a complex, integrated, inter-dependent and truly amazing system of inorganic and organic material. Historically, it was perhaps an inevitable, but nevertheless a serious mistake to view this inter-dependent complexity as a vast, but loosely assembled group of independent life forms which was freely available for whatever profitable use or consumption that could be devised by human beings organised in hierarchical mass societies and responding to the desires of their elites. Consequently, in the later chapters, (8, 9 and 10) the main outlines of the transition from a 'natural', ecologically balanced, hunter-gatherer economic mode of producing (N-M-G-R + A-D), as with all other forms of life on earth, to a hierarchical mass society, unnatural, social form of producing (N-M-G-R + A-D) was outlined not only to indicate its effects upon life on earth in general, but on its tragic effects upon humanity also.

Almost from its most persistent inception, in the ancient Mediterranean region, hierarchical mass society thinking, in the form of its elites, taught itself and those under their influence and/or control, to view life on earth as a limitless supply of separate organic and inorganic resource materials. From such a view, religions were constructed which imagined that these natural materials were gifts from gods and could be legitimately used and exploited in whatever ways could be devised by a presumed 'intelligent' (sic) human form of manipulation. From that point on wherever hierarchical mass societies were formed (or exported by colonisation), life on earth and the natural bio-chemical process of (N-M-G-R + A-D) was being interfered with and artificially manipulated by large-scale human communities.

This was accomplished by selecting and administering the quantity, quality and timing of nourishment (N) and thus learning how to control the processes of plant and animal Metabolism, (M), Growth, (G), Reproduction (R), Ageing (A) and Death (D). This was achieved during the empirical processes of agriculturally based production and by selection of grains, fruits and roots on the one hand, and livestock confinement, selective breeding, killing, rendering the corpses and the consumption of other life forms, on the other. With the creation of slavery – sections of the human species itself – became treated like the domesticated (enslaved) animal life forms. They too were locked up, placed in chains, their nutrition restricted and their reproduction controlled. However, like human enslavement in all its forms, the seemingly harmless 'selection' of plants and their seeds, began to have (and continues to have) negative consequences to life on earth.

"Plants are, of course, the basis of almost every food chain, and by developing methods of farming that almost entirely eradicate weeds from arable fields, such that crops are often close to pure monocultures, we have made much of our landscape inhospitable to most forms of life." (Dave Goulson, Silent Earth: Averting the Insect Apocalypse (HarperCollins, 2021 quoted in 'Insect Apocalypse' Part 4. Ian Angus. Climate and Capitalism. April 19th 2023),

For several thousands of years, that process of hierarchical mass society building through the wilful, self-indulgent paradigm of elite human control and manipulation of natural resources has continued to undermine the millions of years of natural evolution. During that relatively short period, between ancient hierarchical mass societies and modern ones, there has hardly been any recognition that this hierarchical form of human society building might be as problematic for life on earth in general as it has been for the majority of men and women who were subjected to the whims and fancies of the armed elites controlling these societies. As was noted in chapter 9 and 10 the 'vale of tears' for men, women and children of the working and non-working poor during that entire period has registered in human consciousness as either an inevitable product of an invisible God's will to punish them for some anthropocentric invented 'sin', or because of their own lack of education or energy. In actual fact 'the valley of tears', was then, and continues to be now, the intended and unintended consequences of the hierarchical mass society system itself. Until the late 20th century, the accelerated destruction of other life forms such as plants, insects and non-human animals has more often than not failed to intellectually register as more than an occasional moral or local economic supply problem rather than as a fundamental, bio-chemical and therefore structural interference, with life on earth. Until recently, any concern for animal and plant welfare has been marginalised and dismissed as part of a minority of 'tree hugging' type idealists, rather than as individuals drawing attention to a serious and ever expanding problem brought about by anthropocentric arrogance and greed. Therefore, the fact that the hierarchical mass society form of human production and consumption could be seriously undermining an essential, integrated ecological balance for the continued existence of life on earth has never been seriously considered.

The most recent form of hierarchical mass society to develop during the last 6,000 year period has been based upon what is generally known as the capitalist mode of production. Although the European capitalist system had successfully challenged the Feudal aristocracy in the UK in 1640 and in other European countries later, it wasn't until the commencement of the Industrial Revolution that excessive productive capacities became globally problematic. Commencing around 1760 in the UK and then becoming established in Europe and the USA by 1840, the hierarchical mass society system mode of capitalistic production then began to outpace the natural rate of reproduction of global plant and animals used as raw materials. Using steam and then electricity the capitalist mode of production quickly began to exhaust European sources of inorganic and organic raw materials and to overstock existing markets, with commodities. The hierarchical mass society system went fully global. Having already privatised land and resources in Europe into the hands of those elites with sufficient capital this system was exported everywhere and progressively re-assigned the ownership and control of the main means of production - (i.e. organic and inorganic nature) in the form of agricultural land and pasture, buildings, infrastructure and machinery everywhere, to a global capitalist class.

It needs to be remembered that until the onset of hierarchical mass societies no previous human groups have identified natural species and natural inorganic material as objects to be owned and absolutely controlled. Ancient mass society elites in the near east, first began this local ownership and/or control of organic species and inorganic material and Medieval elites continued it throughout Europe. However, after the 19th century this latest iteration of hierarchical mass society economic forms, operating the capitalist mode of production, were now able to purchase nature and the living and none-living contents of nature with surplus amounts of money. Money, in the form of accumulated capital, has not only purchased (for exclusive elite use), almost all the available land globally, (i.e. nature) which is the source of all the necessary organic and inorganic material for life on earth to survive, but has also purchased more. This control of the essentials of life has also enabled the representatives and beneficiaries of capital to purchase the loyalty of the armed recruits needed to physically retain and extend this ownership and control of the earth's natural resources. The period known as the middle-ages was the long interval between the ancient hierarchical mass society formations considered in chapter 9 and the modern period of industrial capitalism. During the European Civil Wars, (correctly classed as political revolutions) the rising capitalist class merely displaced the feudal class as the dominant elite and took over control of the land and state power structures. They then modified and extended the hierarchical mass society state apparatus they had inherited from the absolutism of feudal aristocracy.

When that political revolution was finally completed in Europe, it is essential to understand that the actual fundamental economic revolution in the mode of production and the means of production - had already occurred. It did not occur by the later politically orchestrated transfer of titles, castles and land to a new elite via the 18th and 19th century European Civil Wars, as some historians have mistakenly assumed. The revolution in any mode of production in any period is started on a small scale by groups of human beings achieving their combined (N-M-G-R + A-D) processes of living by doing these processes differently. It becomes socially revolutionary when such initiatives are successful and are copied. In the case of the capitalist mode of production, it was the earlier transfer of peasant workers into landless wage workers on the one hand and the earlier transfer of a new source of motive power for the means of production away from wind, water and muscle power (animal and human) to the burning of fossil fuels, on the other. Hierarchical mass societies by the abolishment of serfs and peasants, land purchases and 'commons' enclosures of course, provided the human socio-economic foundation for the rapid development of mass production, but steam and then petrochemicals only provided the technological means to promote the capitalist mode of production when it had already become established on a small scale.

Medieval water wheels, windmills, oxen and horses were sources of limited and intermittent power, and dependent upon weather and animal and human rest for energy renewal, but coal and later oil could be burned whatever the weather and machinery didn't need either food or sleep. All that was then missing for mass production to exponentially expand was robust and nimble machinery and a class of people with no alternative means of making a living to complete their (N-M-G-R + A-D) processes. The machinery was soon provided with new metals and designs during the period known as the above noted 'industrial revolution' in Europe. With the capitalist mode of production already established, the three subsequent innovations of hungry landless workers, abundant fossil carbon energy sources and advanced power driven machinery, the era of 'dark satanic mills' and 'colonial expansion' was ushered in. A new elite capitalist class by accumulating capital in Europe used it to satisfy the wealth-hungry bourgeoisie and expanding petite-bourgeoisie.

Once these successive transitions in how human societies organised their (N-M-G-R + A-D) processes are sufficiently understood, it is hierarchical mass societies and their latest transformation into mass production/consumption for profit, that are revealed as the originating and operating causes of the current climate, pollution and ecological destruction problems. Not only that but this understanding also reveals them as the accelerators and dispensers of social tensions and disturbances by trade wars, military wars and now by global poverty. Recently there has been considerable debate as to exactly when humans began to sufficiently interfere with the natural evolution of life on earth to cause the current and future existential problems. The dating of the commencement of what is currently termed the Anthropocene (defined as excessive human interference with the ecological balance of life on earth) has caused considerable friction among those engaged in that debate. I suggest seeking such exactness in this regard can be something of a distraction taking attention away from the longer evolution of hierarchical mass societies and their continual and progressive destruction of local communities (human and non-human) by their international commercial expansion in the late middle-ages and onto global domination in the 20th century. I suggest it is more important to fully understand the effects of the social changes to the (N-M-G-R + A-D) processes of certain modes of production, rather than determining an appropriate commencement date, within what amounts to an erratic but increasingly steep upward destructive momentum. Undoubtedly, industry and carbon fuelled global expansion during the 19th, 20th and the early 21st centuries and ever since has given an increasingly steep upward curve to a previously slowly rising graph of global production and consumption and a corresponding steep downward curve on a graph of global human alienation and further ecological destruction.

Capitalist elites, through their wealth, influence and power, have been able to ensure much individual and institutional effort is put into convincing most people that working long hours for little pay and then handing their salaries and wages back to another section of the capitalist class for housing, eating, drinking and entertainment, was far better than the previous lives of tied-cottage and strip farming peasants. As we have seen, evidence from the colonial period contradicts that bourgeois pro-capitalist ideological self-serving perspective. Moreover, this transfer of the working populations from forms of serfdom to wage slavery was not done voluntarily but by violent forms of compulsion. Subsequent generations of bourgeois elites have also convinced themselves (and others) that this waged and salaried system of exploitation is a natural and desirable state of affairs, when clearly, as the historical evidence indicates, it is not. Being an obedient and subservient part of the hierarchical mass society system is constantly advocated and loudly celebrated as the best of all possible worlds, by upper and middle-class Dr Pangloss type elites - even though their system is impoverishing millions of their citizens and non-citizens. Although very few of them mention that it is now known to be destroying the ecological and climatic balance of the planet whilst producing what the elites prefer to consume and what the logic of their system requires. However, the biosphere to be able to sustain 'our' supposedly higher forms of life into the long term future, the higher life forms must ensure it's own economic activities do not undermine all the essential life forms that support and sustain the biosphere.

Of course, the question of whether ancient or modern hierarchical mass societies were any better than each other is largely academic for choice within hierarchical mass societies for the non-elites has never been an option. In contrast, the question of how bad hierarchical mass societies had become by the 20th century is more easily answered. The reader need not trust their own judgement or my own revolutionary-humanist evidence-driven perspective and opinion, because something of a collective judgment on human rights was actually made in the wake of the Nuremberg Trials in 1947 and 'officially' publicised by pro-capitalist elites at the close of the Second World War. It was an implicit judgment broadcast by means of a 'declaration of human rights'.

The Declaration of Human Rights.

In an article on the United Nations Human Rights Commission published in (1947/48) by one of its members, Eleanor Roosevelt, made the following candid admission;

"..systematic and deliberate denials of basic human rights lie at the root of most of our troubles and threaten the work of the United Nations. It is not only fundamentally wrong that millions of men and women live in daily terror of secret police, subject to seizure, imprisonment, or forced labor without just cause and without fair trial, but these wrongs have repercussions in the

community of nations. Governments which systematically disregard the rights of their own people are not likely to respect the rights of other nations and other people and are likely to seek their objectives by coercion and force in the international field."

The final sentence in the above quote could be levelled at any hierarchical mass society elites from ancient Sumer, Egypt, Greece, Persia, Rome or any of the ancient Islamic Caliphates through the middle ages and on to their 21st century counterparts. So this represents an outstanding public but unrecognised admission of the symptoms of such societies from any elite member of the capitalist form of hierarchical mass society. This was no isolated opinion and in a rare moment of truth, was endorsed by a panel of 18 other elite members of the international bourgeois 'establishment'. The final declaration of the commission itself endorsed this view because in one of its opening statements it asserted the following;

"WHEREAS disregard and contempt for human rights have resulted in barbarous acts which have outraged the conscience of mankind, and the advent of a world in which human beings shall enjoy freedom of speech and belief and freedom from fear and want has been proclaimed as the highest aspiration of the common people,"

The contrast between the above rhetorical part of the opening statement and the contemporary reality of the European, North American and Israeli governments contempt for the human rights of the common people of Palestine in Gaza, the West Bank and the diaspora couldn't be starker. The Declaration of Human Rights is often presented as a high point in human fairness and sensibility, yet by the commission's very words it represents the candid recognition of the complete opposite. Its 30 'articles' record over 40 forms of oppression that the bulk of humanity was still suffering after the five thousand year (plus) career of hierarchical mass societies (so-called 'civilised') existence. Furthermore by the 20th century, people were still being routinely killed and injured for no particular reason, hence the need to assert a 'right to life, liberty and security' (Article 3), others were still being made slaves hence the need for (Article 4), and being tortured hence the need for (Article 5); people were still being discriminated against, hence (Article 7), arbitrarily arrested and exiled, hence (Article 9); presumed guilty without evidence, hence (Article 11); their movements constantly restricted hence (Article 13); females forced into marriages, hence (Article 16); regularly suffering confiscations hence (Article 17); subjected to 'politically correct' thought control, hence (Article 19); deprived of rest and leisure, hence the need for (Article 24). Moreover, human beings in hierarchical mass societies were being denied access to the basic (N-M-G-R + A-D) life processes of food, clothing and shelter hence it was felt necessary to assert in Article 25, that;

"1. Everyone has the right to a standard of living adequate for the health and well -being of himself and of his family, including food, clothing, housing and medical care and necessary social services, and the right to security in the event of unemployment, sickness, disability, widowhood, old age or other lack of livelihood in circumstances beyond his control."

Can it by any stretch of imagination, be brought to mind - backed up with reliable evidence - that such a declaration would have been necessary to circulate among any of the hunter-gatherer peoples considered in chapter 8 or any of their antecedents in pre-history? In the above noted article 25, it is tacitly admitted that what all other forms of species life on earth, during their long evolution have obtained naturally – (i.e. 'a naturally available standard of living' that was adequate to their health and well-being) – was by the 18th and 19th centuries, still being routinely denied to millions of members of the human species. That is to say, denied to a large section of people in the most modern technically advanced forms of hierarchical mass societies. It is now over seventy years since the hyperbole of that declaration was broadcast to the world at large and yet anyone in contact with news coverage in the 21st century cannot fail to have registered the fact that it is still the case that in Eleanor Roosevelt's words, *"millions of men and women live in daily terror of secret police, subject to seizure, imprisonment, or forced labor without just cause and without fair trial,'* and if you live in Gaza, Ukraine, and a few other countries - subjected to much more, in the form of bombs.

Indeed, one of the declarations opening assertions that; *"disregard and contempt for human rights have resulted in barbarous acts which have outraged the conscience of mankind,"* still rings true in 2024 as I write these words. Despite its recognition of "outrage", it is interesting and revealing, but not surprising to me, that no attempt was made by the above noted 'Commission' to analyse exactly why this descent into destruction and its bottoming out into a nihilistic barbaric abyss during the two world wars (and incidentally in the Gaza 2023/24) had only routinely happened to the human species during the flourishing of hierarchical mass societies. The 18 privileged elites who formed the above noted Commission, as with other privileged elites in hierarchical mass societies in general, had insufficient understanding or motivation to radically criticise the very mode of production that perpetuates itself by the means of such barbarous acts and by actual contempt for human rights. And it is the 'system' which incidentally is the economic basis for continuing to provide those elites and their modern counterparts with their privileges to make occasional declarations.

Sufficient evidence exists within this book and in general to indicate that the human species, along with every other species of life on earth, had managed to exist and evolve for millions of years without needing a formal (elite group) type of organisation to protect the natural treatment and existence of each individual organism within each species. With the exception of the relative few predatory species, common sense or the obvious unspoken 'golden rule' ('do not do to others what you would not like done to yourself') has been sufficient to ensure the life cycles of (N-M-G-R + A-D) of everything living from single celled organisms to the most large and complex multi-cellular forms of life on earth were overwhelmingly achieved. Moreover this natural evolution over multiple millions of years and hundreds of thousands of years for hominids and homo sapiens, was achieved without any previous form of imprisonment, secret police, torture, or forced labour. It should be obvious by now that, despite occasional wilful blindness by elites, hierarchical mass societies and their privileged elites cannot function without the systematic infringement of basic evolutionary natural (human or animal) rights of those life forms that they extract surplus value from whether by the means of direct extraction or by the indirect means of tithes or taxes.

They cannot function otherwise because denial of these natural biological (N-M-G-R + A -D) process requirements for non-elite citizens, were built into the hierarchical mass society model from their inception, and remain so. Moreover, those additional species which in direct contact with nature obtain or produce all the materials and services (oxygenated air; energy rich nutrition; decay recycling etc.) which the human species needs to survive are not viewed as having a right to live naturally but are viewed as so much useful or destructive raw material to be killed, processed and transformed into elite forms of wealth. It is also now becoming obvious that the hierarchical mass society modes of production are being driven into such a productive frenzy by the owners of financial, commercial and industrial capital that the very organic and inorganic foundations of all life on earth (unpolluted water, air and soil, sufficiently abundant forest plants and insects) are being depleted, debased and destroyed on an ever increasing scale.

Hierarchical divisions of labour.

The extended division of labour in hierarchical mass societies means that nearly everybody within them - in one way or another - plays some crucial part in the annual production and consumption of the goods and services that the entire society needs for its survival and maintenance. This has been the case since this form of hierarchical mass society began thousands of years ago. The goods and technological means to produce them may have changed but the social relationships within them are still invariably structured into the original three broad but distinctly unnatural (i.e. social) groups of citizens currently designated as classes. Numerically speaking, the elite classes constitute a relatively small number of citizens. Below these in wealth and privilege is a larger numerical group of administrative petite bourgeois or 'middle-class' citizens. At the bottom of this socially constructed pyramid in all hierarchical mass societies (both ancient and modern) are huge numbers of labouring or working class citizens. Although arranged in occupationally diverse groups, economically speaking the working classes are the only class which consistently and continually work 'productively'. Although most human physical and mental efforts produce something, not all of it, socio-economically speaking, is 'productive'. Within hierarchical mass societies working 'productively' is the form of economic (N-M-G-R + A- D) based activity which produces essential products and services for everyone in society - even for those who do not produce those essential prerequisites for living. This production as a whole enables two essential forms of consumption to take place in hierarchical mass societies. The first form is production for immediate daily/weekly consumption (food, clothing etc.) which is produced by those who work productively for themselves and who produce enough surplus production for the rest of society so that they can engage in other forms of non-productive activity. The second form is surplus production set aside for current and future maintenance, repair, replacement, contingent and emergency needs.

In other words in hierarchical mass societies, the 'productive' working classes (whether slaves, serfs, peasants or wage workers, produce all the goods and services annually needed, not just for themselves but also those goods needed by every non-productive class member of each hierarchical mass society. Therefore, the working people of each hierarchical mass society also create a mass of production which is not only surplus to their own needs but in addition they produce a **surplus** for the 'needs' of others to consume. As a further addition, these essential workers produce further surplus production for replacement, contingency reserve or development purposes. Each advance in technological, administrative and scientific efficiency has generally increased the rate and volume of this surplus labour and thus the volume of surplus-production which becomes available for many other purposes. Those 'other' purposes, however, are still decided upon by the elites in every form of hierarchical mass society. Thus in modern industrial modes of production, the essential goods and services for everyone plus some luxury goods are produced by the productive activities of the workers occupied in mass-production industries, factories and workshops located in many different countries.

All the other non-essential and luxury goods and services are produced by specialist craft or high skilled industrial workers of one form or another. This extensive division of labour and the advanced technical (industrial) means of production to achieve it, (machinery etc.) therefore, allow the other two non-productive classes to increase in numbers and to occupy themselves in non-essential forms production. Therefore, the hierarchical mass society system still allows the non-productive classes to consume the type of production which is essential to complete their (N-M-G-R + A-D) process of life on earth, whilst enabling them to focus on ruling, administering or entertaining. The ancient and medieval kings along with their *Minstrel's* and *'Fools'*, fed and housed by the local peasants and slaves, have now been replaced by the modern capitalists and the billionaires of the 'Facebook', 'Twitter' and 'Netflix' industries, who are fed and supported now by a global class of human beings who, apart from voting time, are treated as unimportant and precarious wage-slaves. Unsurprisingly, this unequal numerical distribution of classes within hierarchical mass society formations is accompanied by the highly visible unequal distribution of influence and power, and of course the unequal distribution of the annual proceeds of this social form of living, producing and consuming.

Consequently, the numerically smallest class, (the super elites) have individually and collectively, the most power, influence and wealth, which they can (and do) use to support and sustain anything favourable to their standard of living or to change anything detrimental to it. There is a relatively large group of middle-class (professionals) who individually and collectively have a lesser degree of power, influence and wealth within their society, which they are also able to use to maintain or change things favourable or detrimental to their lives. The remaining huge class of workers, spread over, industry, commerce, agriculture and essential services individually have little or no power to maintain things favourable to their lives or change things detrimentally affecting their lives. Their collective efforts to influence things are similarly limited, by their occupational divisions and pay grades and are restricted to defensive campaigns against measures detrimental to them. However, exerting influence by 'striking' (withholding their labour), not only hurts the workers who strike, but it frequently hurts or inconveniences other workers. In this way working people in exerting the limited negative power they have can also hinder or erode any existing or potential solidarity with them from other working people in a similar situation. The only other potential option available to those suffering from the various hierarchical mass society 'systems' within so-called democracies, is to vote for a different set of elites, but of course any future alternative elites will also still have political and economic power over them and will act to preserve the existing unequal hierarchical mass society system. As already noted, the third economic distinction operating between the classes in hierarchical mass societies is that the distribution of the total wealth produced socially each year is divided unequally between the three classes. The elites receive and accumulate, proportionately (per person), the greatest individual share of the total annual wealth, the middle-classes proportionately receive the next largest individual share and the working classes proportionately get, particularly in economic downturn a generally shrinking proportion of the total value they and nature produce annually.

Hence, there is the spectacle, on a national, international and global scale, within every hierarchical mass society in history and in modern times, of various levels of poverty and deprivation of the necessary working people existing within the same community as those with extreme wealth and luxury. In between the two are the middle classes of varying sizes receiving varying levels of economic well-being. The main thing to understand from all the evidence produced in previous chapters is that this hierarchical mode of social production is far from a natural form of species evolution. Among the billions of species of life on earth, there are no other forms of organic life from the smallest single cell organism to the largest multi- cellular organisms on planet earth that distribute the product of their (N-M-G-R + A-D) labours in such differentiated ways. There are no upper and lower caste, or class of individual members of any other species of life on earth.

There are no groups of social insects or animals that exist with some individual organisms living in luxury and others simultaneously existing alongside them in poverty. Another thing to understand from the evidence presented within these chapters is that the human species has not always distributed the wealth it has collectively gathered or produced from nature, in such an unequal and unfair way. In species evolutionary terms this vast discrepancy among the human species, is of a relatively recent origin. Given the unreliable dating of even scientific methods, it is hard to provide exact figures, but in relationship to the multiple thousands of millions of years of evolution of human life on earth it is only in the last five or six thousand years that in certain places, the emergence of one species (humanity) has created societies structured in an unequal class divided form. It is also only then that the elites in those societies began to turn on and routinely kill members of their own species. Of all the millions of species on earth, the social divisions between rich and poor, powerful and powerless individual human beings, is a uniquely human characteristic. Moreover, these characteristics only arose in one or two relatively small areas of the planet and in some cases eventually collapsed whilst others remained functional until the era of colonial expansion. It was only from the 15th century on when these hierarchical mass society forms were exported everywhere.

So it is both an archaeologically established and historically evidenced fact that until the period of European expansion some 600 years ago, the rest of the worlds' human groups continued in classless forms of sustainable, nomadic hunter-gatherer, pastoralist and moderate sized vibrant herding groups which were predominantly egalitarian and remained so. They remained so because for long periods of time calculated in hundreds of thousand year periods, there were no other social forms possible. With restricted group numbers, large expanses of abundant land and resources and with limited methods of social control, hierarchical mass societies controlled by elite men or women, were neither desirable nor possible. In contrast, human hierarchical societies embracing large numbers, needed methods of mass production of (N), large numbers of essential producers; and the elites in charge also needed to wield forms of physical social control and restrict (by gated or other restrictive forms) access to the essentials for the masses to access their (N-M-G-R

+A-D) processes of existence. The early hunter-gatherer bands, groups, tribes and confederations, like those groups of other animals such as Elephants, Horses, Buffalo, Deer, Gibbons, apes, monkeys and gorillas etc., may have not always lived in perfect harmony with each other but they certainly did not routinely perpetrate sufficient physical damage to each other or to the natural environment to create the type of genocidal massacres and huge ecological extinction events, that hierarchical mass societies have consistently produced since they were invented. Furthermore, during the four or five or thousand years of European hierarchical mass society developments, it is only during the last 300 years that the elite classes within them have turbo-charged the scientific and technical level of competitive production and consumption to the current unprecedented and unsustainable global levels.

The technical levels of automated production powered by the use of fossil fuel energy consuming engines that drive complex automated banks of machinery have not only increased levels of production but reduced the time needed to produce them and increased the mass of surplus-value and thus profits for elites, along with the mass of waste products, polluting air, land, rivers, lakes and seas. This elite control has not only promoted large-scale commercial wars of trade for access to markets, and also access to raw materials in order to sell the increased production, but as the evidence in chapter 9 and 10 demonstrates has resulted in military wars of extermination aimed at also destroying social infrastructure, productive capacity and mass populations of other human communities. The two world wars of the 20th century, initiated and urged on by their elites, demonstrated - on all sides - the simultaneous pinnacles of human technological alienation and the deepest depths of human depravity. As noted elsewhere, in the aftermath of the Second World, around 1960, it became obvious to a few observers that unrestricted production and consumption was also beginning to pollute and otherwise undermine and dissolve the very foundations of biological existence (such as contaminated water, soil, air and plants) upon which all life has been sustained and evolved in conjunction with and which is essential to the continuing existence of all life on earth. However, at the same time, during the 20th century, other social changes were also occurring.

During the mid to late 20th century gradual changes had taken place within the ethnic and gender composition of the advanced capitalist based hierarchical mass societies in particular. This took the form of practical and ideological changes to the previous Anglo-Saxon composition of all classes. Gradually, ethnic and gender changes took place first within the composition of working classes, second within the composition of the middle classes and last of all among the composition of the elite ruling classes. Eventually, these changes led to divisions among the elite over what form of governance should be exercised over the now 'mixed' ethnicities of hierarchical mass societies in order to continue to exploit the surplus-labour produced by the 'mixed' working classes into the 21st century. The economic greed of capitalists for exploiting labour to make profits often makes them economically blind to the ethnicity and skin colour of those who have to work for a living, but their class-based consciousness remains sharply focussed with regard to social relationships. The divisions and splits on the basis of these two contradictions reached their most obvious and visible manifestation in the two advanced capitalist countries of the USA and the UK, although they were also evident in practically every country on the planet. The primary struggle within the elite for global predominance in the 20th century was (and is) between the inheritors of the traditional Anglo-Saxon elite pale skinned privileged form of social governance and the 'newly' emerged multicultural elite. Within the advanced capitalist countries this struggle often took the political form of being either for or against, the policy of 'positive discrimination', since then the focus has shifted and it is now around immigration and climate stability. However, locating the source of prejudice and discrimination in any form of skin colour, texture or gender is itself a kind of intellectual ignorance, when prejudice and discrimination has been built into the hierarchical mass society form from the outset and has been maintained within them. Dark skinned, Light skinned, Female ruling elites within hierarchical mass societies have behaved in essentially the same way as each other in upholding their privileges and power, against criticism or challenge.

Similarly, when comprehensively examined, the current elite strategy of pretending to be promoting a solution to climate change, pollution and ecological destruction by 'green' production methods is in reality all form and no real substance. The urge to maximise the amount of production and consumption in order to facilitate the acquisition of profits and to accumulate wealth, lies at the basis of capitalist based economic activity and therefore will still remain the elites' primary concern. The capitalist mode of production to function must daily, weekly, monthly and yearly mass extract material, mass produce commodities, and mass sell and consume them. Since the only materials that can be extracted and made into objects to sell and consume are organic and inorganic substances, then the protection or banning of one organic or inorganic raw material will require the substitution of another. The inorganic materials are relatively finite and the organic materials are frequently limited by their natural reproductive cycles. If the pace of the profit driven mode of mass extraction, production and consumption is faster than the reproductive cycle of the organic material used or can be inorganically replaced, then the result is obvious. The mode of production will soon exhaust it's current material resources and need to find substitute materials, but material substitutes on a single planet also are limited. The perpetual mobile madness of surplus production for elites and the profit driven pattern for capitalist based elites will sooner or later exhaust all substitute resources, organic or inorganic.

This is why there is no real incentive from the current elites and their middle-class supporters to reduce human consumption to a level that allows organic materials to sustainably reproduce. Because in addition to the elite motive of greed, too few of the global population are as yet aware of, or concerned about, the future of life on earth – as a whole - to bother with the serious study of the socio-biological basis of any sustainable human economic system. The level of activist commitment needed to produce a radical transformation to human social consumption to allow the biosphere to evolve naturally is immense and is increasingly unlikely to happen. The history of hierarchical mass societies indicates that extremely powerful, successful and long-lasting elites within human social systems stubbornly and defiantly resist change. The historic evidence available indicates that they attempt to continue as they have until they actually collapse, as the many successful and powerful Empires have done in the past.

The hierarchical mass society system and its monetary and commodified rewards system has, in a sense, captured humanity, physically by monopolising all the natural (N-M-G-R + A-D) processes on the planet. It has captured humanity intellectually by means of education and the habit of ideological conformity to its own elite needs and trapped them socially by eliminating other social forms of living. Immediate anthropocentric gratification, entitlement and self-satisfaction, have saturated the daily thinking and activities of overwhelming numbers of all classes. For example, the desire for unlimited electrical energy has become the equivalent of a social drug for many citizen users; the desire for this has become an intellectually conditioned 'need' and so for some people, any risk to ensure a future 'fix' of electrical energy will be contemplated. Even some on the left have joined the nuclear energy bandwagon on the basis that they would prefer future generations of humans and other animals plus plants and insects to suffer increased nuclear waste contamination rather than humanity learn to manage with less electrical energy and fewer gadgets now and the possibility of a decreased or intermittent supply in future. But that is not the only destructive factor within hierarchical mass society formations.

It is clearly the case that as with many animal species which are social, the vast majority of human beings from birth to adulthood, are part of a small but close community of significant others. This formative social experience reinforces the actual physical and emotional essence of human beings, but of course, as was noted in chapter 9, in some detail, this natural, biological and social existence was distorted by the onset of hierarchical mass society living. After a generation or so of these small groups, permanent close relationships had been significantly altered. They were replaced by the introduction of pre-set economic and social divisions between group members on a scale too large and eventually too fluctuating for close relationships to be maintained. Therefore, for the first time in the evolutionary trajectory of human life on earth, loneliness and insecurity has become a socially constructed dis-ease, leading to forms of illnesses often classed as medical diseases, needing physical, pharmaceutical or psychiatric treatment. In modernity even biological intimacy within small family groups families have become a rarity as families, for occupational reasons, can now be living in separate localities (country wide or in separate continents) that are too distant to be in easy physical contact. Occupational divisions and divisions over control of the mode of production introduced in settled, hierarchical agricultural based mass societies, were noted in chapters 8 and 9 as being a complete socio-economic break with the previous hunter-gatherer modes of production. A small remnant of that lost small scale social character has been resurrected and retained in small group work therapies and in counselling services

In the previous mode of hunter-gatherer production every adult had direct access to the nutrition available to the community and no hierarchical divisions existed between adult members. Any status such as spokesperson or leader was chosen by consensus, was only temporary and the status removed if unsatisfactory to the community. Human societies were thus a natural evolutionary development of the other social species of animals, particularly exemplified by the Simian species, such as bonobo apes, monkeys, orangutan and gorillas. It has become obvious through direct experience and through the information provided in the previous chapters that 'nature' and biological evolution did not create the seven-fold categories of separate *occupations, religions, nations, states, elites, classes or formal politics* among any other species of life on earth. Indeed, divisions between humans based upon the above seven categorical distinctions did not exist in the pre-history of the hominid and Homo Sapien species either. Therefore, such divisions are not the natural result of the bio-chemical evolutionary differences (biological variations) within and between species which have evolved from within the general category of life on earth itself.

The above seven categories (and many more) are in fact intellectually derived, socially constructed - virtual creations intellectually counterposed to natural biologically determined species realities. Within the Anthropocentrically created virtual reality of hierarchical mass societies, the beginning of human life and the very end of human life are the only two periods remaining when human beings are considered just that - human. The new born baby and adults - at the very end of life - are just human beings. They have no direct access to wealth, to privileges, to power and to possessions. The contrast between the external reality of life on earth in general (nature) and the virtual reality distinction of human inherited categories is also starkly revealed by the general intellectual categorisation of every other species of life on earth. This categorisation of non-human species by the representatives of humanity in the natural sciences does not include anything other than bio-chemical based internal and external morphological differences. Consequently, within nature, there are no actual kings amongst lions; no aristocrats among horses, no professors among dolphins; no slave fish among fish species and no ruling organisms among any other forms of life on earth. In other words the above noted class and occupational differences when applied to the human species are pure anthropocentric social disconnections and have no basis in the natural world of life on earth. But these anthropocentric inventions have become the main drivers of the social mode of economic production, which is now capable of undermining the very nutritional (N), metabolic (M) and reproductive (R) basis of the essential species of life on earth.

Moreover, as we have discovered, these hierarchical based categories now applied to modern humans did not originate among all humans and there is no evidence that they existed during the entire pre-history of the human species. These categories are the particular products of historically divided and competitive hierarchical mass societies developed over the last several thousand years. Furthermore, these categories were initially created by influential minorities who for elite partisan purposes imposed them on successive generations of their respective communities. The main historic purposes they serve are to enable the elites to utilise the talents and energy of their communities in promoting or defending their own elite interests. Historically, this ideological imposition of the above seven categories has entered the consciousness of successive generations as a form of socialised common sense within hierarchical mass societies. Yet it is obvious that every time a human child is born it enters the community as a biological entity, without religion, without occupation, without nationality, without elite status, without class or without knowledge that these categories even exist. Therefore each child has to be systematically convinced (taught) that these historically devised, ideologically inspired virtual realities are not inventions and prejudices needing continual political and educational reinforcement, but are 'natural' and are higher common-sense forms of individual identity. The fact of being just another amazing (human) example of the evolution of multi-cellular life on earth is no longer considered as enough identity to be satisfied with. Although a return to previous forms of ancient living for humans may not be possible or desirable, that does not mean dragging all the intermediate destructive and dehumanising forms that have been attached to human evolution for the last several thousand years.

At this point, in considering virtual realities and their supposed common-sense basis, it is worth confronting and exposing a common, but mistaken, yet dominant socio-economic assumption. It is one which is promoted and sustained by those influencers, (ancient and modern) who have failed to fully understand how hierarchical mass society systems function economically. It is the modern ideological assumption that consumer demand in general is the economic force that stimulates and drives production. Therefore, according to this virtual reality scenario constructed by bourgeois and petite-bourgeois intellectual elites, it is the consumers who are driving climate change, pollution and ecological destruction by their demand to consume. Yet this ideological assumption does not reflect the reality of all hierarchical mass societies in their ancient, medieval or modern capitalist forms and once seriously examined such assumptions collapse from their own lack of supportive evidence. Other than their basic survival needs, of food, water, warmth and shelter, the masses in such societies have never routinely initiated demands or campaigned for ever increasing production of commodities and services.

The demand for more production and consumption of the earth's resources has always come directly from the ruling elites in control of these ancient as well as modern societies. The pillaging, tribute collecting, and land exploitation, initiated by elites during the ancient historical period, and highlighted in Chapter 9 and 10 was maintained by the medieval elites and continued by the bourgeois elites under the current capitalist mode of production. Under the capitalist mode of production the elite motive for wealth accumulation comes via the owners of capital who invest it in the production of commodities and services in order to obtain back the amount invested plus a surplus amount (surplus-value/profit) in addition. If this is successful they repeat it again and again. If one particular category of capital investment is not successful in returning profit they search for new avenues for capital investment in production for the same short or long-term purpose of a return of capital plus profit or interest when the production is sold. Consequently they constantly find it necessary to artfully create a desire for ever new products. It is not consumers who drive production, but producers who drive consumption.

The reason why producers put so much effort, expense and expertise into advertisement, cultural events, influencers and sales promotions for commodities and services, is to artfully create a demand that did not previously exist. It is the owners of capital that seek and demand ever more forms of lucrative production – including green production - so they can invest in it for their personal wealth acquisition. This capital investment for profit purposes is good news for the elite but bad news for the ecology, climate and every other species on the planet. This is because, as noted earlier, all investment for production, whether privately funded or publicly funded, requires the consumption of new inorganic or organic materials and energy sources to sustain the manufacturing processes. And of course new materials and energy sources can only come by extracting from our already ecologically exhausted and polluted planet. Once this real world economic system is fully understood - in both its hierarchical pre- and post-capitalist forms - the focus for the prevention of climate change, pollution, ecological destruction and essential species loss, will need to change. The only way to prevent the current mode of production from committing a form of collective socio-economic suicide and species biocide is to end the primary economic system of capitalism along with the underlying social system of hierarchy. Between now and when (or if) that happens, most of the naïve illusions, and deliberate delusions currently promoted as solutions to climate change etc., will have proved sterile or have been abandoned.

However, all these ideological inspired common-sense anthropomorphic constructs are also in direct opposition to the biological and natural social essence of the human species which has evolved only two nuanced biological differences which are essential to the reproduction of the species. Both of these arose on the basis of a two-fold contribution to the sexual form of biological reproduction (R). The evolution of life initially developed individual organisms (bacteria etc.) that self-replicated by cell division. It was only later that bifurcated reproductive genders and separate morphologically distinct species evolved, each with minor or major morphological differences. Every other form of distinction, not actually replicated in the biology of life on earth, is just an intellectualised virtual reality mythical construct, existing only in the neurons, dendrites and synaptic gaps of the human brain. It is only due to the general level of ideologically imposed 'common-sense' social education (indoctrination) by elites along with their prejudices that, like a single lens, this common-sense projects the current world to the brain in the form of an upside down image.

For example, the anthropocentric idea that nature needs humans to control it in order to preserve it is to view the problem completely upside down or the wrong way around. Nature and species life on earth has existed for millions of years by it's own biological self-regulation without any human control. Humanity actually needs to stop trying to control nature and needs to nurture the whole inter-dependent network of nature. That is the only way to preserve its own species. Humanity needs to cease imposing a virtual reality, a socially constructed version of existence upon the evolutionary reality of life on earth. Instead of adjusting the level of human thinking to correspond to the actual intricate and inter-dependent level of life on earth, continuing anthropomorphic arrogance attempts to adjust nature to correspond with current anthropocentric thinking.

Anthropocentric 'science' wishes to interpret and manipulate the actions of the natural world so that they will appear to correspond to the virtual world its alleged 'advanced' intellectual elites have unselfcritically created. But life on earth does actually adhere to human laws; it only appears to do so when human laws approximate reality very closely. However, when they don't or ceases to do so, then it is the 'laws' that need to be adjusted.

The stratification of human societies by the introduction of hierarchical mass society model into human communities has also introduced another practical source of deformed intellectual characteristics to the individuals within them. The division into classes in which one class predominantly rules and lives in relative luxury; another class that predominantly works and exists in relative poverty; and a third class in the middle who oscillate between them has left deep physical, intellectual and emotional scars on all classes of human beings in hierarchical societies. The scars and deformities are different and are not of the same degree for each class or for each individual within each class, but by the structures of their class memberships all have been denied the full possibilities of their species evolutionary potential. However, well adjusted, each individual in each class is living, to a greater or lesser degree, an occupationally deforming existence. The full time existence, from birth to death in one or other of the classes of hierarchical mass societies, creates a one-sided development of their physical, mental and emotional capabilities and responses. A lifetime of dominating others, being dominated by others, or dealing with the schizophrenic contradictions of both being dominated by those above and by dominating those below, has resulted in varying deforming characteristics on the make-up of each individual in each class. The fact that the upper layers of each class may feel compensated for their one-sided occupational development by higher gradients of pay and reward, under the present system, does not alter this fundamental character deformation, however many have become reconciled to it.

This intellectual and emotional deformation is revealed by the uniquely human induced characteristic of self-harming and in the ending of such deeply unsatisfactory forms of living by suicide. Suicide is a pattern which occurs within all classes of humanity.

A constant and vivid reminder of the uniqueness of this hierarchical human condition is the fact that of the billions of other life forms on earth no other species, despite encountering difficulties, has evolved to willingly end its own physical existence by killing itself. Suicide is a characteristic entirely unique to the human species. In the evolution of life on earth, before hierarchical mass societies were formed, any existential species difficulties have been met by organic adaptation, migration or cellular mutation, never by members of a species deliberately ending their own lives or ending other members of their own species existence. The fact that the rich and famous elite classes, with all the so-called advantages this entails, regularly have their own quota of drowning out the pain by drugs and drink before choosing to end their life, by some form of self-determined or self-inflicted suicide, indicates that all is far from well with hierarchical mass society lifestyles. In addition, for those who do not choose to end their lives, the compensation of luxury for the rich and super rich does not entirely remove the stigma of knowing that they are not just fortunate by accident of birth but are actually economically parasitic upon the social production of mass societies. There is a growing awareness by other classes of humanity that the rich, by purchasing multiple mansions, islands and trips to space, are in fact not publicising their self-assumed merits but are actually advertising the extent of their parasitic existence. They are demonstrating that they are not only parasitic upon the majority of human and animal life forms but also on the very inorganic and organic fabric of nature. The more they have and the more they consume, the more they have contributed and are contributing to the depletion and degradation of life on earth. As noted, species life on earth, generically referred to as 'nature', are an interconnected complex web upon which all life-forms ultimately depend. Yet awareness of their parasitic relationship to societies and to nature and to the ecological and climatic implications of their lavish life-styles are things the elite classes studiously avoid confronting.

However, one of the most problematic of the classes produced by the current formation of hierarchical mass societies, I suggest, is the modern middle class. Over multiple generations of these hierarchical social systems these middle sectors have spread downward from the lower regions of the upper classes and upward from the upper regions of the working classes. In doing so many of them have developed a split personality combining arrogance and humility depending upon which of the other two classes they are responding to or relating to. They frequently exhibit, near grovelling deference and humility toward the upper classes and patronising arrogance to those 'below' them, who they actually rely upon for essential goods and services, but consider to be from the lower classes. They have been encouraged to cultivate a myth of individual intellectual superiority and meritocratic ability about themselves, but their intellectual understanding and social position is based upon and dependent upon the intellectually drip-fed needs of the upper classes, whilst their biological needs are met by the working classes. It is the latter who have historically created the socio-economic conditions for the existence of a middle-class strata. The myth of their own individual intellectual or manual skill superiority can only be maintained by ignoring the fact that any achievements they may have obtained have been on the backs of thousands or even millions of other current members of society as well as of previous generations. Individual family and known tutors undoubtedly may have consciously assisted in their development and achievements, but without the continuous provision of food, water, clothing, housing, sanitation, transport, heating and commodities supplied by the almost invisible and unrecognised working classes in each society, the members of the middle classes would have not have had the necessary time or resources to improve their physical or mental skills. Yet the average biological and intellectual attributes of the upper and middle classes are no different to the average of those in the working classes and this is demonstrated by an obvious historical and contemporary fact. When encountering similar favourable circumstances, children of the working classes, both in historical and in contemporary times, have risen to occupy all the same levels of the middle class occupational strata.

The reason why the middle classes in their latest petite-bourgeois form constitute a particular problem for humanity in the 21st century lies in three basic and connected facts. The first is the fact that in modern pro-capitalist mass societies, the sheer size of this class now makes them a considerable political, social and intellectual barrier to any change detrimental to their position. Their numbers in the modern occupational positions of Education, State, Military, Politics, Governance and Health, has grown since the end of the Second World War (1939-45). They now have a substantial amount of voting and influencing power, which is predominantly exercised in their own interests. The second fact is that ideologically they are dominated by a pro-capitalist petite-bourgeois attitude of self and family first. The third fact is that since the capitalist mode of production is dependent upon literacy and numeracy for its bureaucratic management and governmental administration, those who have been educated and trained in these intellectual disciplines have been educated to think themselves superior to those who labour by physical efforts rather than mental efforts. All these factors mean that the middle classes have been trained and rewarded to think anthropocentrically and primarily 'within their own class section' of current hierarchical mass social formations, rather than outside them to their actual effects upon wider biological and biosphere conditions of planet earth.

Therefore, current pollution, climate change, poverty and ecological devastation only stimulate them to occasionally and partially consider solving these species-wide problems from within the hierarchical paradigm of their own middle-class class interests. As a consequence, tidying up (reforming) the worst aspects of the hierarchical mass society socially determined environmental structure we all live in is the most radical many of them can be. Thus considering the need for a complete revolutionary transformation of the entire system of mass society living is – as yet - a physical and intellectual step too far for the middle-classes in general. Thus substantial numbers of them will need to become directly exposed to extreme economic, biological or ecological circumstances before becoming sufficiently critical of the capitalist mode of production to become part of any revolutionary-humanist or radical transformative social movement. Until then most will remain aspirational of their own advancement within the current or any emerging alternative hierarchical system. It is revealing to note in this regard, that the combined shocks of a global Covid Pandemic from 2021, to 2022; the subsequent climate assisted fire and flood destruction of towns and villages in Europe, North and South America and numerous island communities, has been insufficient the for the middle classes, to curb or cease their own polluting activities. Their TV productions, work and pleasure flights foreign holidays, second homes and sea cruises; their 'sports' of competitively driving fast cars and boats - all of which are consuming carbon based fuels, spewing out toxic fumes and disturbing sea, plant and animal life - was resumed with unbridled enthusiasm, as soon as the pandemic restrictions were lifted.

The consequences of the current class compositions in the 21st century are predictable. The elite and their supporters in the middle classes will continue to support the ruling elite to keep the present system producing and consuming as long as is humanly possible. Therefore, token sentiments and empty rhetoric will continue to surface whilst in practice this class will ignore, cover up or fudge any problems and deny or oppose any radical solutions whilst they do so. Social upheavals, strikes and rebellions will be characterised by them as uncivilised, anti-social and even classified as 'crimes' against the system, needing to be severely punished. This is the essence of modern political populism which seeks additional authoritarian measures to stabilise the existing system through the turbulence of any economic, social, financial or ecological crisis, whilst maintaining the class divisions and mode of production. What took place in the 1930's and 1940's social and political crisis in Europe and elsewhere when large sections of the middle-classes backed populist authoritarianism, that identified itself in historical terms with ancient Sparta and the Roman Empire as *Fascista* and became known politically in the 20th century as 'Fascist'.

This symptom also arose among some of the ancient hierarchical mass societies of the fertile Crescent and the Near East, because those ruling elites needed a strong authoritarian armed elite to defend itself against opposition from it's own oppressed citizens and from opposition to its existence by other such armed states within the region. The reason this political symptom is maturing again, lies in the fact that it is a logical outcome of hierarchical mass societies when they reach a certain level of competitive rivalry for scarce resources or when internal dissent threatens to overthrow the system. In such circumstances, protests against the system's unfairness and injustice will be viewed by authoritarians as amplifying the social instability and therefore need to be stamped upon. It is obvious from historical and contemporary evidence that elite and middle-class humanity will not want to entirely undo the division of labour within mass society formations, even if the real world evidence points to the fact that the future of life on earth needs something radical to be done.

Yet, outside of anthropocentric ideological concerns, bringing production and consumption into an ecologically balanced relationship with the rest of life on earth, is what life on earth as a whole needs. But what life on earth - as a whole- needs is not yet at the fore-front of most humanities thinking. Apart from emergencies, the next meal or rent for the poor, the next night out or holiday for the middle-class and the next second mansion, luxury car or aircraft for the rich, tend to dominate much of our hierarchical mass society citizens thought patterns   Since it is the ruling elites, who through ownership and control of capital investments (financially represented stored up social labour) and the technical means of production, are the key instigators of ever increasing production and consumption, evolutionary logic indicates that these elites need to be prevented from doing so. So although the obvious first radical step would be to campaign for ending the ability of the class who are the key instigators of the process of ever increasing production and consumption, to continue doing so, this is unlikely to happen. Furthermore, since the elite will clearly not voluntarily reduce production and consumption to a level compatible with radically reducing climate warming, and ending ecological destruction and pollution, they would have to be forced to do so. However, since this class has acquired control of all the organs of power and influence within its control, they will not voluntarily end or reduce the non-essential luxury production they have become accustomed to enjoy. Therefore, in general the system will have to significantly collapse from its own internal contradictions, before the vacuum, which is then created, will allow small-scale alternative modes of production be developed.

Since, preventing the existing elites from continuing business as usual would require a considerable revolutionary anti-capitalist movement to remove this class and their representatives from those decision-making positions of power and influence, this would most probably involve a huge civil war. Indeed, any such successful revolutionary movement would also need to remove all decision-making positions of power and influence so that the wielding of power - in all its manifestations - (economic, financial, political and military), by a minority could no longer be used to take mass society communities in directions that have not received unanimous community approval. That particular logic is the classical revolutionary anti-capitalist perspective, but this invites a pertinent question. Where is the social force to instigate and implement such a revolutionary transformation to come from? Undoubtedly, the fact is that for generations, a handful of key elite players in each hierarchical mass society has been able to dictate what can and cannot happen to a local community and have been able to drag (as Bush and Blair did) all their citizens into a full scale destructive war, has long been an inversion of the essence of the evolution of humanity. But what will it now take to reverse this historic process of human socialisation? The fact is that a handful of elites in the 21st century can make people homeless by fixing interest rates to suit their 'markets', can still force lockdowns by badly thought out elite dictates, and can even decide to potentially annihilate other human communities by unleashing conventional or Atomic weapons. These symptoms are a further incredible indictment of the hierarchical mass society model of social production. However, this growing list of abominations by the top elites has not yet provoked a middle or working class revolutionary murmur never mind upsurge against them.

That list of problems itself is sufficient reason for wishing to abolish this elite based form, but wishing it to happen is nowhere near acting on it or achieving it. When other key elites from the same class can at the same time facilitate the tearing down of forests, invest in the destruction of fertile open land by mono-cultural planting, fund the over-fishing of entire oceans and undertake the pollution of the deep seas and shallow coasts and at the same time monopolise the essential elements of life such as water, then leaving them in charge of human societies is a form of collective myopia or insanity. But as yet that is the situation. This is why from the perspective of life on earth a revolutionary transition is necessary to the thinking and being of humanity. However, such revolutions do not occur from the conspiracy of a few so-called revolutionaries, who through agitation and propaganda imagine and hope they are able to make them happen! Political revolutions are the result of large scale dissatisfaction accruing among populations who have tried to improve their situation over long periods of time without success. When long term dissatisfaction has turned into desperation for a 'critical mass' of people and when existential problems immediately exist for masses, then a revolutionary political movement can start to form. But even then that does not mean that economic revolutions will follow.

A study of past large-scale revolutionary political changes, (e.g. the English Civil War, the American Revolution, the French Revolution and the Russian Revolution) suggests that an additional factor to the above long term internal tensions which can trigger revolutionary events are the growth of irreconcilable antagonisms and splits (not just rivalry for office) occurring within the ruling elite strata and their supporters among the middle classes. Nevertheless, political revolutions are not identical with socio-economic revolutions and it is the latter which are needed and in reality actually occur well before political revolutions take place. A political revolution can only take place between a class that has initiated and consolidated an alternative socio-economic system, and a class which is defending an obsolete socio-economic system. That was the essential pre-requisite of the bourgeois political revolutions against the aristocratic, land-owning agricultural mode of production. The bourgeoisie in the 17th, 18th, 19th and centuries were not fighting for the idea of instigating the capitalist mode of production. Socio-economically that had already happened a generation previously! The bourgeoisie were fighting to extend the already existing and widespread capitalist form against the established aristocratic barriers and constraints on present and future capitalist expansion. Clearly that is how all socio-economic revolutions by human communities have occurred historically. The transition from hunter-gatherer communities to settled agricultural farming communities occurred whilst both modes were functioning at the same time and often in parallel. The creation of capitalist countries in North and South America, Africa, Asia and Oceania was achieved by creating capitalist based colonist outposts in all those countries and gradually expanding them over generations, until the native populations resisted their extension and a struggle ensued. It was only then, that the superiority of capitalist industry, commerce and weapons technology, harnessed to a de-humanised fighting force proved decisive. This de-humanised result of the hierarchical mass society system continues and is now - harnessed to the capitalist mode of production - at war with itself; with the environment, the climate, and the non-human species of life on earth. This realization indicates to those who are understanding the socio-biological dimension of life on earth, that the present hierarchical mass society system needs to be superseded socially and economically. However, not by a premature civil war but by groups of human beings initiating a new mode of production now! What is needed are modes of productive living which reverse the present class and elite based mode of production and secures its (N-M-G-R + A-D) processes within an ecologically sustainable system. In doing so, however small or diverse they are, such initiatives become models, which others will want to emulate, once the current ownership barriers to nature and its products have been removed.

This 21st century Gaia-centric revolutionary-humanist perspective is now also the only realistic perspective because, the 19th and 20th century concept of political revolution first and the imposition of socio-economic revolution second has repeatedly failed in Russia, China, Cuba and the old Eastern Soviet bloc countries. Being overwhelmingly against something existing on a large-scale, does not automatically bring about collective enlightenment as to what to put in its place and how. That is simply an anthropocentric intellectual fantasy. Furthermore, politically speaking, many things are now radically different than they were in previous centuries. The elites in the 20th and 21st centuries have now created multiple international elite alliances and mutual pacts of elite cooperation and defence such as United Nations (UN) and the North Atlantic Treaty Organisation, (NATO). Although these are ostensibly agreements to defend each member's hierarchical mass society system against rival foreign overthrow and conquest, they are at the same time institutions (clubs) with paid armed mercenaries in which only privileged elites, with their own protection in mind can be members.

As a result, these institutions have been and can be easily used to defend each member's hierarchical systems against internal attempts at overthrowing the hierarchical system. It is a matter of historical record that for close to a century, national elites have been characterising any serious organised internal dissent to their rule as the work of foreign countries or their willing turncoat agents among the indigenous populations. Consequently they continually label and persecute indigenous protesters as enemy aliens. In the event of serious attempts to oust the elite or change the system there is every probability that these elite international institutions will be used to prevent or even reverse such a successful attempt at a revolutionary political transformation. There would therefore, need to be a considerable atrophy or dissolution of such elite alliances for a challenge to the hierarchical mass society formation in any particular country to prove more than temporarily successful. Therefore, until such processes have matured sufficiently the hierarchical mass society system currently dominated by capitalist elites will continue until some form of ecological, climate or military collapse has occurred.

Indeed, I suggest that what is most likely to happen before enough people (a critical mass) emerges prepared to advocate and implement a small or large-scale revolutionary change to the present social forms of production, is that a catastrophic, weather, water or food supply system collapse will be necessary in more than a number of substantial hierarchical mass society formations. This situation might occur due to another destructive world war or a series of ecologically or climatically triggered catastrophes. I would love to be wrong in this latter regard but either way, in the wake of any form of existential catastrophe, or a sudden (unlikely) revolutionary elite-inspired change of direction, sufficient knowledge of actual historical precedent will be essential. Any future construction or reconstruction of human societies will benefit from knowledge of the lessons learned, from the past and present practical ecologically sustainable and humane egalitarian communities. These histories and their outcomes, therefore, need preserving and circulating widely. It would be a tragedy of immense proportions for humanity to continue to make the same historic mistakes yet again and replicate the past pattern of recreating yet more hierarchical mass societies on the self-destructive collapse of previous or present hierarchical mass societies. The alternative form of human societies to hierarchical mass ones is not as difficult to consider or construct as the ideas of sending colonists to Mars when earth has been finally rendered uninhabitable. The alternative is obvious from the logic of a part of the mass society itself. Since the skills and activities of the whole community are needed to allow societies to function, so the whole community should ensure that an effective means of collective decision making - by the whole adult community - is designed and implemented. Of course, that is far easier to think of and write about than it is to achieve in practice.

Such a decision making process could be the obvious arena for all proposals and actions to ensure that present and future production levels should not pollute, damage or deplete any part of the remaining life on earth support system faster than its ability to reproduce itself. This should include work to restore as much as possible of what has already been ecologically lost. Other than that variety and resulting trial and error would ensure that only sustainable and humane practices and methods would be voluntarily copied and extended. Such a community led programme of action producing goods and services for ordinary need rather than for elite greed would also solve the problem of unemployment for there would also be a probable, if not an inevitable, desire among egalitarian communities to correct all the past centuries of neglect and destruction and restore to life on earth, what has been intentionally and unintentionally taken away from life on earth. Producing for sustainability and restoration of endangered or depleted species and environments would allow full employment and with no elites desiring to excessively consume, reduced working hours could become a reality, rather than a dream. It is my hope that this book will be useful as a small part of the store of knowledge and experience necessary for our future children. I also hope that some readers will consider preserving and utilising its findings until circumstances allow future generations to halt and reverse the present decline of morality and the atrophy of the naturally based social humanity of our species.

Meanwhile, in addition to the everyday defence of basic living standards and the welfare of those life forms vulnerable to devastation and destruction, I suggest the task for those who have both grasped the inter-connected complexity of life on earth and the barriers created by the hierarchical system and its elites, is to patiently and persistently share that knowledge with others. Furthermore, I consider that the knowledge that modes of production are actually based upon how social beings collectively obtain and share their (N-M-G-R + A-D) processes of living within the whole spectrum of life on earth, needs to be popularized as widely as possible. Life on earth in general should not be sacrificed either in quality or quantity to fulfil a hierarchical anthropocentric experiment misnamed 'civilisation'. All species contribute to the supply of (N) and extract their (N) from other species and contribute to the biosphere, but this can only be maintained within and upon the basis of a sustainable reproductive (R) biosphere process for all species. Therefore, any socio- economic revolution in any mode of production, as distinct from political revolutions based upon who governs them needs to commence with the alternative mode being practiced on a small scale. That small scale is necessary in order to prove itself to be, not only successful but viable and humane enough to be replicated by others on an ever expanding scale. This requires groups of human beings resisting the recommendations of the elite and refusing to get behind their particular elite pet issue of green reform, as the hierarchically proposed 'solution' within the existing hierarchical mode of elite determined production. As noted, revolutions in modes of production invariably start with something ground-breaking and intentionally new. However, a new way of living and producing needs to be more than theoretical, it needs to be implemented and successful in practice. Succeeding in such practical ecologically based endeavours is the only natural and incremental way that all life on earth has hitherto demonstrated its viability in terms of evolution so far.

However, the previous attempts to create or force elite determined anthropocentric short-cuts and unnatural social forms of organising social production have all eventually failed. As the most conscious and knowledgeable species of life on earth, the time is long overdue for collectives of human beings to re-establish an acute awareness of our responsibility to understand and protect the complexity and inter-dependence of life on earth – as a whole. On the basis of this understanding our species needs to live, produce and consume accordingly. Therefore, every new recruit viewing humanity from the ecologically sustainable standpoint of the rest of life on earth, has become vitally important. The further evolution of our bio-chemically conscious, and species conscious, humanity into a non-discriminatory supporter of life on earth - in all its forms - is a more sustainable and worthy alternative than continuing in the same old hierarchical way. Continuing to be led by the equivalent of a self-indulgent, blinkered elite section of our single species is a self- destructive trajectory. The daily intentional or unintentional destruction of all the essential and (seemingly) non-essential organisms on its own planet, most of which humanity ultimately needs for its own existence, is a recipe for further disasters.

Conclusion: summary.

Throughout the previous chapters in this book all the species which have a social form of existence, that have been considered, all aggregate on the basis of a voluntary membership of the social community to which they belong. No forms of social compunction and/or individual servitude to another organism or species have been encountered. Life in many forms; from bacteria, to fungi, to plants, to insects, and on to animals are found cooperating and associating in small or large groups or congregations but with no separate species or internal species compulsion to do so. The hominid species, from which humanity evolved, replicated the voluntary association of animals for feeding and breeding purposes and formed bands and later tribal confederations which after infant dependence were all voluntary associations of cooperation. Members of these communities could and regularly did switch bands and even tribes for various reasons. Eventually, in a large number of places, members of those voluntary forms of human living banded together in huge numbers and engaged in the most ambitious forms of human cooperation possible at the time. They built megalithic structures of immense size and sophistication, such as Stone Henge in the UK and numerous other such structures throughout Europe, the Middle East and elsewhere. Logic suggests these were voluntary-association building projects because the means to compel such cooperative ways of living and working together were lacking at that time. With very few exceptions, historical evidence confirms that in order to compel animals, (human or otherwise), to do things they do not want to do requires them to be shackled and punished on a 24/7 basis by a separate group of enforcers. Otherwise, the labour force, (again human or otherwise) just, evaporates away at every available opportunity.

Based upon millions of years of the voluntary cooperative association of species of life on earth, from bacteria to plants, to insects and animals, a change away from a predominantly voluntary cooperative way of human living, which had also lasted for hundreds of thousands of years, obviously needed a powerful socio-economic force to deflect humanity away from that natural evolutionary trajectory. In retrospect, therefore, introducing a predominantly compulsive and competitive way of living several thousand years ago was bound to be problematic as the evidence on the introduction of slavery, misogyny and genocide provided in chapters 8, 9 and 10 revealed and confirmed. Moreover it is a model which continues to this day. What has only recently been understood is that the hierarchical mass society form is not only deeply pernicious with regard to its effect upon the human species but now in its capitalist dominated form is also intensively destructive upon the inter-connected web of life on earth - as a whole. Hierarchical mass societies in their modern 20th and 21st century capitalist dominated forms threaten (through repeated acts of genocide) not only the continued existence of human communities, but (through repeated acts of ecocide) many of the key species supporting the whole web of life on earth. It is to be hoped that this contribution to understanding life on earth, will assist the reader to both appreciate the beauty and complexity of life on earth and at the same time understand what needs to be removed and changed if that beauty and complexity is to be allowed to continue for the enjoyment and sustenance of future generations.

www.ingramcontent.com/pod-product-compliance
Lightning Source LLC
Chambersburg PA
CBHW052007070526
44584CB00016B/1652